GIs and Fräuleins

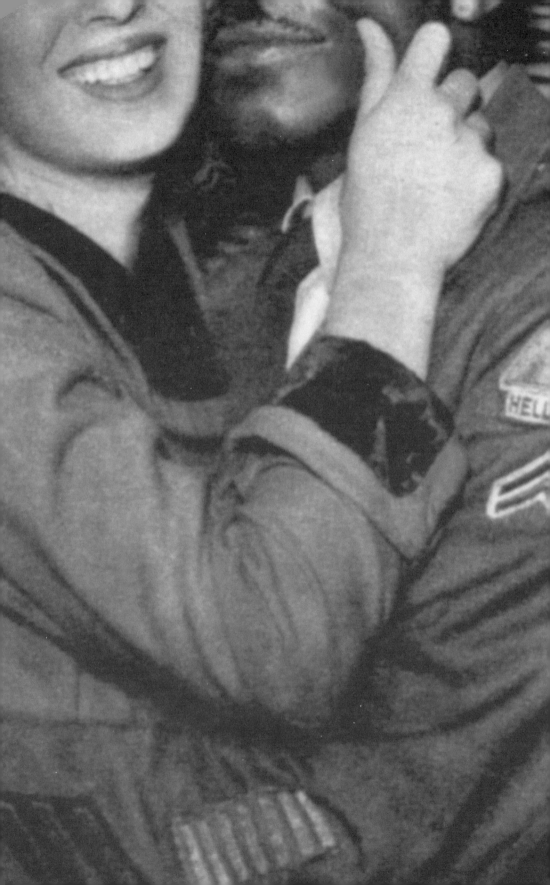

MARIA HÖHN

GIs and Fräuleins

THE GERMAN-AMERICAN

ENCOUNTER IN 1950S WEST

GERMANY

The University of North Carolina Press   Chapel Hill & London

© 2002 The University of North Carolina Press
All rights reserved
Manufactured in the United States of America
This book was set in Carter & Cohn Galliard
by Tseng Information Systems, Inc.

The paper in this book meets the guidelines for
permanence and durability of the Committee on
Production Guidelines for Book Longevity of the
Council on Library Resources.

Library of Congress Cataloging-in-Publication Data
Höhn, Maria (Maria H.)
GIs and Fräuleins : the German-American encounter
in 1950s West Germany / by Maria Höhn.
    p. cm.
Includes bibliographical references and index.
ISBN-13: 978-0-8078-2706-2 (cloth : alk. paper)
ISBN-10: 0-8078-2706-1 (cloth : alk. paper)
ISBN-13: 978-0-8078-5375-7 (pbk. : alk. paper)
ISBN-10: 0-8078-5375-5 (pbk. : alk. paper)
1. Rhineland-Palatinate (Germany)—Social conditions.   2. Rhineland-Palatinate
(Germany)—Economic conditions.   3. United States—Armed Forces—Germany
—Rhineland-Palatinate Region.   4. Germany—History—1945–   I. Title.
HN458.R53 H64   2002
306′.0943′43—dc21   2001058416

cloth   06 05 04 03 02   5 4 3 2 1
paper   06   5 4 3 2

To the memory of my beloved grandmothers,

Anna Höhn and Mathilde München

Contents

Illustrations

Acknowledgments

Over the past few years, the encouragement and support of many individuals and institutions nourished this book to fruition.

During my undergraduate years, Solomon Wank's brilliant seminars first excited me about German history and convinced me that I, too, wanted to be a historian. His friendship and continued interest in my progress as a scholar and teacher are among the great joys of my life. At the University of Pennsylvania, Thomas Childers, Lynn Hunt, and Jane Caplan were inspiring teachers and a most supportive dissertation committee. Since my early years in graduate school, Robert Moeller has been an important part of my intellectual development. He has read most of my work, and his generous and thoughtful suggestions did much to help me navigate the complicated landscape of the Adenauer years. Heide Fehrenbach, Uta Poiger, and Dagmar Herzog have been gracious in sharing their insights into the 1950s and in helping me make better sense of my own discoveries. Maria Mitchell was always gentle when she pointed out the occasional Teutonic sentence structure in my manuscript; she also proved a great resource in helping me understand the CDU's obsession with the *Abendland* (Christian Occident). Volker Berghahn has read sections of this book, and his probing questions helped me reframe some of my key arguments. Hanna Schissler and I discovered many years ago that we share a common interest in Baumholder. Her acute sense of the mood of the town in the 1950s focused my arguments and also assured me that this is a story worth telling. My understanding of *Fräuleins* and

GIs has been tremendously enriched by Annette Brauerhoch's willingness to share her insights on how postwar films depicted these relationships. My New York *Frauen*—Bonnie Anderson, Dolores Augustin, Rebecca Boehling, Renate Bridenthal, Jane Caplan, Belinda Davis, Atina Grossmann, Amy Hacket, Deborah Hertz, Young Sun Hong, Marion Kaplan, Jan Lambertz, Molly Nolan, Krista O'Donnell, and Nancy Reagin—have, on a number of occasions and with great vigor, picked my chapters apart. Atina Grossmann and Molly Nolan especially did much to help me find my own voice.

My years in graduate school and my research in Germany were a most enjoyable experience because of generous funding from the Mellon Foundation in the Humanities. The German Historical Institute in Washington, D.C., has also supported my endeavors in many ways over the years. Thanks are also due to Professor Dr. Winfried Herget of the Interdisziplinärer Arbeitskreis für Nordamerika Studien (IANAS) at the Johannes Gutenberg Universität in Mainz for inviting me to join the Nachbar Amerika (Neighbor America) project and for funding my stay in Germany. I am fortunate that Vassar College has consistently supported my summer research since my arrival there in 1996. A generous grant from the National Endowment of the Humanities last summer ensured the completion of this book.

At the Bundesarchiv in Koblenz, Frau Jakobi, Frau Kaiser, and Herr Scharmann were instrumental in helping me discover material related to the German-American encounter. Dr. Stein and Dr. Rummel at the Landeshauptarchiv in Koblenz were excited about my project from the beginning and willingly declassified many records. Dr. Stein also shared some of his insights on Dr. Detmar Schnapp and the Baumholder prostitution trial records. Working together with Ute Ritzenhofen on the Nachbar Amerika project at the Johannes Gutenberg Universität was not only an intellectually enriching experience; it was also was the beginning of a treasured friendship. In terms of my archival research, I owe the biggest debt to the employees of the Verbandsgemeinde and Kreisverwaltung Birkenfeld. Verbandsbürgermeister Manfred Dreier convinced the Landrat to give me access to still unsorted files stored in the basement. Had it not been for Karl Löffler from the Jugendamt Birkenfeld, I never would have found the folders "Berichte aus Baumholder," which turned out to be a key source in making sense of the Roaring 50s in Baumholder. Karl Löffler dug through dusty boxes with me and provided an office and access to a photocopier. His willing cooperation and his good cheer made my life so much easier. Walter Schuh from the Heimatmuseum Birkenfeld entrusted ten years of newspapers to my care so I could work at my leisure in the evenings. Christa Rühl Schneider's honesty allowed me unprecedented insights into welfare work in Baumholder during the 1950s. At the Stadtverwaltung Baumholder, Herr Weber took an immediate interest in my work and shared many hilarious anecdotes. Good fortune brought Fritz Licht my way. Without his knowledge of the social and political landscape of Baumholder and his willingness to talk about his hometown during the Nazi years, the Baumholder story would have been less than adequate. I am also grateful to his daughter, Ingrid Schwerdtner, and her husband Gerd for providing home-cooked meals and helping my project in so many little and big ways.

At the University of North Carolina Press, both Lew Bateman and Ron Maner were supportive and patient editors as I struggled with the revisions of my manuscript. Thanks are also due Kathy Malin. Her careful and thoughtful copyediting spared me considerable embarrassment.

All of my friends have shared their life experiences graciously and helped me emotionally during the long and sometimes frustrating process of writing this book. For their friendship I thank them with all my heart. Andrea Kihlstedt's brilliant pragmatism and solid advice, Barbara Wank's beautiful pottery and care of my soul, and Heike Bloom's gourmet meals and newspaper clippings related to anything German or anything having to do with the arts have made my life so much richer. Julie Sneeringer and Maria Mitchell always know just the right thing to say to cheer me up or cheer me on. Since coming to Vassar College, Olga and Andy Bush and their two sons, Sasha and Daniel, have made my husband Charles and me feel at home in Poughkeepsie, even as Olga and I dream of European plazas and sidewalk cafes. Norma Torney brings laughter and sparkle to my life. Her optimism about life and her sense of humor have brightened many a dreary Poughkeepsie winter day for me.

Friends have been lifesavers and so has my family. My brother Winfried Höhn, my sister-in-law Elke, and their son Mäthi are my anchors in Germany. They read ten years' worth of *Rheinzeitung* with me and did it all in good cheer. I thank them for being so generous with their love and for always making me feel as though I never left home. Finally, without the sweet love of my husband Charles Geiger and our sons, Christian and Gian, this book could not have been completed. I thank them with all my heart for their patience and wonderful senses of humor; their presence in my life was a much appreciated reminder that there is life beyond the Adenauer years.

Abbreviations

The following abbreviations are used throughout this book. Additional abbreviations used only in the notes are listed at the beginning of the notes section.

BJP   Bundesjugendplan (Federal Youth Plan)
CDU   Christlich-Demokratische Union (Christian Democrats)
EUCOM   European Command
DNVP   Deutschnationale Volkspartei (German Nationalist People's Party)
DP   Displaced Person
FDP   Freie Demokratische Partei Deutschlands (Free Democrats)
HICOG   Office of the U.S. High Commissioner for Germany
HWG   Häufig wechselnder Geschlechtsverkehr (individuals with frequently changing sex partners)
IANAS   Interdisziplinärer Arbeitskreis für Nordamerikastudien (Interdisciplinary Working Group for North American Studies)
KFV   Katholischer Fürsorgeverein für Frauen, Mädchen und Kinder (Catholic Welfare Agency for Women, Girls and Children)
KPD   Kommunistische Partei Deutschlands (Communist Party of Germany)
LRO   Land Relations Officer
MP   Military Police
NATO   North Atlantic Treaty Organization
NSDAP   Nationalsozialistische Deutsche Arbeiter Partei (National Socialist German Workers Party)
SPD   Sozialdemokratische Partei Deutschlands (Social Democratic Party of Germany)
USAREUR   U.S. Army Europe

GIs and Fräuleins

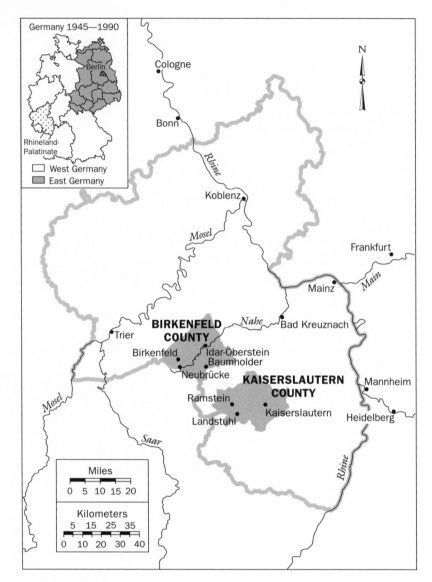

Rhineland-Palatinate

Introduction

In October 1952, the German Bundestag declared a large stretch of Rhine-land-Palatinate—a poor, rural state in the southwest of Germany—to be a moral disaster area.[1] The legislators resorted to this dramatic step because the buildup of American military personnel in West Germany in the wake of the Korean War had allegedly wreaked havoc in the provinces. The American troop deployment, they complained, instead of creating a bulwark against Soviet expansionism, had brought striptease parlors, prostitution, common-law marriages, and unprecedented levels of illegitimacy. The Christian Democratic legislators, who dominated the debate, were equally distressed to report that in one small town alone, 343 German women were neglecting their children because they were in the employ of the American occupation power. The counties of Birkenfeld and Kaiserslautern, home to the garrison communities Baumholder and Kaiserslautern, were identified as the key trouble spots. Convinced that the American-induced economic boom had rendered the rural population oblivious to the moral emergency, the conservative Christian Democrats demanded federal intervention. With great dismay, the Bundestag resolved that West Germany's military rearmament underway in Rhine-land-Palatinate needed to be accompanied by a moral rearmament of the state's population.

Discovering this anxious Bundestag debate during the preliminary stages of my research significantly changed the direction of this book. When I first began my project on the American military in Rhineland-

Palatinate, I set out to explore how West Germans had negotiated their transition from Nazism into consumer democracy during the 1950s. I had chosen my topic because I speculated that the extensive presence of American military personnel and their injection of the "American way of life" would produce a rich collection of sources to comment on those crucial founding years of the Federal Republic. My exploration of the German-American encounter was to provide insights into how economic, social, and cultural changes after 1945 played out in the everyday life of people. How did Germans, after the experience of Nazism, manage to establish a successful democracy in West Germany? Moreover, I hoped that the German-American encounter would reveal how Germans assessed the transformations in their lives. Would they agree with those historians who dismiss "Americanization" as an explanatory model by insisting that the transformation of German society after 1945 was part of a larger process of modernization that had been long underway and was merely disrupted by World War II and the postwar suffering?[2] What would Germans living in close proximity to the American military bases have to say to the Westernization scholars who do not ignore America's impact on postwar Germany but nonetheless stress that the Bonn Republic succeeded because West Germany's political and cultural élites abandoned their resistance to the "Western" liberal tradition?[3]

The anxious Bundestag debate convinced me that I had discovered a much richer story than initially anticipated; it also taught me an invaluable lesson. Since I had grown up in Rhineland-Palatinate during the 1960s and 1970s, I was confident that I brought a certain expertise to my research topic. Growing up, I daily encountered American soldiers maneuvering their huge tanks through the narrow streets of my village. American women shopped at the corner bakery, and American children attended local kindergartens. As a matter of fact, living in close proximity to such a large number of Americans seemed so "natural" to me that it was only while traveling to Düsseldorf in the early 1960s as a six-year-old, that I discovered that not all Germans had American neighbors or American playmates. Because of my extensive exposure to this American presence, I assumed that my role as a participant-observer would allow me special insights into how Germans and Americans interacted during the 1950s. The Bundestag debate quickly disabused me of any such notion. I was born and raised in what the parliamentarians had declared the "epicenter of immorality" and did not even know it.

This book, then, started as a story of how Germans experienced and assessed their encounter with the American military during the founding years of the Federal Republic. The final product is something quite different. While the sources I have uncovered have much to say about my initial query, they also brought to light the desperate struggle of religious and political conservatives to keep the new age at bay. Deeply ambivalent toward their new democracy and the social and cultural implications of consumer capitalism, German conservatives interpreted the economic and social changes brought on by the American troop deployment as a process of Americanization. Because conservatives tried to contain the alleged Americanization of daily life primarily by controlling the sexuality of women, my book also offers a fascinating gender history of those important years. Moreover, the German-American encounter during the 1950s reveals how German racial attitudes evolved in the wake of National Socialism. Because the American military brought segregated troops and Jim Crow practices to these communities, the garrison communities in Rhineland-Palatinate are key sites to observe how the sexual containment of women and German and American racial attitudes interacted.

GIs and Germans

Since 1945, more than 15 million Americans have lived and worked in West Germany, and the great majority of those individuals have spent their time in Germany as members of the American military.[4] Yet, we know almost nothing about this extraordinary encounter of Germans with American military personnel and the American way of life they brought to German communities. For the most part, historians of the German-American relationship have focused on the years of American military government (1945–49), when American influence was considered most pronounced.[5] Work that explores German-American relations beyond those years usually remains at the level of high politics as conducted in Washington and Bonn. That scholarship has been tremendously important in showing how American policies influenced the democratization of economic, social, and political structures after 1945, and how West Germany grew into the Western military and political alliance. The emphasis on institutions and high politics, however, precludes insights into how most Germans negotiated the Federal Republic's alliance with and reliance on America.[6]

By exploring the encounter of American GIs and German civilians during the 1950s in Rhineland-Palatinate, my study shifts the focus of inquiry from Washington and Bonn to the deepest provinces. American GIs have been stationed in Rhineland-Palatinate since 1950, when the outbreak of the Korean War initiated a dramatic American military buildup in Europe. Although it was part of the French zone of occupation after World War II, this economically depressed, rural state west of the Rhine emerged as the American military's most important supply base in Europe in the effort to contain a possible Soviet attack. Within just a few years after the outbreak of the Korean War, Rhineland-Palatinate, one of the smallest and poorest of the newly created West German states, became home to some of the largest American military installations outside the United States. Since that fateful year, millions of American soldiers, their family members, and tens of thousands of civilian employees of the U.S. Department of Defense have passed through the garrison towns of Rhineland-Palatinate.

The living together of these two cultures was not always easy; all too often it was more a living side-by-side. Yet the fifty-year military presence left an indelible imprint on the landscape of the region and the lives of the people who reside around the American military bases. Despite the drastic reduction of the American military presence in Europe after the collapse of the Soviet Union, almost 70,000 soldiers and their dependents can still be found in Rhineland-Palatinate.

The largest number of American GIs came to two communities. Baumholder, a town of just 2,500 inhabitants when the Americans arrived in 1950 became home to a military base and training camp for 30,000 American soldiers. Kaiserslautern, a provincial city of about 80,000 inhabitants, had to accommodate some 40,000 American GIs and their families. Although most Americans and Germans hardly know of these two towns, American military planners assigned them primary strategic importance. During the Cold War, both Kaiserslautern and Baumholder were key assignments for any military officer hoping for a career on the Joint Chiefs of Staff.[7]

Tiny specks on the map of the Federal Republic, Kaiserslautern and Baumholder have much to say about the complexities and ambiguities of the German-American encounter. The two communities are also gold mines for the historian interested in the continuities and changes in German history, because within just thirteen years Baumholder and Kaiserslautern had to accommodate three very different military deployments. The military installations that the Americans took over in Rhineland-Palatinate in 1950 were first established in 1937–38, when the Nazi regime constructed the *Westwall,* its Western line of fortification. Since Rhineland-Palatinate was part of the French zone of occupation, the French military government took possession of these installations in July 1945, only to return them to the American military in 1950 when the American troop presence in Europe was dramatically increased. Germans in these garrison communities thus had ample opportunity to contrast the economic and social changes in their lives brought about by the German troop deployment to changes inaugurated by the French and Americans. Moreover, these communities provide a fascinating locus for exploring German racial attitudes since the 1920s. For many older Germans, the injection of African American GIs in the 1950s evoked memories of the 1920s Rhineland occupation, when the French had brought colonial troops from Senegal and Morocco to their *Heimat* (homeland).

In exploring my topic, I consulted local, state, federal, and church archives, as well as the extensive press coverage produced locally and nationally regarding the American presence. I was also fortunate to have access to the rich collection of oral histories that the Interdisziplinärer Arbeitskreis für Nordamerikastudien (IANAS) at the University of Mainz had gathered to document the fifty-year presence of the American military in the state.[8] Among the seventy people interviewed were former mayors and city council members, and individuals who rented apartments to American families or worked for the Americans on one of the many military bases. These videotaped oral histories were complemented by another twenty-five interviews that I conducted with former mayors, police personnel, judges, and welfare workers, while I was researching in these communities. To balance the German perspective, I consulted American military records at the National Archives and the Center for Military History. I also integrated the recollections of some fifty American GIs who were stationed in Germany during the 1950s. These interviews proved a wonderfully rich source to complement my German sources. However, since the GIs' experience in Germany was transitory by nature, these interviews can offer merely glimpses of a particular moment during the 1950s. They are less helpful than the German oral histories in exploring changes in attitudes over the long run.

As Germans interviewed for this project looked back on the 1950s, they could not help but contrast their encounter with the American military to that of the German and French military deployments. Germans recalled that the economic improvement that came with the Nazi rearmament in 1937–38 was short-lived because of the war, and was reversed during the harsh years of French military government (1945–49). Keeping that experience in mind, most Germans remembered the "Korea Boom" as assuring that the traditional poorhouse of Germany was not left out of the Federal Republic's economic miracle (*Wirtschaftswunder*). Their recollections also suggest that, for the most part, the residents of these communities adapted rather easily to the new realities, including the presence of a large number of Americans and the "alien" culture they brought into their midst. The decade is fondly remembered as a time when Americans drove large, shiny cars and Germans marveled at the extraordinary wealth that the dollar's favorable exchange rate created for the American GIs. Residents also commented on the surprising intimacy of their contacts with the Americans in that decade and on the alluring glimpse at a brave and admirable new world of jazz, rock and roll, flashy cars, and consumer riches that the Americans offered and the younger generation eagerly embraced. In contrast to the disenchantment with America that was to come later with Vietnam, Watergate, and the crisis in the 1980s over the deployment of Pershing missiles,[9] the 1950s are remembered by residents of Rheinland-Palatinate chiefly as the "Golden Fifties" or the "Fantastic Fifties."[10]

In working with the IANAS project in Mainz while at the same time conducting my own archival research, I was struck by the dramatic discrepancy between the oral histories that were gathered in the mid-1990s and the responses to the Americans that were registered during the 1950s. For the most part, Germans interviewed by IANAS in the 1990s no longer recalled any sort of anxiety that the injection of such a large and foreign military presence might have provoked. They failed to do so because after nearly half a century of living with Americans, Germans no longer experienced either the "American way of life" or the "American tempo" as threats to local traditions and German cultural norms. Since Germans in these garrison communities have been living with people of color for fifty years now, they no longer recalled the sense of panic that many felt in 1950, when the Americans arrived with still segregated troops and brought "Negro units" to the German *Heimat*.

The oral histories also no longer registered that the American troop deployment evoked considerable political dissension. After being politically and militarily allied with the United States for over half a century, people barely recalled that until the mid-1950s, the Social Democrats (SPD) vehemently opposed the American military mission and the rearmament of Germany that the Christian Democratic (CDU) government under Konrad Adenauer endorsed. Because living with their American neighbors has become so routine, Germans also no longer remembered that in the first few years after the troops' arrival, the most vocal objection to the American military came not from the SPD but from Chancellor Adenauer's most committed supporters in the CDU. Political and religious conservatives, while endorsing Adenauer's reliance on America to achieve political and military rehabilitation for West Germany, were deeply ambivalent about the social and cultural implications that the American troop deployment entailed.

The reaction of German conservatives to the American presence is central to the questions this book explores. Since the end of World War II, the churches and conservative Christian politicians gathered in the CDU were instrumental in defining West Germany's political, social, and cultural life. Conservative Catholics and Protestants, whose relationships in the past had been deeply antagonistic, found common ground after 1945 by insisting that only a return to the traditions of the Christian Occident (*Abendland*) could ensure that Germany overcome the havoc that Nazism had wreaked on society. According to a deeply held consensus, conservatives after 1945 explained the Nazi regime as the consequence of a secular materialism whose roots were in the Enlightenment. In the churches' assessment, it was society's turning away from God that had brought about the "German catastrophe." To overcome that catastrophe, materialism in all its manifestations had to be checked. Zealous anticommunism to contain the dialectic materialism espoused by the Soviet Union and its protégé East Germany was only a first step to ensure the conservative project. Conservatives were equally adamant that American-style consumer capitalism could not but accelerate the secular materialism they so desperately were trying to overcome.[11] Thus, while the dominant clerical voices within the Christian Democratic government accepted America's military leadership, they insisted that certain spheres of German society needed to be protected from the American way of life.

Informed by such a worldview, clerical conservatives, who dominated the policies of the CDU until 1957, assured the implementation of many of the Federal Republic's deeply conservative policies. Crucial for their project of restoring the Christian *Abendland* and keeping materialism at bay was the role conservatives assigned to women. Legislation and social policy after the founding of the Federal Republic assured that women, who had experienced unprecedented autonomy when husbands and fathers were at the front during World War II, were again to accept the authority of the male breadwinner. Conservatives were also convinced that restraining women's sexuality was imperative to undo the humiliating defeat that German manhood had suffered, both at the front and at home. Thus, the sexual liberation many women experienced in the last few years of the war was to be overcome, as was the widespread fraternization between German women and allied soldiers in the Western zones.[12] For conservatives, restoring women to their "natural roles" as wives and mothers was the answer to many of their cares, because conservatives considered the "God-ordained" nuclear family as the key institution to reverse the Nazi assault on German society. In the patriarchal family Germany's young were also to be steeled against the twin challenges facing the Federal Republic: the Communist model of the German Democratic Republic and the looming Americanization of daily life.[13]

Not surprisingly, the national debate on the dangers of materialism and the important role assigned to German women in containing it also reverberated in the provinces. In all garrison communities, Catholic and Protestant clergymen emerged as the most vocal critics of the American military presence, condemning as unacceptable the material Zeitgeist that the American-induced boom had brought to the countryside. For these conservatives, nothing less than a process of Americanization was under-way during the 1950s, and they pointed to the usual suspects to make their case. Drawing on a long tradition of conservative critiques of America going back to Weimar, they complained about American-style consump-tion and leisure patterns and increasing secularization as both men and women kept their distance from the church.[14] These same observers were also convinced that the family, so crucial to their project, could not with-stand the seductions of the American way of life that the soldiers and their families had brought into their communities. The clergy were also the most outspoken critics of the American military presence when they indicted as unacceptable the widespread relaxation of moral values that allegedly followed the troops to the provinces. In all garrison communi-ties, conservative observers conflated the enormous social changes they observed with cultural and racial decline. Catholic and Protestant clergy-men were appalled that Jewish DPs (Displaced Persons), most of them Holocaust survivors from Eastern Europe, followed the troops from the American zone and opened dimly-lit jazz clubs and striptease bars. They also denounced as shameless the numerous prostitutes who arrived in their towns to pursue the American GIs and their seemingly never-ending dollar riches. Even more troubling than the prostitutes were the many German women from respectable backgrounds who nonetheless asso-ciated with American GIs. Their Americanized demeanor and behavior evoked much consternation, and their willingness to live in common-law marriages with white and black American GIs marked them as sexual as well as racial transgressors. Conservatives reserved their greatest outrage, however, for their own charges. Instead of expressing outrage over the goings-on in their communities, the local population was busily figuring out how to participate in the American-induced boom.

Alerted by the clergy, the churches' affiliated welfare organizations—the Katholischer Fürsorgeverein für Frauen, Mädchen, und Kinder and the Innere Mission—brought Baumholder and Kaiserslautern to na-tional attention. Because the Christian welfare agencies dominated the highly influential umbrella organization of German welfare agencies, the Deutscher Verein für öffentliche und private Fürsorge (Verein hereafter), they were able to use the alleged moral crisis in the state to broaden significantly their socially and culturally conservative agenda. It was largely the pressure of the churches and the Verein that led to a short-lived resurrection of sexual norms during the 1950s that most Germans had condemned as too rigid already during the 1920s.

The conservative effort, which peaked between 1953 and 1958, pursued a two-pronged strategy. The Christian Democratic federal and state governments funded extensive social welfare initiatives to protect the local population, especially the young and women, from the seductions of the American soldiers and the American way of life. Secondly, the churches were convinced that the American presence could not but accelerate the greater sexual tolerance they had been lamenting since the 1920s. In an astounding about-face, the churches and the Deutscher Verein presented sexual immorality, rather than Nazism or genocide, as the Federal Republic's central moral challenge. Anxious to distance themselves from their complicity with Nazism, the churches and the Verein riveted on strict bourgeois social norms and sexual decency (*Wohlanständigkeit*) as the cure for the nation's guilt and moral crisis.[15] To assure German *Wohlanständigkeit*, the Christian welfare agencies gathered in the Verein convinced federal lawmakers to broaden significantly the legal definition of what acts constituted prostitution.

The many anxious but also disconsolate reports that the clergy and the Christian welfare agencies relayed to state and federal ministries reveal just how unsettled German society was in the first few years of the 1950s. In Rhineland-Palatinate at least, the 1948 currency reform and the founding of the Federal Republic in 1949 had not signaled the end of the postwar era. Indeed, the first half of the 1950s was marked by social turmoil and a determined struggle among conservatives and more progressive voices over the meaning of West Germany's new democracy. For a few short years after 1953, that struggle seemed to favor the conservative effort to return society not just to pre-Nazi but to pre-Weimar social and moral values. Because the churches and their affiliated welfare agencies riveted on sexual immorality—rooted in Weimar democracy and expressed most appallingly in the postwar years—as Germany's primary moral challenge, women bore the brunt of that conservative campaign.

By exploring local reactions to the conservative project, I show that the moral rearmament of German society is only one aspect, albeit an important one, of the 1950s. By the second part of the decade, conservative observers in Rhineland-Palatinate provided exasperated accounts of their failure to keep the population from eagerly embracing the prosperity and social mobility that the American-induced economic boom entailed. Their accounts also bemoan the fact that the strict morality that the deeply conservative Christian Democratic state and federal governments were trying to enforce through the Christian welfare agencies, the police, and the courts did not play well in the provinces. Most Germans were unwilling to return to the rigid pre-Weimar sexual norms that conservatives wanted to reimpose. The unprecedented prosperity of the Korea Boom convinced all too many that the era of deprivation and self-sacrifice was over; indeed, the time had come to "live for once." In light of their experience with Nazism, many Germans also found the conservative program intrusive and inappropriate for the new democracy. Consequently, the population rejected the conservative effort to stigmatize and punish as prostitutes all women who associated with American GIs. Notwithstanding the concerted efforts of the churches and of state and federal ministries, even in the deepest provinces, attitudes toward premarital sexuality and women's sexual expressiveness outside of marriage relaxed considerably by the later part of the decade.

However, this greater tolerance in sexual matters tells only part of the story. Germans negotiated this overall relaxation of sexual mores by vilifying as unacceptable the sexual relationships between African American men and German women. When Germans, in both East and West, read about the American garrison communities during the 1950s, the focus was increasingly on the "many" black GIs who met "sexually unrestrained" women in the bars that Eastern European Jews made available to them. The prostitution records of Baumholder and the press coverage of the garrison communities reveal that attitudes toward such relationships hardened considerably, especially after Germany regained sovereignty in 1955.

Historians of postwar Germany have only recently begun to explore how racial hierarchies continued to inform notions of German identity. Exciting new scholarship on German reactions to American popular culture and German policies toward the children born of German mothers and African American fathers make important contributions to the field. That scholarship also shows that it would be too simple to assume a straightforward continuity from Nazi racism to racial attitudes in the 1950s. A process of negotiation was at work as liberal policy makers, influenced by social science research in the United States, distanced themselves from the biologically based racial hierarchies of the past. While the language of eugenics disappeared, this did not mean that racial hierarchies ceased to matter. German policy makers, for example, drew on this psychologically based language of difference to condemn jazz and rock and roll for undermining proper class, race, and gender boundaries.[16]

My book contributes to this work by expanding the exploration of German racial attitudes beyond those of politicians and policy makers to include such debates at the grassroots level. The fact that millions of black GIs have spent time in Germany since 1945 makes it clear that German racial debates after 1945 did not take place in a vacuum. Because of the national attention the garrison communities received throughout the 1950s—not just in Germany's tabloid press—these debates on race also did not remain just local affairs but engaged the country as a whole.

We know from Heide Fehrenbach's important work that during the late 1940s and the 1950s the German liberal discourse on race shifted from a preoccupation with Jews to an overwhelming concern with blacks.[17] However, in the garrison towns, that shift is less manifest for a number of reasons. Most importantly, debates on race are not driven by the self-conscious efforts of national policy makers to overcome the shameful Nazi past. Just the same, despite the murderous rage of the Nazi regime, Jews were not "absent" from German communities or German consciousness during the 1950s. Germans in these communities encountered Eastern European Jews and American blacks simultaneously and on a daily basis. Consequently, German debates on race were marked by the coexistence of separate but also overlapping discourses on "racial others."

This study is also a first attempt to argue that German racial attitudes after 1945 can be understood only if they are examined in light of their face-to-face interaction with those of the American military. Black GIs, and not just those from the Jim Crow South, experienced in Germany a tolerance and acceptance unknown to them in their own country. Their status, first as conquerors and then as occupation soldiers, made possible unprecedented encounters with white Germans.[18] In *My American Journey,* General Colin Powell gave voice to that experience when he recalled his service in Germany in 1958: "[For] black GIs, especially those out of the South, Germany was a breath of freedom—they could go where they wanted, eat where they wanted, and date whom they wanted, just like other people. The dollar was strong, the beer good, and the German people friendly, since we were all that stood between them and the Red hordes. War, at least the Cold War in Germany, was not hell."[19] Yet the record also shows that side-by-side with this tolerance existed a profound unease and often even resentment over the presence of black GIs.

Nowhere were the limits of German racial tolerance more forcefully expressed than in the condemnation evoked by the relationships between black GIs and white German women.

Observing the deep reluctance, if not outright opposition, in the American military toward the relationships between German women and black American soldiers convinced many Germans, and not just conservatives, that their own racial prejudices should not mark them as Nazis. Thus, when Germans during the 1950s condemned the relationships between German women and African American soldiers, they cited the model of racial segregation of their American mentor as informing their own convictions. Germans were able to do so with ease because American opposition to interracial sexuality and interracial marriage was so similar to their own pre-Nazi models of racial exclusion. Thus Germans could reject the racial excesses of Nazism while at the same time invoking racial hierarchies of exclusion that were based in timeless laws of nature and tied firmly to the Western liberal tradition.

The following chapters provide a worm's-eye view of the German-American encounter in Rhineland-Palatinate and the excitement, ambivalence, and panic that marked this encounter. The first chapter follows Baumholder from the 1920s through the Korea Boom of the 1950s to show that the Americans brought an unprecedented prosperity to Rhineland-Palatinate. The next chapter describes how the American military expended much effort to pull reluctant Germans into the Western alliance. Americans also worked hard to be good neighbors and to encourage friendship between the troops and the German population. Germans responded enthusiastically to the economic boom, and many of them, especially the younger generation, eagerly embraced the consumer goods and the more relaxed American style that the GIs brought to the *Hinterland*. Chapter 3 shows how the presence of black GIs confronted Germans and forced them to explore their own racial attitudes. Because the military arrived with still segregated troops, bringing Jim Crow practices into these German communities, this chapter also describes how German assumptions about race interacted in a complex manner with American racial attitudes. Chapter 4 describes how religious conservatives indicted the local population for its obsession with material goods and for ignoring the loosening of morals that came with the troops. This chapter also clarifies that conservatives merely gave voice to a broadly agreed-upon narrative that indicted black GIs, "sexually unrestrained" women, and Jewish bar owners for having brought degeneration to the countryside. Chapter 5 discusses how efforts to contain the side effects of the American troop deployment focused foremost on criminalizing prostitution and broadening the definition of what acts constituted prostitution. In Chapter 6, I describe how conservatives convinced the federal and state governments to grant generous funds to church-affiliated welfare organizations to protect the population from the social and cultural implications of the American presence. The failure of this containment is also detailed. Chapter 7 explores the enforcement of the new prostitution laws in Baumholder. This discussion reveals that locals rejected the national effort to rein in the moral decay in their communities by arresting any woman in the company of a GI as a possible prostitute. The chapter shows that—because of the complex interaction of German and American assumptions about race—this greater tolerance was accompanied by a racialization of prostitution. Chapter 8 is an exploration of events in Kaiserslautern during the 1957 Bundestag election, when the controversial deployment of Nike atomic missiles led to an outcry by both the CDU and SPD over the sexual and racial transgressions of African American GIs and German women. My conclusion returns to my initial inquiry to argue that Germans assessed the changes in their lives as a process of Americanization, rather than Westernization or merely modernization. That discussion also integrates my findings on German and American racism to question the triumphant narratives that the models of Americanization, Westernization, and modernization entail.

1

". . . And Then the Americans Came Again"

In the course of 1950–51, more than 100,000 American soldiers and their dependents came to Rhineland-Palatinate, a largely rural state in the southwest of Germany. The American military arrived in Rhineland-Palatinate to facilitate an extensive American military buildup after the outbreak of the Korean War increased fears among the Western Allies over possible Soviet expansion in Europe. As a consequence of the Cold War tensions of the superpowers, Rhineland-Palatinate—mostly known for its fine Nahe, Moselle, and Rhine wines—was to emerge by the end of the decade as the center of NATO's allied air defense and as the main supply depot for the United States Army in Europe.[1] Since that fateful year, millions of Americans have passed through the Rhineland-Palatinate on two- or three-year tours of duty, as soldiers, dependents, or civilian employees of the U.S. Department of Defense. While most Germans at the time speculated that the American troops would be in their communities for at most ten years, history has shown otherwise. The people of Rhineland-Palatinate have been living with their American neighbors for more than fifty years now, and despite the overall drop in the number of American troops in Europe after the collapse of the Soviet Union, Rhineland-Palatinate still hosts some of the largest American military bases outside of the United States.

The deployment of the American troops in Germany, which was financed through a West German defense contribution, had tremendous implications for the future of the young Federal Republic. Without the Korean War and the Cold War security concerns it generated, the debates on German rearmament that culminated in the 1955 Paris Treaty, the abolition of the Occupation Statute, and Germany's rearmament and inclusion in NATO would not have been possible so soon after the end of World War II. That distant conflict, then, helped fulfill the most cherished goals of West Germany's Christian Democratic (CDU) chancellor, Konrad Adenauer: it made possible the first steps toward a political and military rehabilitation of his nation, greater equality among the Western Allies, and the attainment of West German sovereignty just ten years after the defeat of Nazism.[2]

The decisions forged in Washington because of the Cold War tensions between the superpowers affected Rhineland-Palatinate and its people as well. Part of the French zone of occupation, Rhineland-Palatinate was among the poorest of the new states that made up the Federal Republic. Only a couple of its cities had more than 100,000 inhabitants, and Ludwigshafen and Mainz were the only large industrial centers. The state was also deeply divided against itself. The French military government had created Rhineland-Palatinate out of territories that shared few historical ties and cultural traditions: the Palatinate, Rhine-Hesse, and the regional governments of Koblenz and Trier, as well as the four Nassau districts east of the Rhine (Ober- and Unterwesterwaldkreis, St. Goarshausen, and Unterlahnkreis). The state was approximately the size of Hesse but had a mere 2.6 million inhabitants in 1946. Not much enthusiasm existed for the new state; it was considered an artificial, test-tube creation.

The deepest division in this new state was religion, with the scenic mountain range of the Hunsrück serving as a demarcation line. North of it ruled a stridently anti-Prussian Catholicism under the conservative Christian Democrat, Peter Altmeier. Although Altmeier was an ardent supporter of Rhineland-Palatinate, some within his party had not made their peace with the new state and hoped fervently for a union with the Catholic Northern Rhineland. The most consistent critique of the new state, however, came from the Social Democratic Party (SPD), which dominated the more industrialized Protestant regions of the Palatinate and Rhine-Hesse. The SPD did not consider the state economically viable and agitated to merge with the more industrialized and prosperous Baden-Württemberg to the south. Pragmatic accommodation between CDU and SPD was possible after 1948 only because of the escalating Cold War and the looming division of Germany. The SPD gave up its opposition to the new state while sections within the CDU tempered their Rhenish patriotism (*Lokalpatriotismus*) to support Adenauer's policy of "West-integration." The decision to move the capital of the state from Koblenz to Mainz was to reflect that compromise, but no love was lost between the state's CDU and SPD.[3] After 1951, the state's deeply conservative CDU was able to rule with a comfortable majority, avoiding any sort of alliance with the SPD.

When the Americans arrived in Rhineland-Palatinate in 1950–51, large sections of the population were still not reconciled to the state's artificially imposed political boundaries. The Americans also reported with much dismay how backward the area was compared to the American zone of occupation. The so-called Korea boom of the early 1950s, however, catapulted the area into an economic miracle that would rival developments in the more industrialized parts of Germany. The American soldiers brought much hardship and many inconveniences, but the American GIs also brought an unprecedented prosperity that not only affected the purses of the local populace but revolutionized their whole way of life.

The Baumholder Story

To show how dramatically the American troop deployment impacted the people of Rhineland-Palatinate, I will describe developments in one such garrison community. The town of Baumholder, in the county of Birkenfeld, serves as a microcosm to illustrate the "Gold Rush" atmosphere that so marked all communities where American troops were stationed during the 1950s. The obvious reason for choosing Baumholder as an exemplar is that during the 1950s the little town emerged as a code word in the national debates on the social changes and social problems that accompanied the American troops to the provinces. But Baumholder was also chosen for other reasons. Baumholder has been host to military troops since the Nazi regime created the Reich's largest training camp there in 1937–38. By tracing the town's fortunes back to the 1930s, I will show that the years of Nazi rule, the war and the dislocations of the postwar years, had already undermined many traditions and institutions that marked the life of Germany's rural communities. But this discussion will also show that the economic miracle of the 1950s was not just a continuation of a process of modernization begun in the 1930s.[4] The American-induced economic miracle of the 1950s differed profoundly from that of the 1930s. Baumholder's rocky path from being a deeply nationalistic and fully Nazified community to becoming a modern consumer society by the end of the 1950s presents a valuable case study of the continuities and changes in German history since the 1930s.

Birkenfeld County, a cold and windy stretch of land located between the hills of the Westrich and Hunsrück, emerged in its present shape only in 1937, when the county of Birkenfeld and parts of the county of Baumholder/St. Wendel were merged. Until then, the county of Birkenfeld, although located in the Rheinprovinz, was not Prussian but belonged to Oldenburg, a state in the northern part of Germany, while Baumholder/St. Wendel had been part of Prussia. In a state where 56 percent of the population was Catholic, the county of Birkenfeld was home to a Protestant majority of 80 percent.[5] The region was a poor one, with only one industrial center, the city of Idar-Oberstein, which was renowned worldwide as a center for the cutting and polishing of precious and semi-precious stones. The city's almost 27,000 inhabitants were dependent on that highly volatile industry, with most of the workers employed in more than 2,000 workshops. Those not employed in the precious stone industry worked in local leather factories. The only other towns of any size were the county seat of Birkenfeld, with about 5,000 people, many of them civil servants, artisans, or small businessmen. Baumholder had 2,500 inhabitants, who made their living as farmers, civil servants, or artisans. Another 50,000 of the county's inhabitants lived in over 100 villages and hamlets. The great majority of farms were minute properties, most of them smaller than twelve acres. The soil was among the lowest quality recorded in Germany, prompting local farmers to describe their daily toil as yielding "many rocks, but little bread." Many of the villages in the county had by the late nineteenth century turned into working-class villages (*Arbeiterdörfer*), where the men traveled to the coal mines of the Saarland to supplement the farm's meager income.[6]

The end of World War I brought unprecedented hardship to a county that had never known economic well-being. Once France severed the Saarland from Germany as part of the Versailles Treaty, thousands of jobs in the mining industry were lost to the county's workers. Farmers suffered as well, because the industrial Saar had been one of the chief markets for the county's agricultural products. The occupation of the Rhineland by the French and their use of colonial troops only furthered animosity toward Germany's archenemy, while also stirring resentment against the Weimar Republic. Before 1929 that resentment was expressed largely through voting for traditionally right-wing parties, such as the Deutschnationale Volkspartei (DNVP). Once the county's precious stone industry collapsed in 1929, voter behavior on the right radicalized much more dramatically than in the rest of Germany. Contrary to what was implied in Edgar Reitz's immensely popular TV series *Heimat,* Nazism was not imported from the city to a hard-working and devout country-side but was a wholly homegrown phenomenon in the Protestant regions of the Rhineland and Palatinate.[7] Among the Nazis marching on the Feldherrenhalle during the 1923 Bierhallen Putsch were a husband and wife from Birkenfeld County who boasted NSDAP membership numbers forty-six and forty-seven.[8]

While the 1928 election in Birkenfeld County had brought the NSDAP only 4.3 percent of the vote, the onset of the world depression would change those numbers radically. Increasingly, the civil servants in the county seat of Birkenfeld, the county's Protestant farmers, the industrialists and artisans of Idar-Oberstein's precious stone industry turned to the NSDAP. In 1931 the NSDAP received 34.3 percent of the county's vote. In the summer election of 1932, the Nazis were able to gain 38 percent of the German vote nationwide, while an astonishing 59.6 percent of the people in the city of Birkenfeld voted for the party. In that election, almost the "whole rural population" in Baumholder also shifted their allegiance from the reactionary DNVP and the *Landbund* to the Nazis.[9] Election results in the rest of the county brought even more stunning victories for the Nazis. In the city of Idar (later to be incorporated with Oberstein), Nazi support reached almost 70 percent. Those numbers were even higher in the neighboring hamlets that were home to the precious stone industry's hundreds of small artisan shops. In the tiny hamlet of Niederbrombach the Nazis received 91.8 percent of the vote.[10] For the most part, the Catholic villages of the county remained true to the Catholic Center Party. In the mining villages bordering on the Saarland, many continued voting for the SPD or the Communists, but up to 50 percent of voters in those villages also turned to Nazism.[11]

The conclusion that Gerhard Nestler and Hannes Ziegler had drawn about the Protestant regions of the Palatinate also applied to the southern parts of the Rhineland and the county of Birkenfeld: for a good proportion of the Protestants in this rural region of Germany, the seizure of power of by the Nazi regime was "not a violent subordination but a voluntary devotion (*Hingabe*)."[12] Mambächel, a tiny hamlet right outside of Baumholder was the first German community to make Hitler an honorary citizen. By April 1933 almost all of the county's civil servants were members of the NSDAP.[13]

As in most rural, Protestant communities, the success of the Nazi party depended largely on its ability to attract prominent local residents (*Honoratorien*), such as wealthy farmers, teachers, or clergy to their cause.[14]

In the counties of Birkenfeld and Baumholder/St. Wendel the NSDAP was able to do that. One of the Protestant ministers of Birkenfeld was not only a member of the NSDAP but also the *Ortsgruppenleiter* (local Nazi leader) and the local leader of the SA (*Sturmabteilung,* or storm-troopers).[15] In Baumholder, the school principal held this prestigious office. Baumholder's Protestant minister was a member of the SA, the SS (*Schutzstaffel,* the Nazis' most elite and racist special unit), and the Deutsche Christen, the faction within the Protestant church that accepted the Nazis' Volkish ideology of establishing a racially pure church.[16]

Despite the overwhelming enthusiasm for National Socialism in both counties, the regime did not bless the region with an expansion of its limited industrial base.[17] The counties were just too close to the bor-der with France. Matters began to look up somewhat in 1935, when the Saarland was returned to the Reich and the construction of the Kusel-Türkismühle railroad began. With the exception of the construction of the Nürburgring racetrack, however, most economic development west of the Rhine came in the form of preparing the border area for the coming military conflict. Part of that military strategy was the building of a stra-tegically important highway, the Hunsrückhöhenstraße; the construc-tion of Germany's largest military training camp (*Truppenübungsplatz*) in Baumholder; and the fortification of the western frontier, the West-wall. These three construction projects brought some prosperity to the depressed area but also much upheaval.

The feverish activity for the construction of the Westwall, a fortifica-tion line of 400 miles along the French border, impacted almost all com-munities west of the Rhine. In May of 1938, 500,000 workers from across the Reich arrived in the rural and backward areas along Germany's west-ern frontier to mix 6 million tons of cement into tank barriers and for-tification bunkers. In this mammoth project, 2.3 percent of the Reich's workforce and 25 percent of all workers employed in the German con-struction industry worked 12- to 16-hour shifts seven days a week until the project was completed in October of 1938.[18] During the construction, Security Police (SD) reports describe at great length just how bitter the local population felt about the disruptions they experienced in their lives. People complained about pulverized roads, tainted or cut-off water sup-plies, and the deadly traffic that resulted from truck drivers being forced to work 24-hour shifts on roads that were not suited to handle the amount of traffic generated by the project. Communities were overwhelmed with demands to house and feed the legions of workers, and the presence of so many single men who were paid high wages and had little distraction other than alcohol caused its share of problems. To the great dismay of the clergy, crews worked around the clock, even on Sundays and holidays, as their tireless efforts changed forever the topography of the local landscape.[19] The presence of the workers in these previously rather isolated villages brought an economic boom but also new mores and a loosening of traditions. Project managers were usually housed with local families and introduced the farmers to the ways of the city. The workers attended dances and dated local women, breaking down the strict lines of religious segregation that defined most of these communities.[20]

The arrogant behavior of the military and outside Nazi officials did little to ameliorate local distress. But people also complained about the level of corruption, rigged subcontracting, racketeering, and what many called the "war-profiteer-1938 style." Nazi propaganda ignored these complaints and presented the project as a wedding of "will and technology" and a brilliant success of the *Volksgemeinschaft* (People's Community). Hitler declared enthusiastically in September 1938 that "behind this front of steel and concrete . . . stands a German people in arms." But SD reports suggest that a deep conflict existed between local interests and national ambition. At the height of the tense international wrangling over the Czech crisis between 12 and 15 September 1938, many residents listened to foreign radio broadcasts, and the SD reported with dismay that the population lacked any sort of war fever, instead hoping "most fervently for a solution that will avoid war."[21]

The counties of Birkenfeld and Baumholder were much affected by the disruptions brought by these huge construction projects for the Westwall. But the construction of Nazi Germany's largest military training ground in Baumholder (Truppenübungsplatz Baumholder; Platz hereafter) provided at least economic advantages that outlasted the short and feverish activity of the Westwall boom. To construct this training camp, the regime demanded almost 29,000 acres of the Prussian county of Baumholder/St. Wendel. Fourteen villages were evacuated, and 4,060 villagers were resettled in neighboring communities or received land around Mecklenburg and Magdeburg.[22] Once these evacuations were completed, the remaining territory of Baumholder/St. Wendel was integrated into the county of Birkenfeld. The territorial reforms of the Gross-Hamburg Law of 26 January 1937 integrated Birkenfeld into Prussia as part of the regional government of Koblenz.

While few people in the region were happy about the loss of arable land and the dislocation of thousands of people, Landrat Herbert Wild, the state-appointed head of the county government, an ardent Nazi who was also the NSDAP county chief (*Kreisleiter*), reported that county residents had only great willingness to sacrifice for the *Volksgemeinschaft* and

assuaged – To make milder or less severe; relieve; ease

the Führer.[23] What further assuaged the discontent of those who did not lose their land was the fact that the creation of the training camp significantly boosted the economy of the region. For these traditionally neglected parts of the Reich the Nazi economic miracle had come late, but once it had arrived, it initiated a substantial boost to the economy. Local farmers found employment with the Wehrmacht, and trade and commerce increased as local businesses and artisans catered to the approximately 10,000 soldiers who rotated through the training camp.[24] Once the war began, the economy experienced another boom as thousands of family members arrived in Baumholder and surrounding communities to say a last good-bye to their sons and husbands. Despite all the upheaval that came with those developments, the presence of the troops and the prestige of being home to the Reich's largest training ground were cheered by most people in this very nationalistic community.

The twelve years of Nazi rule and the dislocations that came with the war had a profound impact on the county and its population. As in the rest of Germany, the regime was able to crush the political left. Socialists and Communists, who represented a minority in most villages but had dominated the mining villages along the border to the Saarland, were arrested and harassed. Many of them spent time in a wild concentration camp in the village of Hoppstädten.[25] Baumholder's small Jewish community also had to endure the full wrath of the regime's anti-Jewish measures. The twenty-seven Jews who called Baumholder their home suffered much humiliation, as few in the community stood up for their fellow citizens. Except for two individuals, all of Baumholder's Jews left their homes and businesses in the years before 1938. While some of them were fortunate enough to escape to the United States, the eleven who merely moved to larger cities in the Reich were all killed in Nazi extermination camps.[26]

The National Socialist revolution also weakened the authority of traditional élites and institutions in the villages.[27] The Catholic clergy, for example, lost much of its hold over the young, as Nazi organizations such as the Hitler Youth or League of German Girls (BDM) offered more exciting fare. One woman who became a local BDM leader recalled why the Nazis had held such appeal for her and other young women: "The priest never allowed us girls to go swimming or camping, or to do anything without a chaperone; the Nazis gave us all the adventures normally reserved for the boys."[28] In Protestant communities, teachers often usurped the moral authority previously held by the clergy.[29] Clergy, both Catholic and Protestant, also lost out because the regime stressed productivity at the expense of religiosity. One of the complaints most often voiced concerned the secularization that came with a regime that forced people to work on Sundays.[30]

Once the Nazi regime invaded Poland in 1939, the upheaval in Baumholder and other Westwall communities only increased. In order to remove the population from proximity to the enemy border, whole villages and towns, including their factories and workshops, were evacuated to Franconia, Swabia, and Thuringia. Evacuees from the Saarland, on the other hand, streamed into the county of Birkenfeld, where they had relatives with whom they could stay.[31] All communities bordering on the Red Zone, a 20-kilometer-wide strip along the French border, were filled beyond capacity with construction workers feverishly struggling to complete work on the Westwall. Added to the tens of thousands of workers was the increasing number of military personnel who were arriving into the area to secure the Western border. Birkenfeld County was saved from one hardship, though. The escalation of war at the homefront did not bring any great number of evacuated women and children from the heavily bombed cities within Germany. The county, just as much as the rest of the region, was too close to the Western front to be considered a safe haven.

The Nazi state, whose foremost aim had been the creation of a racially cleansed *Volksgemeinschaft,* defeated its own purposes when it injected ever-greater numbers of outsiders into these formerly homogeneous communities. After 1940, large numbers of French POWs and slave laborers from the East were sent to the villages and towns of the region. These men and women generally lived not in camps but with "their farmer," and relations often were cordial. Even when the slave workers were so-called subhumans (*Untermenschen*) from the Soviet Union or Poland, farmers generally treated them humanely because they were desperate for their labor. In light of this situation, the strict laws that forbade friendly contacts with the foreign laborers, to ensure the racial purity of the *Volksgemeinschaft,* could hardly be enforced.[32] Even the draconian measures aimed at prohibiting sexual relations between Germans and forced laborers were often ignored.[33]

Devotion to the Führer and National Socialism crumbled quickly once the fortunes of the war shifted, after the defeat in Stalingrad in 1943. The county was bombed heavily because of its proximity to supply routes to the Western front but also because of the military installations connected with the Baumholder training area. Collapse of morale had already set in with Stalingrad, but the actions of the regime and local Nazi officials during the Götterdämmerung of the Thousand-Year Reich only exacerbated this process. In September 1944, the county had to mobilize 1,800 men between the ages of sixteen and seventy to fortify the Westwall.[34] In the waning months of the war, more sacrifices for the *Volksgemeinschaft* were called for when the *Volkssturm* (Home Defense), a motley army of untrained and ill-equipped children and old men, was organized to hold up the American advance. The diary entry of a local woman reveals just how pathetic an attempt this last effort to hold back the American invasion was. Comparing her village's haphazard defense to the popular uprising against Napoleon, she concluded, "This can't be done like 1813. One cannot advance against the most modern tanks with sickles and hay forks."[35]

The end of the war came quickly to this region. As in most other communities along the Western frontier, the population waited in nervous and often eager anticipation for the arrival of the Americans.[36] Despite pressure from local Nazi leaders and the remaining Wehrmacht, people refused to evacuate their communities or to build tank barriers. They prepared white flags, burned their party insignias, and begged the remaining German soldiers to put on civilian clothes. Reading the writing on the wall, the local Nazi leadership, including the Landrat, made their way across the Rhine, leaving the population to fend for itself.[37] After two days of heavy bombing of the military training camp in Baumholder, the Americans arrived on 18 March 1945. The advancing units of the First, Third, and Seventh Armies encountered very little resistance, and consequently there was very little fighting and few casualties.

Contemporary observers noted their sense of wonder as this American "avalanche of steel" conquered their communities: "The soldiers looked stunning, healthy and well-fed, dressed in uniforms of the finest cloth and their boots were made of the best leather. On top of that the fantastic vehicles. We were able to convince ourselves in every aspect of the technical superiority of the Americans. . . . They ate lily-white bread, the likes of which we have never seen, they had chocolates in abundance and smoked constantly."[38] Germans were surprised at this sight, especially when they compared the well-fed American soldiers with their superior equipment to the devastating picture that the retreating Wehrmacht soldiers presented: "Many of them could hardly walk anymore, they threw away coats, helmets, ammunition bags and blankets, as they leaned heavily on their knotty walking sticks and pushed the sad remains of their equipment in wooden carts or baby carriages in front of them."[39] The sight of the retreating German soldiers often evoked tears of sadness among the population. But the soldiers' rowdy and often lawless behavior also evoked tears of anger and much bitterness. German soldiers stole bicycles and carts and looted food and drink. The demoralized troops also harassed and terrorized the civilian population during their retreat. The overwhelming military superiority of the American GIs combined with the rowdy behavior of the German troops disillusioned many a German's belief in their military as a "symbol of German power and might."[40]

As straggling German soldiers retreated east toward the Rhine, the Americans took down the marker for the town's Adolf-Hitler-Straße and replaced it with one reading "President Roosevelt Street."[41] The Americans arrested all those Nazi officials who had not fled and appointed well-known anti-Nazis, many of them Social Democrats, to political offices. Before the cessation of hostilities on 8 May, relations between the Americans and the Germans were marked by an almost "carefree rapprochement" (unbekümmerte Annäherung), and Germans expressed surprise that the Americans treated them much more kindly than Goebbel's propaganda had predicted.[42] To this day, recollections of that first Hershey bar or that first piece of chewing gum handed out by a smiling GI sitting atop a tank hold a prominent place in these people's recollections. The local population also did not forget that "the Amis arrived at 6 o'clock in the morning and by 8 A.M. we were already drinking coffee with them."[43] The worst offenses committed by the GIs were looting of wine cellars and confiscation of cameras.[44] Once the Americans crossed the Rhine and encountered the full horror of the Nazi regime in such places as Buchenwald and Dachau, their attitude toward the Germans hardened considerably.

To the great dismay of the local population, the American occupation was short-lived. In July of 1945, the French took possession of their zone of occupation, and the Americans turned all the military installations in the county over to the French. The years of French military government were grim. The French were traditionally considered the archenemy of Germany, and resentment in the border regions was especially strong. The population also remembered all too well the last French military occupation, in the 1920s, when the French had used colonial troops from Senegal and Morocco. Germans were convinced that the French had used these black troops as an occupation force to humiliate the defeated Germany even further. Vivid memories of that "black horror on the Rhine" and the realization that Germans would now have to pay a price for the harsh German occupation of France led to an anxious anticipation of the new occupying power. When the French arrived in July 1945, the people clearly were not happy; everybody understood that a change for the worse was in store.[45] French soldiers did not hand out candy to local children as American soldiers generally did. Local children who lined the streets to greet the soldiers were spat on, and the humiliation of the civilian population became a daily experience. Unlike the Americans, who fed their own troops and even shared their generous rations with the local population, the French lived off the local population. The French also made few friends when they demanded that the Germans salute the French flag, and Germans resented that the French "acted as heroes in a land that they on their own could not conquer."[46] Although the Birkenfeld Landrat, Social Democrat Jakob Heep, reported that relations with the military authorities were civil for the most part, the population thought otherwise. French telephone lines were cut, the tricolor was stolen from the officers' club, and military installations were vandalized.[47] A common derogatory assessment of the French at the time reveals the level of animosity. The French victory over Germany was explained in this manner: "A couple of Frenchmen put on American uniforms, get into tanks delivered by Anglo-Americans, have their Moroccans and Senegalese march behind them, and the matter of the 'grand nation' is achieved."[48]

The French, on the other hand, also had no lost love for Germany. France had suffered greatly under German occupation between 1940 and 1944, and the French were intent on returning the favor. The secret reports of the county's Landrat are full of laments about impossible French requisition demands. Allotted food rations for the local population were as low as 600 calories per day, while the French exported locally produced agricultural goods to France. After all the French had suffered under German occupation, they aimed at the fullest economic exploitation of their zone. For a region whose agriculture had not been self-sufficient even before 1939, this policy had devastating consequences. A 1948 memorandum by the British consulate in Baden-Baden suggested that the French policy might be legally sound but predicted that it would also "lead to the utter devastation of the French zone."[49]

The mood among the population reflected the hardship suffered under the occupation, and a concerned Landrat Heep reported that attitudes toward the new democracy were very conflicted as a consequence. Heep, who had endured much persecution during the Nazi years, despaired that the "great suffering robs a large part of the population of the ability . . . to understand . . . that it was the Hitler years that caused the current circumstances." Instead, Heep complained, the great majority of Germans saw themselves as victims of the occupation and incompetent German administrators.[50] Because of the low caloric intake, few people were willing to expend energy on any sort of labor activity. Infractions of the law had become a daily occurrence because the black market seemed the only solution to the food crisis.[51]

Rebuilding democratic institutions proved a much greater challenge than anticipated. Political parties from the left to the right had a hard time getting people to join, as too many felt burned by the experiences of the

Nazi regime.[52] Strengthening democratic attitudes within the population also was much harder than many had thought. People remained suspicious of a democracy that had brought only empty bellies, and the population accused German officials for having become slaves of the occupation. To an ever greater degree, anonymous letter writers accused local authorities of being traitors to their country and even threatened violence. The occupation force, on the other hand, was accused of being intent on the "destruction of the German *Volk*." To the great dismay of Heep, more and more people, especially the young, questioned whether the "*Volk* could achieve ordered and healthy circumstances through democratic means."[53] Occasional voices emerged that suggested, "If we had a Hitler again, things would turn around for us." Heep was appalled by just how few people took a courageous stand to condemn such comments.[54]

Wow!

The contradictory and often inconsistent denazification policies of the American and French military governments produced mixed results at best. The Americans had interned all individuals who had been high-ranking members of the party or members of the SS, SA, or Gestapo. Compromised civil servants and those who had been ardent Nazis were laid off.[55] The French did not trust the denazification efforts of the Americans and submitted all civil servants to yet another round of investigation. Since the greater part of the county's civil servants had been members of the NSDAP before 1 April 1933, French officials conducted a wholesale layoff. Civil servants were replaced by little-trained substitutes and, as a consequence, the local administration came to a virtual standstill during the French evaluation process.[56] Because of the unpopularity of the denazification efforts, fewer and fewer Germans were willing to serve on the denazification commission. The French desire for the most efficient exploitation of their zone also undermined a more successful denazification of German society. Since only a highly efficient bureaucracy could assure such an economic exploitation of their zone, lower military government officials began to ignore the rulings of the German denazification commissions. Even the Social Democratic Landrat Heep was anxious to rebuild the county and to forge ahead. This he could do only with experienced civil servants.

A more determined reckoning with the past was also subverted because the newly established political parties were anxious to find voter support among former Nazis. All political parties, including the SPD and KPD, urged leaving the past behind and looking to a more democratic future instead. In their efforts they were joined by the local clergy, who refused to denounce former party members and helped many get a *Persilschein* (laundry certificate) that cleared their name.[57] The clergy in Birkenfeld and Baumholder who had been ardent Nazis were relocated to new parishes and the local circuit court received a new judge, but the great majority of former Nazis were more fortunate. By 1947, former members of the NSDAP returned in droves to their old positions, and by 1948 even the Délégation Supérieure, the commission in charge of denazification, came around to this view. By 1950, in line with a zonewide trend, almost all tainted civil servants in the county had been cleared and returned to their former positions.[58]

Despite the easing of the denazification efforts, the local mood and attitudes toward the French did not improve when Birkenfeld County, barely eight years old, suffered yet another devastating loss. In 1947, 20.8 percent of its most fertile farmland was annexed by the French military government and integrated into the Saarland. In this manner, the county also lost 17,000 of its inhabitants. The French separated the Saarland from their zone of occupation to merge it into an economic union with France, and Birkenfeld became a border region. This development interrupted the area's traditional trade routes, further depressing an already precarious economy.[59]

Like all counties in the French zone, Birkenfeld was spared some of the challenges faced by counties in the other zones of Germany. The French had rigorously repatriated all of the 175,000 slave laborers in their zone by the fall of 1945.[60] The French also refused to accept any refugees or expellees into their zone because they had not been part of the Potsdam deliberations on the expulsion of Germans from the eastern parts of the Reich and from Poland, Hungary, and Czechoslovakia. Consequently, the French did not feel bound by this treaty. The French allowed entrance into their zone only for the purpose of reuniting expellees with their families. Thus, while the British and American zones experienced the influx of approximately 11.8 million expellees and refugees, a mere 110,000 had made it into the French zone by 1950. The state of Rhineland-Palatinate thus received less than 1.4 percent of the overall refugee and expellee population. The great majority of those who arrived before 1950 had come illegally.[61] A French observer commented on just how fortunate a development this was for the local population when he suggested that although the Germans in this region lived in "a miserable zone," it was "not yet flooded with refugees from the East."[62]

Thus, even though the county was spared the additional burden of housing and feeding refugee masses, the situation was not auspicious. Matters did not seem to have improved much in this traditional poorhouse of Germany even after the 1948 currency reform and the establishment of the Federal Republic in 1949. The revival of the precious stone industry after the currency reform had improved the economic outlook, but the loss of the Saarland continued to hurt this heavily agricultural county. Local trade and commerce had virtually come to a halt. Unemployment stood at more than 10 percent countywide and at more than 20 percent in Baumholder. In March of 1950, the mayor of Baumholder described the mood of the population as "not confident in light of the abysmal economic situation," noting, "Few people take any interest in political affairs; everybody is merely concerned with their own economic hardship."[63] All that could be sighted on the roads were an "occasional truck, a horse-drawn cart, a motorcycle, or a bicyclist, hardly ever an automobile."[64] Because the French soldiers stationed on the Platz had very little money to spend, they were rarely seen in or around town. Some of the French soldiers traded food with the locals, but the people of Baumholder agreed that "the French had nothing"; indeed, many recalled, "They were as poor as we."[65] Very few local people were employed by the French military and thus able to supplement their incomes. The French had even returned large tracts of the Platz to local farmers for agricultural use. There was so little activity on and around the Platz that a newspaper report asserted that Baumholder was ready to revert to its "pre-1937 sleeping-beauty slumber."[66]

Hell on Wheels

All this changed dramatically when the Americans returned in 1951 with "Hell on Wheels," the United States Army's Second Tank Division. The soldiers and their machinery arrived with a roar like thunder to establish what they called their "Baumholder Community of Victors," a community that would by the end of the 1950s be home to 8,000 permanent American troops and their dependents and approximately 30,000 troops who rotated during year-round maneuvers.[67] For the next four decades, the 80,000 inhabitants of the county of Birkenfeld would live in close proximity to 40,000 Americans stationed in one of the many military bases that dotted the countryside. What consequences this military deployment had on the lives of the local people is best exemplified in the words of the town's official history: "[When the] first American units came to Baumholder, nobody could foresee that this change of scenery initiated a development that would in just a few years completely change the face of the town and the spiritual outlook of the population."[68]

Whereas the Nazi regime's description of the land of the Westwall construction had focused mostly on the themes of military might and sac-

people's community

rifice for the _Volksgemeinschaft,_ the coverage of the area in the 1950s had a very different tenor. National press descriptions of the Baumholder-Kaiserslautern area as the "Eldorado [_sic_] of West Germany" or as the "Alaska on the Westwall" always stressed that this was "the land where milk and honey flow, that is, where the $ and the DM roll."[69] The press coverage also always stressed that the injection of the American military was bound to have larger implications for the people of the state. As a writer for _Der Stern_ put it, "[Nobody has to] travel across the ocean anymore to find the land of unlimited opportunities. It is right here in the Palatinate."[70] The author of these lines clearly understood that the mammoth construction program that accompanied the shift in the American military mission was bound to bring more changes to this poor and backward state than merely a new and modern infrastructure to house the thousands of soldiers. The New World had arrived in Rhineland-Palatinate and confronted a world that perhaps more than other regions of Germany had known very little of unlimited opportunities and even less of the American way of life.

Just fourteen years after the disruptions brought about by construction of the Westwall fortifications, a new military buildup swept the population and local officials into the forefront of high politics. In what was generally described as a breathtaking "American tempo," troop movements, land requisitioning, and huge construction projects went hand in hand.[71] In Baumholder, the plans of the American military called for the expansion of the Platz beyond its existing boundaries. Existing Wehrmacht barracks were renovated and expanded to house the troops transferred from the American zone and to accommodate newly mobilized GIs from the United States. Additional housing for civilian personnel and the thousands of dependents who were expected to join the soldiers was to be constructed as well.

The ambitious military plans for Baumholder affected the whole county. In Idar-Oberstein, the county's only good-sized city and industrial center, the French military command turned over former Wehrmacht barracks to the Americans, and the construction of new barracks and family housing was also begun. Just outside of Idar-Oberstein, large tracts of land were requisitioned in Nahbollenbach to build one of EUCOM's (European Command) largest depots. In Neubrücke, a small village located between Baumholder and the county seat of Birkenfeld, 100 acres of land were confiscated to build a modern, thousand-bed hospital. A whole mountaintop forest was razed, and the discovery of an ancient Celtic burial site slowed construction only long enough to recover a few artifacts for the state museum in Trier. The hospital erected on this historic site

In this 1954 photograph, the contrast between the traditionally rural life of the farmers in Baumholder and the gleaming American city on the hill could not be starker. Courtesy of Stefan Moses, photographer; originally published in *Neue Revue*

was intended primarily for war emergencies, but it was also to provide medical services for the troops stationed in the region and their family members. Another 100 acres was confiscated in the neighboring village of Hoppstädten to allow conversion of a former Wehrmacht airstrip into a small airport. Requisitioning of land continued throughout the 1950s, as missile bases, rifle ranges, radar stations, and other military installations were built. More land was needed when family housing, schools, churches, shopping centers, officers' and enlisted men's clubs, and golf courses were added to the military installations.[72]

The speed, but also the sheer suddenness, of all these developments took many by surprise and evoked diverse responses. These ranged from despair over the loss of ancestral lands to a palpable sense of excitement over the prospects that this military buildup entailed. A newspaper described the new situation as "a gamble, exciting and unpredictable, just like the big lottery." It went on to describe how suddenly a couple of jeeps could be sighted on county roads and remote farm roads. Land surveyors were seen, and the next signs were the "big American automobiles of high-ranking American officers" that appeared in the "tiny and poor villages." All this feverish activity attracted the young of the town as well. According to this report, the boys of the village gathered with great interest and excitement as they inspected the American vehicles. "Finally the day arrived," and the first construction crews showed up. The boom could begin. As soon as the first trees were felled, the prices for rooms in the village inn skyrocketed, because military personnel and construction supervisors needed accommodations. Miraculously, American cigarettes, coffee, and dances were offered in the local inns. Very quickly, too, "women with garish makeup" who followed the American troop movements across Germany appeared in the hinterland. The regional paper *Die Rheinpfalz* reported with much excitement that in all these communities, the "dollar rolled." There were losers and winners in this exciting game. "[Those who] lost their land, moan; others are jubilant." The newspaper described the money that could be made as being "like a jackpot" and concluded, "Today Baumholder, Landstuhl, Kaiserslautern, and Birkenfeld are places that every occupation soldier knows better than the cities 'in God's own land.' . . . In the end, everything is 'OK' and the Americans do their 'shake-hands.'"[73]

Despite all the excitement of the future prospects that this description suggests, the invasion of "yet another occupation" entailed plenty of difficulties for those involved. Often enough, neither state, regional, nor local government was informed by federal authorities or the Americans of ongoing plans. Because the appearance of American troops and the

vis-à-vis 1. face to face
2. in relation to; compared with

construction crews that accompanied them was often so sudden and unexpected, the response they evoked was often one of anger.[74] A Birkenfeld council member, for example, angrily asked the mayor to explain why the city council learned only through a newspaper report of the impending confiscation of land at the local brick factory to build permanent barracks for the American military. The factory was the city's largest employer, and the land to be confiscated contained the clay that the factory used to produce its bricks. A confiscation such as that planned would mean the loss of many jobs. The mayor admitted that he too had only just been informed by the owners of the factory, who in turn had themselves only recently been notified of the planned confiscation. An angry city council also reminded the mayor that to date no state agency in Rhineland-Palatinate had been informed of the planned confiscation or construction of barracks. Just as West Germans were hoping that their defense contribution would be winning them greater autonomy, local officials were not even informed of impending confiscations. Such treatment by the occupying authorities created considerable anger among city council members, who did not wish to be viewed as lackeys of the occupation. The members of city council expressed their surprise that "six years after the cessation of hostilities" such procedures were still possible.[75]

Such misunderstandings arose not necessarily because of disregard or thoughtlessness on the part of the Americans. More often they were caused by bureaucratic snags. Matters were also complicated by the fact that local German officials were not allowed to deal directly with the Americans. All communications with the Germans were supposed to be channeled through the office of the local French délégué (representative of the French High Commissioner). Records indicate that while the délégués were often flexible, permitting German officials to negotiate directly with the Americans, these were individual decisions, not standard procedure. In 1953, Landrat Heep complained to the Kreistag (county commissioners) that the local délégué had been "using methods" that had not been in style since 1945–46. Heep had approached the Americans directly, and the French délégué had reacted in outrage, forbidding any further direct communication between Germans and Americans. Heep seemed little impressed by the délégué's anger, however, and announced that he planned simply to ignore such orders. While the French were jealously guarding their declining status as an occupation power vis-à-vis the Americans, the Germans were emboldened by the new role they were to play in NATO's defense strategy. A member of the Kreistag gave voice to the new confidence when he suggested that it was time to "show the French some teeth."[76]

In German encounters with the American military, the personality of the individual American military commander was as important as that of the French *délégué*. Landrat Heep, for example, acknowledged that over the years most contacts with the occupation powers had been polite, but he complained that once in a while he encountered military commanders "who hated the Germans."[77] When such antagonism existed, relations between the Americans and Germans could be frigid. Cooperation between American and German officials was further complicated by the fact that military commanders rotated at very short intervals. While most tours lasted one year, some commands changed after only a few months. A degree of mutual trust and friendly contact thus had to be built anew with every change of command.

Farmers' Despair

While the city of Birkenfeld was able to ward off the planned requisitioning at the local brickyards by offering an alternative tract, local officials were not able to protect farmers from losing their livelihoods. To accomplish the American mission in the state, large tracts of arable land were requisitioned, causing an outrage among local farmers. Unlike in 1937, when no one dared to oppose the confiscation of over 27,000 acres of land to create the Platz, tempers flared in the years after 1950.[78] Significantly, farmers were not always notified in a timely manner that their lands were to be taken. A farmer could well find his fields ripped open by the excavators of the German construction crews employed by the American military without ever having been notified that his land had been requisitioned.[79] Indeed, a 1952 newspaper report suggested that German construction companies had been caught up in "the American tempo." Once fields and woods were appropriated, farmers often had to wait an average of ten to twelve months to find out how much compensation they would receive.[80] Why, a 1952 newspaper essay asked, is there money for building but no money to compensate the farmers? The local occupation office (*Besatzungsamt*) was so swamped with requests, reported a concerned Landrat, that "forty to fifty percent of the employees of this office were on sick leave due to physical or mental breakdown."[81]

Even when farmers themselves were not affected by confiscation, the American presence could spell trouble for them. It was not unusual for farmers to arrive at their fields to discover that their property was being used to store earth-moving machinery and construction materials. The fact that a year's harvest of potatoes was in the ground counted for little.

fallow—

Other farmers were surprised to find that the access roads to their fields had suddenly been blocked off by barbed wire, with signs declaring the territory off-limits.[82] To the great dismay of the Social Democratic Landrat, the Communist Party, before being banned in 1956, took advantage of such discontent to agitate among local farmers. During another round of extensive land annexations in 1952, farmers in East Germany urged local farmers to fight the "war-mongering imperialistic powers" and to work toward a "united democratic, peace-loving Germany." Even though there were no members of the Communist Party on the city councils of Birkenfeld or Baumholder or in the Kreistag, the Landrat expressed concern over an impending "Baumholder Revolution."[83]

In 1955, a similar revolutionary spirit was suspected when farmers drove a surveying team off their land.[84] At the time of the discussions for the Paris Treaty, which was to be the foundation for Germany's coming sovereignty and full integration into NATO, more land was being confiscated to expand military installations. Representatives from the Communist Party traveled to the region and spread the rumor that the federal government would be leasing local lands to the Americans for ninety-nine years and that further confiscations were imminent. At a time when most people assumed that the Americans would be stationed in Germany for at most another ten years, this rumor caused much concern. Because of the growing uncertainty, a great number of fields lay fallow. Farmers were unwilling to plant crops on land that might be gone the next day. Landrat Heep, who hardly minced words when he criticized the French or the Americans, had equally little patience when this kind of grumbling was incited by the Communists. He expressed his dismay at these activities, and he was convinced that a "regular Communist spy ring existed in Baumholder."[85]

The inconvenience resulting from the expansion of the existing military facilities and the construction of new installations was hard on the local population. Aside from the huge construction projects underway in and around Kaiserslautern, Baumholder was the largest construction site in Germany. Companies from all over the country made bids to cash in on this opportunity, and the "boom" of 1951–53 brought more than 6,000 workers to this sleepy little town.[86] The military construction projects involved the razing of entire forests. Trucks and earth-moving equipment clogged the streets of Baumholder and the surrounding communities. Intermingling with the German construction vehicles were the huge excavators and bulldozers of the United States Army Corps of Engineers. In light of the endless traffic, parents often were afraid to allow their small children out of the house to attend school, let alone to play. Farmers were

bivouacked

reluctant to travel to their fields. How were their oxen- and horse-drawn vehicles to compete with the never-ending roar of the machines?

In the past, the county's roads had accommodated mostly wagons drawn by oxen, pedestrians, motorcycles, and a handful of cars; now they were overwhelmed. The tires of the construction vehicles and the chains of the bulldozers and the military tanks hurled red clay all over the county streets, often making roads impassable. Baumholder's streets, according to contemporary observers, were covered with a slow-moving mudflow. Streets could not be crossed unless one wore high rubber boots. The German press as well as the American GIs jokingly referred to Baumholder as "Schlammholder," or "Mudholder."[87]

The whole atmosphere that accompanied the building boom was, in the words of one resident, like a "movie set of Dodge City." All the rooms rented out by the local population at steep prices were insufficient to accommodate the thousands of workers, nor were there enough local inns to feed them. Thus, wooden barracks popped up everywhere to house the workers, and seven temporary cafeterias appeared as if from nowhere to feed the thousands of men employed with construction companies from all parts of Germany. The largest of them, the Hilfszug Bayern, served 700 lunches daily.[88]

While farmers were still defending their fields with pitchforks and the construction of the military installation was proceeding at a feverish pace, thousands of American soldiers were already moving into the region to start conducting maneuvers on the Platz. Without sufficient base housing, thousands of these soldiers bivouacked in tents on the slopes of the training camp overlooking the little town.[89] A never-ending column of tanks of "Hell on Wheels" arrived in Baumholder from the American zone by train. In Baumholder they were unloaded at the local train station and then driven to the Platz. The town's streets turned into rubble under this assault. Often, though, the tanks, trucks, and jeeps arrived by road, damaging not only the streets of the communities bordering the Platz but the surfaces of the county's roads as well. The newspapers regularly filed stories of roads turned into mud or "heaps of rubble" and of farmers' fields completely destroyed by the heavy chains of the tanks.[90]

"The Americans Brought the City to the Village"

Many of the residents of Baumholder who looked around their town in the early 1950s must have had a sense of déjà vu. To a large degree, many of the upheavals of 1951 were a repetition of the developments that

dousing
unprecedented

had accompanied the boom Baumholder experienced during the Westwall construction in 1937, when "houses, depots, and barracks shot like
mushrooms out of the ground . . . and columns of trucks and cars carried
construction materials through the narrow streets of the city . . . which
turned into a sea of dirt and mud."[91] There were many similarities with
1937, to be sure, but the local inhabitants also recognized tremendous differences. If 1937 was a mere wake-up call from the town's "sleeping-beauty
slumber," 1951 felt more like a dousing with a bucket of cold water.[92] For
a number of reasons this latest modernization effort was different in kind
and in scope. No matter how inconvenient the Wehrmacht construction
of 1937–38 must have been for the locals, that push toward modernization was not experienced as drastically as the changes that came in 1951.
In 1938, it was German soldiers who were stationed in Baumholder, and
their presence was a source of tremendous pride. While German soldiers
had brought prestige, the American soldiers were experienced as occupiers; they were also a bitter reminder of the lost war and Germany's
continuing lack of sovereignty. But even more importantly, the modernization in the 1950s was not only experienced as "foreign"; it was also
of much greater velocity. Moreover, the economic benefits of the Wehrmacht boom could not be enjoyed for a prolonged period of time, because the economic advancement was disrupted by war. The boom of the
1950s, on the other hand, lasted into the early 1970s, thus initiating an
unprecedented opportunity for growth and change in this region.

Unlike their German and French predecessors, the American military
and its soldiers had money, lots of money, and the luxury and chrome
of the 3,000 American *Straßenkreuzer* (fin-tailed limousines) that clogged
the narrow streets of Baumholder were only the most obvious displays
of this wealth.[93] Unlike the French soldiers, who had seldom been seen
about town, the American GIs quickly became a visible presence. As the
local residents were soon to learn, the American dollar and the prosperity that followed in its wake were to change profoundly the existing
town/military relations as well as the way of life in Baumholder and the
entire county.

"Hell on Wheels" and its thousands of soldiers had brought not only
muddy roads and the confiscation of fields to Baumholder and Birkenfeld. They also brought a sense of excitement and great prosperity. When
the Americans first came to Sembach, just outside Kaiserslautern, to construct an air base, the local commander proudly announced to the local
people in a press conference, "In two years you will not recognize Sembach anymore."[94] The same statement could have been uttered by the
commander of the Baumholder "Community of Victors." The injection

of money that the transfer of American troops brought into the local community changed not only economic structures but also social structures. "The Americans," as one local man put it, "had brought the city to the countryside."[95]

In this traditionally neglected region, the American construction program had, according to American military assessments, "psychological and economic effects" because "the spending [of] hundreds of millions of Deutsche Marks . . . was a life-giving tonic" to the local economy. The military buildup in Rhineland-Palatinate was so substantial that it even impacted the national economy profoundly. Between 1950 and 1953, a total of DM 2.364 billion of German tax funds was spent on American construction sites in Germany, and about one-third of that sum, almost DM 800 million, was spent in Rhineland-Palatinate. Baumholder itself was the recipient of some DM 80 million of that money.[96]

In the county, the building boom had an immediate impact. Whereas in March of 1950 the mood of the population in Baumholder had been described as abysmal and lacking in confidence, suddenly everybody had "the feeling that things were moving forward."[97] As one resident recalled, the pace of life was "exciting; nothing ever stood still anymore."[98] The tenor of this exhilaration can be found in much of the coverage by the local press as well. The breathless headline, "Small Village has a Great Future / Big City Traffic in Hoppstädten / Construction Sites Everywhere / 1,000 Bed Hospital Nearing Completion / Planes on the Local Air Strip / Local Business Is Booming," is just one such example.[99] The local people obviously appreciated this injection of funds, but they also understood that the German taxpayer was paying a high price for West Germany's defense contribution to NATO and the country's political rehabilitation. Thus a visitor to the new military hospital outside Hoppstädten commented on how expensive the installation's luxurious interior must have been by adding in a slightly ironic tone that he was convinced that the "Americans spend the money for this project as gladly as it if had been their own."[100]

The huge construction programs had an immediate impact on the local unemployment statistics. Before March 1950 the unemployment rate in this traditionally depressed region had been 10 percent, and the numbers for Baumholder were even grimmer, reaching as high as 22.4 percent.[101] Within a matter of months, unemployment simply vanished. Indeed, the farmers' organizations of Nahe, Mosel, and Rhine issued protest after protest that they were losing their workers to the allied construction sites all across Rhineland-Palatinate.[102] Not only did unemployment drop to 1.4 percent, thousands of new jobs were created. Between 1950 and 1955, the number of employed individuals in the county grew by 6,648.[103] Initially, many farmers and their sons worked as construction laborers to supplement their meager incomes from agriculture. Once the construction projects were finished, many of these men did not return to their farms. The military base needed stokers at its three heating plants, as well as a great number of maintenance workers. In light of these new opportunities, many farmers chose a steady paycheck over the unpredictability of working the land.[104] Wages for laborers as well as for professionals were generous by local standards. Professionals who worked for the Americans reported that they earned much higher incomes than they could have demanded on the German market.[105]

But it was not only men who quickly found employment with the American military forces. Local women, who had traditionally helped on the family farm or worked as farmhands, now ventured out on their own. Young and not-so-young women began work in the cafeterias and kitchens or in one of the many stores on the base. One woman recalled how she had worked at the soda fountain in the American snack bar in the early 1950s. She was paid DM 198 per month and to this day recalls how proud she was when she counted out the first money she had earned herself.[106] A significant number of women also worked as maids for American families, preferring such work because American housewives offered up to DM 15 per day in wages, while the local farmers paid a mere 50 Pfennig (one-half DM) an hour.[107] American housewives often also paid in highly desirable American goods, such as coffee, cigarettes, and chocolates. The *Wall Street Journal* even commented on the "fairy-like salaries paid to German maids by the fantastically rich female Americans, who can do exactly nothing or almost everything, who are slender and elegant and spend their time talking about fashion and family relationships."[108] Local women also worked in professional capacities. A woman hired as a secretary/translator for the local commander in 1953 made the "dream wage" of DM 350 a month; she was the envy of all her friends.[109]

By 1954, 4,500 Germans from Birkenfeld County, a full 17 percent of the workforce, were employed by the American military.[110] The Americans were not only the largest employer in Baumholder but the largest in the whole county.[111] During the 1950s, when all national social policies were aimed at returning women to the home, the number of employed women in the county increased 130 percent.[112] While everybody was delighted that the number of employed men in the county increased by 51 percent, the increase in jobs for women evoked very different responses. At a time of nationwide efforts to overcome the dislocations of the war and postwar years by restoring traditional gender roles, women's increas-

German women working in the American post exchange in Ramstein. For
many German women in these rural communities, employment on the American military bases offered a much-welcomed opportunity to earn their own
paycheck. Courtesy of IANAS, Johannes Gutenberg Universität, Mainz

ing employment caused many a raised eyebrow and much hand-wringing
over the fate of the family and the future of Germany. The fact that the
majority of these new wage earners made their livings on the American
military bases of the county did little to ameliorate anxieties.[113]

Another sector of the population that experienced a boom through
the stationing of American troops was that comprising local artisans and
owners of small business. While local firms were too small to have submitted bids for the construction program, they nonetheless prospered
from the crumbs that fell from the tables of the large general contractors.
Many artisan establishments in the area experienced rapid growth. Once
the construction program was concluded, the American military called
on local establishments to repair and maintain the military installations.
Within just a few years, contracts with the American military amounted
to over 50 percent of local artisans' business.[114] On top of the DM 80 million that were spent on construction projects, the county benefited from
the infusion of DM 92 million between 1951 and 1955, money from the
state and federal government for wages, rents, and other expenses associated with the American military. By 1955, a clearly pleased Landrat Heep

concluded that the Americans had become a substantial economic factor in the county.[115]

The American presence not only eliminated unemployment; American soldiers and their families also spent freely in the German economy. At a time when the average monthly income of a skilled worker in this region was DM 250, an American at the lowest military rank earned $100. With an exchange rate of DM 4.20 to the dollar and free room and board, it is easy to imagine just how rich even a corporal was by German standards. Higher-ranking enlisted men and officers had even greater resources. A sergeant's monthly income was the equivalent of around DM 1,000, and a lieutenant had about DM 1,400 to spend.[116] Because an American corporal earned as much money as a French colonel, American GIs had significantly greater resources than French soldiers to escape the confines of the barracks.

With their pockets full of dollars, GIs were eager to explore their surroundings. Local pubs and inns prospered from serving the GIs, who had plenty of money to sample Wiener schnitzel and German beer or to take their wives or German girlfriends out for an evening of entertainment. New pubs and inns were built to accommodate relatives of the GIs visiting from the United States, and inns that had in the past accommodated tired farmers as they talked politics over a glass of wine or beer quickly adapted to their new customers, offering "rum and cola" instead. The owner may still have been standing in his slippers as of old behind his new fancy chrome bar, but the dimmed lights and the "foreign" sounds that blasted from the latest model jukebox announced to all that a new age had dawned.[117]

Many fortunes were made by enterprising individuals who quickly adapted to the "tourist" mentality of the American soldier. Souvenir shops advertising their goods, often in broken English, sprang up on every corner. As early as 1951 the "Black Forest Shop," a little wooden shack attached to an old farmhouse, catered to the American soldiers.[118] The windows of these shops offered a variety of typical German crafts— such as cuckoo clocks, madonnas, and beer steins—for American GIs to send back home.[119] Stores that previously had sold butter and eggs now offered earrings, necklaces, cheap baubles, and expensive jewelry.[120] A former town council member jokingly recalled that "Germany's first McDonald's" also sprang out of nowhere. This fast-food-type cafeteria clearly aimed at an American clientele with its big advertising sign that read in English, "Here good food—all drinks."[121] But older, established stores prospered as well. American soldiers had plenty of money to buy German porcelain, glassware, cutlery, and furniture, all treasured for their made-in-Germany reputation for high quality. By 1955, American GIs were spending $4.9 million a year on goods and services in and around Baumholder.[122]

In the boomtown atmosphere that lasted until about 1955 in Baumholder, fortunes were made overnight, many of them legitimately,[123] but racketeering also thrived, as revealed in court records in all communities with American troops.[124] Whole train- and truckloads of construction materials disappeared at American construction sites. Tires were stolen, and the American gasoline "pipeline" was tapped.[125] U.S. government–issued blankets, pots, pans, dishes, as well as cans of food and whole sides of beef, found their way by illicit paths into many a German home. Because of the large construction projects, all these communities experienced an increase in theft, and many a German ended up before the local judge for having "organized" some building materials for his garden shed. A common joke in this region suggests that barely a house was built in the 1950s that did not contain some materials intended for the American construction program.[126]

Wherever American troops were stationed, the black market boomed, and cartons of American cigarettes could be found in most every home. The black market flourished to such an extent because American GIs had almost unlimited access to duty-free liquor and cigarettes, items coveted by the thousands of workers building the military installations as well as by the local populace. The *Rheinpfalz* reported on a "brisk traffic with Chesterfield, Luky Striks [*sic*] and Camel as well as coffee."[127] The customs station established in the county after the French separated the Saarland in 1947 had to be enlarged. Customs officials whose job formerly had been merely to check the baskets of farm women and the coat pockets of small children when they crossed into the Saarland to visit relatives now faced greater challenges. Living up to the German ideal of thoroughness, customs officials often went to extremes. Whole new sections of the population were criminalized, as individuals were arrested for owning even a couple of American cigarettes. A member of the Kreistag denounced the fact that Germans working for the Americans had been indicted for accepting a couple of cigarettes or a couple of ounces of coffee. During the same session an angry member of the SPD reported that a young woman had been indicted for merely receiving food from an American family for whom she babysat.[128]

Many in the local population displayed few scruples when it came to taking advantage of the naïveté of young GIs, many of whom were away from home for the first time. Immediately after the war, cutters and polishers of the precious stone industry from neighboring Idar-Oberstein had produced the most "marvelous rubies, emeralds, and diamonds" from bottle glass. These were then traded with American GIs for food.[129] It is probably not too far-fetched to suppose that many a GI in the 1950s sent home "precious jewels" he had exchanged for cigarettes or coffee. There were also many who cleaned out their grandmothers' attics to sell family heirlooms in exchange for American coffee and chocolates. In those days many more "heirlooms" were sold than could possibly have existed. Americans were no longer enemies, but they were also not yet friends. A former city council member remembered, "In the beginning we viewed them [the Americans] as tourists; and tourists pay more all over the world."[130]

Many local people, including a number of the angry farmers who had lost their ancestral lands, also started to cash in on the boom by renting housing. Whole families moved into their kitchens to be able to rent the rest of their house or apartment to the GIs. Soldiers rented apartments and rooms to escape the barracks during weekends, but young American couples also sought apartments "on the economy," as the GIs called it, because of the lack of sufficient housing on the base.[131] But the classified ads in the 1950s were also filled with requests from American soldiers looking for housing for their "German fiancées," and this, as will be shown later, caused much concern among the local clergy and also in the federal ministries. In light of this demand for housing, a secondary building boom was initiated in the surrounding villages. Barns were transformed into apartments; attics were expanded into apartments; additions were built onto single-family homes. Homeowners did not hesitate to take out mortgages, because they knew that dollar-wielding GIs were ready to pay any price for decent housing.[132] In the early 1950s Americans were willing and able to pay rents that were four or five times higher than what had been the going rate. At a time when the average monthly rent for a two-room apartment was DM 60–80, a local family was able to charge DM 350 for two rooms, a kitchen, and a bath. One landlady recalled that the American officer and his wife who rented from her were so desperate for an apartment that they were even willing to share the family's outhouse in the yard.[133] In a region where traditionally even workers had kept some sort of small farm animals, residents now faced the choice of whether to "keep a pig or an Ami."[134] Many regretted not having decided "in favor of the Ami" before the latter part of the 1950s.[135]

A whole new service industry emerged because the Americans, with their abundant financial resources, preferred to ride in taxis. The first taxis in Baumholder came with the Americans from Giessen.[136] Obviously having little faith in the purses of the French soldiers who replaced the American troops in Giessen, the taxi drivers packed up and followed the dollar. In Baumholder alone, about fifty taxis were registered within a few months. Many of them were owned by the sons of local farmers, who preferred driving an automobile to walking behind a plow. To this day, taxi drivers delight in telling stories of how during the "Golden Fifties" Americans were so well-off that they could afford a taxi to transport them from one pub to another, even if the distance was a mere fifty yards. Those GIs who did not have their cars shipped from the United States relied on taxis to take them for wine-tasting tours at Moselle vineyards or on sight-seeing trips to one of the many castles along the Rhine. On and around payday, especially during the initial years when leisure facilities on the bases were not yet complete, GIs did not even hesitate to call a taxi to visit Munich, Paris, or Amsterdam.[137]

Enterprising individuals arrived in town and made fortunes. A young woman used all her savings to buy a Volkswagen "Beetle," which she rented to American GIs for DM 45 a weekend. Within a short time, she had made enough money to buy another car, and before long she was the proud owner of a fleet of twenty-five Beetles; these she rented solely to GIs, because no German could have afforded her fees.[138] Local residents also understood that the Americans' love of cars could bring great financial rewards. Garages appeared offering maintenance service, and the owners with their entire families also washed and waxed American cars. Even teenagers quickly understood how to benefit from the American penchant for comfort. To the great dismay of the youth social workers, teenage boys hung around the military barracks and delivered beer and sandwiches to GIs too worn out to bother visiting the cafeteria or a local pub.[139] Another enterprising young man represented the regional Coca-Cola plant, selling their product in front of a military barracks. He quickly realized that GIs could not live by drink alone. Together with his brother and mother he prepared sandwiches with an assorted offering of German sausages. His delicacies quickly became a hot item among the GIs, and he was able to sell 800 sandwiches in the morning and another 800 at night. He soon had made enough money to support himself while attending university.[140]

The town's tax base increased substantially through all this feverish business activity. While the creation of the Platz in 1937–38 had already begun the shift from an agricultural to a commercial and trade economy, the "second invasion" of the Americans in 1951 accelerated this process greatly. In 1938, income from trade taxes was RM 10,626, but by 1952 this tax supplied the town's treasury with a staggering DM 360,649. Even after the building boom subsided, the trade tax income of Baumholder remained at around DM 300,000. Apparently, American soldiers were also much thirstier than the German soldiers had ever been. The 1938 beverage tax collected in Baumholder was RM 2,000; in 1953 the town collected DM 54,874. American soldiers also seemed to have had more fun, at least as measured by commercial entertainment. The town's income from the entertainment tax, which was charged to establishments that sponsored music and dance events, ballooned from a mere RM 400 in 1938 to a mind-boggling DM 36,035 in 1953.[141]

By late 1953 most of the construction in the county and in Baumholder was complete. The wooden barracks and canteens and the tent city of the Americans, which had given Baumholder the flair of an American frontier town during the gold rush, had largely disappeared. Most of the construction workers who had arrived from all over Germany had left. In a newspaper essay in 1956, the writer recaptured how just four years ago he had had to "wear rubber boots to be able to cross the muddy streets that were torn up by tanks and construction vehicles." All this had now changed, and his "shoes were clean as he crossed meticulously maintained asphalt streets." With the worst of the construction over, the mood in town was more optimistic, and people were much more polite than they had been four years before. He concluded that the "people in this town had proven that they could deal with any challenge that life has to offer."[142] A 1953 American assessment of troop morale came to a similar conclusion when it suggested that the completion of the construction program had "contributed to a reduction in the number of internal and external 'incidents' . . . because dry billets and more recreational facilities had replaced tents and substandard quarters."[143] Local authorities as well as the police also breathed a sigh of relief that the "turbulent days of the first few years had passed."[144]

How much the initial upheaval and disorder had subsided is best exemplified by the results of a readers' survey conducted by the local press in 1956. The population agreed that its former rhythm of life had been destroyed but that the community had become more modern and progressive. The standard of living had improved significantly, and people felt that they were more open-minded and ambitious than before. Optimism was expressed in the sentiment that even though people could not return to their old ways, their new rhythm of life was not worse, only different.[145]

Press coverage of the developments also suggests that the locals took a lot of pride in their new and much changed community. Baumholder's 1957 town fair special in the local paper, for example, described the "new Baumholder" in glowing words: "When the visitor arrives here by night . . . he is greeted by thousands of lights as if it were a fairy-tale city. An enchanting picture captures the visitor." The visitor would even be more stunned, according to this account, after encountering the excitement of the inner city at night, which sported "stores with splendid displays . . . drinks and food of every kind . . . and chrome-decorated street cruisers that roll majestically through the narrow streets." Baumholder, it crowed, "has become the City of Light."[146]

While people were aware of the fragility of a boom that was wholly reliant on the Cold War tensions of the superpowers, the advertisements in their newspapers beamed with confidence. Whereas the classified ads of 1950 still had people trying to borrow tents for camping trips to nearby mountains, after 1955 the newspapers were advertising vacations to the sunny beaches of Italy. A local department store reflected the same optimism when it compared itself to Wanamaker's in Philadelphia and Macy's in New York.[147] The many newly registered cars that now competed with the more than 3,000 cars of the American GIs are perhaps the most obvious indicator how much the economic situation had changed in the county. Between 1950 and 1955, the number of cars in the county increased from 635 to 2,802; the number of motorcycles also more than quadrupled, to 4,728.[148]

West Germany's economic miracle had arrived in the provinces, and the Germans in this region attributed their unprecedented prosperity solely to the American military presence. While just a few years earlier farmers had been upset about land confiscations, the new jobs and steady incomes convinced many in both Birkenfeld and Kaiserslautern counties that the "Amis have brought us prosperity." At the height of the American construction boom, many in the region rejoiced at the economic prospects that a long-term American presence offered them. The continued feverish pace of construction convinced many that the boom was not just a short-term phenomenon. During the early 1960s, just ten years after those first dreaded signs had appeared in Baumholder announcing that fields and meadows had been confiscated, a beaming mayor of Baumholder reported to the visiting president of the state assembly that he "had good news to report, because another battalion was scheduled to arrive in Baumholder."[149]

continuity –

Conclusion

After undergoing years of hardship under the French military government, the residents of communities with American bases saw the American military as the agent that "brought prosperity" to the region and inaugurated the rebirth of a hitherto stagnant economy. The excitement over the new prosperity and the sheer sense of elation that "things were moving forward" cannot be underestimated. Even the defense ministry in Bonn celebrated the state's new prosperity in 1955 by gushing, "Rhineland-Palatinate has never been so well off . . . as it is now."[150] The new prosperity came at a price, though. Within just a few years Rhineland-Palatinate was dotted with huge military installations, a fact that earned the region the dubious honor of being called the Federal Republic's "aircraft carrier." Because so much federal and state money was invested in military installations, the state remained Germany's stepchild when it came to funds for industrial development. Instead, the military emerged as one of the foremost industries in the state.

In many ways, one could argue that the 1950s were a mere continuation of a process of modernization that began in 1937 when the Nazi regime established the Baumholder Platz. For the many farmers who worked on the Platz for the German Wehrmacht and later for the French and then the American military, such a conclusion may be all too obvious. When people assessed the new state of affairs in the initial years after the arrival of American troops, they at times compared their new prosperity to the changes in their lives during the 1930s, suggesting that this sort of prosperity would also have come to their communities if German soldiers were still stationed there. For many Germans in these communities, then, the 1950s were a continuation of the "good old days" of the Nazi regime when the Saar was returned, the economy saw a marked improvement, and rural infrastructures experienced a modernization boost because of the Wehrmacht construction.[151] Regrets were expressed not over the region's enthusiastic embrace of Nazism but over the fact that the improvement in the quality of life had been interrupted by war, defeat, and the humiliating years of French occupation.

Acknowledging this continuity should not blind us to the many ways in which the 1950s were markedly different. On a most basic level, the modernization of economic structures during the 1950s occurred at a much faster pace; it also affected broader segments of the economy. The American military was intent on providing its soldiers and their families with all the amenities that life in America would offer them. To ensure that comfort level, the American military relied exclusively on local labor. Germans maintained the military installations; they cooked and cleaned for the soldiers, ironed and sewed their clothing and uniforms. Germans ran the barbershops, the bowling alleys, the movie theaters, and the many clubs on base that catered to the GIs. Even more importantly, the Americans carried their leisure and consumption patterns into these German communities. Germans did not act like country bumpkins but accommodated their spoiled customers. By 1953, the American military had brought such a level of prosperity that a newspaper gushed that there was "luxury, luxury wherever the eye glances." The author asked in wonderment, "When have there ever been so many modern automobiles in our city or so many well-dressed people?"[152] A store owner expressed a similar enthusiasm when he declared, "Never before have things been this good, not even during the time of the Westwall construction."[153]

While the occasional observer insisted that this sort of prosperity would have come with German soldiers as well, most knew better. The soldiers of the Wehrmacht had lived a very "soldierly" life and were almost self-sufficient. The 10,000 who had trained on the Platz had had to peel their own potatoes and wash their own dishes. Sections of the local artisan community had benefited from delivering goods and services to the German military base and farmers had delivered hay for the thousands of horses on the Platz, but the population of Baumholder at large did not prosper from the soldiers' presence. Because the German soldiers (*Landser*) received meager wages compared to the American GI, there was no explosion of the entertainment industry in the 1930s as there was in the 1950s. The *Landser* who came to Baumholder after 1938 had a mere eleven pubs to frequent; many of those sported the Nazi slogan, "You are nothing, your *Volk* is everything." There also was almost no expansion of the service industry. So poor were most of the *Landser* who trained on the Platz that the population felt pity for them. When German soldiers marched through town in the 1930s and 1940s, parents would give their children money so they could buy cigarettes and hand them to the soldiers leaving for the war.[154]

Because the modernization of economic structures was so radical during the 1950s, social structures revolutionized as well. Communities grew not only substantially larger and richer; they also became much more diverse. Their streets and overall appearance became more international and their populations more heterogeneous. By the end of the 1950s, children of more than fifty different nationalities attended schools in Baumholder.[155] Even more importantly, living with Americans changed the mentality of the local population in a most profound manner. The greatest discontinuity between the 1930s and 1950s was the basic fact that people experienced the modernization of the 1950s not under a totalitarian dictatorship but under a democracy. It was in their day-to-day interaction with the American military that Germans in these communities grew into the Western alliance and often learned to overcome their ambivalences about the freedoms implicit in a modern and democratic consumer society.

2

Living with the New Neighbors

When assessing German-American relations, observers generally refer to the 1950s as the "Golden Years."[1] The humiliating years of military government were over, and under America's watchful eye West Germany was slowly but surely being readmitted into the family of nations. Just ten years after the end of World War II, the country that had wrought so much destruction and suffering would emerge as a crucial ally in the defense of the West. Dean Acheson called these years before 1955 a "period of not only settling differences but of growth and understanding" between the United States and West Germany.[2] Surveys conducted at the beginning and end of the decade suggest just how much progress was made in that decade. By 1961, 70 percent of Germans believed that the United States saw them as friends and only 10 percent believed that Americans still viewed the Germans as enemies. This was a dramatic turnaround from just ten years earlier, when a full 60 percent of Germans were convinced that the United States considered Germany its enemy, and only 20 percent believed that the United States was Germany's friend.[3]

The interactions between Americans and Germans in Rhineland-Palatinate provide a fascinating looking glass for exploring how the former enemies became committed allies and often even friends during the 1950s. The more formal interactions between military leaders and German officials reveal that the punitive years of the occupation were clearly over. These interactions also show America's commitment to nurturing West Germany's fragile democracy by fully binding the country into the Western alliance. In the more informal interactions between the former enemies, one can observe the growing attraction of the United States as the best guarantor of freedom and of assuring a standard of living and a way of life that the communist model of the East could not provide. Although many Germans still thought of bombing nights when they encountered Americans, those sentiments were increasingly balanced by the helping hand extended through C.A.R.E. packages, the Berlin Airlift, the Marshall Plan, and the United States' contribution to assuring the freedom of Western Europe in an increasingly bipolar world.[4] Younger Germans, as we will see, were less concerned with questions of national security but admired the American soldiers with their abundant consumer goods and ease of life as harbingers of a better future.

Military Integration

When the Americans first arrived in Rhineland-Palatinate in 1950, their biggest concern had been to erect the infrastructure that would assure their new mission in Germany. The logistical aspects of creating a bulwark of defense west of the Rhine were quickly joined by an even more daunting challenge. The military had to convey to the Germans in this area a conviction that this huge American military presence was the country's best hope of containing communism and of assuring West Germany's political and military integration. Since the Rhineland-Palatinate was dominated by the Christian Democrats (CDU) and its president, Peter Altmeier, was one of Adenauer's staunchest supporters, this should have been a relatively easy task. Altmeier, whose views were based on a devoutly Catholic and deeply conservative vision of the Christian *Abendland,* was both anticommunist and antinationalist, and he was committed to the goal of Germany's political and military integration within Europe. Because of his supranational vision, but also because of the geographical location of the state, Altmeier saw himself and his state as mediators between Germany and the West, but especially between Germany and France. However, Altmeier was also concerned over the viability of his young state. Since West Germany's Basic Law (*Grundgesetz*) contained a provision that the state boundaries created by the allies might be revised in the future, Altmeier viewed any annexation of land for military purposes as a threat to the physical integrity of Rhineland-Palatinate. He complained ad nauseum to the federal government about the burden that was being placed on his state. Although Altmeier fully supported Adenauer's goal of West-integration, he nonetheless demanded an equal sharing of the defense burden among the West German states. Through-out the 1950s, he balked at every American request for more land and tried to negotiate relief for his rural constituency. The records of the American Land Relations Officer (LRO) in Mainz are full of complaints about Altmeier's "intransigent behavior."[5]

The Americans biggest struggle, however, was to convince the Social Democrats in the state that the U.S. military presence was the Federal Republic's best hope. During the late 1940s and for much of the 1950s, large sections of the German population feared that Adenauer's policy of West-integration would undermine any chance of German unity. The most outspoken critic of Adenauer's policy was the Social Democratic Party (SPD) and its chairman, Kurt Schumacher. The SPD objected to Adenauer's West-integration because it hoped that a neutral West Germany would leave the door open for a future unification of East and West Germany. Thoroughly disillusioned by their country's militarist past, SPD members were also deeply opposed to the remilitarization of West Germany. A growing number of leaders within the Protestant Church and many Germans also shared these views.[6] The U.S. military was fully aware of that stance and very anxious to convert these Germans to the U.S. vision of weaving Germany into a Western military and political alliance.

The deeply antagonistic visions of Adenauer and Schumacher over West-integration also reverberated on the local level, albeit much more softly. Because of the economic boom that came with the Americans, no clear-thinking politician could afford to malign the source of the new prosperity. Even more importantly, before the 1956 ban of the Communist Party (KPD), the SPD in these garrison communities was anxious to distance itself from the virulent anti-American propaganda that the West German Communist Party spread in the region. The activities of East German Communists, who were posting handbills that depicted Chancellor Adenauer as a traitor to German unity and called the local population colonial slaves to U.S. imperialism, made that effort even more urgent.[7]

On the municipal level, no representatives—neither those from the CDU, the FDP (Free Democrats), nor SPD—questioned the federal commitment to the United States. Nor did they question the overwhelming American military presence in their communities that was the guarantor of that Western integration. When KPD council members raised questions regarding the U.S. military mission, the SPD, CDU, and FDP members dismissed them as concerns of "high politics," which had no place in city hall.[8] Even in the SPD stronghold of Kaiserslautern, the Social Democratic *Die Freiheit* defended Adenauer's policy in 1951 by suggesting that "no clear-thinking individual in West Germany can ignore the necessity of the defense preparations" going on in the Palatinate.[9] The Rhineland-Palatinate SPD also worked hard to overcome the Americans' preference for conducting business with the more conservative CDU. When Adenauer traveled to the United States in 1957, the SPD in Kaiserslautern responded by showing a film covering the U.S. trip of Erich Ollenhauer, the SPD's new chairman. The title of the documentary, "Shaking Hands with America," indicates that the SPD did not want be left behind.[10] The SPD in these garrison communities developed a more consistent critique of the American military mission over the deployment of Nike nuclear missiles only after the KPD was banned in 1956.

Converting the Germans to the American Mission

The American military was fully aware that many of the Germans in Rhineland-Palatinate needed to be reconciled to the U.S. military presence. They also understood that appeasing the political leaders in the state would not suffice. Thus, they set out first and foremost to win the hearts and minds of the population at large. In the first years of the decade, the Americans faced an uphill battle. By late 1952, 58 percent of West Germans believed that the U.S. forces should remain in Germany to ensure the country's security. But what to do with the 20 percent of Germans who wanted the U.S. forces to leave, and the 22 percent of Germans who professed to have no opinion at all on the matter?[11] Throughout West Germany, the U.S. State Department and its representative, High Commissioner John McCloy, relied on a wide variety of formal and informal contacts between German and American groups and institutions to tie these reluctant Germans into the Western block.[12] But these efforts were not limited to the Office of the High Commissioner. Because of its close proximity to and daily interaction with a large number of Germans, the American military took on a major role in this endeavor as well.

The military's Public Information Office attributed the lack of enthusiasm for the American mission among 42 percent of the German population to the fact that "there is still a tendency on the part of the vast majority of the German people to refer to American Defense Forces in Germany as occupation troops." The office was convinced that such an outlook was detrimental to winning the hearts and souls of the German population over to the Western military alliance. One way to convince the Germans that the U.S. military was no longer an occupation force but was instead a protective force was to stress the united defense strategy of NATO. Military commanders were instructed that "every opportunity

American military parades, such as this one in Kaiserslautern in 1957, were a powerful expression of America's Dual Containment strategy of providing security *for* Germany and security *from* Germany. Courtesy of Professor Walter Rödel, Mainz

should be made in Germany to show the troops of the United States, Great Britain, France and Benelux countries marching together as a symbol of Western unity." To avoid offending German sensibilities and to erase painful memories of the occupation years, the military reduced the number of English-language signs and posters around military installations. The Public Information Office further suggested that the wording on the license plates of the more than 60,000 military vehicles be changed from "US Forces Germany" to "US Forces in Germany."[13] The Federal Republic was in fact no longer occupied, but Germans were not to be made to feel as though their country were a mere colony or satellite of the United States.

Removing English-language signs and paying more attention to avoiding offensive language were just first steps toward convincing Germans that the Americans were allies, not occupiers. Another way to tie reluctant Germans into the Western alliance was to court local officials. Commanders always invited the town's dignitaries to attend American military ceremonies as guests of honor. The commanding general of the Western

Area Command, Miles Reber, for example, invited the mayor of Kaiser-slautern to a commemoration of the first anniversary of the Rhine Military Post in 1952. The Germans were clearly pleased at this shift in U.S. policy. The Social Democratic mayor expressed his gratitude for the opportunity to stand as an equal with the French governor of the Palatinate and the American general during the review of troops.[14]

Images of this new alliance between the former enemies were also carried into the German communities with the aim of reaching a large audience. The military leadership instructed military commanders to hold parades through the neighboring towns and cities "as often as possible to celebrate national holidays or for any other good reason."[15] The military always invited community leaders to attend these parades and the American Armed Forces Day celebrations and to sit as guests of honor on the reviewing stand. On these days, large military parades filed through the German garrison towns, while thousands of people lined the streets. So impressed were German observers with the "reverberating sound of the fanfare and the beating of the drums," as well as the columns of vehicles of all sorts, that an exuberant newspaper article reported, "These picturesque images will remain with the participants for a long time."[16] These military parades with their display of American military power probably warmed the heart of many Germans who missed the pomp and glory of German soldiers marching. But they also reminded the Germans and the rest of Europe that the U.S. presence served a dual purpose; it contained the Soviet Union while simultaneously providing security "from" and security "for" Germany.[17]

During the early 1950s, the American military was also anxious to convey to the Germans that the United States would not pull out of Europe in case of a Soviet attack on Germany, that it was firmly committed to defending the West against Communism. In 1952, surveys had indicated that "around one third of West Germans believe that America will leave Germany 'in the lurch' in time of emergency." The military's Public Information Office was concerned that "it is precisely where American troops are most plentiful (the American and French zones) that the greatest mistrust of this sort exists." That office also concluded, "The individual soldier has done a good job in creating liking for Americans as persons; but this may not be enough. The next step is to create confidence in America's world aims and particularly America's commitment not to abandon Germany."[18]

The American military faced another, and perhaps more daunting challenge. Just a few years after their triumphant defeat of Germany, the Americans found themselves in the awkward position of having to convince the Germans of America's military prowess. The American military was appalled by surveys that indicated in 1951 that only 42 percent of Germans believed that the Americans could stand up to the Soviet threat. The Korean War improved that outlook significantly; in 1952, 54 percent of Germans expressed confidence in the United States' fighting spirit. The Americans were even more stunned to hear that the Germans showed a general skepticism toward the "size, equipment, and psychological readiness of American units." Military commanders were thus instructed to impress the German population with the fighting qualities and discipline of the Army and Air Force by employing "mechanized equipment" and "'fly-pasts' by our warplanes."[19] The military also always invited the German press when conducting maneuvers. Since most of the press reporters were war veterans, the American officers hoped that the former Wehrmacht soldiers would be impressed by the Americans' sophisticated equipment and training opportunities. In 1952 the military's Public Information Office was anxious to convey to local American commanders that although "in the previous period, the problem was to convince West Germans that the American soldier was a friendly, tolerant person who wished them well," the current task was different: "The time has now arrived for stressing the fighting qualities of the troops, their desire and ability to hold back an invasion."[20]

Because the United States believed that Europe could not be defended without the assistance of German manpower, fostering German acceptance of rearmament was also a crucial challenge during the early 1950s. Nationally, Eisenhower built morale in January 1951, when he met with former Wehrmacht generals whom he had affronted during the German surrender. He reconciled many a German when he declared that he had "come to know that there is a real difference between the regular German soldier and officer and Hitler and his criminal group." According to McCloy, Eisenhower's commenting that he did not think that "the German soldier as such had lost his honor" and that he was ready to say, "Let by-gones be by-gones," left a very favorable impression on the Germans.[21]

Efforts to rehabilitate the German military could also be observed on the local level. Because the SPD dominated in both Kaiserslautern and Birkenfeld Counties, the Americans worked even harder to overcome the Social Democrats' objection to the ongoing rearmament of West Germany. One important way in which this objective was achieved was through the honoring of the German soldiers who died in the two World Wars. In 1955, a representative of the Western Area Command attended such a commemoration for German soldiers and expressed outrage when Altmeier, the president of the state government, did not at-

In 1957, the American military called on Elvis Presley, its most famous soldier in Germany, to help overcome widespread German unease over the rearmament of West Germany. Presley took part in the relocation of this World War I Memorial dedicated to "Heroes 1914–18." Courtesy of UPI/Corbis-Bettmann.

tend.[22] American troops also participated in honoring the German war dead of the two World Wars during West Germany's national day of mourning (*Volkstrauertag*). American efforts to treat Germany's war dead with the same respect accorded to U.S. soldiers left a tremendous impact. When the U.S. military and representatives of the other allied forces laid wreaths at monuments in a number of different communities, the local population expressed "great satisfaction."[23]

After the establishment of the German Bundeswehr in 1956, American efforts to honor fallen German soldiers did not cease. The construction of the war memorial in Birkenfeld to commemorate dead soldiers of World War II would have been doomed for lack of funds had it not been for the help of the American soldiers.[24] American soldiers also planted a tree at the local memorial for the German dead of World War II. Birkenfeld was no exception in this regard. In numerous communities, it was the labor and machines of the American Army Corps of Engineers that helped create war memorials for their former enemies.[25] To publicize their commitment to honor German soldiers, the American military even called on its most famous soldier in Germany, Elvis Presley, to help relocate a World War I memorial dedicated to "Heroes 1914–1918."

The newly inducted soldiers of the Bundeswehr received instant legitimacy among wide sections of the population when they started participating in the annual American Armed Forces Day celebrations and the German-American friendship weeks. The report of the Land Relations Officer for one week during May 1957 provides a glimpse of what sort of activities Germans and Americans participated in to foster the German-American military alliance and to convey that alliance to the public at large. Joint activities during that week included the following: "'a flying day' in which German and American pilots participated; a 'Summer Day Parade' in Germersheim in which US soldiers, Bundeswehr representatives and members of the civilian community paraded through the streets; an assembly of German and US Fire brigades in Sembach; an 'Arbor Day' celebration in Mainz in which the OB [mayor] planted a tree in honor of an American friend and the US Army band from Bad Kreuznach gave a concert; an 'International Children's Day' drew 800 children to the Sembach airbase."[26]

These friendship weeks fostered German-American bonds and legitimized the new German army, but they also reinforced the message to the Germans *and* other Europeans that Germany was a viable part of the West and NATO. To reiterate that message, the U.S. military encouraged events that included other NATO members stationed in Germany as well. For example, during the American-sponsored Armed Forces Day in 1957, German, Canadian and French troops all participated. The NATO association was stressed by exhibiting equipment from the different NATO partners, while the most up-to-date aircraft were brought in to entertain the spectators. Germans from the surrounding communities were picked up by military buses and taken to a baseball game, and a Canadian-French soccer game attracted a large German audience. The event had special meaning for the Germans in this community, because it was the first time German troops participated in the Armed Forces Day celebrations. This fact, reported a satisfied Land Relations Officer, "lured many persons into joining the onlookers."[27]

Winning the Hearts and Souls of the German People

The U.S. military used any and all opportunities to convince the Germans that the United States was no longer an occupation force, that the United States was ready to stand up to the Soviet threat, and that the new German army was safely contained within the Western alliance. But the military also worked very hard to convince Germans of the "American mission." In 1952, the Public Information Office of the U.S. Army in Europe expressed much concern over persisting anti-Americanism in Germany, estimating that about 10 percent of Germans were openly hostile to Americans. While this antipathy toward Americans could be found among all social groups, it was most widespread among former officers and the well educated. Another 15–25 percent of Germans were indifferent to Americans, neither liking nor disliking them. The military was concerned about these people, but they worried even more about those Germans who generally liked Americans, reporting, "It is clear that the West Germans are much more friendly to Americans as people than they are to what they consider American national aims to be." The military worried that too many Germans, but especially the Social Democrats, believed that American aims in world affairs "are such things as world domination, economic control of the world, making other people do their fighting for them." The military concluded that "there are a few more strongly anti-American Germans than average in the Rhineland-Palatinate area." The military was convinced that much of this antipathy toward the United States existed because "American units have moved into this area fairly recently and have not yet been accepted by the population to the same extent as in other areas."[28]

To overcome these sorts of reservations, the military had to do more than invite local dignitaries and community leaders to the occasional base dance or military parade. The Americans had to engage the community at large; the soldiers had to become good neighbors. In light of the challenges at hand, the military high command instructed its commanders that "German-American relations be nurtured to the highest possible degree."[29] The military hoped to achieve this goal through mutual church celebrations, leisure activities, educational tours, American involvement in charities, as well as by inviting the German population onto the military bases for "Open Houses."[30] Such official involvement of military personnel in community affairs and projects as well as more informal contacts between Americans and Germans were to forge lasting bonds of friendship.

The military received help in its efforts to win the population over to the American mission through the extensive cultural exchange programs sponsored by the U.S. State Department. In 1952, the Amerika Haus (America House) in Kaiserslautern opened its doors and quickly established itself as an active and popular institution.[31] In the first year alone 17,000 people attended seventeen different concerts. Another 5,600 individuals showed up to listen to sixty-seven different lecturers from the United States, who spoke on a wide variety of topics, while screenings of 277 films were shown to an appreciative audience that totaled 43,900. Within its first year, the Amerika Haus sponsored 2,560 events in Kaiserslautern and the outlying communities, and 270,840 German locals rewarded these efforts with their attendance. The Amerika Haus was proud that it did not appeal only to the educated groups of society; the audiences at these events as well as the tens of thousands who frequented the institution's library came from all social classes and age groups.[32]

This sort of cultural exchange seems to have left its mark. In 1955, the Birkenfeld Landrat complained that the films that the Amerika Haus had made available to German youth were unsuitable for German tastes, since local tastes preferred the German *Kultur Film*.[33] By 1960, however, the German-American committee in Birkenfeld was much less critical of the American cultural imports. The German committee members proudly announced that one of the main attractions at the upcoming German-American friendship week was a movie for the young guests, preferably a "cartoon or a Western."[34]

The Kaiserslautern Amerika Haus made sure that its offerings did not benefit only the urban population. They sent many of their attractions as well as a wide selection of library materials into the most remote communities. The bookmobile that toured the countryside on a regular schedule brought American literature into even the tiniest hamlet, and it was an eagerly welcomed sight for many. The local papers were especially impressed that the "New World" that the bookmobile introduced to the population had no room for Wild West stories or cheap romance novels. According to the local paper, German women looking for a Hedwig Courths-Mahler novel may have been disappointed at first, but they quickly found new favorites in Margaret Mitchell and Pearl S. Buck. The bookmobile visited Baumholder and its environs every three weeks and counted 3,200 adults and 1,100 children among the regular readers of its collection of 7,000 books.[35]

While the Amerika Haus was sponsored by the State Department, the military also had a rich cultural program that it offered to the Germans during the 1950s in all communities of Rhineland-Palatinate. The military command viewed the Seventh Army Symphony Orchestra as its most successful ambassador, and German audiences, especially the older generation, wholeheartedly agreed. Whenever this orchestra played, auditoriums filled, and many Germans credited the talented musicians with having "removed many of the reservations against the occupation."[36] Aside from offering hours of entertainment, the orchestra served the important function of convincing many in this region that Germany did not have a monopoly on culture. At a time when most Germans believed that "Europe meant old culture and America meant civilization, refrigerators, and jazz music," the local residents expressed surprise at the high quality of the soldier-musicians' performances.[37] Newspaper reports of that time all reflect a certain astonishment that the young soldiers from the New World were able to express in their musical performances the soulful sentiments of the Old World. One commentator even reminded the readers that the Old World snobs should not forget that "nobody in Europe was building cathedrals anymore, nor was anybody writing a *Faustus* or a *St. Matthew Passion*."[38]

Another much beloved performer of classical music was the soldiers' choir called the Red Diamonds, which toured military communities and won the hearts of the audience in the "Pa-Pa-Varieté" in Baumholder when it performed Italian, French, and German arias. The audience was especially taken with the fact that the choir showed finesse and skill even when performing a difficult masterpiece like *Tannhäuser*. A special treat of the evening was the performance by the Spiritual Quartet. The *Rheinzeitung* reported that the quartet sang a "happy plantation song" and that the biggest applause reverberated when the young soldiers performed old German folk songs (*Volkslieder*) and "sang them without a trace of accent." The evening closed with a selection from Gershwin, and for a long time the people of Baumholder remembered this splendid evening of Old and New World cultural treasures.[39]

The American military forces were, in many ways, in the forefront to win the hearts of the German people to the American mission.[40] In daily interactions with the Germans they could forge bonds of friendship, but they could also convey to the Germans the superiority of the American way of life. One way of doing that was to give Germans a peek at how Americans lived and worked. Beginning in 1951, the American military command in Birkenfeld initiated "open houses" so that the German people could see how their new neighbors worked, lived, and played. Aware that the military had brought many inconveniences, the commander reminded the visitors at the opening ceremony of the first open house of the many benefits of the Americans' presence, especially the economic improvement in the region. By opening their installations, the military commander hoped for "more openness from the Germans and more possibilities for individual contacts, especially with German families."[41] While older people at these open houses were not particularly surprised at how modern the American installations were, they marveled at how tidy and clean everything was. The very young were less concerned

During the annual open houses held at U.S. military installations, German and American children (the American boys recognizable by their crewcuts) were often given rides on tanks. Courtesy of Bundesarchiv Koblenz (183/64503/11N)

with such matters and delighted instead in the friendly soldiers, who took them for rides in their jeeps and showed the visitors games of softball and football. So many visitors showed up on this first open house that the organizers were totally unprepared for the deluge. They had to use the soldiers' field rations, intended for maneuvers, so that none of their guests would go hungry.[42]

These open houses became very popular events with the local population. In 1955, tens of thousands visited the American installation in and around Kaiserslautern on Armed Forces Day; 20,000 went to Ramstein alone.[43] As time went on, these affairs became ever more elaborate, culminating in the German-American friendship weeks, which were usually held in May. Aside from the local town fair, the friendship week became the highlight of the yearly calendar of community activities. American military bands took turns joining local bands in entertaining the crowds that arrived from even the most remote villages. The American bands played a wide selection of music that ranged from Sousa to Gershwin to Elvis Presley, while the bands of the local clubs performed such favorites as the Radetzky March and German folk songs. When German bands played the beloved *In München steht ein Hofbräuhaus*, the Americans sang along as best as they could and always called for an encore. A special attraction for the young were the displays of airplanes, helicopters, and tanks, which they were invited to inspect. Children were treated to rides in tanks, and they could even sit in the cockpits of the bombers and cargo planes.[44]

The Fourth of July was another occasion when Americans invited their German neighbors to join in mutual celebrations. The hosts introduced the Germans to square dancing and country and western music, and games of baseball and football were organized. The grand finale at these celebrations was a spectacular display of fireworks. At all these events, Americans distinguished themselves through their love of children, and the German visitors marveled at the generosity of the Americans, who dished out gallon after gallon of American ice cream.[45] Children especially loved the fact that soldiers never seemed to mind that they kept coming back for refills. "Hamburgers, hot dogs, ice cream," recalled one woman, "they all went like hotcakes."[46]

The military commanders also encouraged mutual religious celebrations as another way to strengthen the bonds of friendship. As early as 1951, the combined choirs of the Kaiserslautern military community performed a Christmas cantata in the Kaiserslautern Stiftskirche for German and American audiences. Church services, especially on holidays, were often led by both German and American clergy, while German and American choirs provided the musical offerings.[47] On World Prayer Day for Women in Baumholder, reported Der Weg, the "prayers of American and German women rose up to God, and the joyous glory of Easter as well reverberated in unison." The American military also provided the funds and facilities so that Handel's Messiah could be enjoyed by Germans and Americans alike at the Americans' largest auditorium in Baumholder.[48] American troops regularly participated in the religious celebrations of the Catholic communities. Soldiers in dress uniform walked in the Corpus Christi processions, and they also participated as individuals in the local processions to Marian shrines.[49]

Whenever a hand was needed, the churches knew that they could count on the Americans. During the synodal youth day in Birkenfeld in 1955, the local military unit provided the meals for all 500 participants, and the military's contribution was widely praised as having made the event a successful one.[50] But extending a helping hand could also serve a political purpose. The Protestant minister from Alsenz, for example, appealed to the Americans to transport a new set of bells from Bochum to Alsenz. To make his request more palatable to the Americans, the minister suggested that through such a grand display of American generosity, the Social Democratic members of the city council, who were still very critical of the American presence, could be embarrassed. The Americans agreed, and the presence of General Miles Reber of the Western Area Command and a representative from the state church council (*Landeskirchenrat*) during the dedication of the church bells lent the event an added touch of pomp.[51]

Through the initiative of the military command, German-American friendship committees were founded to foster a neighborly communal life and also to provide a safety valve for resolving local conflicts. For the early years few formal records of these committees exist, because, according to a former member of one such committee, "we just met at a local pub, had a couple of beers with the commander, and worked things out."[52] Issues brought before such meetings included concerns over drunken GIs who were pulling flowers from the window boxes of German townspeople and the question of whether German children should be allowed to use the playgrounds belonging to the American housing areas.[53] The American military was concerned enough over some of the complaints of drunken and noisy GIs that they at times ordered a midnight curfew. But German authorities did not single out only young American GIs for such excesses. Local innkeepers, who could not get enough of the GIs' precious dollars, were also blamed for selling alcohol to GIs who had already had enough.[54] The military commander at times declared the pubs where most of the incidents occurred off-limits to the GIs or instructed the military police to patrol those places on a tighter than usual schedule.[55]

The friendship committees were also often able to resolve other local conflicts. Americans, for example, found it perfectly acceptable behavior to go into the local woods to cut their own Christmas trees. The Germans were appalled at this, but they also responded pragmatically by offering inexpensive trees for sale in front of the American post-exchange.[56] Another sore point in relations was the fact that Americans parked by local creeks and rivers to wash their cars. The Germans feared for their environment and complained bitterly. While the American commander could not understand all the fuss about polluting local creeks, he nonetheless agreed to instruct his troops to cease this practice. Commanders also instructed their troops not to litter when they picnicked in the local woods and not to disturb the peace by blasting their radios.[57]

Aside from resolving such misunderstandings, the friendship committees also encouraged the founding of clubs with joint German and American membership.[58] The Americans, for example, helped with necessary work at the Birkenfeld County ski resort and joined the ski club. In all communities, Americans were members of the local tennis and horse-riding clubs as well. Americans were invited by German hunters and fishermen to join them, and Germans in turn joined the Rod and Gun Club on the American military bases.[59] But the American presence also led to the founding of new clubs, for example, the many square dance clubs and the gospel and spirituals choirs.[60]

American efforts to foster relations with their German neighbors did not stop at the founding of clubs. The Americans understood the German love of soccer and so organized their own soccer teams. This effort was crowned when the team of one military unit in Bad Kreuznach advanced into the Kreisliga B (minor soccer league), an admirable feat for the young soldiers. The somewhat shamefaced German observers concluded that the Americans did so well because their background in American football gave them unheard-of strength and endurance. The skill and force of this American team was respected by everyone and even feared by some.[61] Despite the vigorous competition, the soldiers made many friends by sending buses or trucks to pick up to their German opponents, whose clubs often could not afford their own transportation. German beer and American whiskey and cigarettes ensured that even an American victory after such a game could be celebrated and enjoyed by all.[62]

Another great source of enjoyment for both sides was the German Mardi Gras season (*Fasching*). For many Americans, who had never heard of *Fasching,* the rambunctiousness of these days "was even more fun than Christmas."[63] The American appreciation of *Fasching* spilled into every aspect of how the season was celebrated in their host communities. The American soldiers transformed military vehicles into large floats with which they participated in the local *Fasching* parades. Where just a few years earlier modest floats had been drawn by horses or oxen, the new floats were extravagant, motorized colossi. During one *Fasching* season in Ramstein, the soldiers went overboard in their enthusiasm and planned to include in the parade "Atom-Anni," a 280mm-long barrel cannon. The Germans insisted that such a show of force was contrary to the spirit of *Fasching,* and while the Americans were disappointed, they nonetheless relented and offered a more peaceful contribution to the festivities.[64]

During these parades, individual soldiers also delighted in decorating their large and much admired American "street cruisers" with streamers and inviting the local youth along for the ride. To ride in an American tail-fin limousine was not an everyday event, and the young men and women of town sought eagerly to be the first in line. Where just a few years earlier the local *Fasching* princess and her court had traveled atop a hay wagon,

During a parade for Neubrücke's town fair in the early 1960s, GIs in their Thunderbird added a touch of flair, while the army military band provided American tunes. Courtesy of Heinrich Brucker, photographer, Birkenfeld

they now rode amidst the cheering crowds in an American convertible driven by a dashing GI in dress uniform. The Americans' enthusiastic embrace of *Fasching* also substantially increased the amount of candy and chewing gum thrown into the crowds at these events, and this was no small matter in the German children's system of priorities.[65]

The motto of the 1955 *Fasching* season in Kaiserslautern was "From Kaiserslautern to the Banks of the Mississippi, *Fasching* Forges the Bonds of Friendship," and the committee was clearly intent on topping the events of the previous year. A "Munich beer hall" was erected, and Colonel Ascani from the 86th Fighter-Interceptor Wing flew a helicopter displaying advertisements above the cheering crowds. The crowning touch occurred during the grand finale of the week-long celebration, when the *Fasching* princess and the lord mayor of Kaiserslautern descended by helicopter into the festive crowds. This was considered a major coup by all, and everywhere the helicopter landed, it was greeted by cheering American and German crowds awaiting the princess's grand entrance.[66]

American Philanthropy

Intent on convincing the German people that it was no longer an occupation force but a protective one, the American military expended considerable effort making sure that good deeds reinforced its new mission. The military helped financially strapped communities by giving them full access to the much more generously funded fire departments on base, and agreements were signed for mutual aid in cases of emergency.[67] If there was a fire or any other sort of emergency, the American fire engines and ambulances were always the first to arrive. The American military hospitals, while intended only for military use, also opened their doors to German patients when an emergency arose. When accidents occurred, the American military ambulances usually arrived before those of their German colleagues. In January of 1958, the U.S. Army donated 15,000 antipolio shots in the state.[68] But aside from these formalized exchanges of help, there were also more informal channels. A number of individuals recalled that young American doctors who lived in town treated German children without charge because the military hospital had medical technology not yet available in German hospitals.[69]

Despite the economic boom that had come with the Americans, many communities were still struggling. Because of war damage, schools were in still in need of rebuilding, and new housing had to be created for the expellees and refugees who had arrived in the state after 1950. In light of these demands on municipal budgets, few funds were available for the so-called "luxuries" of life, and so the Americans came to the rescue. In the state of Rhineland-Palatinate hardly a soccer field exists that was constructed without the volunteer services of the American Army Corps of Engineers.[70] Outside of Kaiserslautern, the community of Otterberg saved DM 250,000 when its soccer field was built through the voluntary help of American soldiers who showed up with their equipment and a lot of goodwill.[71] In Hoppstädten and Thallichtenberg, plans for soccer fields had been languishing for years for lack of money, until the generous help of the Army Corps of Engineers made possible the realization of these soccer clubs' dreams.[72]

The Fritz Walter Stadium in Kaiserslautern, the home of many of the players who won the 1954 soccer world championship, was built with generous labor and funds from the American military. The city of Kaiserslautern also received financial assistance and the services of the Army Corps of Engineers for construction of the Technical University. Because the Americans brought an unprecedented number of vehicles onto the streets of Kaiserslautern, they supported the construction of a bypass with a grant of DM 750,000. Machinery and money were also donated for construction at the north railroad station in Kaiserslautern, saving the city an estimated DM 180,000.[73]

But the men and their machines also offered their free time to help build kindergartens and schools and to restore church towers that had been destroyed by American and British bombs.[74] In Morlautern, a small community outside of Kaiserslautern, American bombing raids had destroyed 40 percent of the buildings, and the local people were delighted that only eight years after the war it was American soldiers who were helping to restore the destroyed schoolhouse.[75] When the local hospital in Baumholder was being expanded and the community was short of cash, the Corps of Engineers volunteered its services, saving the city hundreds of thousands of marks.[76] All the military commanders ever asked in return was that their soldiers be served a "good German schnitzel and plenty of German beer."[77]

Americans did not merely extend help in building and construction. They also became a prominent source of philanthropy for many charitable causes. The generosity and the goodwill of the Americans were at times cited by the local press as a reminder that even though it is not ideal for any country to have foreign troops within its borders, "the occupation is not such a 'scourge' as some people like to portray it."[78] The fact that the local citizenry had to be reminded at times of all the advantages they enjoyed because of the Americans suggests that despite the extensive efforts on behalf of local military commanders, not all Germans had come to embrace the presence of their new neighbors. Many continued to keep their distance.

Despite these clearly existing reservations toward the American presence among certain segments of society, the sheer scope of American charity surprised the German population and won many hearts. American soldiers were involved in all kinds of charity events, as were their wives through their numerous philanthropic clubs. The American Officers' and Civilian Wives' Club established a foundation to permit a gifted and needy student in Baumholder to attend an institution for secondary education. The trust fund of DM 3,360 was to pay school fees, books, and transportation expenses.[79] During the harsh winter of 1952–53, Americans distributed coal among the poor and disadvantaged of the town.[80] Clothing was collected for the poor, for orphans, and for refugees.[81] German youngsters at that time were mad for these American hand-me-downs. Even among those who were not needy, the used American clothing was much sought after. Among teenagers, American clothing, especially blue jeans, conveyed a sense of the "New World" with which German clothing could not compete.[82]

Even the youngest members of the military community were involved in charity efforts. The Baumholder Girl Scouts sponsored a party for the Berlin children who were spending their summer vacations with local American families.[83] That same year the Girl Scouts had collected donations and visited the German kindergarten to shower the tots with boxes full of books, dolls, teddy bears, and mechanical toys. The teachers had their hands full to contain the excitement of the children. The young Girl Scouts brought even more cheer by treating the children to home-baked chocolate-chip cookies and bars of Hershey's chocolate.[84] At a time when most Germans of this region were just emerging from the hardship of postwar deprivation, the relative wealth of the Americans that the favorable exchange rate of the dollar provided gave the population a first glimpse of the coming consumer paradise.

Soldiers did not leave the charity work to the wives' clubs and Girl Scouts but became patrons of the local kindergartens themselves. In Baumholder, GIs collected DM 1,200 to buy toys for the kindergarten, and the sheer volume of the toys "took away the breath of many a young one." When the children were also served "ice cream, hot chocolate, cookies, and candy, their joy could hardly be contained." To the great delight of the young crowd, the pleasant afternoon was concluded with the showing of three American cartoons.[85]

This kind of largesse was not a onetime event but became a neighborly way of life. Every year soldiers from all units donated money to sponsor Christmas parties in orphanages and retirement homes, where generous gifts were also distributed. In 1952, more than 200,000 West Germans and refugees received gifts from American military personnel.[86] In 1953, the American soldiers of the Western Area Command alone donated DM 35,000 to charity, and this sum does not reflect the many donations in kind. The soldiers hosted more than 100 Christmas parties that year, and their commanding general, Miles Reber, encouraged them to do even better in the coming year.[87] In 1955, the Air Force soldiers of the Hahn air base alone sponsored twenty-four Christmas parties for 2,000 orphans, nursing home residents, and refugee children.[88] The American soldiers were so intent on guaranteeing German war orphans a joyous Christmas that the military clergy had a hard time finding institutions that had not yet benefited from the soldiers' largesse.[89]

Christmas parties were also given to entertain the children of the local communities and the children of employees who worked on the bases, and the memories of these events still evoke glowing depictions of plenty and cheer. The contemporaneous descriptions of these Christmas parties reveal that those memories of abundance and excess were well founded. They also show how quickly these two cultures adapted their traditions to suit each others' needs. At one such event in Hoppstädten, 600 children spent the anxious time before Santa Claus's arrival by watching a "film on the Newyorker children's zoo [*sic*]." The children waited with eager anticipation because they still remembered how generous the American St. Nikolaus had been the previous year. The long wait was duly rewarded when the base siren began to wail. The children's eyes lit up, because they knew that the sound of that siren meant that "St. Nikolaus had passed the main gate to the base in a sled." Since elves were not a familiar part of German Christmas traditions, Santa's usual helpers were replaced with angels. The sled in which "St. Nikolaus and his angels" traveled was pulled by reindeer, in the American tradition, but since German observers were unfamiliar with such creatures, the children were told that the sleigh was being pulled by four roebucks. The joy and excitement of the children were so overwhelming that nobody seemed to mind or even notice that Santa's sleigh was really just a camouflaged military jeep. After a towering Santa and his angels distributed generous gifts, the children were spoiled with hot chocolate, sweets, and fruits.[90]

The Christmas parties sponsored by the American military community in Baumholder offered even more grandiose displays of splendor. Thousands of children and adults from Baumholder and neighboring villages gathered on the town's soccer field, and all eyes were turned heavenward. The children knew that the Santa Claus of Baumholder descended not by sleigh but, just as in previous years, by helicopter. The most excited among the crowd had arrived early, standing for hours and straining their necks in the hope of getting the first glimpse of St. Nick. When the roar of the helicopter was heard, the children's cheers and cries of delight almost drowned out the noise of the rotors. After the successful landing, which took place amidst riotous jubilation, a tired and weary Santa, towering above the children at six feet four inches, emerged from the helicopter. He was then rushed atop the biggest available fire engine, which, with horns loudly blasting, drove to the theater on the Army post where the actual Christmas party was to take place. After all the German and American children arrived at the base theater, they treated their elders to German and American Christmas carols while Santa made sure not to forget any of them with generous gifts of toys and sweets.[91]

In Kaiserslautern, the military staged similar celebrations for the German population. The local commander supplied the town with an almost life-sized, fully illuminated nativity scene each Christmas season so that "all people understand that true peace can be had only if we follow the Prince of Peace."[92] The American penchant for "bigger is better" was also noted: the Christmas trees that Americans put up for Germans and Americans to enjoy were taller than any other Christmas trees in town. They also ravished the eye with their sheer excess of color, lights, and ornaments.[93] Just as Americans became regular visitors at the German Christmas market (*Weihnachtsmarkt*), so German families would take their children to delight in the splendid decorations that marked many of the homes among the American base housing.

The impact of the American largesse was immense. At a time when most Germans in this traditionally poor region of Germany were just beginning to imagine what prosperity the emerging economic miracle might hold for them, the American generosity of those years left an indelible mark. After all these years, many residents still remember with great delight the new sounds, smells, and tastes, the enticing glimpses of American wealth that these events provided. But the Americans also opened a whole new world for the local children. At the American-sponsored celebrations, German children, who had been taught that the spirit of the Christmas season is best expressed in song with the reflective and solemn *Silent Night,* learned a whole new way of celebrating the season. Many adults shuddered at the Americans' preference for celebrating Christmas as a "joyous birthday party," and they also remained unconvinced that "girls dancing the can-can side by side with German fairy-tale characters" was an appropriate way to celebrate the birth of the Savior. When planning for one such communal Christmas party, the German organizers finally put their collective foot down, insisting that "cowboy songs and 'hilly-billy music' do not belong in a Christmas pageant."[94]

German children were also exposed to American traditions by the many American children who attended the German kindergarten beginning at age three.[95] American parents came regularly to explain to the young the meaning of Thanksgiving or Halloween, telling the children how the American people celebrated these holidays. Thanksgiving was also a time when Germans who worked on the military bases or who had American tenants would be invited to officially sponsored celebrations on the base or to more casually organized meals in private homes.[96]

German families tried to return all the favors bestowed on them, and they often invited single soldiers to celebrate Christmas in a German home.[97] Many extended these invitations on their own, but local mayors and clergy also issued appeals for families to invite soldiers to their homes to return some of the kindness that these men had brought to the local communities throughout the year. These appeals seemed to have made a difference. In 1951, only 20,000 families invited an American soldier for Christmas celebrations. Just a year later, 175,000 families shared their holiday cheer.[98] When invitations slacked off, local newspapers urged people to open their homes. The *Rheinzeitung*, for example, expressed frustration over the fact that many Germans seemed to keep their distance from their American neighbors. The editor urged local families to invite soldiers by suggesting that "the 'Christmas-activities' cannot be a one-way street." He reminded the readers that hundreds of local people "make their living with those 'Amis' and that uncountable friendships already existed" between Germans and Americans. "Together they play sports, together they hunt or play chess and ping pong."[99] All the Germans who responded to these appeals by taking soldiers into their homes over the holidays were in turn invited to a reception by the American base commander to honor the Germans' hospitality.

Military commanders also sponsored dances to which the local population was invited. A former commander of the Birkenfeld air base remembers how the young women from the outlying villages arrived in buses that the military provided to spend an evening dancing to American tunes with the GIs. At the end of the evening, the buses collected the women and brought them back to their villages.[100] Despite the still glaring gender imbalance as a result of male casualties in the war, the local men were often displeased with this American competition. One man recalled that he and his friends had to travel far beyond his hometown to avoid having to compete with American GIs for the favors of German women. Fistfights between German men and American GIs at village dances, especially after the consumption of too much alcohol were often the end result of this competition for women.

German women, it seemed, were little deterred by their countrymen's hostility toward the GIs. Because of the continuing "lack of men" but also because German women found American GIs attractive, relationships between American GIs and German women became ever more common.[101] American men, according to one German woman, "were generous, complimentary and thoughtful in such a casual way, which was a totally different behavior pattern than that of German men."[102] A number of marriages between American men and German women arose out of these encounters, and as the decade progressed, those numbers steadily increased. Of the 1,865 marriages conducted in Baumholder between 1954 and 1962, 936 of them involved an American spouse. The number of German-American marriages in other communities also showed a steady increase throughout the decade, averaging about 20 percent of all marriages.[103]

Because of the prohibitive expense of transatlantic travel, marriage to an American during the 1950s often meant that parents would not see their daughters again for years to come. Not surprisingly, parents were apprehensive, no matter how fond they might have been of their future son-in-law. Despite these hardships, by 1955, daughters of some of the best families in town were among the brides headed for the New World.[104] When the 12 March 1955 edition of the *Rheinzeitung* announced four weddings, three of those involved a German-American union. During the 1950s, it was not unusual to find families in which more than one daughter had married a GI. One of the most prominent farmers in Heimbach and the owner of the village's construction company "lost" three of his four daughters to dashing GIs.[105] In the neighboring village a respected railroad civil servant saw four of his daughters pack their bags to follow their American husbands to America.[106] One father whose two daughters married American GIs recalled his horror when his eldest daughter first started dating a GI in 1953. "When Bob would come in through the front door, I would leave by the back door," he said. But he also recalled that it did not take long before Bob and his friends were welcomed and respected visitors in his home.[107] Soldiers who were stationed in Germany during the early 1950s recall that "these were the best years of my life," since it was "in Germany that I became a man." Another man agreed, because "when I arrived I was eighteen years old; when I left I was twenty-one and I had a beautiful German wife and a son."[108]

Bringing the American Way of Life into the Villages

The following discussion about the often intimate living together of Germans and Americans during the 1950s is by necessity the story of only those individuals who reached out to each other. Recollections by these Germans and Americans suggest that individual soldiers and their families were even more successful than the officially sponsored friendship events in breaking down existing barriers. When American families moved into German communities, they became the best ambassadors of the American military and the American way of life.[109] These individual Americans were also able to ensure that contacts between Germans and Americans during the 1950s were intimate and plentiful. Just as importantly, the physical presence of the American GIs, their families, and the American way of life that they brought into these communities greatly contributed to what Kaspar Maase has called the "informalization" of West German society during the 1950s.

Because the military never was able to provide sufficient base housing for its personnel, many of the military personnel lived in the towns and villages surrounding the military bases. American soldiers and their families who were stationed in Baumholder or Birkenfeld found domiciles in eighty-seven different villages of that area, sometimes moving beyond the county line or even beyond the state border of the Saarland once it was reunited with West Germany in 1957.[110] Those soldiers whose military rank was below that of sergeant were not eligible for base family housing. These individuals also sought housing "on the economy" once their wives followed them to Germany. Thus, while many Americans lived the segregated "ghetto existence" generally associated with American military bases in Germany, many others ventured willy-nilly into the local communities.[111] Around the military bases it was not unusual to find communities where up to a third of the population was American; in some communities this ratio was even higher.[112] Just how intimate this living together could be is best exemplified by statistics from Sembach, a small community bordering on the Sembach airfield. During the 1950s an average of 300 American families lived in the village, while 50 American children attended the German schools. In the four years after the Americans' arrival, 125 German women from Sembach and surrounding communities married American soldiers.[113]

Cultural barriers existed, but when an individual American set out to find a place for himself in the community, those efforts were much appreciated by the local people. Throughout the years of the American presence in Germany, but especially during the Golden Fifties, contacts were intimate. Soldiers and their wives could be found eating in the local pub and shopping in the towns' bakeries and meat markets. It was not at all unusual to find that an American soldier played for the local soccer club. One GI played for the team in the town of Hoppstädten for three years, until he was transferred back to the States.[114] American GIs played in the local firemen's band and sang in the church choir. That kind of involvement declined with the devaluation of the dollar and the introduction of a professional military in the 1970s, but in the 1950s and 1960s such affiliations were not at all unusual.[115]

Even when GIs did not become formal members of local clubs, strong ties developed between the Americans and the local population. In one town, two GIs volunteered to teach English at the local school.[116] A professional clown who was serving in the military hospital in Neubrücke was among the favorite *Fasching* attractions of local clubs.[117] A GI named Morris is still remembered in the small village of Nohen. Not only was the young soldier the very capable goalie of the local soccer club, but when the local school was built he sent crawler tractors and excavators to assist in the construction effort. Just prior to his return to the States, he donated two bicycles to the village and hosted a Christmas party for a hundred children, showering them with chocolate, a rare and much sought-after treat in the early 1950s.[118] Thus, not only projects directly sanctioned by the military were accomplished. Individual soldiers also "organized" many little projects on the side to help local communities as well as their German friends.

The young people of the towns were especially quick to befriend their new neighbors. And many of the older citizens who rented to Americans accepted their new tenants without much ado, especially when there were small children in the house. Due to the housing shortage in the 1950s, it was not at all unusual for homeowners to rent just one room to an American couple, sharing with them the kitchen and bathroom. In such an intimate setting, it was unavoidable that people learned about each other and from each other.[119] A former mayor of Baumholder recalled that he and his parents had arrived as refugees in Baumholder without anything but the clothes on their backs. They were assigned an apartment, but they had no furniture. The local furniture dealer advised them to rent their living room to an American family and to use the rent money to buy furniture from him on the installment plan. The advice was taken, and while living space was confined as these two young families lived in two rooms and a kitchen, the physical proximity led to a new openness of mind. The former mayor recalled how quickly he learned about the excitement of American capitalism while their American tenants introduced him and his parents to the game "Monopoly."[120]

When Germans and Americans lived together, there were linguistic barriers to overcome, and they often "talked with hands and feet," which could lead to misunderstandings.[121] A local man recalled with a chuckle how he had tried hard to learn some English to speak with his new tenants. His pronunciation must have been less than perfect, for when he said to the young American wife, "Excuse me," she understood him to say, "Kiss me," and promptly reported the offense to the man's wife.[122] Such small setbacks, however, were seldom a deterrent, and even limited language skills did not prevent most Germans and Americans from socializing together.

During the 1950s many Germans in that region still slaughtered a pig once a year, and American tenants were always invited to help and celebrate on this day.[123] At such celebrations Germans were able to teach their American friends that the local cuisine included more than the quintessential Wiener schnitzel, although not all Americans were favorably impressed with such "archetypal German" offerings as Palatine liver dumplings or "Palatine pig's belly."[124] The German housewives taught their American counterparts how to cook their favorite dishes, while the Germans still remember their first turkey, pizza, or French fries that the American women prepared for them in return.[125] The fact that American husbands at times helped in the kitchen or that American women could talk on the phone while cooking caused much wonderment among the German housewives.[126]

Germans and Americans shared meals even when owners and tenants did not have to share a kitchen. Americans invited their landlords not just for holiday meals, but they also introduced their German hosts to the American ritual of the outdoor barbecue.[127] The Germans in return invited their tenants to help color Easter eggs and bake Christmas cookies. They also took their tenants along to the yearly village fair and taught them to waltz and to sway together arm in arm while singing their best-beloved drinking songs. The Americans returned this kindness, once inviting the entire populace of a small hamlet to the air base's *Oktoberfest,* at which Marilyn Monroe entertained the troops.[128]

American children raised in the villages of the region often learned the local dialect as easily as their mother tongue, English. Because the people who rented to the Americans often acted as substitute grandparents for the couples' young children, it was not unusual for children to be raised bilingually.[129] A woman recalled how both members of the young couple who rented from her were at work during the day, and how their little son Stevie called her "Mama."[130] Another German woman was called "Mama Edith," while her husband was known as Grandpa (*Opa*) to the American children who grew up in her home.[131] The children went to the German kindergarten and "spoke a perfect Palatinate dialect," and when African American children spoke the local dialect, people were even more enchanted.[132] Another woman recalls "that our [American] children went to the German kindergarten and thus learned German very quickly; it was a sheer delight."[133]

This intimate living together had advantages for the German children in the home as well. They often learned English before they went to school.[134] Parents encouraged this language development, and many German and American children acted as translators for the parents. Beginning in 1951, American children began taking German language lessons at the American schools on base as a means of facilitating communication. While German observers were very satisfied that the "occupation power" took this step to introduce the youth of America to German culture and the German way of life,[135] Germans also adapted to the new circumstances. A local newspaper reported that "to be able to communicate with Americans is today the most important goal of many people." To perfect English already learned in school and to initiate the novice without any English at all, the newspaper recommended the book *How to Learn American English.*[136]

Individual Americans also invited their German friends to spend time at the local Enlisted Men's Club or the Officers' Club, and special events at these clubs were advertised in the German newspapers so that Germans might attend.[137] Even today people recall their surprise at the luxury of these institutions and the American ease with this comfort. Germans loved these clubs "because there were always outstanding bands, and we hardly knew of hamburgers and Coca-Colas."[138] And while it was mostly younger German couples and young single men and women who frequented the clubs, it was also not unusual to "find respectable married couples in their forties and fifties."[139] At these clubs the German guests made their first acquaintance with bingo and slot machines.[140] They also learned how to eat corn on the cob and how to tackle an American T-bone steak. They were delighted with the variety and quality of entertainment that was offered, and they remembered with a chuckle their first encounter with pizza, thinking at first that it was an "American version of a pancake."[141]

To the great dismay of German conservatives, rural teenagers embraced with much enthusiasm the popular culture and the consumer goods that the American GIs brought to the Hinterland.[142] The young invested the American goods with a meaning that helped expand their narrow and provincial world. One man remembered that during the early 1950s, "Coca-Cola was one of the most sought-after goods for the Germans. Today, Coca-Cola is a company, in those days it was a Weltanschauung."[143] Another recalled that American soft drinks like Coke were already known and accepted before the war, but that even during the 1950s mixed drinks were still considered the "embodiment of sin."[144] Instead of ordering a beer or a glass of wine, the young Germans now insisted on mixed drinks, considering themselves ever so sophisticated, if not downright decadent.[145] One man marveled that for him such drinks were a taste of the wide world that lay beyond his little village (*der Duft der großen weiten Welt*).[146]

Young Germans were not only enjoying drinks that had thus far been considered decadent; they were also listening to music that until a few years ago had been called degenerate and were delighting in it. Teenagers listened to American jazz and to rock and roll on the American Forces Radio, and in the clubs and bars of the military base, the rural population of Rhineland-Palatinate had a chance to attend concerts by such stars as Bill Haley, Elvis Presley, Ella Fitzgerald, and Louis Armstrong.[147] Bands, both famous and not so famous, played every weekend in the American clubs, and local teenagers attended these events regularly. One man recalled that this exposure to American music was "for us teenagers from the countryside the non plus ultra."[148] But the German population also had at these American clubs the opportunity to listen to popular German entertainers, such as Max Greger, Conni Froboess, Caterina Valente, and Silvio Francesco, who probably would not have found their way into the provinces had it not been for the American presence.[149]

Because so many Americans lived in German communities and frequented the pubs there as well, they quickly made friends with the local teenagers. Because American music was played in all the German inns and bars where soldiers spent their free time, going to the pubs where Americans congregated became a favorite pastime, "because where the soldiers went, their music was played."[150] One man remembered that it was "because of rock 'n' roll that he found America so attractive."[151] American music and the newest dance fads that the American GIs brought to the local pubs and clubs was a breath of fresh air for many of these rural teenagers. "Rock and roll just spilled over," recalled one woman, "[It was] soaked up as if we were sponges . . . especially since things had been so strict in the past with jazz . . . which was forbidden."[152] American GIs often brought the hottest new singles directly from the States and asked local pub owners to include these records in their jukeboxes. In this manner, the newest musical trends at times appeared in the provinces before they made it to the big cities via the regular channels of the international mass media.[153]

At local dances and in the village inn, it was not just the young women of town who took notice of the soldiers in their snazzy uniforms and shiny cars. The young men of these communities also often made friends with the GIs. A man recalled how the simple fact that the Americans had fast cars made them appealing to younger Germans. Young men also felt "how it was like an incredible high for a young person [in the 1950s] to be able to drive the fast cars of the Americans, and that all these things made it extremely easy for soldiers to make contacts."[154] Another recalled the Americans' big cars, and "how just getting to ride in one of them was such a big deal for us." When one was lucky enough to have an American friend and thus access to an American car, he said, "We felt like on a different cloud, like we were in a different world."[155]

American clothing, music, and consumer goods were extremely popular among the local teenagers. Consequently, German products were no longer desirable. Teenagers would ask GI friends and American tenants to buy original American Levi's jeans for them. Wearing the American jeans was by no means even primarily a matter of practicality for these young people: said one, "We were crazy for the clothing that they brought over here, starting with the jeans."[156] Another man recalled that "we only had the hots for American clothing . . . we felt like kings, when we were at least dressed like them, . . . nice plaid swimming shorts, not the old wool rags that we had."[157] Even Germans who were no longer teenagers saw in the American clothing a sophistication that German styles could not offer. American tenants also supplied young farm wives with stylish petticoats and the most up-to-date accoutrements, including bobby socks and saddle shoes.[158] People who were teenagers in the 1950s preferred the American clothing because to them it represented a sense of "freedom, of the taste of the big wide world out there."[159] Those who could not get their hands on American-style clothing to experience a taste of that world had to make do with American cigarettes. Instead of smoking German brands of cigarettes, the younger generation insisted on "smoking Lucky Strikes."[160]

The recollections of people in Rhineland-Palatinate suggest that this daily exposure to the American soldiers convinced Germans that the Americans' easier life was also intimately bound up with a different experience of freedom. According to one woman, the Americans had not only brought prosperity, they had "opened a fantastic new world to us."[161] Another woman reiterated that sentiment when she recalled that to the teenagers of the 1950s, "the GIs symbolized a piece of freedom. . . . Even the GI of lowest rank had plenty of money in his pocket, and we all felt, yes, this is the true freedom."[162] How closely even more restrained observers equated American-style consumption with freedom is exemplified in a 1951 newspaper description of the GIs that concluded that their "opportunities were unlimited [because] they have the newest cars and the newest cigarettes."[163]

The younger generation was crazy for American consumer goods, but they also admired the much more relaxed American approach to life. Local teenagers recall that "the [soldiers'] whole way of carrying themselves, their clothing, their mode of behavior had a tremendous impact" on them.[164] While most Germans had plenty of opportunity to observe and mimic American idols such as Marlon Brando, James Dean, and Elvis Presley, the teenagers in this region experienced the much-admired American "cool casualness" (*Lässigkeit*) on a daily and much more intimate basis. Much as male teenagers throughout Germany copied the American role models of the big screen because "American actors possessed a physical presence that their German counterparts lacked," so the teen-agers in Rhineland-Palatinate observed the confident seesaw walk of the smartly dressed GIs around them. They marveled at the laid-back manner of the American GIs as they walked the streets of town "with their hands in their pockets." Walking with hands in pocket, sitting backwards on a chair, putting the feet up on a table, all these gestures became a new way to express an informalized habitus that set the younger generation apart from the more inflexible and formal world of their elders.[165]

The fact that this relaxed style prevailed even when young GIs inter-acted with their superiors was noted by many Germans and commented on in the press.[166] While the American military was hardly an egalitar-ian institution during the 1950s, German observers from all age groups nonetheless experienced it as such, especially when they compared the American soldiers to the soldiers of the Wehrmacht. According to the *Rheinzeitung* in 1955, "The German visitor [to the military base] notices immediately the incredibly casual manner of interaction between superi-ors and subordinates. Without doubt, there is plenty of hard discipline here as well, but one gains the impression that it is only demanded when necessary. That the beds . . . are not fixed as tidily as in the German Wehrmacht does not evoke condescending smirks; we find it quite like-able."[167] A former German Wehrmacht soldier who interacted closely with the American military echoed those sentiments: "The German offi-cers were tough nuts (*Komissköpfe*)," he reported, while American officers were much more relaxed.[168]

After years of enduring the discipline of Nazi Germany, the young were especially taken with the casual American manner. One young woman recalled: "What impressed me personally . . . to an incredible de-gree was when you saw . . . these young GIs, who were so relaxed when they put their hand to their cap in their casual manner, while I still had all this zack! Attention and heel clicking in the back of my head. That's how they were . . . such comradely relations that the subordinates had with their bosses. . . . I was incredibly impressed by that."[169]

Already in 1951, the *Pfälzische Volkszeitung* thoughtfully concluded why it was that the American soldiers appeared so attractive when it com-mented that "the uniforms are young and powerful," and that they "can't be measured by the standard of the 'Old World.'" The military caps that the soldiers wore so nonchalantly and jauntily on their heads "revealed vitality and an unrestrained joy of life." Because the soldiers strode about in a seesaw manner, their walk expressed "confidence." The young sol-diers were so appealing, reported the newspaper, because "rhythm is their 'way of life,'" and that had implications for all. This exuberant report relied on the language of the "New World" to equate the GIs' vitality with their music: "'Jazz first class style, hot jazz' is the expression of the most pronounced happiness—'not just for an hour, not just for a year, but always'—now and today—forever!'" It was because of the American music that these young soldiers brought to the provinces, concluded the newspaper report, that the "respectable vertical line of the 'Old World' had been dissolved in favor of an awry (*schiefe*) horizontal line—'Don't fence me in,' don't tie me down!"[170]

But people also noted that despite this more relaxed style, the Americans were not the "effeminate Yankees" that the Hitler propaganda had always talked about. The oft-repeated Nazi propaganda that the American military could not possibly win the war because "the German soldier marches, while the American soldier dances" seems to have been overcome through living with the GIs.[171] Interacting with the GIs on a daily basis convinced many a German that "they were tough soldiers once you got to know them."[172] At a time when German men were not yet allowed to wear soldier's uniforms but debates about German rearmament were seriously underway, the gushing article by the *Pfälzische Volkszeitung* presented American soldiers as the new model of Germany's citizen soldier. Their informal manner may not have been as awe-inspiring as the German uniforms of times past, but the newspaper's admiring description suggests that the Nazi dictum that the "rooted individual—even the young one—does not dance to Jazz . . . and also senses that Jazz and uniform are incompatible" was no longer fully accepted.[173]

The impact of the American presence in economic terms, the largesse of the military, its willingness to be involved in the communities, as well as the many friendships that developed as people lived and worked together, created much goodwill. Just two years after the Americans first arrived for the second time in the Palatinate, the local newspaper celebrated the fact that "nobody stared at them anymore" as if they were a "some sort of exotic animal." People supposedly also no longer believed in the stereotypes that "America is merely the land of cowboys, gangsters, and long-lost rich uncles." These stereotypes were overcome, according to this report, because "the American military has brought with its people and infrastructure a piece of America right into the Palatinate."[174] The U.S. Army Europe expressed similar euphoric sentiments over its efforts at forging friendships with the Germans, reporting that the relations between German civilians and American soldiers "are as friendly and wholesome as have ever been enjoyed by any body of troops residing on foreign soil, anywhere, any time in history."[175]

The mostly cordial German-American relations in Rhineland-Palatinate during the 1950s are unique in many ways and were possible for a number of reasons. The area had traditionally experienced large-scale emigration of its impoverished and land-hungry population to the United States. People thus felt a certain kinship with the American soldiers that they did not necessarily share with the French. The fact that the state was a border region of Germany's traditional archenemy France and had suffered severely under the French military occupation only enforced that sense.[176] The region was also unique because of the intimate living together in this mostly rural setting. Americans stationed in the American zone in such urban centers as Berlin, Frankfurt, or Munich lived very secluded lives, sheltered from the rest of German society. Their "little Americas," already established in 1945, provided for their every need. In Rhineland-Palatinate that separate infrastructure existed only by the later part of the 1950s. Because the military never provided sufficient on-base housing for its soldiers, GIs and their families continued to live on the German "economy." The withdrawal behind the safe walls of the "little Americas" would come in Rhineland-Palatinate only later, with the devaluation of the dollar in 1971 and the rash of terrorist attacks on American military bases during the late 1970s. For most of the 1950s and 1960s, Germans and Americans in the villages and hamlets of Rhineland-Palatinate lived as good neighbors and often became friends.

3

When Jim Crow Came to the German *Heimat*

The preceding chapter provides a mere glimpse of the extensive and often cordial German-American relations that made the 1950s such a unique decade in Rhineland-Palatinate. Clearly, those Germans and Americans who sought out each other largely drove the narrative of those encounters. It is much harder to get a sense of the experience and attitudes of Germans who remained ambivalent, if not hostile, to the American presence. Oral histories are a wonderfully rich source for detailing the everyday encounters between Germans and Americans and for recapturing the wonder that many young Germans experienced in their interactions with the Americans. However, they are less helpful in revealing what anxieties Germans must have experienced over this dominant foreign presence and its social impact. Much of what appeared alien and threatening to local life and German traditions in the 1950s has since become routine and part of everyday life for Germans in these communities.

Recapturing the full spectrum of the German and American encounter during the 1950s is thus a complex challenge. The fact that both Germans and Americans were undergoing dramatic social change during that period only further complicates such an endeavor. Not only were Germans making the difficult transition from fascism to democracy; they were also experiencing radical changes in their way of life due to the American presence. At the same time, the American military faced its own dilemmas. Deploying any such large contingent of single young men into a foreign country was a tremendous undertaking. The social revolution emerging in the United States over civil rights only complicated the military's task. Arriving with segregated troops in 1950, the European command spent the better part of the decade trying to overcome centuries of racial discrimination. That experience was probably no less dramatic for many of the American soldiers than were the profound changes Germans experienced in their way of life.

This chapter complicates the mostly positive narrative of the preceding one by exploring the social and cultural anxieties that marked the German-American encounter during the 1950s. As will be seen, not all was well in the provinces. While business people delighted in their new prosperity and German teenagers were dazzled by the glimpse that Americans provided into a new and desirable world, others felt overwhelmed by the Americans' alien culture. In the first few years after the troops' arrival, woeful expressions over the loss of *Heimat* (the homeland) existed side by side with exhilarated coverage of the modern military installations and the luxurious interiors of the American homes on the base. The record also indicates that for many Germans, black American soldiers were the most visible and disturbing sign of just how unsettled their lives had become.

By exploring in particular the face-to-face interaction of Germans and black GIs, I will show that German attitudes toward the black soldiers were multifaceted. While Germans expressed little open hostility toward black soldiers, the presence of single black men nonetheless evoked considerable anxiety. Thus, even as Germans grudgingly accepted the black families who moved into their towns, ate in their restaurants, or shopped in their stores, most Germans condemned as unacceptable the relationships between German women and black American soldiers. Germans were assured of the righteousness of their beliefs by the complex manner in which German and American racial attitudes interacted during the 1950s. Rejecting the language of Nazi racism, Germans drew instead on the example of American racial segregation to justify their own opposition to interracial relationships.

"We Have Lost Possession of Our *Heimat*"

Despite the good will of the American military, many Germans, especially before 1955, were bitter about the presence of U.S. troops, complaining, "We are still not masters in our own house and thus cannot define our own life."[1] For much of the decade, Germans continued to see the GIs as occupiers, and American soldiers at times received the cold shoulder. In particular, many Germans on the Left continued to reject Adenauer's policy of West-integration and rearmament as the country's best hope of regaining its place in the family of nations. For these Social Democrats, the American presence was proof that Germany had learned little from its militarist and murderous past.[2]

Perhaps most troublesome to Germans were the daily annoyances of having to live in close proximity to such a large, foreign military presence. Continuing land confiscations, damage caused by military maneuvers, the deafening noise of low-flying jets, and the daily barrage of shooting from firing ranges became a normal part of the lives of people in all military communities. Just as difficult was the fact that small rural communities like Baumholder had to integrate tens of thousands of American GIs. All communities with American GIs saw increased levels of crime and violence.[3] Moreover, as far as the Germans were concerned, the Americans also directed too much attention toward local women. Especially around payday, GIs often approached women alone at night on the streets. GIs sometimes had difficulty taking no for an answer, and the local paper reported that women were occasionally harassed. Such incidents, rare though they were, raised the ire of local people. Many Germans were also annoyed by the GIs' jovial habit of calling every woman "Frollein" and their practice of inviting women for a "joy ride" or an evening of fun. The Birkenfeld police chief reported that his own wife had been accosted in this manner, and the mayor of Kaiserslautern had no better news to report.[4]

The Americans also brought into those communities cultural norms that jolted the sensibilities of the German population. Thus, even when the soldiers were on their best behavior, many Germans judged the American military an alien presence that threatened their way of life and undermined German identity. In a typical account that regretted this development, a Protestant clergyman complained that Kaiserslautern, with its "abundance of American tailfin cars (*Straßenkreuzer*), American street signs, and men in American uniforms," was no longer a German city but an American one.[5] Others complained that the city's streets teemed with "overly casual" and "undisciplined" men, who made up for their lack of German language skills by gesticulating wildly and speaking too loudly. German streets were not only populated with "alien" people; formerly sleepy German communities were allegedly also caught up in the "American tempo."[6]

Germans at times expressed their anxiety over the drastic changes by

macadamized
razed

American military housing appears to loom oppressively over the little town of Baumholder. Courtesy of Karl Edinger, photographer

objecting to how the physical landscape of their *Heimat* had changed due to the military construction program. They complained that whole hills were flattened, forests razed, and blooming meadows macadamized into airfields.[7] Small communities like Baumholder found themselves surrounded by block upon block of military barracks and American family housing. Observers eyed with anxiety the intimidating and sprawling American bases (*Amistädte*) that hovered over the simple homes of the sleepy towns and villages. These new structures, considered "dull and monotone" by some Germans, dominated the rural landscape in an almost threatening manner, evoking fears that nobody could escape their "hot and restless breath."[8] For many, the huge American military communities stood as stark reminders that Germans had lost control over their own destiny. One commentator gave voice to that sentiment when he bemoaned, "Here we have been alienated from our *Heimat;* here we have lost possession of it."[9]

Conservative clergymen were the most outspoken critics of the cosmopolitan character that many of these provincial towns took on due to the American presence. They complained about the increase in traffic, the glittering neon lights, and the many foreign businesses that catered to the

GIs. A Kaiserslautern clergyman expressed how alienating these changes were when he reported gravely that "the far east and the wild west meet here; there is the Cafe Brodway [*sic*] and only fifty yards over is the Chinese Restaurant Juang-Tung."[10] Conservative clergy, at times even drew on the racially charged language of the Nazi past to describe the new situation as an "over-foreignization (*Überfremdung*)."[11]

In a widely published proclamation entitled "It concerns all of us," the Kaiserslautern Synod probably expressed the sentiments of many a disgruntled German in 1954: "*We have to blame ourselves most of all,* when foreign masters have much power and great influence in our city and our *Heimat.*" The wording of the synod's proclamation does not reveal whether Germans should accept blame for their support of Nazism, since it was this eager embrace of the dictatorship that had led to the current political situation. However, the synod's recriminations make clear that the time for passively standing by was over. The authors admonished the population that something needed to be done: "It has to concern each and every one of us, that foreign white and colored soldiers dominate the appearance of our streets by day and even more by night."[12] While this appeal mentioned both white and black soldiers, most other observations focused almost solely on the black soldiers who allegedly dominated the appearance of the local streets.

Encountering African American GIs

When black GIs arrived in Rhineland-Palatinate, first in 1945 and then again in 1950, it was not the first time that the local population had encountered people of color. Indeed, when the Americans arrived with all-black units, it must have seemed like a replay for many older Germans. After World War I, an estimated 14,000 to 25,000 French colonial troops served as part of the French occupation forces in the Rhineland. Observers at the time reported little antagonism against these troops among the population; unlike the French, the soldiers from Morocco and Senegal did not view the Germans as their archenemy and thus tended to treat them more kindly. Nonetheless, the presence of these "colored troops" at the very moment when Germany had suffered a humiliating defeat and lost its status as a colonial power caused considerable hostility. Although the colonial troops perpetrated no more offenses against the German civilian population than did their white French counterparts, a nationally organized political campaign depicted them as "wild beasts" intent on destroying the German race. Foremost in this hateful propaganda about the

"*Schwarze Schmach*," or the "Black Horror on the Rhine," was the image of the black rapist defiling German womanhood and thus German honor. This racist image had been a staple of Weimar election propaganda not just for the National Socialists, but for all parties except the Independent Socialists (USPD) and the Communists (KPD). Nazi propaganda during the Weimar years went even further, linking the presence of black soldiers on German soil to a Jewish conspiracy aimed at destroying the "Aryan" race and German morality.[13]

In the counties of Birkenfeld and Kaiserslautern, the memory of the highly politicized *Schwarze Schmach* lived on long after the troops left. In the Palatinate, the NSDAP had been able to gain a large share of the vote by exploiting the population's resentment toward the French and their use of colonial troops.[14] During the Third Reich, the regime directed its racial hatred mostly against the Jews. However, the presence of the "Rhineland bastards," and the regime's campaign to forcibly sterilize them, kept alive the German encounter with blacks as a racial "other."[15] In the last months of the Second World War, the Nazis hoped to draw on those sentiments when they intensified their racial propaganda against black Americans. Hoping to shore up German resolve before the impending collapse, the regime evoked memories of the "Black Horror on the Rhine" but failed to mount a large-scale propaganda campaign. The impact of the regime's antiblack propaganda in the last months of the war seems to have been limited, though.[16] Unlike in the East, there was no mass flight from the advancing Americans. On the contrary, on the Western front, people refused last-minute evacuation plans during the waning months of the Nazi regime.

While Germans along the Western frontier were grateful to be conquered by American instead of Soviet troops, most probably harbored some anxiety over the prospect of black troops. When the first black American troops arrived in these regions of Rhineland-Palatinate in March of 1945, however, such trepidation and fear were quickly overcome. Black soldiers distinguished themselves through their generosity and friendliness toward the Germans.[17] Lutz Niethammer suggests that this positive encounter with African American troops disrupted widespread anticipation of racial violence, allowing many Germans an opportunity to rethink their racial worldview.[18] The experience of black GIs in postwar Germany makes possible an exploration of Niethammer's intriguing thesis.

Germans were stunned at how well the black soldiers treated them, but black soldiers were equally amazed that most Germans approached them with much more tolerance than did white American soldiers. In the aftermath of Germany's bitter defeat, many Germans preferred the black GIs to the white soldiers, because black GIs were more generous with their food rations. Black GIs also did not approach the defeated Germans with the sort of arrogance that many of the white soldiers displayed. Because of the humiliation of their defeat, Germans also experienced a certain kinship with the black GIs, convinced that black GIs, just like themselves, were treated as second-class citizens by the white Americans.[19]

The encounters of black GIs with Germans were so positive that the African American press in the United States repeatedly described the experience of the GIs in Germany to indict American racism at home. *Ebony,* for example, reported in 1946 with much surprise on how cordially most Germans treated blacks: "Strangely enough, here where Aryanism ruled supreme, Negroes are finding more friendship, more respect and more equality than they would back home—either in Dixie or on Broadway." While providing wide selections of photos of interracial fraternization, *Ebony* concluded, "Many of the Negro GIs . . . find that democracy has more meaning on Wilhelmstrasse than on Beale Street in Memphis."[20] William Gardner Smith, who had served in Germany and contributed numerous articles on the experience of black GIs to the African American press, gave voice to these widely shared sentiments in his novel, *The Last of the Conquerors.* One of the protagonists, speaking for many black GIs at the time, declared: "I like this goddamn country, you know that? . . . It is the first place I was ever treated like a goddamn man."[21]

Because of their extensive and cordial relations with much of the German population, black GIs came to believe that Nazi racial propaganda had not left a deep impact on German attitudes toward blacks. When black soldiers experienced racism in Germany in the postwar years, one GI recalled, it was generally "marked, 'made in the United States.'"[22] The American military's newspaper *Stars and Stripes* commented on this unexpected German tolerance when it reported in late 1945 that "the most serious source of racial propaganda against the Negro people" was white GIs.[23] The message of German tolerance versus American racism was brought to a wider audience in the United States when *Newsweek* reported in 1946 that in "their attitude toward Negro troops, many Americans are more virulent than a large number of Germans."[24] Black observers who toured Germany several times during the occupation to investigate the status of black personnel reported much the same. They found "no carry-over of Nazi racial ideologies directed against the American Negro soldier," stressing that the "expected ideological difficulties in the use of Negro troops in Germany have not materialized."[25]

Because of their status as American occupation soldiers, black GIs experienced their military service in Germany as a time of liberation. For the first time in their lives, black soldiers could enter any pub, shop in any store; they could even date a white woman. If their ability to do so provoked sullen service in pubs and stores or rude stares from Germans, it did not expose the soldiers to arrest or physical violence. A black soldier in *The Last of the Conquerors* expressed how profoundly this experience in Germany affected him: "Now I know what it is to walk into any place, *any* place, without worrying about whether they serve colored. . . . You know what the hell I learned? That a nigger ain't no different from nobody else. I had to come over here to learn that. I hadda come over here and let the Nazis teach me that. They don't teach that stuff back in the land of the free."[26]

The commanding general of the U.S. Army in Europe suggested that this positive experience convinced many black soldiers to extend their tour of duty in Germany. According to Lt. General Clarence Huebener, the "German attitude toward American Negroes immediately after World War II was notably tolerant, a factor in the popularity among Negroes of assignments to Europe."[27]

It would be too simple to dismiss the widespread acceptance of black GIs by Germans as a survival strategy during the years of military occupation. A tour of duty in Germany remained one of the most coveted assignments for black GIs even after the founding of the Federal Republic in 1949. Military investigations conducted during the early 1950s showed that black GIs encountered no discrimination when they frequented German stores, pubs, and restaurants. After observing a German town with a substantial presence of black GIs for one week during 1952, the military investigators concluded their report by stating that most Germans considered blacks "friendly, fun-loving, and generous." They reiterated that Germans treated the black GI in a friendly manner, considering him "ten times more pleasant than the Russian."[28]

Black soldiers who arrived from the United States, where communities around military bases—not just in the South—were still segregated, were, in the words of a former soldier, "hard put not to make invidious comparisons with the American scene."[29] The Department of Defense also expressed surprise when it concluded in 1954 that "it is paradoxical that the Negro citizen in uniform has frequently been made to feel more at home overseas than in his home town."[30] Unfortunately, no surveys on how black soldiers assessed their time in Germany were conducted during the 1950s. However, the results of a 1965 survey are telling in a number of ways. As late as the mid-1960s, when German postwar suffering was long over and Germans had long since gained national sovereignty, 64 percent of black GIs still believed that they experienced more racial equality in Germany than in the United States. Only 6 percent of black GIs thought that they were treated better in the United States, while 30 percent saw little difference between the two countries.[31]

A white soldier stationed in Germany during the 1950s expressed his surprise at how easily Germans accepted blacks when he reported that he "saw and heard of little prejudice on the part of the Germans, consequently the black soldier could readily socialize and integrate with the civilian population."[32] Another white soldier was equally amazed when he learned just how much black GIs enjoyed their tour of duty there. Complaining to a black soldier in the mid-1950s about being homesick, he found little sympathy. The black GI responded: "You just don't understand, Leland, I have it a lot better here."[33] For many black GIs, then, their military service in Germany expanded their world and helped them reimagine their own place in the world. One black veteran recalled, "Before going to Germany, I felt like a prisoner in the United States. Germany opened my eyes to the variety of reactions a black could expect when dealing with whites. I was surprised at how friendly some white people were over there, especially older people."[34] Upon returning to the United States, black soldiers reported with great dismay their shock at having to "deal with Jim Crow" again after experiencing a "three-year breathing period" in Germany.[35]

The way in which black soldiers experienced their time in Germany as a liberating experience should not blind us to the widespread racism that existed side by side with the overall tolerance toward black soldiers. After the horrors that Germans had committed in their quest for racial purity, many Germans seemed to have been willing to question a Weltanschauung based on rigid racial hierarchies and exclusion. Heide Fehrenbach's work on the liberal German discourse on how to treat the children born of German women and African American GIs reveals a self-conscious effort to overcome the legacy of racism.[36] That same sort of self-conscious effort can also be found on the local level. Thus, the occasional newspaper report delighted in the new racial heterogeneity of local communities by stressing that "where just a few months ago children gawked at black-skinned women and their dark-colored children," nobody took notice anymore.[37] Much more common than this celebration of diversity, however, was a sense of shock over the presence of black Americans.

Because Germans in these communities have been living with white and black Americans for more than five decades now, none of the people interviewed for this project mentioned black GIs specifically when recalling the 1950s. The interviewees recalled their sense of unease over the black GIs in the 1950s only after the interviewers specifically inquired about how alien this aspect of the United States presence must have been. Once prodded on the topic, however, Germans recalled their anxiety over the encounter with black GIs vividly. Fifty years after the first blacks began moving into German villages and towns, people recalled "that it was scary"[38] and "that they were afraid."[39] They explained their apprehension and fear by insisting that "one did not know what the blacks would do to us."[40] Because of widespread unease over this alien presence, people "entered with strange feelings into relationships and conversations with the black GIs."[41] Although none of the women interviewed reported a special fear of black GIs, a number of men suggested that women were especially afraid of the "dark-skinned," since "women did not know whether [blacks] might assault them."[42] Another man suggested that no woman had been able to go out at night anymore because the town had become "a dangerous spot because of all the blacks."[43]

The manner in which the presence of American troops in Rhineland-Palatinate was problematized throughout much of the 1950s makes it clear that for many Germans single black GIs were the most troubling aspect of the American presence. The reporting in local and national news papers reveals that most Germans assumed that black soldiers caused the major share of problems associated with the American military. News headlines always mentioned the soldier's race when the offender was black. Even when there were no witnesses or evidence, it was all too common for the local news report to assert that the perpetrators were black soldiers. Statements such as "The soldiers, especially the Negroes, seem to enjoy the shatter of broken windows" and headlines that screamed, "Baumholder: Who is the next victim of such willful disregard—Every colored American soldier carries a knife!" reveal this all too clearly.[44] Indeed, in neither of these two cases was there evidence that could substantiate the claims.

German anxiety over the presence of black men is expressed most clearly in press coverage of the sexual threat that the soldiers allegedly posed to local women and youngsters. These sorts of reports were generated mostly in the first few years after the troops' arrival, and they reflect a long tradition of European racism that associated blacks with both sexual aggression and male weakness.[45] In one such report, the mayor of Koblenz suggested that the "occupation soldiers, but especially the colored soldiers with their well-known uncontrolled passions (*Triebhaftigkeit*), presented an immense danger to our young generation."[46] Youth welfare agencies were convinced that black GIs posed a danger not only to women and girls but also to young men and boys. According to their anxious reports, young boys were in danger of homosexual seduction be-

cause it was not always easy for the "Negroes . . . to establish relationships with women." Because of the GIs' consumer goods, but especially
because of their flashy cars, German boys were judged easy targets. In
Kaiserslautern, a "22-year-old soldier with a Cadillac," allegedly seduced
all members of the boys' club, where he volunteered, into homosexuality.
The police suggested that this incident represented just the tip of the ice-
berg because "homosexuality tends to be hidden."[47] Having little hard
evidence at hand that confirmed these speculations, the social workers
and police nonetheless suspected that "*indecent acts between occupation soldiers and children* seem to be going on around the barracks to a much
larger degree than can be ascertained."[48]

Another charge directed at black soldiers was that they employed children as procurers of women. The GIs were supposedly paying the children to bring them their older sisters or perhaps a female neighbor. A
police report on this alleged phenomenon closed by admitting that so
far none of these matters had been proven but that it was highly likely
that these things were going on.[49] Most of the concerns that were voiced
were clearly mere speculation or else extrapolations from perhaps a single
incident. In an effort to stop such wildly flying rumors, the *Allgemeine
Zeitung* informed its readers in 1953 that none of the stories that "Negroes
were offering money and sweets to children so that they organize women
for them" were true.[50]

Encountering Jim Crow

The fact that the Americans arrived in Rhineland-Palatinate with segregated troops and all the social problems associated with the ongoing integration of the military only helped to reinforce German prejudices against
the black soldiers. Despite Truman's 1948 Executive Order 9981, only
7 percent of black soldiers in the European Command were deployed in
integrated units in 1952.[51] Pressure to integrate the European Command
came largely from the Department of the Army in Washington once the
State Department realized that the Soviets as well as the West and East
German Communist Parties were exploiting the continuing segregation
of troops as an embarrassment to America's alleged mission of defending
democracy.[52] Communist propaganda relentlessly attacked Americans as
hypocrites and informed the German public that "lynching is the standard treatment of Negroes in the United States."[53] The "American Dilemma," to use Gunnar Myrdal's words, had been imported into Europe,
and the American government was keenly aware that something needed

to be done. By 1951, the Department of the Army became convinced that a segregated military provided "a constant embarrassment in foreign relations, [but] also jeopardizes the effective maintenance of our moral leadership of the free and democratic nations of the world."[54] Integration in Europe, according to Assistant Secretary of Defense Anna Rosenberg, was a "living example of democracy in action—the only answer to communist propaganda."[55]

The secretary of defense had a difficult time convincing the commanding officers of the United States Army Europe in Heidelberg of this necessity. The commanders in Heidelberg opposed integration, warning that the positive experience with integration in Korea could not be transposed to Europe. They argued that the problem in Europe "was complicated by social relations not only between white and Negro but between the Army as a whole and the civilian population." The officers thus seemed to suggest that it might be offensive to German sensibilities to have integrated troops. They also pointed to another source of conflict that complicated matters in Germany—namely the "competition between white and Negro troops for German girls, and some of the serious problems that were to arise if the troops were integrated"—as a major reason for their opposition to integration. Despite these objections from the military leadership, Washington insisted that General John W. Handy and his officers in the European Command revise their view that integration would be possible only in 100 years.[56]

Integration of the military proceeded rapidly once the command in Heidelberg gave permission to proceed. By April 1953, 83 percent of black troops were deployed in integrated units. For the most part, integration on the military base was a rather peaceful process. However, many of the white soldiers, a disproportionate number of whom came from the South, were unwilling to extend integration to their off-duty time.[57] In the words of one black veteran, who was an officer during that period, "We were integrated in bodies, but not in spirit."[58] Throughout the decade and even into the 1960s, troops continued to spend their leisure hours in a strictly segregated manner.

To avoid or limit social contact with blacks, white soldiers employed a number of strategies. On base, white soldiers succeeded in keeping black soldiers out of their clubs by playing only country and western music instead of jazz and boogie-woogie.[59] Off base, white soldiers introduced Jim Crow laws into German communities, just as they had done in Great Britain during the war. Segregated facilities were of course illegal in Germany, because the German Basic Law assured equality of the law regardless of race. By using economic pressure, however, soldiers convinced pub or bar owners that catered exclusively to GIs not to open their establishments to black GIs.[60] In general, the soldiers threatened the owners by telling them that all white members of the unit would boycott their businesses if they served blacks. In response to this, black soldiers also sought out their own places. In this manner, all establishments in close proximity to American military bases that catered *exclusively* to American GIs were segregated by race.[61]

A November 1952 essay in the *Saturday Evening Post* informed the American public of the ongoing integration of the European command by stressing the relative ease with which it was being accomplished. That same article also hailed Germany as a test case for a future racial integration of the communities surrounding military bases in the United States.[62] The reality of integration during the 1950s was often not that rosy. According to a former GI, integration was a "very scary and painful process . . . tensions were high since many of the soldiers hailed from the South."[63] For example, the first black Air Force soldier stationed in Birkenfeld slept in his truck for four weeks because he feared the antagonism of his white roommates.[64]

Because of the military's commitment to racial integration after 1952, commanders severely penalized soldiers who tried to sabotage integration on base. In order to avoid possible demotion, white soldiers thus expressed much of their opposition over the ongoing integration in their off-duty hours, that is, in the German communities surrounding the military bases. Black soldiers, not surprisingly, also carried many of their frustrations over the slow pace of integration and the emerging civil rights struggle in the United States into these German communities.[65] For most of the 1950s and even into the 1960s, when soldiers came into town to socialize, they arrived in groups that were strictly segregated by race. Germans observed as the black and white soldiers went out of their way to avoid physical proximity to each other. White soldiers often crossed the street so they would not have to pass black GIs on the sidewalk. Sneers and derogatory comments aimed at the black soldiers who refused to budge were also part of this ritual of intimidation. Germans recall their surprise as they encountered the deeply troubled racial relations of the soldiers being played out in the streets of their towns and villages.[66] For many, these scenes may have been ugly reminders of the sort of humiliation Germans had inflicted on the Jews during the Third Reich.

Physical violence between the soldiers was not the exception but the rule, especially on the American payday. Tempers often flared when either party had consumed too much alcohol or, as the military had feared, when the parties were in competition for German women. Violence levels were especially high during the early 1950s, when many of the soldiers from "Hell on Wheels" arrived in these communities after serving in Korea. Brutalized by the war and its deprivations, the soldiers were ready to have a good time. The many new sergeants who had earned their stripes in Korea had a particular reputation for hard drinking and fighting.[67] Racial incidents in and around Baumholder probably were also aggravated because Baumholder was a training camp. The soldiers were removed from the usual routine of their home base, encountering units with whom they shared long histories of competition or antagonism.

While military commanders acknowledged that most of the racial conflict between the soldiers took place off base, they were also anxious to convey to the Germans that expressions of racial strife were most likely just "fights over German girls."[68] Germans in these communities, however, had a different story to tell. According to German police records, most of the increase in violence that all garrison towns experienced in the 1950s was caused by the ongoing integration of the American military.[69] Violence erupted regularly when soldiers new to the community failed to observe the rigid racial segregation of local pubs. One black soldier, after entering a "wrong" place, was told by the waitress that she had no problem waiting on him, but she also warned him that if he stayed "too long," he was "going to have a problem because the 101st [Airborne] will be here in full force soon."[70] Black GIs who ignored such warnings could expect the full wrath of their white compatriots. During one such incident, it took fifty military police and German police officers to form a human chain to separate the fighting soldiers.[71] On a number of occasions, GIs demolished whole interiors of bars while defending their space from intrusion. During one of the bloodiest such incidents, the famous New Year's Eve battle of 1955 in Baumholder, a number of GIs were killed, and scores were wounded as hundreds of white and black GIs battled each other in the middle of town.[72]

As suggested earlier, tensions between white and black soldiers escalated regularly during the decade because of the emerging civil rights struggle in the United States.[73] Whenever a confrontation occurred in the United States over civil rights, German authorities and the American military police were put on alert to deal with the expected clashes between the soldiers. During one such confrontation in Butzbach, a small village in neighboring Saarland, a great number of soldiers were hurt and much property damaged in town.[74] Violence also erupted in Baumholder

truncheon — The club carried by a police officer; billy club

in 1956 when black soldiers reacted with anger over the refusal of the University of Alabama to admit Autherine Lucy, a black student.[75] The crisis in Little Rock, Arkansas, in the fall of 1957 brought about a series of street battles between black and white soldiers in both Baumholder and Kaiserslautern.[76]

As the civil rights struggle intensified in the United States, violence increased in the garrison towns because black GIs were less willing to accept the strict racial boundaries that white GIs had imposed on local bar owners. In 1958, black soldiers staged a sit-in in a Baumholder bar that had put up a sign informing guests that the place was closed to "colored soldiers." The confrontation was especially jarring for the black GIs because the owner of the bar was an Eastern European Jew, who himself had been a victim of Nazi racial persecution. The soldiers demanded service, shouting at the waitress, "Where do you think you are, in Little Rock?" The soldiers erupted in anger when the waitress informed them that the owner was only doing what everybody else was doing in the United States when he refused service to them. Because the soldiers were not willing to take no for an answer, the owner called the American military police. Instead of defending the soldiers' rights to equal treatment, the military police arrested them for disturbing the peace. The local paper condemned the owner for putting up the sign but was even more upset when it learned that the captain of the military police had brutalized the arrested soldiers in the Baumholder military jail with his truncheon and a water hose.[77]

The violence between white and black soldiers and the outright contempt that many white GIs expressed toward the black GIs shocked many Germans, especially those who admired the United States as a progressive and democratic model.[78] Just as surprising to these Germans were the institutionalized aspects of American racism. The Army, for example, insisted that it could do nothing about the development of Jim Crow in German communities, since the "men seem to want it that way." Worse than this acceptance of racial segregation was the fact that commanders at times consciously condoned segregation. Investigations by civil rights advocates even found that in a number of bases commanders "used their authority to reinforce racial segregation and other forms of off-base racial discrimination." The military police (MP), for example, recognized and enforced the racial boundaries the soldiers had created.[79] A white soldier, newly arrived in Baumholder, reported that after he accidentally went to a "black bar" he was told by a white MP sergeant to "drink up and leave!" The sergeant informed the soldier that within a few hours his would be the "only white face in the crowd" and that he "didn't need any more

Cartoon of the Kohlenkeller bar in Baumholder. Germans and white Americans assumed that black-only bars were places of sexual excess and violence. From *Der Fröhliche Westrich,* 1956; courtesy of Stadtverwaltung Baumholder

trouble today."[80] Even worse, in some garrison communities, military police even put soldiers on notice that anybody who transgressed those boundaries could expect physical violence.[81] The MP not only refused to protect black GIs who encountered violence while trying to break down these racial barriers; as we have seen, they even removed black GIs from establishments if the owner did not want them there.[82]

The brutal manner in which a predominantly white military police treated the black GIs was probably the most obvious and troubling expression of American racism that Germans in these communities observed. When breaking up confrontations between the soldiers, white military police asked few questions, often using their nightsticks to beat black soldiers into submission.[83] Germans were anxious not to criticize the American military outright, especially because the German Communist Party had made American racism such a critical element of their anti-American propaganda. After the KPD was banned, however, the local press indicted American racism more energetically. In 1958, the *Pfälzische Volkszeitung,* for example, described the "race hatred and the brutal methods . . . à la Little Rock" of the military police and stated that such behavior was unacceptable in democratic Germany. The paper was appalled to report that the commanding officer had asserted that a "dago [was] as bad as a nigger" and that he had called an American Indian a "son of a bitch."[84]

Observing the deeply troubled racial relations in the U.S. military in their own backyards provoked a number of responses among the German population. Germans stood back with amazement but also a good deal of Schadenfreude as they surveyed the widespread racism of their American mentors. The fact that the German Basic Law did not allow for racial discrimination proved to many liberal Germans that they had overcome their own racism.[85] At the same time, the very presence of the military and the white GIs' efforts to introduce Jim Crow into German communities allowed many other Germans to channel their own racism by drawing on the American model of segregation. Ironically, it was the American military with its segregated troops that confirmed for many Germans their own racist convictions that black soldiers somehow were not "real" Americans.

The labels that Germans used when talking about American GIs reveal this pattern of racial exclusion. German commentators generally distinguished between "American soldiers" and "Negro soldiers" (*Amerikanersoldaten* and *Negersoldaten*). When welfare agencies referred to "occupation babies," they at times also relied on racial categories rather than national categories. One such report distinguished between "French babies, American babies, and Negro babies" (*Franzosenkinder, Amerikanerkinder, und Negerkinder*) with the last category presumably encompassing both American and French fathers.[86]

The widespread popular identification of African American GIs as "*Mockchen*" reveals that Germans hardly needed the Americans to give them lessons in racism. When Germans called black GIs "*Mockchen*," a name given to the black soldiers from Morocco during the 1920s Rhineland occupation, they were drawing on long established racial attitudes.[87] Still, we cannot ignore the complicated manner in which German and American assumptions about race intersected in the daily encounter of German civilians and American soldiers, especially at a time when the United States' impact on German life was tangible. The discrimination that black GIs experienced in German communities related mostly to being denied housing or access to bars and pubs. Civil rights investigations by U.S. authorities in the late 1950s and early 1960s found that GIs encountered these problems primarily in the communities immediately surrounding American military bases. Soldiers who left the American-dominated environment encountered no problems when entering pubs or restaurants. These same investigations stressed that discrimination in the garrison communities existed because Germans "began to adopt the

garrison

discriminatory practices of their conquerors."[88] In 1965, General Paul Freeman, commander of the United States Forces in Europe, was the sole commander willing to admit that racial discrimination existed on overseas bases. However, he also made very clear that the racial discrimination black GIs encountered in Germany was largely imported from the United States.[89]

Until the mid-1960s, the American military in Germany resisted intervening on behalf of African American soldiers for fear that such actions would force the military to intercede in the communities surrounding the military bases in the United States, especially the American South. In 1955, the Department of Defense (DOD) reiterated that it could not intervene on behalf of black GIs because "community mores with respect to race vary . . . and such matters are largely beyond direct purview of DOD."[90] The department repeated that line in 1959 when a black soldier in Germany was denied housing, and in the early 1960s investigators found that "local military commanders seemed unwilling to take the matter [of discrimination] seriously."[91] Demands from civil rights leaders to address these abuses brought only negative responses from the military commanders.[92]

The unwillingness of the American military to adjudicate on behalf of black soldiers stood in stark contrast to the military's usual concern for its troops. The military, for example, occasionally made German swimming pools off-limits to GIs and their families because the quality of the water was not up to "American standards." At times, the military declared German pubs or bars off-limits for GIs if they did not fulfill the military's standards of hygiene.[93] No such action was ever forthcoming when local bar owners denied service to black GIs or when German landlords refused to rent apartments to black families. Unwilling to become involved in matters of race, the military command generally interpreted the discrimination that black GIs experienced in German communities as anti-Americanism rather than racism.[94]

Attitudes within the military changed only in the mid- to late 1960s. In July 1963, on the fifteenth anniversary of Truman's executive order, the Civil Rights directive of the Department of Defense was extended to assure integration of communities surrounding military bases in the American South. Beginning in 1964, the military started using economic sanctions to enforce this policy, and in 1968, the Open Housing act was passed.[95] Pressured by the Civil Rights movement, the American military in Germany also took on a more active role to assure racial equality, even if this meant interference in German communities. For most of the 1950s, however, the white soldiers' hostility toward integration and the military command's laissez-faire attitude were not lost on the Germans.

Drawing the Line

As the discussion has shown so far, the experience of black soldiers in Germany in the 1950s was multifaceted. For many, their tour in Germany offered an unprecedented level of prosperity, social mobility, and freedom. Single black soldiers were able to date white German women without having to fear the sort of violence they would have encountered in their own country, especially in the South. When black families moved into German villages, friendships often developed with landlords and neighbors, especially when there were children in the home.[96] Yet, we need to be careful not to overestimate the depth of German acceptance of black GIs. The fact that many black soldiers experienced their time in Germany as a moment of liberation probably says more about the level of discrimination that blacks faced in the United States than about German racial tolerance during this period.

The records also make painfully clear that German tolerance toward the black GIs found limits from which most Germans would not budge during the 1950s. The great majority of Germans did not approve of the relationships between white German women and black soldiers. "Many segments of the population," reported one mayor in 1952, considered the "fraternization" between black soldiers and German women to be especially offensive.[97] If anything, attitudes toward these relationships actually hardened as the decade progressed. In 1957, the minister-president (governor) of Bavaria did not merely complain about such relationships but went so far as to inquire of the U.S. military whether it was possible to send only "married colored troops" to his state.[98]

A man interviewed for this project, who was in his early twenties in 1950, believed that young Germans, who were socialized during the Nazi regime, understood their racial attitudes in those years as a legacy of the Hitler years:

> You have to keep in mind that the people who were 15, 19, 23 years of age [in 1950] were raised during the Hitler Reich by the Nazis, and racism was even taught in the schools. That's how we grew into this. Of course, young people were told that blacks were other human beings, that they were wild beasts from Africa [sic]. These young people, who had internalized all that, with their hate toward all that was different, now found themselves stand-

vitriolic—

ing face to face with a nigger [*sic*] in Baumholder. My God! All of a sudden, there was a beautiful blond woman walking with a colored and she married him. In the beginning that was just awful.[99]

While the years of Nazi racism clearly left an impact on many Germans, especially those Germans who were wholly socialized during those years, it would be too simple to interpret German opposition to interracial relationships solely as a legacy of the Nazism. When conservative commentators condemned interracial relationships during the 1950s, they drew on racial hierarchies that long predated the Nazi regime. These commentators did not regard their convictions as residual racism inherited from Nazism but understood them as "natural" or "God-given" notions fully compatible with Western values and their new democracy. Letters to the editors of local newspapers or editorials made that point when they condemned interracial relationships by evoking divine law. In a 1952 editorial published in the *Pfälzische Volkszeitung,* a Protestant minister warned that "the racially mixed marriage presents a danger . . . and that God has made the different races and wants them separate accordingly."[100] The author of a 1953 letter stated that a "racially mixed marriage is against nature and culture," because "true love could not exist between the two, only sexual confusion."[101] Another letter to the editor in 1954 informed the readers that the "overwhelming majority of Germans rejected the mixing of races." The female author speculated that out of a "thousand parents, perhaps one would be willing to tolerate the marriage of his/her daughter to a Negro." The letter closed by stating that "nowhere in Germany has a Negro ever been harassed, but that in certain affairs there are limits, and these have been drawn by God himself."[102]

The idea of a sexual relationship between a white woman and a black man was clearly offensive to many Germans. White Americans, not surprisingly, confirmed them in these attitudes. In the immediate postwar years, the military command found that the "absence of a color bar—in particular the American Negro soldier's freedom to associate with white civilian girls—stirred most southern whites and many northerners to vitriolic anger."[103] The former national commander of the American Legion was so appalled by interracial fraternization in Germany that he informed General Eisenhower in 1946, "These Negroes . . . likely are on the way to be hanged or to be burned alive at public lynchings by the white men of the South."[104] Not surprisingly, opposition to interracial relationships did not disappear after the armed forces integrated. In 1952, the military command speculated, for example that black soldiers would not fit again into the segregated society of the South once they returned home. How "were blacks to understand that they have to step down from the sidewalk when they encounter a white woman"?[105]

Throughout the 1950s and for much of the 1960s, white American soldiers shunned and stigmatized as "Nigger Lover" any German woman who associated with a black soldier.[106] Many white GIs seem to have shared the convictions of the military police official in William Gardner's novel, *The Last of the Conquerors,* who tells a German woman walking with a black GI, "[You must] know that the colored man [is] not like everybody else, and that an American white woman could never go out with one . . . the colored man [is] dirty and very poor and with much sickness."[107] The 1957 comments of a white military police officer in Kaiserslautern confirmed that prejudices toward interracial relationships still existed despite the almost decade-long effort at desegregation. Observing German women and black soldiers together, he snarled, "At home in Alabama they would take care of [such excesses]."[108]

Germans had plenty of opportunity to observe the hostility white GIs expressed toward interracial relationships; Germans also noticed the institutionalized aspects of these attitudes in the military. While the American military no longer frowned upon German-American marriages, they did not encourage them either. The application process for a wedding permit was not an easy one, even if both partners were white, but thousands of couples saw it through. During the 1950s, more than 5,000 German women married American soldiers each year despite the cumbersome process. Before 1954, the soldier could apply for the permit only after he had been stationed in Germany for eighteen months, and then it took on average another five to eight months before the permit was granted. The woman had to undergo a barrage of rigorous interviews to test her "morals" and intelligence. Unless the woman came from a respectable local family, military commanders suspected that many of the women willing to marry GIs were opportunists at best, prostitutes at worst. Permits could also be held up for health reasons or because the woman had been a member of a Nazi organization.[109] Women who were expellees from the eastern parts of the former *Reich* or refugees from East Germany faced special hurdles. Not only did they have a hard time producing their birth certificates, the Americans also suspected that they might be spies sent by the Soviets or the East German government. Chaplains counseled these young couples with special care, warning the soldier that such a marriage could have a detrimental impact on his career.[110] They also cautioned women of the hardships that living in the United States would entail for them.[111]

While the military command had committed itself to equal treatment before the law regardless of race, the decisions to grant marriage permits were up to local commanders. The military headquarters in Heidelberg had delegated the decision making to the local command level to expedite the process but also to prevent young and often naïve soldiers from making rash decisions. However, for a black GI this policy could also spell doom, especially if his commander hailed from the South. Due to the miscegenation laws that still existed in twenty-four American states until 1967, many commanders were reluctant to grant wedding permits for black GIs and German women.[112] In 1952, when Luise Frankenstein interviewed 552 women who had children with black soldiers, she found that 20 percent planned to marry their partner. Yet, out of all these couples, only four had been granted wedding permits.[113]

To prevent such interracial marriages, commanders would at times reassign the soldier to another command in Germany or even ship the soldier back to the United States.[114] This strategy was used even when the woman was pregnant, earning black GIs the reputation that they abandoned their babies. A soldier could appeal his transfer, but that usually involved another lengthy delay. Chaplains took special care to counsel interracial couples and to explain to them the "facts of life that they may have to face" upon their return to the United States. Young black soldiers were confronted with the harsh reality that they could not return to their homes and families in the South after their military service if they married a German woman. Soldiers also could not be deployed to a military installation in the South with their new wives because of the existing miscegenation laws. In 1952, when one interracial couple returned to the United States, they were imprisoned for violating that statute in one of the southern states. Only after the military promised to send the soldier to a base in the North was this ordeal resolved for the young couple.[115] When the Second Armored Division transferred from Germany to Fort Hood, Texas, in 1957, the military had to separate thirty-one black GIs and their German wives from their units and reassign them to a military base in the North in order to ensure their physical safety.[116]

Another hurdle that the military imposed was the provision that the soldier had to prove his financial ability to "keep" his wife, so that she would not become a public charge. Although that rule applied equally to white and black soldiers, it left plenty of room for discriminatory practices. Since the military regulations did not specify what financial resources this mandate entailed, it was up to the individual commander to assess the soldier's future ability to be a good provider. As late as 1957, some commanders granted a wedding permit to interracial couples only if the soldier had enough financial resources to return his wife to Germany should the marriage fail. In light of the expense of transatlantic travel at that time, that provision proved an almost impossible barrier to surmount. This was a particularly harsh burden for lower-rank personnel because the military also did not pay for their wives' transfer to the United States.[117] The marriage plans of one soldier were thwarted when his commander demanded that he deposit $2,000.[118]

Recollections of a man born to a German mother and an African American father in the mid-1950s suggest that his parents' experience prompted them to draw painful comparisons between their life in Germany and that in the United States:

> My parents lived together in Germany where they wished; they traveled together where they wished; they ate together where they wished; and they had many German friends. It was when they returned to the United States that my mother and father were forbidden from traveling in the same cabin; it was when they returned to the United States that they couldn't be stationed in most military bases; it was when they returned to the United States that we feared as a family when we traveled together during daylight.[119]

In light of these problems, many of the interracial couples chose to stay in Germany rather than return to the United States, after the soldiers' military service expired.[120]

Germans at the time were fully aware of the military's ambiguous attitude toward the social implications of integration, but especially toward interracial relationships. Thus, when Germans expressed their opposition to interracial relationships during the 1950s, they often cited the American model of race segregation as informing their own views.[121] Doing so allowed them to "normalize" aspects of their discredited Nazi past. While these commentators rejected the genocide of European Jews by the Nazi regime, their line of argumentation suggests, nonetheless, that not all aspects of Nazism were tainted. Observing the American military's widespread opposition to interracial marriages convinced these Germans that Nazi racial segregation, codified in the 1935 Nuremberg Laws, was not an aberration but wholly compatible with a Western democracy. A 1953 editorial in the *Rheinpfalz* makes this point succinctly. In explaining his objection to mixed race marriages, the author rejected the most recent German past during which "racial pride" (*Rassenstolz*) perverted the "timeless principle of decency" (*zeitloses Prinzip der Wohlanständigkeit*) into "revolting barbarity." To overcome Germany's descent into barbarity, he encouraged the readers to treat "black occupation babies" with respect and dignity. However, the author was equally adamant that a return to decency

(*Wohlanständigkeit*) did not entail any approval of the racially mixed marriage. He concluded that it was well known and scientifically established that "human capacity is impaired" by the mixing of the races. He also suggested that nobody could fault the Germans for wanting to copy the American model of racial segregation.[122] Just a few weeks later, a letter to the editor of the *Pfälzische Volkszeitung* criticized an American officer who had labeled German parents racists for not allowing their daughter to marry a black soldier. The German letter writer rejected mixed marriages as violations of nature and culture, while also lecturing the American officer at length on the American miscegenation laws and the American practice of lynching.[123]

Exploring this complicated constellation of German and American attitudes toward race reveals that it would be too simple to draw a straight line from the racism of Nazi Germany to that of the Federal Republic. In their day-to-day encounters with the American military, Germans were able to examine and renegotiate their racial attitudes. The record indicates that Germans left this encounter with a variety of lessons. Observing the widespread racial discrimination within the U.S. military convinced liberal Germans that racism was a universal problem, not a peculiarly German one.[124] Since Germans had made racial equality a touchstone of their new democracy and had anchored that commitment in the constitution, these liberals could also insist that the Americans had much to learn from the Germans. The fact that some of the interracial couples preferred to stay in Germany rather than return to the United States only confirmed for these Germans that they, unlike the Americans, had overcome racism. Encountering American racism thus allowed these liberals to efface their country's own racist past. A letter to the editor of the *Rheinpfalz,* in which the author asserted that the "presence of black troops had pushed the racial question into the foreground in Germany as well" revealed this shift all too clearly.[125] Many other Germans, and not just conservatives, drew a very different lesson from their encounter with American racism. Because of the military's marked ambivalence toward the social implications of integration, these Germans could insist that opposition to interracial sexuality should not mark Germans as Nazis. Interacting with American racism thus allowed Germans to rescue pre-Nazi models of racial exclusion that were based in laws of nature and firmly tied to the Western liberal tradition.

4

Heimat in Turmoil

In the first few years after the troops' arrival, Protestant and Catholic clergymen emerged as the most outspoken critics of the American military presence when they denounced the social and cultural implications of the troop deployment. Above all, clergymen pointed to the dark side of the new prosperity when they indicted as unacceptable the explosion of the entertainment industry that catered to the troops. Clergymen were outraged that Displaced Persons (DPs), most of them Holocaust survivors from Eastern Europe, followed the troops from the American zone to open dimly lit jazz clubs and striptease bars. They also condemned as shameless the numerous "professional" and "amateur" prostitutes who arrived in their towns on the American payday to pursue the GIs and their seemingly never-ending dollar riches. The clergy reserved their biggest outrage, however, for their own charges. They complained that local officials and most of the population were oblivious to these developments because they were too busy trying to figure out how to participate in the American-induced "Gold Rush."

In all garrison communities, clergymen were at the forefront of reiterating a language that associated the population's new prosperity with sexual disorder and racial decline. In their anxious accounts to their church hierarchies, but also to state and federal legislators, the clergy described a society that had not yet overcome the disorder of the war and postwar years and had then lost all moral bearing when the dollar came calling. In doing so, they depicted developments in Germany in the 1950s as a worse catastrophe than any other to confront the country, thus completely obliterating the country's murderous Nazi past. Some clergy drew on racial categories that have traditionally defined German notions of bourgeois respectability when they charged that the population was in danger of degeneration (*Verwahrlosung*), or reverting back into a state of nature (*verwildern*).[1] While conservatives considered both white and black soldiers as the source of this sexual disorder, it was the ability of black GIs to associate freely with white German women that occupied the most prominent place in the unfolding drama of cultural and racial decline. Clergy also drew on a long tradition of European antisemitism when they indicted the Jewish owners of the entertainment industry for bringing the sexual excesses of the city to a formerly virtuous countryside. While conservatives blamed Jews for facilitating interracial relationships, they were most anxious to reiterate that the real villains were the German women who aggressively sought out the black GIs.[2]

Conservative clergymen were the most outspoken critics of the new age, however their racialized language merely gave voice to a more common topos around which different groups debated the American presence. When communities such as Baumholder and Kaiserslautern made national headlines during the 1950s, it was largely because of the alleged moral degeneration that had developed due to the American troops. Although opinion polls conducted in 1953 had shown that only 15 percent of Germans objected to the American troops on grounds of morality, the discourse of sexual and moral degeneration nonetheless came to dominate much of the national press coverage of the U.S. presence.[3] Even respectable newspapers, church publications, union papers, and opponents of rearmament relied on the scandalous reporting on sexually unrestrained women, "sex-starved" black GIs, and "greedy" Jewish bar owners to criticize the American military presence. The obsession with the threat that "outsiders" posed to German morality and respectability suggests that racial hierarchies remained a powerful organizing principle by which Germans reformulated and expressed their national identity.[4]

Rhineland-Palatinate as a "Moral Disaster Area"

During the 1950s, Baumholder and Kaiserslautern became synonymous with the upheaval and "Gold Rush" atmosphere that the American troop movements brought to the hinterland. In the debates in the Bundestag, as well as in reports of the national press and the tabloid press, those two provincial towns became code words for indicting the social costs entailed in the continuing "occupation" of Germany.[5] Indeed, Baumholder became so widely known throughout Germany that in a 1954 collection of state-of-the-nation essays, a chapter titled "*Amerika Ante Portas*" ("America at the Gate") was dedicated to the goings-on in this little provincial town.[6] Even more Germans heard of this little town in 1955, when the movie *Die Goldene Pest* (*The Golden Plague*) brought the Baumholder story to a nationwide audience.

Baumholder received this sort of attention because the boom that accompanied the American military had given villages and towns in Rhineland-Palatinate a touch of the city and, with it, all the social problems associated with urban life. The Americans had brought the advantages but also the "deviance and sexual excesses" traditionally associated with the city. The presence of tens of thousands of young soldiers had led to an explosion of the entertainment industry and what was perceived to be a general loosening of morals. Because of what conservative German observers considered an overly lax military discipline, soldiers were out and about town, ready to spend money and have fun. Conservatives expressed fears that the "Americans with their unrestrained freedom were ruining the German population," which was not used to such license.[7]

In all communities with American troops, as if out of nowhere, a whole new industry emerged to entertain the thousands of GIs in the evenings. During the building boom, buses were converted into mobile bars in which waitresses tended to every need of the soldiers and the German workers.[8] An enterprising individual who had arrived in Baumholder from Saxony erected a huge tent, like those seen at the circus, by the town pond, accommodating a couple of thousand people. Dollar-wielding GIs wandered into this tent at night to drink, play cards, dance, and be entertained by the young women who had arrived from all over Germany and other parts of Europe. This tent, reported a visitor to Baumholder, "exuded its jazz rhythms without interruption until deep into the night."[9] The offerings in the tent also included "mud wrestling for women" and women's bicycle races. The young women, dressed in shorts and tight sweaters, bicycled on stationary bikes, while the platform on which they pedaled rotated like a merry-go-round. The bicycle races were one of the favorite attractions among the workers and GIs.[10] The tent was up only until 1953, when it was replaced by more permanent fixtures that catered to the GIs after the military construction project was finished and the workers were gone.

Another new kind of enterprise that suddenly appeared in the villages of both Kaiserslautern and Birkenfeld counties was the nightclub. Until 1951, the only nightclubs this region had ever heard of were those that

German soldiers had visited during the occupation of Paris. A nightclub, or "bar," as the Germans called these establishments, was associated with the big city and a debonair clientele. However, when the thousands of GIs arrived, the local farmers did not act like country bumpkins. The same men who just a bit earlier had raised their pitchforks to defend their fields and meadows quickly made their peace with the new situation. In Baumholder, three local farmers leased their barns to be transformed into fancy clubs offering American jazz, pretty German waitresses, and mixed drinks. Within just a few months of the Americans' arrival, bars with such fancy names as Manhattan Bar, Atlantic Bar, Hawaii Bar, and Flamingo Club were established. Many of these clubs sported not only fancy names but also luxurious interiors and variety shows that could compete with any big city establishment.[11] The entertainment offered was so enticing in the first few years that even local people attended these bars occasionally.

Most of these bars catered solely to GIs, however, and once owners realized that young soldiers were not such demanding customers, they cut back on their expensive interiors and entertainment programs. What distinguished all the so-called *Ami-Bars* from "solid middle-class inns or wine pubs" was that they were all marked "by a rather dark interior." Particularly offensive to middle-class German tastes was the "red light that prevailed, the indispensable jukebox, and the bar with its barstools, which rounded out the picture of a nightclub of the lowest sort." The presence of *Animierdamen,* young women whose job it was to induce the young GIs to buy overpriced drinks in the hope of affection, was especially offensive to the guardians of morality.[12] Some of these bars even offered the occasional striptease, usually advertising such performances as "beauty dances." Within just a few years, more than forty bars dotted the streets and byways of Baumholder.[13] Even though the great majority of the bars in Baumholder were leased to outsiders, local owners profited handsomely, since farmers charged as much as DM 1,500–2,000 per month to rent their former barns.[14]

The nightclub-like establishments that popped up in every community with American GIs were a novelty in these rural towns. Descriptions and photos of these bars stressed the jarring dissonance between "steaming manure piles in front of century-old farm houses [that] sit side by side with the most elegant nightclubs offering *variété* programs normally found only in the city."[15] Concerns about the impact these bars could have on local children and teenagers were widespread in light of the close living quarters in most communities. Youth welfare workers especially were concerned about what sort of influence such places might have on the town's young. These places, they feared, would attract the local

The American street cruiser sits awkwardly between the Atlantic bar—with its jazz and rock and roll—and the manure pile and outhouse of the farmer who owns the building. The movie *Schwarzer Kies* was filmed at the Atlantic. Courtesy of Photoarchiv Stern

teenagers, who would respond to the "exciting and stimulating interior" and succumb to the "overly loud and hot music and alcohol."[16] Allegedly, the "police force has its hands full to keep male adolescents away from the doors of the *variétés* in the evenings," where they were gathering to watch the striptease dancers.[17] Another factor that caused much concern, especially in the very early years of the decade, was that children gathered at these bars to beg for money or sweets from American GIs.[18] Indeed, this practice was so common that the military leadership complained that the soldiers "were followed every step by begging children."[19] Aside from embarrassing Germans' sense of pride, it was feared that children might be seduced into acting as procurers for love-starved GIs.

The fact that many of these bars were leased and run by outsiders did little to lessen concerns over the impact of such establishments in the provinces. In all garrison communities, former DPs (Displaced Persons) arrived with the Americans. The presence of these DPs, most of them Holocaust survivors from Eastern Europe, was a rather new phenomenon for these counties. None of the Nazi regime's concentration camps had been located in this area, and the French had been so rigorous about repatriating Eastern European and Soviet slave laborers from their zone that by late summer of 1945 almost no DPs remained.[20] Thus, when DPs arrived with the American troops, their presence in these communities was largely associated with the American military.

Most of the former DPs who arrived with the troops had survived the Nazi death camps only to experience violent pogroms when they tried to return to their homes in Poland after 1945. They had made the bitter choice to flee to the country of their tormentors because the Eastern European Jews perceived the American military government in Germany as their best hope to facilitate emigration to Palestine or the United States. The influx of these Jews into the American zone led to a widespread resurgence of anti-Semitism, much of which found expression in charges that the DPs controlled the black market. While the great majority of Eastern European DPs left Germany by the late 1940s for Israel or the United States, some decided to stay on. Among those were a number who had prospered by running pubs and bars for the American soldiers in the American zone.[21] When the troops were deployed from the American zone to Rhineland-Palatinate because of the Korean War, many of the DPs simply followed the soldiers.

Just a few years after the violent deportation and murder of many of the Jews who had previously lived in these communities, the presence of these Jews caused a good deal of controversy. Not only were these individuals considered outsiders to the *Heimat,* their alien status was further magnified by the fact that most of them were Eastern Europeans. Even more importantly, the presence of these Jews revived long-standing anti-Semitic stereotypes that blamed Jews for undermining German national integrity by promoting sexual deviance. While these sorts of allegations had been employed most viciously in Nazi propaganda, they were hardly unique to German anti-Semitism. In fact, they were part of a larger tradition of conservative nationalism in Europe that associated Jews, modernity, and national decline.[22] It was this larger European consensus that allowed many conservative Germans after 1945 to reject the "excesses" of the past while still relying on anti-Semitic stereotypes.

The proliferation of bars that were leased and managed mostly by Jewish survivors caused an outrage among the clergy and conservative segments of society. One clergyman expressed the sentiments of many when he proclaimed that the "variétés and striptease" in these establishments made the soldiers so "horny and lascivious" (*geil und lüstern*) that no decent local woman was able to walk the streets anymore.[23] Clergymen were even more appalled by the influx of the many single women who followed any American troop deployment in Germany. Because the American military, unlike the German Wehrmacht and the French military government, did not provide brothels for its soldiers, "professional" and "amateur" prostitutes arrived on the American payday to satisfy the soldiers' desires.[24] Many of these women arrived from such places as Frankfurt, Mannheim, or Munich; during the boom years of 1951–53, they even came from as far away as the Netherlands, France, and Belgium.[25] As soon as the women came to town, they rented a room in one of the local hotels or inns. With such an influx of women, available rooms filled up in no time, and the women were forced to explore housing possibilities among the local population. While many locals were appalled by the women's inquiries, others were happy to let a room for the night, as long as the price was right. In light of the housing shortage, some of the women even set up shop in buses, while others camped in the woods surrounding the military installations. By the time darkness fell, the streets of communities such as Baumholder were filled with the chatter and laughter of young women making their way to the favorite hangouts of the young soldiers.

Not surprisingly, municipal authorities in Rhineland-Palatinate were hardly thrilled with these developments, but they were also realistic. Officials were not happy that most of the owners of the so-called *Ami-Bars* were not local people, since it complicated the background checks necessary to grant concessions to run such establishments. However, they were also pragmatic about the proliferation of the bars, arguing that they were a logical side effect of such a large concentration of soldiers. The bars also did much to increase the tax base of the town. Furthermore, local officials were convinced that the *Ami-Bars* "concentrated vice." The Birkenfeld Landrat, for example, considered the many bars a bulwark against the corruption of communal life because, as he put it, "If we were to close our public places, the soldiers would go into our private homes, which we cannot control."[26] The bars, then, served to steer American GIs away from the daughters and wives of the local burghers. The bars also ensured that GIs were concentrated in known locations, which allowed the local German police and the American military police to keep an eye on them and the women who congregated there.[27]

Religious and political conservatives were appalled by the municipalities' laissez-faire attitude. For these conservatives, the explosion of the entertainment industry was the very antithesis of the Christian Germany to which they aspired. They were even more distraught that most Germans tolerated the many new bars about town and at times even frequented them. Moreover, most people did not seem to mind the women's pilgrimage to the American dollar. For the most part, the local population may have looked askance at the lifestyle of these women, but that did not prevent them from renting rooms to the women and their GI customers. Instead of expressing outrage over the goings-on in their town, the population was busy figuring out ways to participate in the boom.[28]

The Bleeding Wound of *Amerikanismus*

The clergy and church-affiliated welfare organizations became the most outspoken critics of the American presence when they indicted as unacceptable the social and moral side effects of Germany's integration into the Western political and military alliance. The churches in Germany have traditionally seen themselves at the forefront of protecting public morality and the sanctity of the family. Having failed during the Nazi years to speak out against the terror unleashed against the political left, the gradual exclusion of Jews from German life, and finally the murder of European Jewry, both the Catholic and Protestant churches sought to claim the moral high ground after 1945. Taking advantage of a short-lived revival of religiosity that set in after the 1943 defeat in Stalingrad, the churches managed to present themselves to the Allies as the only institutions not tarnished by the Nazi experience. After 1945, with wide segments of German political life completely discredited, the churches assumed a tremendously powerful role as arbiters of not only moral but also social and cultural values.[29]

The conservative restoration of all aspects of society during the Adenauer years was due in large measure to the immense influence wielded by the Christian churches. To distance themselves from Nazism and their own complicity with the regime, the churches, their publicists, and conservative politicians promoted strident anticommunism and a rigid sense of decency (*Wohlanständigkeit*)—grounded in traditional petit bourgeois social mores and strict adherence to sexual sobriety. This single-minded focus on *Wohlanständigkeit* as a cure-all for the country's moral crisis allowed the churches to avoid any serious engagement with the Nazi past. It also created the sexually repressive climate that so marked the recollections of young Germans coming of age in 1950s West Germany.[30]

In Rhineland-Palatinate the churches' efforts to assert the moral high ground were complicated for a number of reasons. Their overly enthusiastic embrace of National Socialism had compromised many Protestant clergy. While the most ardent supporters of Nazism had been denazified, this generally meant only a transfer to a different parish, rather than dismissal from the church. However, even Protestant clergy in both the Rhineland and the Palatinate, who had resisted Nazism, felt under siege because the area had experienced a tremendous loss of religiosity due to the popularity of the Nazi regime and the success of its mass organizations. The yearly reports of the Protestant clergy are filled with woeful descriptions of empty church pews and the unsuccessful struggle to attract people back to the church. According to these internal memos, even the most "devout villages" had been "completely transformed because of National Socialism."[31] In Landstuhl, for example, less than 40 percent of the population attended Sunday services in 1953, and most of those who did were women. By 1959, church attendance had decreased to less than 8.5 percent.[32] The fact that the struggle of the church for the faithful took place in a state dominated by political Catholicism only increased the Protestant clergy's anxiety to make their voices heard.

The Catholic clergy felt empowered after the war because of the dominance of the CDU in the state, but their struggle to recreate their Catholic milieu was an uphill battle nonetheless. Nowhere had the assault on the Catholic churches been more severe than in the Palatinate under the ruthless regional Nazi leader Gauleiter Josef Burkel. While Catholics had for the most part remained steadfast under this assault, the Catholic milieu was nonetheless severely disrupted. Catholic villages in the Palatinate had been forcefully evacuated during the war, and their priests had been arrested.[33] The general upheaval of the postwar years, the influx of mostly Protestant refugees beginning in 1949, and the American deployment in 1950 only further complicated the Catholic effort.

The clergy, both Protestant and Catholic, understood all too well that the population's preoccupation with things material and the relaxed attitude toward sexual matters were not postwar phenomena. The clergy had expressed concerns over these developments already during the Weimar years. When Protestant clergy had supported the Nazi regime, they did so because they hoped the new regime would overcome the "Godless secularism" and "impudent immorality" of the democratic Weimar Republic. Catholics were more leery of National Socialism, but they also rejoiced at the prospect of a regime promising to restore traditional family values and sexual decency.[34] As we have seen in Chapter 2, the Nazi regime did nothing of the sort. If anything, the regime's policies increased the trend toward modernization and greater secularization. To the great horror of the churches, once the war began the regime even encouraged illegitimate motherhood, to ensure a steady supply of soldiers. Thus, when the local clergy decried the "bleeding wounds" inflicted by *Amerikanismus,* they referred to changes in attitude that were long underway before the Americans arrived.

When German conservatives turned their eyes toward Rhineland-Palatinate, they could see much more clearly than in the rest of the country that the conservative project was doomed. While the occasional clergy report made reference to the impact of Nazism on people's materialist and secular outlook on life, most focused their public laments on the present. Drawing on a rich German tradition of conservative critique of *Amerikanismus* dating back to Weimar times, the clergy complained about the "American tempo," the rootlessness of American culture, the fear of American-style consumerism, and the "hypersexuality" resulting from such a way of life.[35] The clergy drew on these stereotypes to indict the American-induced prosperity as the root of the moral degradation they reported on so dejectedly. People who cared only about making money and buying a new TV had few scruples over the source of their new wealth.[36]

The churches' goal of reclaiming lost authority over their charges was being thwarted as Germans eagerly embraced their emerging consumer society. While the clergy delighted in the fact that their flocks had by the early 1950s abandoned their "political passions," their joy was tempered by the fact that those passions had been replaced by an unrestrained consumerism whose focus was "what else needed to be bought" or "how one could best enjoy life."[37] One exasperated Protestant minister concluded, "Demon Mammon has taken hold of the hearts . . . and all people care about is how they can make their lives as comfortable as possible and what they still need to buy for themselves."[38] Not only were people making consumption the center of their lives, they were willing to tolerate the "sexual immorality" that came with the American troops to the provinces. According to the outraged clergy, "marriage scandals, common-law marriages, and illegitimate children," defined local life, and the clergy indicted "money and Amis" for having "contributed much to this deterioration of morality."[39]

The view that Baumholder and similar garrison communities were the Sodom and Gomorrah of the new Federal Republic was so widespread that a film was made in 1954 to expose the population's dance before the golden calf. *Die Goldene Pest* (*The Golden Plague*) was a first-rate production that dramatized the effect of the American troop deployment on West Germany's rural communities. The story took place in the hypothetical Dossenthal, a small village that stood for Baumholder and all the other small communities experiencing large concentrations of American troops.[40] In the film, the good people of the village are caught up in the Gold Rush. Anxious to make money off the soldiers, they are willing to break the law and forgo traditional standards of morality. Karl Heinz Böhm plays Karl Helmer, the son of the town's church organist. Having spent a few years in the big city, he returns when the Americans arrive to make his fortune in his *Heimat*. He borrows money from a mysterious "straw man" in the city who carries all the stereotypes of the Jewish profiteer. By opening a huge amusement tent for the GIs, Helmer manages to bring all the excitement of the city to his little Dossenthal, including hot jazz and beautiful women. He also convinces many others in the village to follow his lead. To open bars and businesses that cater to the GIs, local farmers borrow money from the same "straw man" who had financed Karl Helmer. One local farmer, egged on by his wife, prospers by turning his former barn into a fancy bar sporting a Hawaiian-theme interior. Another farm wife pressures her husband into transforming their barn into a new hotel, renting rooms to "prostitutes" from the city and American GIs. Others in the community participate in the boom by renting any spare room available for outrageous rates by the hour, asking few questions and closing their eyes to the obvious goings-on.

In *Die Goldene Pest*, the locals lose all sense of right and wrong when they default on their loans. Hounded by their creditor and desperate to get out of debt, Karl Helmers and other villagers get ensnarled in all sorts of shady deals. Even Helmer's unsuspecting grandmother becomes corrupted in the process. Her souvenir store's favorite item, a tacky reproduction of the famous Idar-Oberstein *Felsenkirche* (mountain church), is desacralized by serving as a container to peddle cocaine to the GIs. The situation in Dossenthal escalates into violence when Helmer and others in the village attempt to tap the American gasoline pipeline to pay off their creditor. The community is saved from its own greed only when a large fire consumes Helmer's amusement tent and Helmer is killed by an American military policeman.

In the film, the American GIs appear mostly as passive and good-natured extras with their fists full of dollars; the focus of the film is on how formerly decent people lose all sense of morality when the dollar came calling and profits could be made. The culprit was not so much the individual American GI as the age of materialism and the loosening of traditions and morals that accompanied him to the countryside.[41]

The 1953 Baumholder *Denkschrift*

In the first few years after the troops' arrival, clergymen played a key role in keeping the German public informed about the moral upheaval in the new garrison communities. One of the documents most important in bringing Baumholder and similar communities to national attention was the 1953 *Denkschrift* (memorandum or admonition to ponder) titled "Save Baumholder," drafted by a Protestant clergyman in Baumholder. The author of these lines was a committed anti-Nazi who, during the Third Reich, had belonged to the Confessing Church—members of the Protestant church who, unlike members of the Deutsche Christen, viewed Nazi racial ideology as a violation of Christian teachings. He had been assigned to Baumholder to replace the town's former clergyman, who had been compromised through his all too eager embrace of Nazism.[42] The *Denkschrift* reflects succinctly conservative views on the ongoing dramatic changes in the region. The complaints raised in the *Denkschrift* reveal that conservative commentaries on the American-induced changes drew on a long tradition of German conservative thought that associated modernity with cultural and racial decline.

In this widely published *Denkschrift,* the clergyman expressed his disgust with the new materialism he observed in his town. He reported that the "monstrous and unrestrained false gods" of "work-money-pleasure" that came with the Americans to his town were "in reality a rape of the little Europe that has lost touch with its roots."[43] He identified the secular materialism and hedonism displayed in Baumholder as "apocalyptic" and representative of the whole of Europe.[44] Exemplifying the prevailing conservative opposition to the emerging consumer society, the pastor concluded that matters were bad because the local population had forgotten its Christian roots and worshipped the new idols. He then attacked the secular powers of the town and demanded, in an attempt to halt the immorality that had engulfed them all, that tax-hungry and business-crazy city councils no longer grant licenses to bar owners. He called on the town's officials to stop the avalanche of "prostitutes known under the name 'Veronikas' or '*Amizonen*.'" He also pleaded for stricter measures to limit the level of prostitution that occurred around the American payday in the infamous "dollar forest (*Dollarwäldchen*)," a patch of woods bordering a bar frequented by black GIs.[45]

The author echoed prevailing sentiments among conservative Protestants of the time who still hoped for a third way that would defend Germany from both the dialectic materialism of the Soviet Union and the practical materialism of the United States. He concluded that no difference existed between the two "punishing rods of God," namely on "one side America and on the other side Russia." In his *Denkschrift,* the clergyman managed to portray Germany as a "defeated and unfree people (*unfreies Volk*)," now a victim of the "youthful American world domination." Completely overlooking the destruction of Europe that had been committed by Germans less than a decade ago, the clergyman described Germans as the true victims. He charged that the entertainment industry that came with the Americans was "nothing less than a rape of the local population and the German land."[46]

Drawing on a long tradition of bourgeois notions of respectability, this committed anti-Nazi condemned as outsiders all those who transgressed proper gender and racial boundaries. He diagnosed the alleged sexual disorder of these communities by singling out the black soldiers and the German women who actively and eagerly sought out the GIs in one of the many new bars about town. He bemoaned the noisy goings-on in the bars with "their music that whips everybody into a frenzy, the striptease, the taxi-girls, the roaring jungle noises of the black soldiers" and the German women who "finished off (*fertigmachen*)" the American soldiers. He concluded that the American soldiers were "overpaid, overfed, and underworked" and that matters would not improve as long as "one Negro can spend more money in one night than a German worker with three or four children makes in a month."[47]

Germany's Wild West

Throughout West Germany, and even in East Germany, the GI bars, the young women who came in search of the dollar, and the Gold Rush atmosphere in these towns came to dominate the public discourse on West Germany's "continuing occupation."[48] Alerted by the Baumholder clergy, the tabloid press sent one reporter after another into the area to bring the German reader yet another titillating account of the goings-on in the southwest of Germany. One of West Germany's weeklies specializing in this sort of scandalous reporting, *Wochenblatt,* had the following to say about the situation in Baumholder: "The older generation faces speechlessly the sociological collapse. . . . Baumholder is the meeting place of international soldiers' sweethearts." The weekly called Baumholder the "oozing wound on the body of morality" and reported that the local judge was busy trying to "prevent the final collapse of the human social order."[49]

It is probably not surprising to find such exaggerated reports in the pages of the tabloid press. What makes the "Baumholder Story" so interesting is the fact that even respectable publications drew on the tale of unrestrained and illicit sexuality to indict the American presence. In *Die Pfalz klagt an,* published in 1954, a Protestant minister from Frankfurt used the "Baumholder Story" to indict as immoral the American deployment of Nike atomic missiles in Germany. The clergyman attacked American militarism and the rearmament of Germany by suggesting that, instead of defending the last values of the Christian West, the American military mission in Rhineland-Palatinate was actually destroying them. Intent on inciting passions, he reported that matters could not be worse, for "by day and by night the German people, women and men, the elderly and children were assaulted, beaten, battered, raped, and hunted down with dogs." He topped these outrageous charges by drawing vivid pictures of the moral degeneration that came with the Americans, that is, the bars and the avalanche of women that had followed the troops.[50]

Less than ten years after the defeat of Nazism, this Protestant clergyman used the alleged crisis of morality in Rhineland-Palatinate to attack the American military mission in Europe and, in his view, to set the historical record straight. First, he redefined the meaning of the "German catastrophe" by asserting that the country's nadir was not its most recent Nazi past but the 1950s, when, due to the Americans, the "moral derangement of a whole state was taking place."[51] From his perspective, matters concerning morality were so grim in the state that he described the situation as "the end of all values." He then went on to belittle the horrendous crimes committed by the Germans, equating the relaxation of morality in these communities with the genocide committed by Germany's military in Eastern Europe and the Soviet Union during World War II. The anonymous author shamelessly asserted, "Those things that went on under German occupation during World War II in France or other countries . . . can in no way be compared with the situation that has become a daily fixture of life since the Americans came here three years ago."[52]

Whereas the initial press coverage on such communities as Baumholder and Kaiserslautern focused on all sexual transgressions of German women with American GIs, by 1954 only the most deplorable aspect of the situation made headline news—namely the racial transgressions of German women and black GIs. We have already seen that opposition to these interracial relationships was widespread. The author of the *Denkschrift* was, thus, hardly a lone voice; he was merely articulating publicly what many others also viewed as the most scandalous and threatening aspect of the American presence. A September 1957 photo essay in *Die Bunte* magazine, entitled "A Cry for Help from Kaiserslautern" indicted the situation by showing ten pictures of American GIs and German women. Of those photos, eight showed German women in the arms of black soldiers.[53] Considering that at most 15 percent of American troops during the 1950s were black, the disproportionate coverage of the behavior of German women and black GIs in the German media speaks volumes.

The editor was so appalled by the openly affectionate behavior of this "Veronika" and her GI boyfriend from "Hell on Wheels" that he disguised their identities. Photo from 1954 *Neue Revue;* courtesy of Stefan Moses, photographer

When Germans, in both East and West, read about the American garrison communities during the 1950s, the focus was increasingly on the "many" black GIs who met "sexually unrestrained" women in the bars owned by Eastern European Jews. This story of interracial sexuality in Germany's boulevard press became a staple means of enticing readers into vicariously experiencing forbidden pleasures. According to such publications, the women willing to "sell" their bodies to black GIs were duly compensated. Black GIs supposedly spent DM 72 million for "fast kisses," and Maureen, the Kaiserslautern "queen of the Negro lovers" (*Negerliebchen*), reputedly drove about town in her own Mercedes.[54] But these stories also encouraged readers to condemn such shameless behavior. A 1954 report on the boom in Baumholder entitled, "The *Volk* Must Pay the Price," shows a beautiful and vivacious blonde woman tenderly embracing a very happy black soldier from "Hell on Wheels." So shameful was their act considered that the editor blacked out the eyes of the young couple.[55]

These moralistic and condemnatory reports also found a wider audience in more respectable newspapers and publications. In *Das Land Ohne*

Träume, which is a 1954 assessment of life in the Federal Republic, the author describes the evening hours in Baumholder where "the Negroes, whose heavy bodies have not been tired by their duties, prance about like bears." The author adds, "Some of them already have their girls with them, others are busy looking for one, which is not hard, because they flow out of alleys and nooks."[56] Even the left-leaning newspapers resorted to stories about interracial couples to keep their readers informed about the American troop presence. The union newspaper *Welt der Arbeit* took upon itself the task of visiting Baumholder and reported that in the GIs' hangouts rock and roll was booming from the jukeboxes while "bleached-blond Fräuleins pressed their luscious bodies against the sinewy bodies of black-skinned gentlemen."[57]

While both white and black American GIs went to such establishments, it was predominantly the bars favored by black GIs that attracted national attention. Because most of the *Ami-Bars,* but especially the so-called *Neger-Bars,* were leased and managed by Jews, the outrage over developments in the American garrison towns became even shriller. A 1955 headline in a Mainz newspaper announcing "The Root of All Evil is the 'Frolleins'—A Trip with the Base Commander through Mainz's Negro bars" probably reminded many a German of Hitler's diatribe: "It is the Jew who brings the Negro to the Rhine."[58]

Talking about the "Negro-bars," the black GIs, and the German women who associated with them allowed Germans from different political persuasions to oppose American policies or to bemoan publicly Germans' lack of sovereignty without having to attack head-on the country's foremost ally. While people may have objected to the new reality for very different reasons, they expressed much of their opposition in language that stressed the moral and sexual degeneration that the Americans, but especially black Americans, allegedly had brought to the countryside. This language of moral and racial threat reverberated widely among very diverse strata of the population. Indicting the sexual excesses of the black GIs allowed Germans on the left, for example, to express opposition to the American-sponsored rearmament of Germany or to the stationing of Nike missiles.[59] Lamenting the immorality that came with the black GIs also gave voice to nationalists and those conservatives who still hoped for a Third Way for Germany between the capitalist materialism of America and the dialectic materialism of the Soviet Union. Even those Catholic and Protestant conservatives who strongly supported the American-sponsored integration of West Germany into the Western alliance relied on the language of racial threat, because for much of the 1950s they judged the social and cultural implications of the American presence as undermining their conservative project. Finally, one cannot help but be struck by how indicting the Americans for destroying German morality allowed Germans to express woes over "poor Germany" while also belittling the horrendous crimes committed during the Nazi regime. Attacking their senior ally for immorality allowed Germans to repress the guilt for their own murderous past.[60] The fact that Germans framed their debates on the developments in Rhineland-Palatinate by identifying traditional out-siders to their nation—namely Jews, blacks, and sexually unrestrained women—suggests that racial hierarchies continued to inform notions of German identity.[61]

5

Controlling the "Veronikas"
and "Soldiers' Brides"

When conservative observers surveyed developments in their communities during the early 1950s, they could not but be appalled. Formerly rural villages sported fancy jazz bars and nightclubs, while the narrow streets were abuzz with the chatter and laughter of young women who arrived regularly on the American payday, leaving only when the GIs' dollar supply was exhausted. Even more troubling than the prostitutes, however, were the German women who flocked to these communities because they had followed their American boyfriends or fiancées from the American zone. Their Americanized appearance and demeanor evoked almost as much consternation as did their willingness to live in common-law marriages with their American partners. For local guardians of morality, little distinction existed between the women who were in committed relationships with American GIs and those who arrived on the American payday to sell their bodies. In the initial panic after the troop's arrival, every woman who associated with an American GI was given the derogatory name "Veronika" or "soldier's bride."

Local municipal authorities did not necessarily appreciate the influx of these single women into their communities. However, unlike the local clergy and church-affiliated welfare workers, they did not perceive the women as a force capable of undermining the country's still fragile democracy. For most local officials in these Social Democratic counties, the women who came in the wake of the American troops were the logical side effect of any such military presence. Consequently, they were not so concerned with the threat these women and their lifestyle posed to the Christian *Abendland,* but they were most anxious to avoid an increase in the prevalence of venereal disease (VD).

State and federal efforts to deal with the alleged moral corruption in Rhineland-Palatinate went much beyond local ambition. For the Deutscher Verein für öffentliche und private Fürsorge—Germany's umbrella organization for church-affiliated, private and public welfare agencies and one of the most influential organizations to affect social policy at the federal level—the "Veronikas'" lifestyle could not be explained away as being simply postwar developments. The Verein believed that the roots of the morality crisis were to be found in the Weimar years, when traditional gender roles started to break down. The dominant Catholic and Protestant welfare agencies in the Verein used developments in Rhineland-Palatinate to halt a loosening of morals that, while long underway, had accelerated dramatically in the postwar years. Their answer to Germany's continuing moral crisis was to revive sexual norms that had already been judged as too rigid during the Weimar Republic. By focusing on women's sexual transgressions as an impediment to restoring German respectability during the 1950s, the churches and their affiliated welfare agencies avoided an engagement with the enormous crimes committed by Germans during the Nazi regime.

"Veronikas," "Amizonen," and "Soldiers' Brides"

When the American soldiers arrived in Rhineland-Palatinate from their military posts in the American zone, they brought not only their tanks and artillery; in the wake of the soldiers came also an avalanche of young and single women. We have already seen that the dollar attracted professional and "amateur" prostitutes from across Germany and Europe to the new garrison towns. Not surprisingly, the American troop deployment brought a whole variety of other women to the provinces as well. Many of the American GIs arrived in these communities with their German girlfriends or fiancées. Because American soldiers could marry their German partners only four months before the GI was to return to the United States, many of these young couples were engaged and cohabiting without the legal sanction of marriage.[1] Often, these couples already had a child or two, and their marriage had been delayed only because the U.S. military had not yet granted a wedding permit. During the early 1950s, if the GI was black, it was often almost impossible for him to get a marriage permit from his military commander, due to the miscegenation laws that still existed in many states of the United States.[2] Because these young couples were not married, they also were not eligible for base housing. Thus, when German-American couples arrived in the provinces looking for housing "on the economy," conservative guardians of morality were appalled.

Another group of women following the troops created even more of a stir than the women in committed relationships. In all garrison towns GIs arrived from the American zone with their German mistresses to set up house. While many of the women in these relationships may have secretly hoped for marriage, plenty of the GIs had no plans to marry, often because they already had a wife in the United States. The arrangement between the woman and the soldier was one of short-term convenience, which often ended when the GI left for the United States. These sorts of arrangements were similar to those that can be found to this day around American military bases in Korea or the Philippines. Such women kept house for the soldier and were able to live rather indulged lives in exchange for sex and companionship. Often, when the soldier returned to the United States, the woman would find a new partner, thus bringing the phenomenon of serial monogamy to the provinces.

Young women also flocked to the garrison communities because they had read colorful descriptions in the national press of the never-ending dollar supply of the American GI. The descriptions of Baumholder as the "El Dorado of West Germany" or as the "Alaska on the Westwall" in the national press always stressed that this was "the land where milk and honey flow, that is, where the $ and the DM roll."[3] At a time of high unemployment, especially for women, many desperate souls responded to these enticing tales. Young women hoped for employment as a maid with an American family or as a waitress or dancer at one of the many establishments that catered to the GIs. Others came hoping to find a rich GI to rescue them from a life of poverty. Among these individuals were women who had lost homes and parents in the war. Others were expellees from territories in the East or recent refugees from East Germany. None of them had yet found a niche in the new Republic, and they came with hopes for a better life.

The labeling of all of the women who associated with American GIs as "Veronikas"[4] is surprising, given that the phenomenon of the "Veronika" is usually associated with the "hunger years," those immediately postwar years of scarcity, not the 1950s.[5] A "Veronika" was a woman who had sexual relations with American GIs despite the harsh fraternization laws enacted by the American military government in its zone. The name "Veronika" emerged as a code word for "fraternizing" women when, as the immediate consequence of this widespread sexual contact, a tremendous rise in venereal disease occurred among American soldiers. Military commanders were quick to act in response to this health crisis and put up posters on the military base showing photographs, names, and addresses of infected women. To warn soldiers of the dangers of infection, military commanders also put up large billboards that depicted a woman in a trench coat with the letters "VD" stamped on her chest. It was only a short time before the acronym "VD" became popularized as "Veronika, Dankeschön" in an American hit song of that title.[6]

By the early 1950s, when American troop strength in Germany was augmented, the worst of the hunger years were over, yet in many ways the early 1950s still seem part of the postwar years. Because of the so-called "excess of women" after the war, the flood of refugees from East Germany, and the high rate of female unemployment, the phenomenon of German women seeking out American GIs for love and/or material support was not uncommon.

An extensive 1952 newspaper essay that addressed the "Veronika phenomenon" in Birkenfeld County reveals how problematic the label "Veronika" was. The author reminded local authorities that the women known by the name "Veronika" could not all be judged by the same standard. Many of the women, he suggested, "may have entered into relationships that cannot stand up to strict moral principles," that is, they were living with a soldier without being married. While this author did not explain that a German woman could marry an American soldier only four months before his return to the United States, he did point out the recent and numerous marriages that had taken place between German women and American GIs. He also warned local authorities that, in light of the reality of having thousands of single men in the county, a stricter persecution of these women was not without danger, arguing, "These women protect our own [from the sexual advances of the American GIs]."[7]

A somewhat more lighthearted contribution in the same newspaper made the same argument, namely that the women who had followed the troops served an important function. A short blurb that was clearly published as an April Fool's joke states that "3000 V[eronika]-Dankeschön" would be stationed very soon at the training camp in Baumholder, "so that the girls and women of our town may walk the streets after 9 P.M. without an escort during the summer months."[8] While this may have

proletarianize — to convert or transform into a member or members of the proletariat — middle class

been an April Fool's joke, its sentiments actually reflected the convictions of local authorities, namely that these women protected the wives and daughters of the local burghers.

While the writer of these lines expressed the prevailing view of the Landrat as well as that of the police, others in these counties were appalled by what they saw. The judge at the Baumholder lower court, who was also a prominent member of the Verein, rejected this pragmatic view and expressed outrage at what he considered a flooding of Baumholder with what he called "secret" prostitutes. While the women living with American GIs did not consider themselves prostitutes, the judge was of a different mind. He included them in the category of HWG individuals (*häufig wechselnder Geschlechtsverkehr*), women who allegedly had constantly changing sex partners. He called the women "most crafty prostitutes" and concluded that in the "narrow confines of village life their way of life is no secret."[9]

The judge's harsh assessment of these women compelled the Birkenfeld Landrat to defend them, or at least some of them. He pointed out that many of the "soldiers' brides" who had arrived in Birkenfeld came from respectable backgrounds. Most of them, he concluded, were refugees, "wives of officers, industrialists" who were killed in the war, and he pointed out that, "many of these relationships end in marriage."[10] The Birkenfeld chief social worker agreed with the Landrat that most of the out-of-wedlock relationships between GIs and German women were "committed relationships." While she insisted that these women were neither professional prostitutes nor "secret prostitutes," she nonetheless agreed with the Baumholder judge that the women presented a tremendous "source of unrest in the small villages."[11]

Dangers That the Women Pose

After the perceived social leveling of the Nazi regime and the proletarianization experienced by wide strata of the middle class because of war and the subsequent postwar displacement, German conservatives were anxious to restore bourgeois norms. At the core of this class-based bourgeois society was to be a patriarchal, nuclear family based on traditional gender roles. German women, in this Weltanschauung, were not to transgress gender and class boundaries, let alone those of race. The women who appeared in the garrison communities of Rhineland-Palatinate failed on all these counts. While the local population might have considered the behavior of the new citizens about town as audacious and perhaps even shameless, the clergy and the church-affiliated social welfare workers viewed the women's lifestyle as having much larger implications. In their assessment, the women's behavior was not only morally offensive; it was a threat to political stability and national integrity.[12]

It is easy enough to see why the women walking hand in hand with American GIs or taking rides in their fancy American cars transgressed many rules in these rural communities. Many of the women had arrived via the American zone from places such as Munich or Frankfurt and thus brought the tastes of the city with them. The women wore American-style clothing and makeup, and this caused many a stare. The soldiers' brides dressed like American women, but even worse than that was the fact that they began acting like American women. Observers were appalled that the women paraded "in pants and garish colors, smoke cigarettes and chew gum."[13] At a time when the Nazi slogan, "The German woman does not smoke," still resonated in many ears, the behavior of these women probably offended many a sensibility.[14] One observer complained bitterly, "The girls already feel half like foreigners (halbe Ausländer) and do not bother with German laws."[15]

Conservatives were also appalled by the women's pragmatic approach to their romantic relationships. Not only did they leave parents and loved ones behind to follow their GI boyfriends to an uncertain future; they seemed to revel in the independence that their relationships with the GIs allowed them. Conservatives were horrified by the matter-of-fact approach many of these women brought to their sexuality. Not only did these women choose to "live in sin," they often flaunted the pleasure and enjoyment of their sexuality. Women also did not hide the fact that they preferred the GIs to German men, saying they found the Americans "more manly and sexually attractive."[16] One of the complaints most often uttered by conservatives, was that the women believed that they "had a right to their way of life" or that "they could live as they pleased."[17] Not surprisingly, bourgeois and church-affiliated social workers were appalled.[18]

Conservative observers reserved even greater scorn for the women who associated with black GIs. Under the Nazi regime, the so-called betrayal of race through miscegenation (termed Rassenschande, i.e., racial disgrace, and defined as any sexual act between a German and a Jew or Eastern European) had been considered one of the worst offenses a woman could commit against her Volk. Just a few short years after the fall of the Nazi regime and the abolition of such laws, it was the women in the company of black GIs who appeared to many observers as the worst offenders. Social workers pointed to the black GIs' willingness to adore

abnegation — The act of relinquishing or giving up a right or denying oneself some rights; convenience

and indulge their German partners as one of their main attractions. But social workers were also convinced that German women actively sought out black soldiers because they found them more attractive as sex partners than white GIs. In making this choice, the women allegedly became sexually "enslaved" (*hörig*) to the soldiers, and "could not find their way back to a white partner."[19]

At a time when conservative political and religious leaders still decried the dangerous impact that American-style materialism was having on West Germany, but especially on youth and women, American GIs showered their German girlfriends with all the luxuries the American consumer paradise had to offer. For conservative observers, it was this flaunting of American consumer goods that exposed the cash nexus of these relationships. For most of them it was impossible to imagine that any such union was founded on affection or love. In their worldview a woman proved her love through self-abnegation and self-sacrifice to her husband and children. The German project of rebuilding the country after the destruction of the war demanded rational consumption. The German woman was to scrimp and save for her home and family, not to squander precious resources for clothing, makeup, and rides in fancy cars.[20]

While many of the comments on the indulgent lives of the soldiers' brides suggest a good deal of green envy, they also reveal that middle-class observers were appalled that women from the lower classes were able to blur the boundaries of respectability because of the wealth of their American boyfriends. The "Veronikas" traveled in more luxurious cars than the most prestigious members of the German middle class could afford; they were also able to rent some of the nicest real estate in these communities. The local paper expressed outrage that "the ladies" were "living like 'honorable citizens' among the local population," spending their days in "sweet laziness and boredom." But this same article also pointed out how murky the whole debate on women cohabitating with American GIs had become. The article suggested that it was difficult for the "layman to decide which woman was respectable" and which woman took on employment "merely to cover up" her prostitution activities (*Scheinarbeitsverhältnis*).[21] The soldiers' brides might be living the unrestrained sexual life that the middle class has traditionally associated with the lower classes, but their access to the Americans' consumer goods and powerful dollar allowed them at least a measure of outward respectability.

Lower-class women were not the only ones to blur traditional markers of respectability. While social welfare officials have traditionally associated lower-class women with unrestrained sexuality, they were horrified to observe that many of the women associating with white and black Ameri-

German conservatives were outraged that the "Veronikas"
traveled in more luxurious cars than the respectable German middle class could afford. This couple lingers beside a
street cruiser outside a bar in Lautzenhausen. Courtesy of
Photoarchiv Stern

can GIs came from the respectable middle class. Because the women from
the middle class also wore American clothing and make-up and often indulged in what conservatives considered sexualized, American-style dancing, conservatives viewed them as sexual aggressors. Indeed, middle-class
women seemed to have adopted sexual norms previously associated with
the working class, a trend that emerged during the Weimar Republic and
accelerated during the war and postwar years.[22]

The comments on the threat that the so-called soldiers' brides posed reveal that constraining these women was not just a matter of assuring sexual sobriety (*Wohlanständigkeit*) and containing racial boundaries. Echoing nineteenth-century bourgeois convictions, conservative observers immediately linked these women's consumer-oriented lifestyle to unrestrained sexuality that could affect all other women as well.[23] Social workers were convinced that local women would not be able to resist temptation and would also yearn for "the 'pleasant,' spoiled life, the new clothing, the rides in the tailfin limousines that sparkle with chrome."[24] Farmers' daughters, whose own lives were characterized by "hard and laborious work," were not the only ones judged vulnerable.[25] Social workers concluded that even "good bourgeois daughters were in danger of 'degeneration' (*Verwahrlosung*) and to succumbing completely to prostitution."[26]

Anxieties over the dangers that the "Veronikas" posed to local life went even further. The women were described as a danger that "could develop into an epidemic for the entire *Volk*."[27] Conservatives feared, not without reason, that the "Veronikas'" example of fast and easy money would seduce the whole population into becoming accomplices to her lifestyle.[28] Indeed, the Protestant minister of Miesau reported that every member of his congregation had succumbed to the temptations that the dollar and the soldiers' brides presented. The class and political divisions that had so marked and divided German social and political life in the past were apparently overcome by the power of the dollar. The minister reported that "farmers and workers, rich and poor, pious and nonbelievers, communists and devotees of the Third Reich" all were sponsoring immorality by renting rooms to these women and their American boyfriends.[29]

While the Baumholder judge insisted that only "asocial" families rented to GIs and their girlfriends, this was clearly not the case. Even devout Protestant and Catholic families from the middle class "forgot" their scruples when the dollar came calling. Attitudes toward sexuality and morality, according to the concerned clergy, were increasingly secularized. The Catholic priest in Landstuhl, for example, reported, "With regret one has to watch how even Catholics have become contaminated by the greed for money and the neo-pagan spirit, among them even a number of families with good Catholic tradition, of whom one would have expected differently."[30] Even the most steadfast church members and church elders in Miesau wanted to take part in the housing boom, asking few questions and closing their eyes to the obvious.[31] In another small community outside of Kaiserslautern, the daughter-in-law of an honorary church elder not only ran a bar for GIs but also rented rooms by the hour to "black soldiers and their girls."[32] The Protestant minister from a nearby town reported no better news. The longtime church organist and director of the choir, a local dentist, was renting to not just one but three different soldiers' brides.[33]

People in the village tolerated the "concubinage" within their houses for economic gain, and if pressed on the matter by the clergy, their laconic answer was always, "They will get married soon; they already have their [wedding] papers."[34] The fact that plenty of people had no scruples in renting housing to interracial couples caused even greater consternation. A Birkenfeld social worker reported with a great deal of indignation that some families in town not only rented to interracial couples, but were living with the "girls' Negro boyfriends in great harmony, even going for rides with them in their car."[35]

The commentaries on the women who had followed in the wake of the troops show that it was not at all clear, even to the most astute observer, who was a prostitute, occasional girlfriend, or "legitimate" fiancée.[36] Even women working for the American military who socialized with their American bosses or coworkers were at times included in the anxious reports.[37] That ambiguity, however, did not prevent outraged observers from passing unforgiving, even cruel, judgment. Because of the continuity in personnel involved, much of the rhetoric from the Nazi years carried over into the deliberations during the 1950s. It was not unusual at the time to find reports by clergy, welfare workers, and other self-appointed guardians of morality that called the women "*arbeitsscheu*" (disaccustomed to work) or referred to them as "vermin" (*Ungeziefer*) that lived the existence of "parasites."[38] The Protestant minister from Miesau especially did not mince words. In a letter to the federal government in 1952, he described women who dated black soldiers as "whores" (*Huren*) who represented a "dangerous invasion of asocial, immoral, destructive, and infectious forces" to the parish and family life.[39]

Controlling Vice in the Village

Action to contain the dangers posed by the "Veronikas" generally came from local clergy. The churches and their agencies were outraged that officials of county governments and municipalities took the position that the "Veronikas" were necessary, that it was useful that they be "available for the troops, because otherwise the daughters of our *Bürger* (burghers) would have to suffer."[40] After exhausting their appeals to local mayors and city council members, individual clergymen alarmed the national press, and they turned to their superiors as well as to the state government to report in great detail about the moral upheaval that was unfolding before their eyes. This did not necessarily sit well with town officials. During a conference of mayors in October of 1953, Birkenfeld's Social Democratic Landrat told the mayors in attendance that he had only one wish—that he never see the name of Baumholder in the national news again. An agitated mayor of Baumholder fully agreed with this sentiment. He reported that in the past week alone, he had had to expel four senior editors of major publications from his office. He was also furious about all the attention being paid to his town by church publications of both northern and southern Germany. The angry mayor faulted one man for creating these problems for the community; he accused the local Protestant minister of disparaging the community and criticized him for writing directly to American officials.[41]

Local clergymen wrote to the Protestant state council (*Landeskirchenrat*) as well as to the Social Ministry. In their appeals they commented on the "destruction and perversion of the village spirit" that came in the wake of the troops and the "Veronikas."[42] They described the women who had come to the region as a "locust plague" responsible for putting the community in acute danger of "reverting to a wild state" (*verwildern*).[43] In response to these letters, the Protestant Landeskirchenrat in the Palatinate initiated concerted action. It warned the state government that the situation around the garrison communities signaled the "destruction of all bourgeois and moral order." The church leadership bemoaned the "stream of white and colored occupation troops" into the village and expressed hope that help would be available for the few righteous souls who still had the willpower to "withstand the flood that has engulfed us all."[44]

In addition to alarming state authorities, the church leadership also appealed to the Americans for help. In a meeting with the military leadership in Heidelberg in February of 1952, the Protestant Church of the Palatinate informed the American military of the "girl problem" that had come with the troops. While most of the focus during that debate was on the women who had arrived in the wake of the troops, the church representatives also acknowledged that the "relations between white and colored soldiers to the women and girls of our communities" were an unpleasant side effect of the recent developments. They framed their request by reminding the Americans of the responsibilities that both Germany and the United States had as the "bearers of culture in the past as well as in the present."[45] Exploiting the Cold War hysteria of the Americans the church representatives also suggested that West Germany's fragile democracy might be at stake. They warned the Americans that the

Nihilism - Total rejection of established laws and institutions

d. Anarchy, terrorism or other revolutionary activity

immorality induced by the large number of troops in the Palatinate was
the "best precondition for communist propaganda and the spirit of nihilism."[46] After reminding the Americans that their troops' sexual exploits
might weaken German resolve against communism, they escalated their
strategy even further. As a last desperate measure, the Protestant Church
of the Palatinate informed the American women's organizations of the
"dangers" their husbands and sons faced around their military bases in
Rhineland-Palatinate due to the "Veronikas" and the many bars. The
church leadership was convinced that the American women's organizations had the necessary muscle to impress upon the military and political leadership of the United States the fact that something needed to be
done.[47]

While the local clergy and their church leadership were alarmed about
the influx of professional and "secret" prostitutes, local police chiefs as
well as municipal and county government officials were convinced that
these women protected their own wives and daughters from the advances
of lonely GIs. Local officials did not condemn prostitution per se; as a
matter of fact, they acknowledged that wherever there are soldiers there
are prostitutes. What they did object to was the "freelance" character that
prostitution and the many variations of relationships with the soldiers
had taken in the countryside. Foremost, local authorities hoped to keep
prostitution manageable. To limit the influx of single women attracted
by the American dollar, while also controlling the spread of VD, they
put their hopes in brothels. Consequently, local governments as well as
a number of clergymen appealed to the American military command to
establish brothels for its troops.[48]

The American military was not willing to give in to German demands,
not only because prostitution was illegal in the United States but also
because it did not want to get entangled with the American women's
rights organizations.[49] Consequently, it refused to establish institutionalized brothels for its troops.[50] The military leadership was not happy
about the after-hours entertainment choices of their troops, but it forcefully rejected any suggestions that the presence of American troops led to
a "moral endangerment of youth."[51] If anything, the military command
suspected that many of the women flocking to the new military bases
were actually communist spies sent from East Germany. The Protestant
Church of the Palatinate was all too eager to exploit the Cold War hysteria of the American military and confirmed these suspicions to the military chaplains.[52] Despite concern that the sexual exploits of their troops
could endanger the fighting prowess of the American military and fears
that the troops might be exposed Communist spies, the Americans were

unwilling to give in to German demands. Even the occasional taunt in a German newspaper that the American generals feared only McCarthy and the American women's organizations could not persuade the military to change its policy.[53] The military handed out condoms to its soldiers, reinstituted bed checks in the barracks, and agreed to have military police assist German police officers on vice raids that were conducted regularly. Other than that, they insisted that the "girl problem" was first and foremost a German problem.[54]

While local officials understood that not every woman who associated with an American was a prostitute, they were also eager to get a handle on the situation. Legal avenues for the police and local courts to battle "immorality" in the provinces were limited, since prostitution was legal in Germany. According to the German Criminal Code (§361 No. 6a–c), courts could indict prostitutes for transgressing certain boundaries. To limit street solicitation, prostitutes could be charged for behaving in an offensive manner. It was also against the law to solicit in the close vicinity of churches or in an apartment or house in which children between the ages of three and eighteen resided. Furthermore, prostitutes could be indicted if they conducted their business in the vicinity of schools or in homes where youth between the ages of three and eighteen resided *and* where they presented a moral threat to them. Finally, the law provided that communities with populations of less than 20,000 could be declared off-limits to prostitutes by executive order of the state government.[55]

Before the Americans arrived in Rhineland-Palatinate in 1951, the section of the Criminal Code that outlawed prostitution in communities under 20,000 inhabitants had never been invoked for any of the communities in the state. Because authorities were convinced that it was the never-ending supply of dollars that attracted the female camp followers, it was only with the American troop movements that the prostitution debate emerged in these communities. This is not to say that prostitution did not exist in the countryside before the Americans' arrival. However, under the previous masters of the military installations, rural prostitution had a very different face. When the Baumholder training camp was under German sovereignty, the Wehrmacht supplied a brothel for its troops, and there was little need for freelance prostitution.[56] When the French military took over the installation it provided in the same manner for its troops, setting up segregated brothels for white and colonial soldiers.[57] Thus, prostitution had been in the countryside since the establishment of the Platz in 1937, but it had been controlled and regimented; the women conducted their business out of sight, in facilities provided by the military. Prostitution had a very different face in the 1950s. Prostitutes were visible in town because they sought out the GIs in the many bars that had sprouted around town.

As soon as American troops and the first of the so-called "Veronikas" arrived in the counties of Rhineland-Palatinate in the course of 1950–51, local authorities investigated with their state government the possibility of reinstituting brothels. In a letter of 4 March 1950, the president of Rhineland-Palatinate asked the Ministry of Justice whether brothels or brothel-like institutions could be tolerated. The Ministry of Justice informed the president in April of 1950 that it was not possible for them to persuade the attorney general's office to tolerate any such institution, because the Venereal Disease Law Reform of 1927 had outlawed the establishment of brothels.[58] While Himmler had reestablished brothels by 9 September 1939, that decree was invalidated by the American military government in October of 1945.[59] Thus, the 1927 Law that prohibited brothels was once again in force.

Having been denied the possibility of a more regimented form of prostitution, the towns' next step was to attempt at least to obtain better control over the influx of suspect women. Legislation was passed providing that anyone arriving in a locality with troop concentrations had to register with the local inhabitants' registration office (*Einwohnermeldeamt*) within twenty-four hours instead of the standard seven days.[60] Signs were put up at the train and bus stations to inform any newcomer to town of the new law.[61] The provision was passed "so that investigations can be initiated immediately to determine who the arriving individual is." The other aspect of the stricter registration law was to identify immediately local families who took in boarders.[62] The problem of the "soldiers' brides," however, was not necessarily solved by this measure, because many of the women simply did not register with the local office at all, despite the threat of a jail sentence.[63]

Even though the existing legal situation limited local authorities as to what could be done about the "soldiers' brides," no steps were taken initially to appeal to the state government to outlaw prostitution. The Birkenfeld Landrat and police echoed the sentiments of most county and municipal government officials when they agreed that there was "no interest in getting rid of the 'Veronikas' since that would probably mean that our wives and daughters would become fair game for the American soldiers."[64] Much as the clergy in small villages were horrified by what they called the "inflation of morality," they too did not reject prostitution as such but instead called for institutionalized, and thus controlled, prostitution. What they rejected was the nonregimented and uncontrolled nature of much of the sexual relations in the countryside and the fact that these women had invaded the homes of the respectable middle class (*Mittel-stand*).[65]

All this changed in 1951, when a new judge was appointed in Baumholder and came to the help of the Protestant minister in town. Dr. Detmar Schnapp was a brilliant judge whose distinguished career culminated in his appointment as the chief justice of the state's supreme court. Although he studied law during the Third Reich, he had passed the bar only after the war. Schnapp had joined the NSDAP in May of 1933 when he was only eighteen years old, long before career demands might have made such a move a necessity. According to former colleagues, Schnapp was "arrogant and tough as nails" and obsessed with his mission to make Baumholder "*hurenfrei*" (free of whores).[66] That outlook not only reveals a deeply misogynist stance, but the language is also reminiscent of the Nazi effort to make Germany "*judenfrei*" (free of Jews). In public statements Schnapp was more guarded, insisting that his "utmost goal was to remove from the local communities the influx of inferior (*minderwertige*) elements."[67]

Schnapp was not only a dedicated judge, he was also a prominent and vocal member of the Deutscher Verein für öffentliche und private Fürsorge and viewed his tenure in Baumholder as an opportunity to ensure that "decency, discipline, and order define us as Germans." Moreover, he was committed to influencing national legislation to fulfill this ambition.[68] On 1 October 1951, just a few weeks after he was appointed to the local court, Schnapp appealed to the Landrat in Birkenfeld. In a letter, he asked that the Landrat petition the state government to outlaw prostitution in communities smaller than 20,000 inhabitants, as provided by the Criminal Code. According to the judge, matters in Baumholder had just become too scandalous to put up with any further.

Prodded by the judge, the Landrat met with a number of clergymen and mayors from the county to hear their opinions. Participants at this gathering approved in principle the idea of outlawing prostitution in the county but some feared that such a step could expose local women and girls to the "aggressive pursuits of the troops, especially of the Negroes stationed in Baumholder."[69] The meeting of the county youth welfare committee that followed came to a similar conclusion. The mayor of Birkenfeld as well as the former judge in Birkenfeld pointed out that matters in Birkenfeld were vastly different from those in Baumholder. Their comments are revealing in that they demonstrate how broadly the label "Veronika" was applied to a variety of women but also because they illuminate how tightly the definition of prostitute-like behavior was tied up with race. The mayor and the judge argued that in Birkenfeld "not all

'Veronikas' are prostitutes according to the letter of the law," because in Birkenfeld [where predominantly white air force personnel were stationed] "'genuine relationships' existed and ten marriages had taken place in the last few weeks, with forty-six more pending approval by the military." In Baumholder [where a number of black army units were stationed], however, there could be found the "worst of the worst . . . of the prostitutes (*Dirnen*) in the western regions of Germany."[70]

The *Landräte* and the police of both Kaiserslautern and Birkenfeld counties still were not wholly convinced that outlawing prostitution was a desirable solution, but increasing pressure from the local clergy and the national efforts of Dr. Schnapp forced a decision. Furthermore, alarmed by the clergy and church hierarchies, the welfare organizations of both the Protestant and Catholic faiths had become activated, since they were convinced that local municipalities could not handle this challenge on their own. These organizations as well as the clergy increased pressure on the local population to repent. In December 1951, the Catholic priest in Landstuhl, for example, used his Sunday sermon to speak out against all women who cohabited with American soldiers. In the same tone of fury, he condemned all those who rented rooms to these women.[71] The Protestant clergyman in Baumholder did the same.[72] Furthermore, the Landstuhl priest visited every Catholic family that rented a room to one of the so-called "Veronikas" with an appeal to their Catholic consciences; as a result, families terminated their leases with fifteen women.[73]

Finally, on 27 November 1951, the Birkenfeld Landrat gave in to the pressures from the clergy and the ambitious Dr. Schnapp and appealed to the regional government in Koblenz to petition the state government to outlaw prostitution in the county of Birkenfeld.[74] This request was scarcely a wholehearted one, because in a memorandum dated 12 December 1951, the Landrat's office was still considering the idea of allowing "wild brothels," that is, tolerating privately run houses of prostitution. This solution, it was believed, would "make it easier for the police to control" the prostitutes so that they would pose neither a health nor safety threat. Most importantly, the memo suggested, this solution would ensure that the "foreign soldiers do not satisfy their needs with our local women."[75]

The half-hearted request of the Birkenfeld Landrat to outlaw prostitution was forwarded by the regional government in Koblenz to the Ministry of the Interior of Rhineland-Palatinate. The ministry ordered a conference that the Landräte of the counties of Kaiserslautern and Kusel were also to attend. Also invited were the police chiefs, representatives of the three "democratic parties," and the representatives of the city and county welfare offices.[76] On 9 January, the Landrat of Kaiserslautern joined the Birkenfeld effort and formally appealed to the regional government of the Palatinate to outlaw prostitution in the county. In his letter, the Landrat ignored the past when he presented prostitution as a novel phenomenon in the countryside. He also urged that the local youth of the region had to be protected from the bad examples set by these women.[77] On that very same day, the Ministry of the Interior of Rhineland-Palatinate responded to the appeals from the regional governments of the Palatinate and Koblenz and invoked §361 No. 6c, which outlawed prostitution in communities of fewer than 20,000 inhabitants in the counties of Birkenfeld, Kusel, and Kaiserslautern.[78]

The decree of the Ministry of the Interior stated that "the congestion of people in the southwestern part of the state and the proximity of training camps of the Allied troops" had led to an increased influx of persons "who practice prostitution." The decree was passed to protect "the sensibility of morality of the population" and to ensure the protection of the youth as well as "public decency." The decree specified that prostitutes be punished with jail sentences of up to four months while also providing for the application of §42 of the Criminal Code. This meant that women could be committed to the workhouse for up to two years after serving their prison term.[79] If women were sentenced a second time, they could be punished by up to four years in the workhouse.[80] In a letter accompanying the decree, the regional governments of both Koblenz and the Palatinate instructed localities to make generous use of the workhouse provision because jail terms were viewed as a mere "vacation at the expense of the state, while the workhouse was despised by all prostitutes."[81]

National Action

While local communities were convinced that they had done enough by getting the executive order passed, others were of a different mind. By October 1952, developments in the garrison towns of Birkenfeld and Kaiserslautern Counties had also become a matter of debate in the German Bundestag. Convinced that local municipalities were unable or perhaps even unwilling to understand the gravity of the situation, Maria Dietz, a CDU representative from the state of Rhineland-Palatinate, brought the situation to the attention of federal legislators. Dietz's report made clear that she was much concerned about morality, but she was also convinced that generous federal grants could ease much of the pain. Dietz reported that the construction boom had brought many women who were "kept" by the soldiers and workers and that these women presented a great danger to the young male workers who had come to work in these locales. She called for the construction of youth dormitories, so that the young men who had arrived in search for work would have a place to live. Dietz feared that the young women who had come to these regions had done so for reasons less savory than looking for work. She immediately assumed that any woman who arrived in these communities was in danger of slipping, and to protect these young women from themselves, "asylums" rather than dormitories were needed. She concluded her petition by declaring that her state had "in light of the moral and ethical endangerment of youth become a disaster area."[82]

Dietz's impassioned petition provoked a number of responses from the women deputies of the major parties. The deputy from the FDP, Herta Ilk, expressed concern over these women that was never voiced in the communities in question. She worried about the moral decay in these communities but also repeated an often-used accusation of the immediate postwar years, namely that it was sexual relations of German women with occupation soldiers, rather than the country's murderous past, that were the source of Germany's disgrace. She charged that these "carefree women and girls" were creating the "wrong picture outside of Germany," by suggesting that the "mass of our female youth has become addicted to a less than wholesome way of life." She then distinguished these women from the great majority of young German women who were "diligent, clean, and decent and healthy in body and soul."[83] For Friederike Nadig from the SPD, the developments in the localities with troops were not of a moral nature. She pointed out that an increase in prostitution was always linked to socioeconomic causes, and she listed the present extremely high rate of unemployment among women as one such cause. But she also suggested that the specific problems of the time contributed to the problem, namely the still-occupied country and the "excess of women."[84]

In an unusual alliance, Grete Thiele from the KPD wholeheartedly agreed with her colleague from the CDU. However, rather than blaming irresponsible and immoral women for the recent developments, she connected the whole problem of the "moral disaster" to the fact that the entire region had become a "war preparation area." Thiele agreed with the recent findings of a conference of welfare workers in Düsseldorf, which concluded that it had been "centuries since our youth has been in such danger."[85] She suggested that the only way to end this moral disaster was to call for a complete withdrawal of the occupation troops in West Germany. Despite great consternation over the many problems posed by the troops, none of the deputies took this last suggestion seriously. Thiele's proposal was interrupted a number of times by the bell of the presiding president as well as by angry calls from the floor.[86]

Although concerns over the moral state of affairs in Baumholder and Kaiserslautern were debated in the Bundestag on just three occasions, the Deutscher Verein für öffentliche und private Fürsorge (Verein hereafter) kept the counties of Birkenfeld and Kaiserslautern on the front burner throughout the decade. The Verein was one of the most influential voices at the federal level on matters of social policy, and its members presented a variety of views, with clerical voices predominating. The Verein had been alerted by its members, the church-affiliated welfare organizations, of the moral emergency at hand. But Dr. Schnapp's prominent position in the Verein probably also contributed to the Verein's interest in the goings-on in Baumholder and Kaiserslautern. Many of the debates within the Verein on the so-called "Veronika" problem were dominated by representatives from two church-affiliated welfare organizations, the Katholischer Fürsorgeverein für Frauen, Mädchen und Kinder (KFV), associated with the Catholic church, and the Protestant Innere Mission. Developments in these regions offered a rich opportunity for these organizations to expand and consolidate their welfare mission and to increase their influence regarding social policy at the federal level.

The Verein had been interested in the affairs of these communities ever since the first troops arrived. It was Elizabeth Zillken, a KFV member and one of the leading voices of the Verein, who pressured the Ministry of the Interior in Bonn to act. Zillken had been one of the foremost voices of the KFV since 1916 and had defined much of its agenda ever since its founder, Agnes Neuhauser, died in 1944. Zillken's long and uninterrupted career was not at all unusual; most of the personnel in the church-affiliated charities as well as the Verein had been involved in welfare issues during Weimar and the Nazi regime. The chair of the Verein, Hans Muthesius, for example, had initially lost his post in the Verein between 1933 and 1935 but joined the NSDAP in 1939 and held a prominent post in the child welfare division of the Nazi regime. Even though Muthesius was deeply compromised through his involvement in setting up concentration camps for youth, he was able to assume his leadership in the Verein after 1945. While most of the structures and personnel of these institutions were the same in the 1950s, the political landscape was of course a vastly different one.[87] The responses of the Verein to the crisis in Rhineland-Palatinate provide a rich source to explore how attitudes carried over from Weimar and Nazi Germany played out in this new political constellation.

For the Verein, the many "illegitimate" relationships in the localities with American troops and the population's acceptance of these develop-

antipathy — a natural, basic or habitual repugnance, aversion

ments were not new challenges. Indeed, the Verein had been trying to rein in more relaxed sexual mores and to redefine the meaning of prostitution ever since World War I had brought an increase in prostitution and VD. In those debates the dominant Christian welfare organizations within the Verein insisted that the increase in prostitution could not be explained by socioeconomic changes or the suffering of World War I. Instead, they explained prostitution as indicative of the modern age, which they saw as a process of corruption and decline that had begun with the Enlightenment and the French Revolution. It was the individual's turning away from God and absolute truths that had led to atheism, individualism, materialism, immorality, and, finally, the revolution of 1918. Due to the Christian organizations' deep-seated antipathy toward democracy and modernity, they invested most of their efforts in the 1920s toward reversing parliamentary democracy. Because of their rejection of Weimar as a godless and immoral republic, they welcomed the authoritarian renewal that the Nazis promised. Although the Catholic charities were much less enthusiastic about the Nazi seizure of power than the Protestants had been, they too embraced a regime that promised to restore decency and order. In May 1933, Zillken had welcomed the new regime by declaring: "If the state combats godlessness . . . , if it wants to use its power to end the impudent immorality of the past few years, then we have reason to be thankful to it."[88]

The Christian welfare organizations that initially delighted in the Nazi regime's crackdown on socialists, communists, and "sexual immorality" soon found out that the Nazis were hardly the harbingers of the religious awakening they had hoped for. Although the regime did not lead a full-scale assault on the church-affiliated institutions, the Christian charities lost much of the influence and power they had gained during Weimar due to the principle of subsidiarity. The regime also failed to deliver on its promise to restore sexual decency and order. While illegitimacy rates and prostitution decreased once the economy improved due to the regime's rearmament drive, that trend was short-lived. Once the war began, youth crime rates, adolescent sexuality, and illegitimacy rates all began to rise again.[89] The regime also offended many Catholics in 1939 when it encouraged single women to have children with soldiers departing to the front to ensure future soldiers for their Führer. The last years of the war and the harsh suffering of the postwar years drove not only VD rates but also illegitimacy rates to levels previously unheard off.

When members of the Verein turned their eyes toward Baumholder, they realized that all their efforts and hard work since 1918 had failed. The trend toward greater sexual freedom that had begun with World War I

subsidiarity- serving to assist or supplement

rearmament-

had not been reversed at all but had only accelerated. After World War I, the increase in premarital sexuality, which social welfare workers throughout the Weimar Republic conflated with an increase in secret prostitution, had been mostly a phenomenon of the cities. Now, after World War II, that relaxation of morality had spread to the countryside. According to one study in the early 1950s, 80 percent of high school girls in the southwest of Germany had not only reported sexual activity but had done so in the most matter-of-fact way.[90] Just as troubling to the Verein was the fact that the relaxed attitudes toward sexuality also affected more strata of society. Unlike the post–World War I era, when most of the alleged "HWG women" came from the lower classes, the so-called soldiers' brides came from all social backgrounds.[91] A conference on how radically the war and postwar years had impacted women's sexual norms confirmed the worst suspicions. Studies showed that 47.5 percent of the women judged to be HWG individuals came from the lower middle class (*Kleinbürgertum*), while an astonishing 16 percent came from families in which the father was a professional.[92]

The crisis of morality in Baumholder and Kaiserslautern thus provided the Verein with the necessary ammunition to expand a social policy agenda going back to World War I that aimed at redefining the proper sexual conduct of women.[93] In the Weimar years, that agenda of the church-affiliated welfare organizations had largely failed because of the opposition of liberal and Social Democratic policy makers. During the deliberations of the 1927 Venereal Disease Reform, when the KFV spearheaded an effort to redefine as prostitution "any immoral way of life that provokes offence or injures a sense of shame," it was rejected as too rigid even by the reactionary DNVP.[94] The general relaxation of sexual mores during World War II and the postwar years, which showed no sign of abating in the early 1950s, convinced conservative Catholics and Protestants within the Verein to give it another try. The fact that the federal government was committed to a Christian social and cultural agenda presented a new opportunity to redefine what exactly constituted proper and improper sexual conduct. Developments in such communities as Baumholder and Kaiserslautern, then, provided an unusual opportunity for the Verein to get the debate on women's sexuality back on the front burner.

The Verein responded to the challenge with unusual vigor because its members were convinced that "neither the cities nor counties in Rhineland-Palatinate appreciated the problem in its full extent and implications." In light of this, Zillken called for a "word of authority from the federal government to activate the initiatives of the welfare agencies . . . and of the municipal and county governments."[95] The positions of the Verein were expounded most comprehensively in the May 1953 meeting of the Verein's committee on the "Nonsettled and Uprooted" (*Nichtsesshafte und Entwurzelte*), of which Dr. Schnapp was also a member. Among the individuals invited were psychiatrists, social hygienists, judges, representatives from justice and police, and representatives of private and public welfare institutions.[96]

Speakers at the conference were officials from the cities of Mannheim and Frankfurt, home to large concentrations of American troops since 1945. They quickly established just what was at stake. A representative from the municipal administration of Mannheim, a city that had received considerable notoriety because of its large number of black units and its high rate of "colored occupation babies," reported that the debate on prostitution was no longer primarily a question of the "protection, salvation of the prostitute" but one of saving "our youth and our families."[97] The question of brothels was irrelevant, the speaker concluded, because the new enemy is not the professional prostitute but the secret prostitute or the HWG individual.[98] The chief social welfare worker of the city of Frankfurt also suggested that the professional prostitutes were not the problem, because they knew the rules of the game and played by them conscientiously. Occasionally, these women might attract attention, but the speaker concluded, "It was relatively easy to control their conspicuousness." The much greater danger was posed by the HWG individuals, because these women were "convinced that they have a right to their way of life." While the professional prostitute represented order, the "unrestrained life" of the HWG person created a public "annoyance" and thus presented a great source of disorder.[99]

The Frankfurt social worker completely ignored how certain policies of the Nazi regime—for example, the encouragement of motherhood outside of marriage—may have changed attitudes toward sexuality. Instead, she focused on the war and the hardship of the postwar period as contributing much to the increase in the HWG phenomenon. But even more importantly, she insisted that the real shift began in Weimar with "the demand of the younger generation for greater freedom and independence, for a full life, for the 'same rights for both sexes.'" This last demand, concluded the speaker, did not lead to greater progress, as some feminists may have hoped for, but merely led to the demand by women that they might enjoy men's "freedom in sexual matters" for themselves. It was this assertion by women of their right to greater independence and sexual equality that had led to the destruction of the family and the increase in divorce rates. The sexual liberation of women that emerged in the Weimar years, she added, was "one of the predominant causes for the increase of all forms and levels of prostitution."[100]

After hearing all the evidence, the Verein recommended that the whole question of "who is a prostitute" needed to be redefined. The participants at this conference ignored existing data on the by then significant number of German-American marriages and argued that the "so-called 'engagements' or 'permanent relationships'" at the localities with troop concentrations did not lead to marriage, but were defined by an occasional change of partners."[101] We have seen above just how complicated the situation was for many in these relationships and how hard it was even for local observers to judge the merit of these unions. For the Verein, no such ambiguities existed. While the Verein acknowledged how fluid the boundaries could be between premarital sexual experimentation, HWG behavior, and prostitution, its members were intent on restoring not only decency but also certainty. The clerical members dominating the debate judged these women with the same values that had informed their views during the Weimar years. In that understanding, any sexual union outside of marriage was an act of prostitution.

Just how narrowly the Verein defined improper sexual behavior can be seen in their outcry over a high school senior who had talked about sex as "if it were the most natural thing." The Verein asked in great consternation: "Where is the boundary to prostitution?" in such behavior.[102] Informed by such a worldview, the Verein concluded that the great majority of unions of German women and GIs in the garrison towns lacked a "serious and deeper attachment" and therefore constituted prostitution. The Verein recommended that these sorts of relationships with occupation troops should be prosecuted to the fullest extent under the existing prostitution laws. The Verein also recommended that jail was not sufficient punishment for such offenses. Punishment by assignment to the workhouse should not be for second-time offenders only but should be used generously to punish even first-time defendants.[103]

It would be easy enough to conclude that the members of the Verein merely recycled their idea from the 1920s on reining in social disorder by containing women's sexuality. However, the Verein's deliberations suggest that they had drawn tremendous lessons from their most recent past, the Nazi years. Although they still decried the women's behavior as an outward sign of a spiritual emptiness brought on by the materialism and rationalism of the modern age, they no longer explained the women's sexual behavior as a product of the greater freedom inherent in democracy. Even as most of the participants in this debate remained deeply ambivalent about their new democracy, they nonetheless argued that the

This young German-American couple celebrated their wedding in style at the Landstuhl Non-Commissioned Officers Club. Courtesy of Michael Geib, curator of the Museum des Westrich, Ramstein

women's behavior posed a threat to that democracy. They demanded sexual containment not to reverse democracy, as they had during the Weimar Republic, but in order to protect the "democratic state based on Christian principles."[104]

The Verein's recommendations on redefining prostitution were passed on to the Ministry of the Interior, and Ministerialdirektor Dr. W. Hagen's reaction shows that, although rigidity in matters of morality may have been the dominant mood in the Verein, voices of dissent also existed. Hagen thought the Verein's recommendation out of tune with the times, and he was troubled by the Verein's call to judge relationships between "two consenting adults of the opposite sex" based on the same attitudes that dominated the values of the past. He also questioned whether it was appropriate to prosecute women who were engaged or were involved in committed relationships with American GIs when a greater relaxation in matters of sexuality was underway throughout Germany, noting that at the time 70 percent of all babies born in the first year of marriage in Bavaria had been conceived out of wedlock.[105] A year later, Hagen again raised objections to the Verein's suggestions "because one-fourth of the relationships between German girls and American soldiers ended in marriage." He added that it could not be in the interest of this ministry that such women be prosecuted to the fullest extent.[106]

However, Dr. Hagen seems to have been a lone voice of dissent in the federal ministries of the Christian Democratic government throughout much of the 1950s. Conservative and mostly clerically inspired officials at the federal level seemed intent on undoing the relaxation of sexual mores, if need be through the courts. In a 1955 letter to the Ministry of the Interior, the Ministry of Justice expressed the prevailing tenor, namely that the old qualifications of prostitution were not appropriate any longer in the new climate.[107] The Ministry of the Interior was informed that as early as 1952 individual judges, encouraged by the court decisions of Dr. Schnapp, had begun ruling according to the Verein's recommendation. The Ministry of Justice further reported that "according to the present interpretation of the law," the definition of prostitution should also be applied to the so-called "kept women" in the "regions with great troop concentrations."[108]

The Verein as well as the Ministries of Interior and Justice were of course aware that it was not particularly easy to prove prostitution when a woman had been living with a particular GI over several years and the only reason they were not married was the military's prohibition on marriage until the soldier returned to the United States. Therefore, federal efforts focused on changing a key element of the prostitution law—the term "habitual fornication" (*gewohnheitsmäßige Unzucht*)—into "continuing" fornication (*fortgesetzte Unzucht*). Thus, a woman in a relatively new relationship or a woman who had a second cohabitational relationship could be a suspect because "the defining character of habituation" could be proven, the ministry argued, even if "there is an absence of frequent partners," because the "propensity for prostitution can also be developed through single acts with few partners."[109]

The Ministry of Justice also pointed out that in order to make this new definition of prostitution stick, "a thorough investigation of the way of life of the accused" was necessary. To achieve this objective, the ministry "deemed it necessary that the police and courts pay special attention to the so-called committed relationships in the area of foreign troop concentrations." The ministry also instructed localities "not to make their individual intervention dependent on the still valid letter of the law that states that habitual prostitution is defined by random and frequently changing intercourse."[110] Thus, even though no laws had officially been changed to legalize the new and expanded definition of what constituted prostitution, the new emphasis on "continued" rather than "habitual" fornication was adopted and county governments were instructed by the state and regional governments to apply this new standard. To ensure that the population understood the new parameters of what acts constituted prostitution, local newspapers published the new guidelines. From now on the definition of prostitution was to include the "committed relationship to one occupation soldier, 'the so-called steady boyfriend.'" The article also reiterated the ministries' position that even the acceptance of gifts in kind exposed women to charges of prostitution.[111]

By 1957, when a major overhaul of the German criminal code was being debated in the Bundestag, the Ministry of the Interior asked that §361 be changed accordingly. In a letter to the Ministry of Justice, the Interior Ministry called for eliminating the term "habitual" from the books because that wording made it hard to prove prostitution in "so-called committed relationships." It also called for a much broader definition of "continued" to be used, to battle the new type of prostitute, the "soldier's bride." It further suggested that the other component that defined prostitution, namely "intent of financial gain" (*Erwerbsabsicht*), was fully satisfied in the case of soldiers' brides and HWG individuals. It could be assumed, the ministry argued, that the "kept woman" was engaged in prostitution and insisted that a "frequent change in partners is not an important feature" to address the problem of the soldier's bride.[112]

The ministry also asked to have the age limit in §180 (procurement) raised to twenty-one, to allow the protection of a greater number of women, who could thus be prevented from prostitution. Whereas the procurement law had hitherto pertained to women under the age of eighteen, the ministry argued that it should now be made illegal to rent housing to a woman under age twenty-one if she lived with a man outside of wedlock. The letter also pointed out that the country's highest court (*Bundesgerichtshof*) had already ruled in 1953 against the more tolerant attitudes of some state courts in the postwar years regarding intercourse between fiancées. The Bundesgerichtshof ruling stated that any "sexual act outside of marriage is an offence against the elementary law of sexual discipline (*Zucht*) and is therefore prostitution (*Unzucht*)."[113] The ministry further petitioned that prostitution be punished as an offense (*Vergehen*) rather than as a misdemeanor (*Übertretung*). The authorities also hoped to clamp down on parents who might be renting to "Veronikas." The age limit for youth protected under §361 No. 6a and b (youth endangerment) was to be raised to twenty-one. Thus any parent could be indicted for renting to a soldier's bride if there were "children" under twenty-one in the house. Lastly, the ministry suggested that the endangerment of youth clause provided by §361 should be enforceable before the courts even if no endangerment of the child had actually occurred.[114]

The Ministries of the Interior and Justice seem to have agreed that a woman who lived with an American soldier and was financially supported by him while she managed the affairs of the home was a prostitute. Even when these women worked and were not "kept women," they were considered prostitutes, because their employment was considered a "mere cover-up." When they did not work, at the insistence of their American fiancés or boyfriends, German authorities accused them of being a bad example with their lazy way of life that offered nonetheless great rewards. At a time when the public discourse on women agreed that the life of the homemaker was the German woman's natural calling, the women who lived this life with an American were vilified.[115]

Even more disturbing is the fact that the positions of both ministries and the Verein developed at a time when a great number of German women were living in nonsanctioned common-law marriages with German men. Because under existing legislation war widows who remarried lost all their pension benefits, many widows decided not to marry again but to live with their new partners without the legal sanction of the state. These cohabitational relationships between two Germans were called "uncle marriages" (*Onkelehen*), and according to the records from youth agencies and the yearly church reports of the clergy, such arrangements existed not just in the anonymity of the city but even in remote villages.[116] While these relationships caused their share of concern, they were nonetheless judged very differently from the relationships between GIs and German women.

The Ministry of the Interior informed the Ministry of Justice that any reform of the Criminal Code would be faced with the need to "delineate the *commercialized sexuality* [of the soldiers' brides] sufficiently from committed relationships, which were known under the description '*Onkelehen*' and *Pensionkonkubinate*.'" The distinction had to be made, it argued, because it would be "doing injustice to reality if one were to characterize these forms of nonmatrimonial living together as 'prostitution,'" explaining, "Material considerations were playing a role here as well, but they were the foremost reason for the lack of legal sanction, which would endanger the common household through loss of pension benefits, etc." These committed relationships, the ministry concluded, should not be addressed through the avenues of the criminal law but had to be dealt with through social legislation that would induce the partners to legalize their relationships.[117]

Thus, at a time of prevalent *Onkelehen,* the Verein, as well as the Ministries of the Interior and Justice, agreed to judge women who lived outside of wedlock with American GIs as prostitutes. Instructions that reflected the new "present-day interpretation of the law" were handed down to the state government of Rhineland-Palatinate, which in turn instructed its regional governments. In this manner, the local Landrat, the police authorities, and the local judges were informed about the new definition of prostitution and instructed to apply it.

When the German Criminal Code finally was revised in 1960, the lawmakers rejected as too extreme the suggestions of the Verein and Dr. Schnapp that the defining characteristic of prostitution be changed from "habitual" to "continuing."[118] However, throughout the 1950s, local communities were instructed to judge the women who associated with American GIs as if the Criminal Code had already been revised according to the Verein's proposal. Keeping this rigid interpretation of proper sexual behavior in mind, every woman who dated an American GI bore the burden of proof that hers was a relationship based on love and affection, thus displaying the signs of "deep and serious attachment" that the Verein deemed the defining characteristic of a true relationship. This redefinition of prostitution meant that local officials, if they were to judge prudently, had to keep very close watch on all women in the vicinity of American soldiers. And, indeed, a close web of surveillance emerged to ensure that proper relationships could be distinguished from suspicious ones. In the process, *all* women were affected by the legislation and the containment measures that aimed at controlling the sexuality of the so-called "Veronikas."[119]

Conclusion

This short overview of the national debate has illustrated the degree to which the developments in communities such as Baumholder and Kaiserslautern were discussed in the arena of "high politics." The debates within the Verein and the Bundestag as well as the suggestions drawn up by the Ministries of Interior and Justice reveal a much broader agenda than can be discerned on the local level. To the conservative voices in the federal government, the Verein, and the churches, the "Veronikas"—with their cherry-red lips, colored hair, and American-style dress and manners— were offenders twice over. Their "sexually immoral lifestyle" undermined the conservative project of gender stabilization, and they represented the most offensive aspects of the evils of the secular materialism that conservatives were so desperately trying to avert. At the national level, Baumholder and Kaiserslautern also become a metaphor for the moral decline associated with the continuing "occupation" of Germany. Even more importantly, in that narrative, sexually promiscuous women were portrayed as the real source of Germany's moral crisis. It was the behavior of these women, not the country's murderous past, that were giving Germany a "bad name" in the community of nations.

But Baumholder also became a metaphor for the need for a general overhaul of German mores, the "moral rearmament" of Germany after the disaster of the Nazi years. It was not only the "soldiers' brides" who were to be controlled and punished. State and federal agencies as well as church-affiliated welfare institutions also expressed the opinion that the presence of the so-called "soldiers' brides" and the seductive power of the dollar were endangering the entire state of Rhineland-Palatinate. In the eyes of conservative political and religious leaders, society had not yet overcome the disorder of the country's most recent past. Hoping to halt, if not reverse, a general trend toward greater sexual tolerance, the Verein stressed that its greatest task was to induce in the population at large "the sensibility for what is right and wrong in matters of morality."[120] While these efforts aimed at the population at large, the next chapter illustrates that the foremost targets were women and the young.

6

Keeping America at Bay

The efforts within local communities to contain prostitution and immorality showed that it was largely because of the work of the Protestant ministers of Miesau and Baumholder, as well as the efforts of Dr. Schnapp, that the names of Baumholder, Kaiserslautern, Ramstein, and Landstuhl had been catapulted into the national debate. These men's efforts to involve the nation at large in a public debate over the social costs of the "continuing occupation" of Germany forced these communities to act more boldly. The outlawing of prostitution in rural communities was just one component of a two-pronged attack to battle the "moral emergency" in the state of Rhineland-Palatinate. The nation's "eye on Baumholder" also raised the question of how the young, the future of the new democratic Germany, would survive the challenges at hand.

Throughout West Germany and during much of the 1950s, youth social workers expressed concern over the country's young men and women, and debates over Germany's youth reflected anxieties relating to the past as well as the present. Officials concerned with youth felt that it was the lack of attention to the problem of youth radicalism in Weimar that had resulted in the Nazi nightmare. The impact of Nazi mass organizations on youth, the dislocation of millions of young people during and after the war, and the continuing high youth unemployment had only increased the sense of crisis. The dominant influence of American popular culture that set in immediately after the war added yet another layer of danger that the young faced in the fragile republic. In the communities with American troops, these general anxieties over the country's young were magnified even further.

The fears expressed by concerned clergy, the church-affiliated social welfare agencies, and public welfare workers reveal just how anxious conservative Germans were over the emerging consumer society and the considerably more relaxed attitudes toward sexuality that accompanied this shift. The soldiers' never-ending supply of money and carefree way of life were perceived as a threat to the "traditional structures" of the village as well as to the local population, which was judged not strong enough to withstand this onslaught of "*Amerikanismus.*" Addressing the issue of the prostitutes and "Veronikas" was not enough. A much broader program was needed because the family, the very foundation of the state, was perceived to be weakening before the onslaught of the dollar. Indeed, concerned political and spiritual leaders identified the GIs' wealth as an unwholesome enticement to the whole population. In these anxious debates, it was not just single GIs who represented a threat. Even the American families, with their example of materialism, consumerism, and carefree mobility, contributed to the climate of uncertainty. Conservative clergy, church-affiliated social welfare workers, and bourgeois observers worried incessantly about how the population—but especially women, the young, and the "asocial" classes—could withstand the seduction of the American way of life.[1]

Even by the middle of the decade, when the initial destabilization of the years of the building boom had settled down, the church-affiliated welfare agencies in the Deutscher Verein für öffentliche und private Fürsorge continued to concern themselves with the dangers facing society. The fact that the Innere Mission and the Katholischer Fürsorgeverein für Frauen, Mädchen und Kinder (KFV) continued receiving federal funds throughout the 1950s is perhaps indicative of the degree to which the dangers that the agencies described reflected larger anxieties about the new democracy and the new freedom it entailed. The highly exaggerated reports from the private welfare agencies reveal that their concerns over the U.S. military presence were not merely the expressions of German provincialism. Indeed, a much wider national audience shared the concerns they expressed; the desperate pleas of these organizations were rewarded by generous federal grants to battle the moral emergency in Rhineland-Palatinate.

Getting Federal Funds

Just a few months after the first troops arrived, the Hilfswerk der Evangelischen Kirche der Pfalz (which later merged with the Innere Mission) and the KFV alerted the state government in Mainz as well as the federal government in Bonn to the scope of moral challenge in the areas with troop concentrations.[2] Continuing their long-standing antagonism toward public welfare agencies, the church-affiliated welfare agencies regretted the principle of self-government of the municipalities and county governments that were responsible for the administration of youth welfare. The Christian welfare agencies feared that the regional public welfare offices, because of fiscal concerns, would do very little to help in the current crisis. Conversely, many of the public welfare agencies initially not only viewed the Christian welfare agencies' interventions with great suspicion but also rejected their interference outright.[3]

In February 1952, the Youth Council of the Protestant Church invited representatives from both Catholic and Protestant youth welfare institutions to discuss the "moral situation of the female population in the regions with an especially strong occupation force, and for those regions where rearmament efforts are underway." The participants gathered because they were convinced that police efforts to contain prostitution were not sufficient to halt the decline of morality in the new garrison towns.[4] The representatives at the conference were ready to help but could achieve little without generous funds from the federal government. In light of the challenges facing them, the Hilfswerk decided that funds of the federally sponsored youth plan (Bundesjugendplan, BJP) would be suitable to create an extensive and effective social welfare network in locations with troop concentrations. Money from the BJP would allow the Hilfswerk and the KFV to help contain the "Veronikas" and uprooted women who flocked to these regions. But federal money would also be needed to strengthen the families in the Rhineland-Palatinate against the detrimental side effects of the troop concentrations.

In their anxious pleas for funds to protect Germany's youth, the Christian organizations depicted the situation in Rhineland-Palatinate in the most horrid manner, basing most of their charges on mere speculation rather than fact. According to their accounts, "there were supposedly certain meadows and woods where intercourse was conducted out in the open, even in the presence of children."[5] The Protestant minister from Miesau reported much the same thing to the state government in Mainz when he claimed that children who played in the fields and woods regularly encountered the "whores and their lovers."[6]

Children and teenagers allegedly were not only encountering an indecent way of life, they were also participating in it.[7] The people reporting on these alleged sexual acts between occupation soldiers and German youth seemed convinced that federal authorities would be more generous with funds if they understood the special dangers that the black soldiers presented. According to one such inflammatory report, an eleven-year-old girl whose "parents rent to 3 to 4 whores . . . voluntarily had intercourse with a Negro in a close-by wooded area."[8] Another report describes a fifteen-and-a-half-year-old girl who was allegedly found in the bushes engaged in consensual sexual relations with "Negro soldiers." According to this report, the girl was "so worn out through her intercourse with the Negroes that she could literally neither stand up straight nor walk."[9]

In November 1952, the youth social welfare committee of the German Bundestag traveled to the state so that its members could see just how critical the situation was. The FDP (Free Democratic Party) delegate, Karl Hübner, who reported to the Bundestag on the committee's tour, commented on the burgeoning nightlife in these communities, the number of registered prostitutes in the village, the illegitimate children born to young women who arrived in these communities as well as to local girls. He acknowledged that such temptations had always existed in the big cities, but considerable help was needed in the countryside because it lacked the infrastructure to deal with the crisis. He furthermore added that the new urban atmosphere of the villages was only exacerbated by the greed that many families displayed in letting rooms to unmarried couples. The young in this region, the speaker concluded, were in acute danger of "falling victim to a depraved way of life."[10] But it was not just a matter of "Veronikas" and the occasional striptease in the refurbished barn or chicken coop that caused concern in the Bundestag. The speaker added that in one small town "343 local women were employed with the occupation powers, and because of a lack of day-care facilities, 131 children under the age of fourteen were left at home without supervision." This last comment caused much unrest among the members of the Bundestag seated on the right side of the aisle—the Christian Democrats.[11]

As this debate reveals, the fact that social structures in the hinterland were shifting rapidly caused as much outrage in the Bundestag as did the presence of soldiers' brides and "sleazy bars." Not only were the streets of the villages and towns populated with a great number of foreigners, lawmakers also lamented that working mothers were increasingly absent during the day. Even though two-thirds of those 343 employed women in Baumholder were single women without children, the whole debate about women's employment with the occupation force centered on working mothers.[12] The committee completely ignored the fact that most of these women could rely on extended families for help with child care and instead accused mothers of failing in their duty to ensure that their offspring stayed away from the GIs, the "Veronikas," and the many bars about town.

In light of this crisis, the committee on youth welfare saw as its foremost goal the keeping of "unsupervised and badly supervised youth off the street and away from the bad impressions to which they are exposed through irresponsible adults." The FDP delegate called for extensive funds to aid in the construction of kindergartens, day-care facilities, youth libraries, and youth dormitories.[13] These facilities were needed to ensure that the young of Rhineland-Palatinate would stay away from the "dens of vice of the occupation."[14]

The suggestion for such construction projects drew extensive applause from the right side of the aisle, but the speaker from the SPD also seconded the motion. However, the contribution of the speaker from the SPD also reveals that party's deep differences with the more conservative CDU and the FDP. Although the SPD was hardly the most ardent supporter of the American-sponsored military and political integration of West Germany, it was much less critical of the social and cultural implications of the U.S. presence. The speaker from the SPD completely refrained from the charge that conservatives generally hurled at the Americans, namely that the soldiers and their dollars brought moral degeneration to the hinterland. Instead, he concluded that any such concentration of soldiers would lead to similar problems; but he also stressed that the relative wealth of the Americans exacerbated the problem.[15] He agreed that federal funds should be made available to help these communities. During another debate, the SPD again rejected the narrow focus on sexual containment in the debates of the Christian welfare agencies. To deal with these perceived morality problems they called instead for sex education in the schools and better employment opportunities for young women.[16]

While the local population "expressed a sense of astonishment" over this interest from the federal government, the parliamentarians agreed that money-crazed parents were ill able to judge the dangers at hand.[17] The local young needed to be protected from the soldiers, the bad influences of the "soldiers' brides," and the bad example that many local families set by renting rooms to GIs and their German partners. On the basis of the committee's report, it was decided that large grants from the Federal Youth Plan would be made available to protect the young of the state, as well as the many young men and women who arrived there from the German Democratic Republic (GDR) in search of fortune.[18]

The youth plan had been established in 1950 in response to the hardships that the war and its aftermath had wrought upon the younger generation of Germany.[19] In July 1951, Rhineland-Palatinate began receiving funds to help the state's endangered youth cope with the "concentration of NATO troops."[20] In that first year the state received a mere DM 50,000. By 1953, due to pressure from the Youth Council of the Protestant Church and from the KFV, both members of the steering committee of the BJP, this meager offering had expanded into a grant of more than DM 2.5 million for the creation of extensive youth social welfare programs in Rhineland-Palatinate. These federal funds were also augmented by generous state funds.

Until "Model Baumholder," as the effort to save German youth from the social perils of the American "occupation" was called, funds from the BJP were granted only for job creation and civic education programs for Germany's youth. Because of pressure from the churches and church-affiliated welfare organizations in the Verein, the mission of the BJP was expanded and funds designated exclusively for initiatives in the field of youth social welfare work were granted. Zillken's insistence that "when we speak of Baumholder, we are only referring to the central point of a much larger phenomenon" had prevailed.[21] With a certain amount of pride, the clergy reported that "due to the impact of Baumholder, it was possible for the first time to break the [heretofore] unyielding (*sture*) policy" of the BJP.[22] The moral situation in Baumholder and Kaiserslautern had changed the politics of the BJP tremendously, while also giving the Christian social welfare organizations an invigorating boost. Because of the alleged moral crisis, the agencies were able to significantly expand their infrastructures and their culturally and socially conservative mission in the state.[23] The SPD's objections to the way in which the churches and their affiliated agencies used the situation in the Rhineland-Palatinate to push their conservative agenda had been tuned out.[24]

Strengthening the Family

For the church-affiliated welfare agencies, the loosening of morals and the greater tolerance of out-of-wedlock sexuality that they observed in Rhineland-Palatinate could not be understood solely in the context of the lost war and the Federal Republic's lack of sovereignty. In their analysis, much of that development was firmly tied to the age of materialism and its impact on traditional social structures, but especially on women and the young. Thus, in their view, the age of consumerism and the break-down of old orders that so marked the 1950s, but whose origin lay in the Weimar years, created a climate in which all women were highly vulnerable. Added to such concerns, which marked social debates throughout the country, were the particular challenges faced by the communities of Rhineland-Palatinate. The presence of the American way of life in this region further magnified the general anxiety over the encroaching consumer society and the impact it might have on the conservative effort to restore German society along the principles of the Christian *Abendland*. In the eyes of the church-affiliated agencies, the intersection of unrestrained American consumption and "unrestrained female sexuality" was a matter that could not be ignored.[25]

In light of all these challenges, one of the main goals of the church-affiliated agencies was to strengthen the family in the locations with troop concentrations. In their work with families, the welfare workers assumed an activist and controlling function. Rejecting in principle the Nazi intrusion into the family and distancing themselves from the communist model of the East, the church-affiliated agencies, in close connection with the public agencies, nevertheless set up in practice a system that was just as intrusive, though without being "collectivist." The private and public welfare agencies defended their measures against the model of the recent past as well as against the model of East Germany while still maintaining the same degree of control over people's lives. Not surprisingly, in this anxious debate on the family, the most intrusive aspects focused on single-parent or lower-class families.

The policies designed to strengthen the family were characterized by both beneficent and controlling functions. Throughout Germany, politicians on both the left and right agreed that a woman's foremost obligation should be her role as mother and homemaker. Only a "traditional" family with a breadwinner father and homemaker mother could provide the stability that could distance the young and fragile democracy from the Nazi past as well as from the collectivist model of East Germany. But during the better part of the 1950s, conservatives also envisioned the family as a bulwark against the ever-expanding influence of American popular culture. Mothers were needed at home to make sure that their children did not frequent movie houses or read American comic books. In Rhineland-Palatinate, mothers faced even greater challenges. While workers for the KFV insisted that they did not reject women's working on the military installations in principle, because of the limited opportunities for women's employment in this region, they nonetheless stressed that this sort of work harbored many dangers. The mother was needed at home, demanded social workers, because "parents who usually both work" cannot oppose the "Americanized life in the community" with the "moral values" necessary to protect their young.[26]

The Bundestag Committee for Occupation Affairs was especially harsh in its assessment of working mothers. It called for the construction of day-care facilities for the "loitering children of the numerous mothers who were in the employ of the occupation for high wages and were neglecting their children."[27] This last comment reveals the many layers of concern that were expressed over the situation in Rhineland-Palatinate. Lawmakers attacked women not only for working outside the home, they also maligned them for "being in the employ of the occupation." The committee's finding also completely disregarded the fact that most women had to work to make ends meet and that many of them, especially in the villages, still had extended families to help with child care. Their working for "high wages" was described as culminating in the neglect of their children, the implication of such rhetoric being that these women worked merely to satisfy their selfish material needs.[28]

To protect those children, whose mothers were allegedly negligent in their duties because of their employment with the occupation power, the Ministry of the Interior instructed the regions with troop concentrations to build child care facilities.[29] To the great joy of many a community but also numerous exhausted mothers, the federal government made millions of deutsche marks available for this purpose. The principal impetus behind these programs was not to give women more choices but to protect children from the potential seductions of occupation soldiers or sleazy bars. Furthermore, day care institutions were designed to ensure educational access to the parents while their children were young. It was at the kindergartens that responsible educators were to impress upon the parents the dangers their children faced in the midst of the occupation forces.[30]

These institutions were set up as conservative and defensive measures to contain the worst damage that accompanied the accelerated modernization and perceived Americanization of the region. While their establishment was grounded in a solely conservative agenda, their impact in these traditionally neglected regions of the state had the opposite effect. The creation of these facilities made life much easier for working mothers. Furthermore, it allowed those women who were not yet employed an option they had never had before.

The affected communities also invested a considerable amount of money in expanding or creating leisure facilities. Together with the church-affiliated welfare organizations, they sponsored summer camps for those children and adolescents considered most at risk because of the American presence. These were usually the children of parents who rented rooms to German women and their American beaus. Welfare officials hoped that the time away from their parents and the sinful life conducted in the home would prevent the child's complete corruption.[31] Another effort to battle the moral decline in the state was to expand existing libraries and to send bookmobiles with the German classics into even the most remote villages.[32]

At a time when the records of the juvenile courts of Birkenfeld and Kaiserslautern counties show that the worst offenses being committed by teenagers were traffic violations and cutting school, the KFV reported, "The older pupils in school have reached a horrifying nadir of morality that cannot be reversed."[33] In one of the rare reports that actually addressed young men and women, this situation was ascribed to the fact that pupils spent their free time in pubs with the "occupation forces or with the numerous prostitutes."[34] Federal funds were thus provided to create youth clubs for young men and women to keep them away from the bars and pubs where American soldiers congregated. In these clubs, the young were not just to be protected from the "eroticized atmosphere" around the bars. The programs at these clubhouses were also envisioned as a counter force to the dominant American culture that so attracted the adolescents. The young were to be introduced to good German films, classic books instead of comic books, and traditional German music instead of jazz, which many Germans at that time disparagingly referred to as "Negro music."[35] Despite all these efforts, the local young often rejected the leisure facilities created with the help of the Federal Youth Plan. Teenagers thought much of the programming old-fashioned; they also did not appreciate the strict supervision that prevailed in many of these institutions. In both Kaiserslautern and Birkenfeld counties it was deeply regretted that the young men and women preferred less organized leisure activities, choosing to meet with friends in the back room of a pub to talk, listen to music, or dance.[36]

Protecting Local Teenagers

Church-affiliated welfare workers worried incessantly that parents were not up to the task of protecting their young from the seductions of the dollar. They worried even more over "incomplete" families, that is, families without a father and families from the lower classes. While anxieties over "incomplete families" were expressed in all parts of the new Republic, the presence of American occupation troops raised these anxieties to fever pitch. Although the rates of illegitimacy and VD were lower than the national average and lower than they had been during Weimar, the welfare workers continued to describe the situation in the state in apocalyptic terms.[37] In order to protect young German women from the GIs and their dollars, church-affiliated welfare workers also spun a tight web of surveillance around all those families considered at risk.

As part of the initial reaction to the large influx of foreign troops, guardians of morality speculated that mothers were making a living by pimping their children to black soldiers.[38] Such wild rumors settled quickly into more tempered debates over single mothers' inability or unwillingness to protect their teenage daughters from the seductive powers of the American GIs. Speculation abounded that because the strong hand of the father was absent, there were "plenty of older mothers who did not mind seeing that their daughters have an American boyfriend, and even supported these relationships directly or indirectly."[39] Another observer commented that too many mothers watched quietly while their daughters imitated soldiers' brides and started dating an American GI out of a desire for new shoes and clothing.[40] Just as during the years of occupation, none of the observers ever acknowledged that a young woman might be dating an American soldier for reasons of affection. The assumption underlying all the comments on these relationships was that the GIs were mostly attractive because of the material goods they could offer. German mothers as well as their daughters failed not because of an affliction of the heart but because of their greed for consumer goods.

Social workers spent a lot of energy trying to prevent young women from ever wanting to date an American GI because they were convinced that it was but a small step from being a "girlfriend" to becoming a fallen woman. Even in the counties in which no American troops were stationed, young women were not considered safe because of the great mobility the GIs' cars afforded them. Consequently, counties and towns that were not home to American troops also applied to be included in the "moral disaster area" so that they could receive funds from the Federal Youth Plan. However, funds were forthcoming only if American GIs showed up in great numbers in such communities. Trier was one such community, and according to the KFV, the American troops who traveled to Trier as tourists presented a "strong general endangerment of our women and of our female youth." These KFV reports stressed that the French presented little problem because of their limited financial resources. The Americans, with their large paychecks, their "less than strict military discipline," and their elegant cars, were a different story—"The soldiers arrived in town with one aim, and that was to have a good time." The social workers reported with a heavy heart that girls from all social classes were dating the American GIs.[41]

Social workers considered the American GI so dangerous because he was showing the local youth, "especially the female youth, who are much more susceptible to temptations . . . a standard of living that was not common here."[42] The fears expressed by concerned guardians of morality clearly illustrate how they linked the temptations of a consumer society with unrestrained female sexuality. Social workers were convinced that the girls' "fashion instincts quickly lead to sexual instincts" and thus to contacts with "occupation soldiers."[43] They reported that the most "deplorable appearance of this general moral degeneration (*Verwahrlosung*) is the fact that even younger schoolgirls already get themselves an '*Ami* boyfriend,'" since only the GIs' money could satisfy their desire for "beautiful and conspicuous clothing . . . lipstick . . . and rouge."[44] These observers fully understood that most young women could never afford on their own meager wages the consumer goods that American GIs might introduce them to. Consequently, the only way such a young woman could attain such goods was through prostituting herself.

Social workers condemned the fact that even girls from respectable middle-class families were dating GIs. They reported with great regret that increasingly local girls were being brought to school in Kaiserslautern by their "Ami-boyfriends" in their big cars.[45] The situation in Baumholder was similar. The county social workers reported that a young girl from a good bourgeois home, who was still attending the local high school, was nonetheless acting and dressing like a "little prostitute." The report further listed six female adolescents whom the social workers "were keeping an eye on and for whom [they] had not yet gathered enough material to act."[46]

Although church welfare workers fretted about girls from all social classes, their main effort centered on containing the young women from the lower classes. Social workers were convinced that the "local girls who toiled in the factories learned quickly that nice clothing and good food were not that hard to come by if one was built well and not too shy." The girls from the working class were judged especially endangered because all they could see was that they could make "DM 20 in one evening while enjoying an evening with a big Cadillac, the best music, as well as a handsome young man . . . all the while escaping their dirty, decrepit homes." For these girls, concluded a speaker at a meeting of social workers, "becoming a prostitute or an HWG person was not a precipitous downward slide, but a shallow one. The woman does not crash, but slithers into her fate."[47]

To prevent such a slide into prostitution, authorities called for "an increased social guardianship from the city and the whole of its population."[48] The web of surveillance that encircled the soldiers' brides; the single, widowed, or divorced mothers; and lower-class families expanded ever further to ensure that "order and morality" would prevail. The Ministry of the Interior instructed schools to report to the county and church-affiliated welfare workers those female pupils who were seen in the company of GIs. Legally, this was a highly questionable step in West Germany's new democracy. However, in light of the circumstances, an exception was granted to the Ministry of Culture by the Ministry of the Interior that permitted teachers to provide such information on their students.[49]

A young woman in Birkenfeld who had dated a GI encountered the full force of this surveillance when she found herself before the court for alleged prostitution in 1957. Although the young woman was released in the end, the charges are revealing insofar as they show how closely "families at risk" were placed under observation. The seventeen-year-old woman was not from one of the better families in town, and the fact that she dated an American GI was enough to bring her before the bar. Not only was the young woman forced, under the most humiliating questioning, to admit when and under what circumstances she had engaged in sexual relations with her American boyfriend, but she was also asked what gifts she had received. She denied ever having received DM 20, the going rate at that time for prostitutes, but she did admit that her boyfriend paid for her drinks when they went out. The judge also questioned why she had never saved any of the money she made at her job, what she spent it for, and why she never gave any of it to her mother.[50]

The private lives of residents were also exposed to public scrutiny when neighbors denounced them for allegedly fostering immorality or for procurement (*Kuppelei*). Significantly, those who denounced did so not because they agreed with the nationally sponsored morality campaign but out of personal vengeance.[51] Because of the rigid morality that was being delegated through state and federal offices, these denouncements could result in dire consequences. Especially in cases involving members of the lower classes, judges seemed intent to set examples with their harsh judgments. In a Kaiserslautern procurement trial, a mother was sentenced to three months' probation for allowing her daughter's GI boyfriend "not only in her house, but in her daughter's room."[52] In another case, a fifty-year-old mother received a sentence of six months' probation for allowing the boyfriends of her two daughters in her apartment. Even though the mother pleaded that she had no control over her daughters, who were over the age of twenty-one, the judge showed little mercy. He reprimanded her for not having called the police to put an end to her daughters' assumptions that they "could live their lives as they pleased." The fact that this family was from a "sad milieu" did not help the woman's case.[53]

The coverage in the Social Democratic press and even the centrist press indicates that most people felt that the state had gone too far in its moral purity campaign. When a widowed mother received a one-month jail sentence for allowing the GI boyfriend of her daughter to spend the night at her house, the centrist *Pfälzische Volkszeitung* expressed great outrage at the severity of the treatment this mother had received. Although the GI slept on the sofa in the living room, a "mean-spirited neighbor" reported that the GI visited the girl's room at night. The daughter had in the meantime married the young soldier and was living happily in the United States, yet her mother was punished for neglectful parenting. The paper did not approve of this sort of ruling and complained about the insensitivity of a bureaucracy that cannot be stopped once it is set in motion.[54]

In a scathing critique of these measures, the Social Democratic publication *Die Freiheit* questioned whether the "interests of the state have not exceeded their bounds in light of the aspirations for freedom of the individual in the changed social circumstances of the time." Obviously, not everybody in the garrison communities approved of the strict standard of morality that was being prescribed from above. The paper reported that the question of whether the state has the right to enforce morality was "deeply engaging public opinion."[55]

The leftist press was also a most scathing critic of the state-imposed morality campaign when their papers pointed out the selective enforcement of the procurement laws. The Communist *Freisoziale Presse*, for example, charged that "big *Ami-autos*" were parked nightly in front of the new apartments in the middle-class suburbs of the city and that the "boarding places of the *Amizons*" could be found all across town.[56] Yet the great majority of the indictments for procurement resulted from arrests that occurred in the poorer quarters of the city.[57] The Social Democratic *Freiheit* also indicted this class bias by suggesting that the ambitions of the local Christian Democrats to cleanse the whole city of prostitutes and procurers were sure to find their limit at the "respectable *Privat-Pensionen*" (Bed and Breakfasts) where these things were going on as well.[58]

The furor over the rigid morality that the Christian Democratic state and federal governments and the churches were trying to impose reveal that the story of the 1950s "normalization" and moral rearmament is much more complex than we have previously assumed. For the most part people did not appreciate the rigid morality that lawmakers were trying to impose. Germans also criticized the efforts of state authorities to enforce morality through the police and the courts. The outrage expressed at these procurement trials also shows that this was a selective process. When women of the lower classes were involved or when women allowed black GIs into their homes, many fewer defenders stepped forward. For the most part the *Pfälzische Volkszeitung* spoke up when these laws affected one of its own, that is, a member of the middle class. A more consistent critique of this invasion of privacy and the class bias inherent in the rigid morality only came from the Social Democratic newspaper *Die Freiheit*.

Fear of Americanization

The many anxious reports that social welfare workers sent to the state and federal governments to report on their work reveal that more was at stake in their struggle than simply controlling women's sexuality. These reports are also a tremendously rich commentary on middle-class efforts during the 1950s to rein in the side effects of the Americanization they observed. We have already seen in Chapter 2 how infatuated many Germans, but especially the young, were with the "American way of life," which promised a plethora of consumption but also a different experience of freedom. By smoking American cigarettes, drinking Coca Cola, wearing blue jeans, and listening to American music, young Germans were able to indulge that "breath of fresh air" (*Duft der grossen weiten Welt*) that so many longed for after the years of Nazism and postwar scarcity. Kaspar Maase suggests in *Bravo America* that the eventual triumph of this grassroots Americanization was a long and hard-fought struggle that pitted urban proletarian youth against the guardians of German *Kultur,* the propertied middle class. The following observation from a Kaiserslautern clergyman in 1954 suggests that young, urban working-class males were not the only segment of German society who embraced America:

> The American way of life has strongly affected the outlook of our population. Frugality has become a rare virtue. One wants to imitate the Americans. . . . The primitive classes of our population are not capable of righteous judgment [and] only see the cheerful and unrestrained goings-on and pleasure and money spending of the young Americans removed from

the bonds of family. Thus the desire of German women for regular visits to cafés and movie houses is much more poignant than before. The expenditures of the broad masses for the requirements and silliness of fashion have increased rapidly. In many working-class families, it has become customary for parents to go out on Saturday evenings with their children (kids from the age of 12 years on) and to "live" for once.[59]

The reports from social workers also make clear that it was not only the young who found the American model attractive. These same observers also expressed widespread fears that the population's infatuation with things American profoundly threatened traditional bourgeois class privilege. While such anxieties existed nationwide, efforts to contain the American impact on German social and cultural life would reach a state of extreme agitation in Rhineland-Palatinate and in other regions of Germany where American troops were stationed.[60] Because these communities did not deal with a "figurative" or "imagined America," conservatives did not just brush off the impact of *Amerikanismus* as an "inevitable problem" of the country's ongoing modernization.[61] Instead, debates on Americanization took on a tone of considerable disquiet.

According to the anxious reports of the church-affiliated welfare workers, danger lurked in the garrison towns even when families were intact, with both father and mother present. Both the Catholic and Protestant welfare agencies expanded their initial missions when they asserted that women who worked as maids for American families housed on base required protection from the dangers lurking in the American homes. While welfare workers were anxious about the sheer fact of women's employment outside the home, the exposure to the American way of life at their place of employment increased these anxieties significantly. The welfare workers' comments show that conservative middle-class observers were profoundly leery of democracy and all the freedoms it entailed. They were also most anxious to reverse or at least halt the leveling of social classes that resulted from the war and postwar years. For conservatives, Americanization was not just about big cars, nylons, and lipstick. Americanization also meant a loss or weakening of the gender and class hierarchies that they saw as the necessary foundation of their hoped-for bourgeois social order in a Christian state.

As soon as a young woman between the ages of eighteen and twenty-one registered with the employment office and was assigned a job with an American family, that office passed her name on to public and private social workers so that they might keep an eye on her. This practice was highly controversial, if not illegal, according to the Ministry of Labor.

However, the ministry put its reservations on hold in light of the "special situation in the regions with large troop concentrations" and "in light of the fact that the girls who arrive [in these towns] were lacking the support of their own families."[62] Even though both young men and women were allegedly exposed to danger in these communities, local authorities were only expected to keep an eye on the young women. The "exception" of the federal Ministry of Labor was initially passed to detect the women who arrived in these communities searching for work; not surprisingly, in the end, all women working as maids were affected by this policy.[63]

The social welfare workers' comments on the dangers that German maids faced in the American home also reveal how much the whole debate on "Amerika" in Rhineland-Palatinate was influenced by middle-class anxieties over the continuing leveling of German society. In the American homes, German women encountered not only sexual dangers; they were also exposed to a different experience of freedom and the materialism of the American way of life. The biggest problem, the social workers complained, was that the American people did not have a real understanding of human nature, because Americans foolishly assumed that "human beings were good, that they needed freedom." Social workers were distressed to report that the American families did not understand that young and single women from the lower classes required close supervision. They complained unceasingly that the Americans granted too much unsupervised leisure time to these young women. Because of this lack of a firm hand, the young women faced "terrible dangers" in the American homes. The young women, they reported, spent many hours "reading cheap magazines, watching television, or listening to pop music." Social workers were convinced that the "girls" would make the wrong choices with the new freedom that their American employment provided. For the social workers, it was but a small step for young women from reading cheap magazines to having the American "boyfriend visit" in their rooms.[64]

The social workers from the Innere Mission and the KFV agreed that the simple fact of working in the American homes or on the military base put women at risk.[65] They worried incessantly that the young women would succumb to the temptations of consumerism and be overwhelmed by the range of choices offered them. They reported with dismay that "these girls come from the rural regions, are used to a traditional life, and are suddenly faced with independent decisions and personal choice." Faced with all these temptations, they warned, it was only a small step before the girls "copy the standard of living of the Americans." That "their money is spent quickly, nutrition suffers, eating too little and drinking too much coffee and constant smoking of cigarettes" were just some of the dire consequences in store for these women.[66]

Social workers were so anxious about German women's exposure to the American model because they realized that this exposure undermined their vision of proper femininity. Local women, partaking of American "tastes, comfort, fashions and language," were appropriating these foreign models. Because American women often gave their German maids hand-me-down clothing, the women wearing these "alien" clothes began to look different from other German women: "they appear grotesque and conspicuous in their slacks or colorful silk dresses, as they chew gum and sport long hair."[67] Appropriating these foreign models had larger consequences than changing the outward appearance. German women not only looked like American women, they behaved like American women.[68]

The comments from a social worker's accreditation thesis reveal just how threatening exposure to the amenities of the American home was judged to be for German women from the lower class. The thesis was prepared for the worker's supervisors in her district, and the themes she raises probably regurgitate prevailing wisdom about social work in the garrison communities. The conclusions presented are a fascinating commentary, since they are indicative of just what sort of fears the American presence evoked among the middle class.

According to this thesis, one of the great dangers of women's employment with the Americans was that local women would yearn for the American standard of living. Being in the American home would convince them that they also wanted the "central heating, washing machines, refrigerators, kitchen appliances, canned goods . . . upholstered furniture, hi-fis, and TVs" that adorned the spacious apartments on the base. The thesis argues that impressions of the American home were bound to confuse the lower class's understanding of its own place in society, especially since many of these American employers on base were hardly members of the upper class, the very stratum in Germany that had traditionally enjoyed such privilege. The author worried that being exposed to the American model could convince Germans from the lower class that these sorts of goods should be available to all members of society, not just the privileged middle classes. Having a slice of "Little Amerika" thus available on a daily basis led to such developments as the German population's "demanding luxury as a right." The social worker repeated widespread bourgeois convictions when she concluded that such ambitions were bound to upset traditional class boundaries and lead to a further "process of leveling."[69]

Throughout the 1950s, then, bourgeois social workers were convinced that this daily exposure to American wealth would undermine the class distinctions that bourgeois Germans were intent on restoring. The church-affiliated social workers' reports are full of laments over what dangers the American wealth posed to local women who came from a "simple and arduous life." They were convinced that "the opulent milieu of the Americans corrupted their values, so that they were no longer satisfied with a life lived in modest circumstances."[70] Thus, the church-affiliated social welfare workers expressed anxieties that have traditionally defined conservative German debates on America.

But social workers' comments display not only fears over women's "inappropriate consumption" of luxury goods, too much individualism, social mobility, or personal freedom. Kaspar Maase has shown in his work on the impact of American popular culture how proletarian youth were in the forefront of creating a new "civil *habitus*" through the consumption of American popular culture. He argues that throughout Germany, the embrace of the American style was slowly beginning to undermine the symbolic distance between men and women, between young and old, and between the classes that traditional German élites were so anxious to preserve.[71] The social workers in the garrison communities fully understood the larger implications of this "informalization" of daily life that was being injected into German society during the 1950s, and they reported on it in detail. Social workers were certain that the "American way of life and the more relaxed approach to life" would be pulling young women into "a completely different milieu." This development, they feared, would have dire consequences for a bourgeois social order based on class privilege and a traditional gender order. As a consequence of being exposed to the American model, wrote one worker, "[lower class women] lose all sense of their position in society (*Stand*); and this already was the root of endangerment."[72]

The many anxieties over women living and working in the vicinity of American GIs remained vexing. An exasperated KFV concluded in 1957 that the longer they ministered to their important calling, the more they realized that "among the employees working on the military installations, there is not one girl or woman who is not endangered."[73] Thus even the "girls and women" who worked in the offices, stores, and cafeterias of the military installations were considered at risk.[74] At their place of employment they observed not just different patterns of consumption but also a more relaxed style of authority and interpersonal relationships. Social welfare workers concluded that women working on the base were "detached . . . and under the strong influence of surroundings that were deeply defined by the American point of view."[75] They reported with great dismay, "The local people have adapted to the American standard of living, their clothing, way of living, and way of life."[76]

"The Chaos . . . Does Not Exist"

The evidence from both Birkenfeld and Kaiserslautern counties suggest that these communities were not at all comfortable with the level of attention that the state and federal government was devoting to them. The local Landräte did not object when church-affiliated welfare institutions described their counties as a "moral disaster area" when applying for federal funds from the Federal Youth Plan for day care facilities and youth hostels. Indeed, their offices proceeded in the same manner when applying for funds. But town officials also reacted with disdain to the conservative effort that had landed them in this predicament in the first place. When the state government sent inquiries concerning the morality or lack thereof in the communities with troop concentrations, the Landräte in Birkenfeld and Kaiserslautern were quick to respond that the initial upheaval that had come with the troops and the building boom had settled down and that all was well in the provinces.[77] Responding to an inquiry about the state of affairs in his county, the Birkenfeld Landrat responded forcefully that the "chaos that everybody was talking and writing about does not exist."[78]

The bad press these communities had been receiving over the alleged crisis of morality in the Rhineland-Palatinate only increased the defensive stance of local officials. In 1956, the German-American Committee in Birkenfeld "condemned and rejected most forcefully the horrid depictions in the press, especially the ones that could be found in the boulevard press, that focused on Baumholder." The committee stressed that "in reality the daily life in the military centers of West Germany is completely different" from the picture these publications convey and complained that these sorts of "unbelievable press reports do nothing but besmirch" the town and its people.[79]

In light of the unfavorable portrayal Baumholder had been receiving, the Catholic priest of Baumholder also came to the defense of the population. He stated in 1954 that "the local girls were holding steadfast under the circumstances" and that the local judge was able to tell him "that not one local girl has been before the courts."[80] The new Protestant minister in town took a bit longer to come around to this more tolerant attitude. In an extensive essay published in a church newspaper in 1959, he admitted that the local youth were "more infected by *Amerikanismus*" than other adolescents in Germany—that is, that local "girls probably apply rouge to their cheeks earlier and more generously than in other small towns." But he also defended the young women by suggesting that "their eyes are just as bright, if not brighter," than those of girls in other towns."[81] This assessment of the local young is a stunning reversal to reports of just a few years earlier, when any young woman wearing makeup was considered sexually promiscuous. The clergy probably still did not like the fact that the young women in town wore makeup, but they also no longer viewed the use of makeup as a sign of moral degeneration, and thus a threat to the social order.

The church-affiliated welfare agencies were not willing to accept such assurances, even when they came from the local clergy. Without a moral crisis, no funds would be forthcoming from the federal and state government. Thus, in 1954 the Innere Mission reported an "improvement of the previously very unpleasant conditions" in many localities, but it also insisted that "at other localities the possibility exists that the indecent behavior that was previously displayed in the open was more likely taking place in secrecy now."[82] Reports to the federal government stressed that the low number of women in their care "does not reflect the work that was really being done here,"[83] or that the number of women in their care was deceptive and did not "mirror actual achievements."[84] When the church-affiliated welfare agencies were asked why the number of illegitimate children born was so low despite the moral crisis at hand, social welfare workers insisted that the American GIs were conscientious practitioners of birth control.[85] In light of the missing numbers, social workers seemed to suggest that many failings of local girls were hidden.

Conclusion

By the end of the decade, then, we can discern a dramatically different situation in these communities. Local officials no longer felt threatened by the "alien" presence of the soldiers. Relations between Germans and Americans had become, if not always cordial, at least matter-of-fact. As the Americans became neighbors, and often friends, the local population no longer viewed them as a sexual threat. The anxious depictions of every GI as a potential seducer of German womanhood, which so marked local sources in the first year after the troops' arrival, all but disappeared. The fact that ever more local women married American soldiers greatly contributed to this greater tolerance. Even the clergy came to be much less critical of the American presence. In their day-to-day interactions with the military, the German clergy came to appreciate the deep religiosity of the Americans and the many good deeds they did in German communities.

The conservative effort "to rein in" the local population, which found its high point between 1953 and 1957–58 was also doomed because people refused the interference of the state and the churches in their private affairs. After their experience of Nazism, parents no longer wanted the state to tell them what was best for their children.[86] They also no longer wanted the churches to impose a morality that people thought out of touch with the freedoms their new democracy entailed. After years of being asked to sacrifice for their *Volk* and enduring the deprivations of the war and postwar years, people were ready to give the American model a try. People were all too eager, in the words of a disconsolate clergyman, "to live for once."[87] Having the example of the American way of life available on a daily basis convinced many Germans that such a good life could also be within their own reach. While status-conscious members of the middle class were appalled by that fact, all who yearned for an easier and better life could not but reject the conservative effort to restore a class-based society where lower-class people knew their place.

What we can observe in both Baumholder and Kaiserslautern Counties is that the Christian welfare workers who had dominated the debate were increasingly being tuned out in the last few years of the decade. By 1960, secular and more progressive voices asserted themselves in the debates on youth welfare issues. Those people concluded that matters with the local youth were not as bad as some people would have liked to make believe, because too much of the emphasis when talking about teenagers was on a few bad apples. Defenders of the local teenagers agreed that an increase in traffic violations was hardly a matter of concern over the moral state of the young and that these infractions should not mark teenagers as criminals. Not one youth welfare worker even mentioned what danger young women faced in the garrison communities.[88]

We know that on the national level, the exclusivist rhetoric of the Christian *Abendland* increasingly became the preserve of an unrepentant and reactionary conservatism, as the CDU distanced itself from that language and embraced instead the notion of the "Free West." The CDU came to that revision because, without acknowledging the key role of the United States, the struggle of the "Free West" against Soviet communism was doomed. The conservative debate about materialism underwent a similar modernization due to the exigencies of the Cold War. It was no longer politically viable for conservative German political and cultural élites to reject the American model as completely unsuitable.[89] Once modern conservatives, gathered around Ludwig Erhard, the architect of West Germany's economic miracle, drowned out the religiously inspired conservatives around Adenauer, prosperity, as promised by the American way of life, became an ever more desirable goal. While the most adamant conservatives continued to decry the new consumer republic with its "demons of moneymaking and pleasure seeking," Erhard reminded West German consumers that Germans had manufactured hundreds of thousands of Volkswagen "Beetles" for export. But the new economic powerhouse that was Germany had also managed to produce 100 million pairs of nylon stockings for the domestic market. Stressing the economy's new emphasis on consumption, Erhard urged West German women to quit darning their old stockings and go buy new ones.[90]

With the publication of Erhard's 1957 *Prosperity for All,* the anxious defenders of the Christian *Abendland* who still hoped for a cultural third way for Germany were increasingly tuned out at the national level. At the same time, the emergence of "modern conservatives" like the sociologist Helmut Schelsky shifted conservative attitudes toward consumption and leisure. The new conservatives no longer viewed consumption as threatening to class and gender stability. Instead, they accepted it as a means to overcome the polarization of traditional class society. These modern conservatives admonished the old guard to not recklessly fight modernity but to take charge of it so that they could regulate it.[91] Prosperity, leisure, and pleasure would not destroy the West, they argued: "Enjoyed in good measure, they would actually be a key weapon . . . exposing economic inferiority and lack of democratic choice" in East Germany.[92]

Once "prosperity for all" replaced the defense of the Christian *Abendland* as the national objective, the long postwar years were over. This shift was not lost on our church-affiliated welfare workers. By the beginning of the 1960s, Christian welfare agencies realized that federal money would not be forthcoming if they insisted on their old lament over what dangers the American way of life posed to the local population. While they still fretted over what dangers German women faced through their employment on the American base, they also pointed to West Germany's newest challenge. By 1962, the Innere Mission and the KFV justified their work in the region by insisting that the new danger came from another group of foreign men, the newly arrived foreign workers (*Gastarbeiter*) from Spain, Greece, and Italy.[93]

7

Punishing the "Veronikas"

Throughout the 1950s, the church-affiliated welfare organizations put up a valiant fight to protect the German population from the seductions that the American dollar brought to the hinterland. These efforts were doomed because of the population's wholesale embrace of their new consumer society and their willing acceptance of much of the American way of life that they observed. In light of the experience of Nazism and the dislocation that the regime, the war, and the postwar years had brought, most people no longer viewed the interference of the state and the churches in their private lives as appropriate. A similar drama of control imposed from above and rejected from below played out in these communities when we look at the enforcement of the much stricter prostitution laws that the Verein and the federal and state ministries were trying to impose. Evidence from both Birkenfeld and Kaiserslautern Counties suggests that while the communities with troop concentrations exercised a renewed social vigilance, they were not necessarily willing to live by the values of the past. Despite the often derogatory and careless use of the terms "Veronika," "soldier's bride," and prostitute (*Dirne*), many of the women thus stigmatized never ended up before a court of law.

The population rejected the conservative effort to return to pre-Weimar social values for a number of reasons. For the most part, liberals and Social Democrats rejected the Verein's rigid moral values as inappropriate for the new democracy. People also refused the moral armament campaign once local women began dating and marrying American GIs.

In light of this, many in these communities were anxious to defend their own women against the Verein's blanket charge of prostitution. Finally, most people did not agree with the Verein's convictions that the so-called "soldiers' brides" posed a greater threat to local life than did the professional prostitutes. While church-affiliated welfare workers spent most of their energies trying to locate and rein in the "soldiers' brides," locals evaluated the situation very differently. For local officials and most of the population, the enemy was not the "soldier's bride" who lived in town and kept the GIs dollars in town. The real enemy was the professional prostitute who showed up on the American payday to leave only after the soldiers' last dollar was spent.

The population's greater tolerance toward the women who associated with American soldiers or worked in one of the many bars about town changed enforcement of the prostitution laws in two important ways. By the mid-50s, almost all of the women punished for prostitution in Baumholder were professional prostitutes who arrived in town on the GIs' payday. The greater tolerance toward the sexuality of the so-called "soldiers' brides"—who lived locally—also led to a redefinition of prostitution around racial issues. By 1955, the local population and officials in these communities identified as prostitutes predominantly those women who associated with black soldiers. The prostitution records in Baumholder indicate that this important shift was possible largely because of the complex ways in which German and American assumptions about race interacted. Thus, while both the United States and West Germany had made racial equality a touchstone of their democracies, the activities of lower level German officials and American military personnel reveal the limits of that agenda.

Reining in the "Veronikas"

Reiterating the convictions of the Verein, the church-affiliated welfare agencies, which had set up shop in all garrison communities, made clear that they had very little interest in the professional prostitutes. These women showed up around payday and left after the GIs ran out of money. Because these women observed the "rules" and usually did not live in the homes of the German burghers, they did not present a moral danger to the local community. While the "bad needed to be punished," the real efforts of the social welfare workers throughout the decade were devoted toward "fostering the good" and "protecting the endangered," those who could still be rescued for a life of decency.[1] Thus, the social welfare workers were most concerned with three groups: the "soldiers' brides," women working as maids for the Americans, and women who worked as waitresses in one of the many bars about town.

Much of the work done by the Innere Mission and the Katholischer Fürsorgeverein proved a saving anchor for numerous runaways or luckless seekers of fortune who had heard of the riches to be made in the "El Dorado of the West." The agencies opened shelters for the woman who had perhaps arrived with her beau when he was transferred, only to find herself deserted and without money after he returned to the States. Welfare workers also stood by a young woman if she had to appear before a court of law, be it for alleged prostitution, failure to register with the police, or not carrying a personal identification card.[2] After such women were released, social workers tried to find employment for them or reunited them with their families. If a young woman arrived without work, the social workers often helped her to find work as a maid with a reliable German family, preferably far away from the American troops. They also did much to ensure that American families met the German standard of work regulations, insisting that health and social security insurance be provided to the women employed as maids. For young women employed as waitresses in one of the many bars, social workers also intervened to make sure that work regulations were obeyed and that the women had proper health and social security insurance.[3]

However, the other aspect of the social workers' efforts reveals a degree of control over these women's lives that can be understood only as a profound anxiety over single and independent women at a time of conservative efforts at gender stabilization.[4] Social welfare workers expanded a tremendous amount of effort in tracking down newcomers to town and keeping an eye on those already there. If local authorities wanted to know whether a woman living with a GI was in a "committed relationship" or "dating" a number of soldiers, the woman's activities had to be closely observed. Social workers from the Katholischer Fürsorgeverein and Innere Mission as well as women who worked for the county youth agency interviewed neighbors to determine what kind of company the women kept and what went on in particular apartments. As soon as it was suspected that a particular woman was dating more than one GI, she would be reported to the local judge, who could then decide to issue a warrant for her arrest. Any suspicious act was enough to convince Dr. Schnapp, the Baumholder judge, to grant a warrant to search the woman's home.[5] These searches could be highly embarrassing affairs; the objective was to surprise the woman and the soldier "in the act." The law enforcement officials seemed to have been very successful. Dr. Schnapp reported that "it was continually observed that Americans were pulled out of the beds of these women."[6]

Examples of just how closely the *Amimädchen* (Ami-girls) were watched in the first few years include the case of two women who were suspected of being "Veronikas." Although their landlord stated that the women never had male company for more than a few minutes, the social workers had other information. Indeed, after observing their apartment for a number of weekends, they reported that the women had received visits from two "Negroes who stayed for two hours." After another investigatory visit and intense questioning, the landlord admitted that the two women had been drinking champagne with the "Negroes one afternoon." In another incident, two women who had been observed for a time admitted under questioning that their American boyfriends supported them. However, the women denied that they had had sexual intercourse in their apartment, since that could expose their landlord to indictment as a procurer.[7] The net of surveillance was so tight that social workers reported to the state office of the Innere Mission their estimation of the number of women in various localities who had engaged in sexual relations with foreign men. Aside from American GIs, social workers also reported on the number of women who had relationships with former Displaced Persons (DPs) who worked for the Americans and on those who had relations with French soldiers.[8]

In the daily decisions made as to who was a prostitute, who was an HWG woman, and who was perhaps just slipping for the very first time, the efforts of the church-affiliated agencies, the county social workers, police, and judges often intersected. If the local police and judges wanted to determine whether a suspect was perhaps a respectable, middle-class young woman gone astray as opposed to a hard-core, unrepentant HWG person, they needed the "close investigation of the woman's background" called for by the Ministry of Justice.[9] Thus, a significant degree of cooperation emerged between the formerly competing public and church-affiliated welfare organizations over the "crisis of morality" in Rhineland-Palatinate.

Local Reaction

Conservative efforts to impose a stricter morality by reining in the sexuality of German women who associated with American GIs encountered opposition almost immediately, in large part because of their capacity to affect all classes of society. As the first waves of "soldiers' brides" and

"Veronikas" came to town, local officials conducted raids of hotels and private homes suspected to be "dens of vice." Just how unpopular the initial vice raids were is revealed in an early case of procurement prosecuted in the Birkenfeld court. In 1951, a local innkeeper and his wife were indicted for having rented rooms to the so-called "Frolleins" without much regard for what transpired behind closed doors. After the couple's arrest, the local newspaper expressed the sentiment that the vigorous moral rearmament promulgated by the federal government was inappropriate. Tongue in cheek, the paper asked: "Were the 'Frolleins' creating a tempest in a teapot? Who was going to save the morality of Birkenfeld?" While the prosecutor called for a harsh sentence so that others might be deterred from such behavior, defense counsel suggested that his clients "were doing what many were doing in Birkenfeld." Indeed, he said, "[If a] raid were conducted from house to house, then it would quickly become apparent to all what the sparrows were whistling from every rooftop." We cannot, argued the defense, "demand of our innkeepers that they become guardians of morality."[10]

The Social Democratic newspaper, *Die Freiheit,* took an even stronger stance, reminding its readers that nobody should have any illusions that a garrison city like Kaiserslautern was going to turn into a "strait-laced petit bourgeois idyll." The paper reiterated that prostitution was neither an American nor a postwar invention. The essay also reminded Germans nostalgic for the "good old days" that prostitution existed "even before 1914, when people could expect 'normal circumstances.'" What made prostitution different then was that it was controlled and limited to brothels. *Die Freiheit* also took a stab at the local Christian Democrats, who were the foremost supporters of the American military mission in Europe but who also dominated much of the local moral purification campaign. *Die Freiheit* teased the CDU for supporting economic liberalism while being unwilling to accept the social implications of the free market, suggesting that the present form of prostitution was so offensive to the guardians of morality because "it was conducted according to the principle of the free market economy, from which the Americans were not willing to budge."[11]

While *Die Freiheit* pointed out the class bias inherent in the national purity campaign, the paper was less sensitive to the racial implications of the state-sponsored effort to enforce sexual decency. The records of Kaiserslautern suggest that police conducted raids most consistently in those places where "racial transgressions" allegedly occurred. During raids on twelve different hotels and inns in Kaiserslautern, German and American police officials detected unmarried couples in three places. In the first hotel, "five prostitutes with Negroes" were caught in flagrante delicto. In the second establishment, run by a former Palatinate village councilor, the raid netted "four Negroes and their prostitutes, who were still mostly dressed." In the third location, a private residence in which the owner rented furnished rooms (*Privat-Pension*), "Germans had smuggled in girls at night." In all three cases, the owners were charged with procurement.[12] However, only the hotel owners lost their licenses, and thus their livelihoods. The owner of the *Privat-Pension* was simply told to behave in the future. She did not lose her business license, argued the city's legal adviser, "because in this case matters were not that grave since the incidents involved only Germans," that is, white men.[13]

The police also used §180 of the Criminal Code (procurement) to gain search warrants to investigate indecency in private homes. Although federal ministries instructed communities to enforce procurement laws vigorously, most police officers seem to have looked the other way when solid middle-class individuals rented to the so-called "Veronikas." In Kaiserslautern, most of the vice raids took place in the more marginal parts of town, a fact that *Die Freiheit* repeatedly indicted. Not surprisingly, German women whose partners were African Americans were especially vulnerable, since interracial couples often were able to find housing only in the poorer neighborhoods of town. The fact that it was a black American who was found in the woman's bed or hiding in the bedroom closet was always pointed out in the extensive coverage of these raids in the local press.[14]

The most obvious limit on successful enforcement of §180 in smaller communities such as Baumholder was the fact that public opinion was reluctant to condemn the practice of renting rooms to unmarried couples. The annual reports of the church-affiliated social workers reveal how dramatically attitudes had shifted. With much exasperation they described the situation: "The letting of rooms to unmarried couples is no longer perceived as procurement. Hardly anybody gets annoyed by this practice. Charges are almost never brought." Instead, they complained, "Indecency is no longer on public display" in the streets but "[has] crept like an ever expanding epidemic into the *Volk*."[15]

The instructions of the federal Ministry of the Interior to the Ministry of Justice in Rhineland-Palatinate to contain prostitution more forcefully through the application of §180 of the Criminal Code seemed to have made little difference.[16] Even Dr. Schnapp, no matter how much he railed against "widespread indecency," was not able to criminalize a whole town or village, especially members of the middle classes. Neither were most police officers—often born and raised in these communities—willing to enforce unpopular laws that were considered intrusive and inappropriate to the changed circumstances.

Controlling the *Ami-Bars*

Because of the unpopularity of vice raids that also exposed the middle class to scrutiny, officials became more discerning in their efforts to limit prostitution. In small communities such as Baumholder, law enforcement officers most often relied on controlling the many bars and pubs where American soldiers congregated in order to track down prostitutes.[17] To accomplish this task, German law enforcement officers had to work very closely with the American military police. In the first few years after the troops' arrival, the German police force in these rural areas was not only understaffed, it also lacked the equipment to get the job done. In all of these communities, the German police had to rely on the manpower and logistical support of the American military police. Even more importantly, the German police had to call on the Americans because of West Germany's legal situation vis-à-vis the U.S. forces. Due to the Occupation Statute, German police officers could not conduct vice raids without the assistance of American military police (MP). Unless accompanied by the MP, German law-enforcement officers could not check the identification of a German woman if she was in the company of an American GI. Her male companion merely needed to claim that the woman was his fiancée or wife, and she was thus beyond the reach of German law.[18]

Such was the legal situation until 1955, and the fact that women could thus evade the controls caused much consternation among the German police and judges. Some women enjoyed thumbing their noses at the authority of the German police officers, and this attitude did little to endear them to local authorities. The limits put on their authority was particularly abhorrent to German police officers if the woman was in the company of a black soldier. They complained that "it was especially hard in Negro pubs to take a stand against the customers there" because the "woman often refused to allow her documents to be inspected or created other complications."[19] Police officers also did not appreciate that in the "bars that were frequented by coloreds and their female following" it was possible to assert themselves only "with the help of the military police."[20] Even after the lifting of the Occupation Statute in 1955, American military police continued to participate in vice raids. While German police officers regained greater autonomy after 1955, they still had no jurisdiction over American GIs. However, GIs could no longer protect the German women in their company from the reach of the German police.[21]

In the small confines of towns like Baumholder, controlling the women who might be prostitutes was a relatively easy task. As soon as a single woman was observed in a pub or bar where American soldiers congregated, her identification papers were checked by the police officers, who patrolled these bars every night at regular intervals. In fact, nightly visits by the German and American police were the norm, not the exception, in towns like Baumholder. On and around payday, these visits occurred on an even tighter schedule. The social workers always accompanied the police, and Johanna Wefelscheid, the chief of the county youth office, was as strict as her colleagues from the church-affiliated welfare agencies. The "cry of terror, 'Wefelscheid is here!'" went through the pubs when the much-feared supervisor was sighted, as young women scrambled for the bathroom windows and GIs tried to buy time for them by blocking the doors.[22] If a woman had no ID, or had failed to register, she could be arrested on the spot and sentenced to a short jail term.[23]

For the German women and American GIs in these bars, even more distasteful than the nightly control checks were the large-scale and often humiliating vice raids. The police soon found that the vice raids caused considerable controversy, since daughters and wives from the respectable middle class were at times apprehended during such raids. During one such raid in Kaiserslautern, the police arrested a number of young women from "good and impeccable families." The local paper was stunned to report that most of the women looked like "innocents from the village," who were dressed in "solid skirts" rather than "skimpy outfits."[24] In another frenzied raid, the German police and American MPs even arrested the Baumholder social worker and two of her colleagues despite their loud protests. The social workers were in the bar to check on "their girls" when they were picked up with everybody else, loaded on an American military truck and taken to the police station.[25]

Matters over these indiscriminate vice raids came to a head in Kaiserslautern when an outraged city council member asked his colleagues whether it was appropriate that the "daughters and wives of Kaiserslautern *Bürger* be treated in this manner." His own daughter had been a guest in the Café Atlantik, a bar favored by American officers, when German police conducted one of their routine checks and arrested all the women present. The councilman was furious that, although these women had their identification cards and were with "proper companions," the police still suspected them of being prostitutes. The mayor expressed his displeasure with such methods, as did the city council.[26]

The most outspoken critique of these vice raids came from *Die Freiheit*. In a 1954 essay the paper decried what it called the "state-sponsored hunting down of girls." The writer opined that such behavior was inappropriate in the new democracy, reminding the readers that the "liberty of each individual is sacrosanct." With obvious distaste, the paper reported on a German-American police effort in which "American [military] buses were already filled with suspect women, but ever more victims were being pushed in." Among the many women arrested were "two local girls" whose parents had allowed them to stay out until midnight. Despite their assertion that they were not prostitutes, they were dragged to the German police station and detained until 3 A.M. In the same bar, the police tried to arrest a woman who was not carrying her personal identification card. Her husband, a severely handicapped war veteran, pleaded with them to leave her alone. Only when a third person intervened and identified the woman as the lawful wife of the veteran did this embarrassing situation end.[27]

While *Die Freiheit* was the most outspoken critic of these measures, it was not the only publication that raised questions concerning such practices. The centrist *Pfälzische Volkszeitung* also wondered why only the "girls" were punished, pointing out that in a considerable number of incidents "good girls" who were merely visiting one of the local pubs or bars had been arrested and treated without dignity. The paper agreed that the authorities had an interest in maintaining public order but suggested that the police needed to be more discerning in their judgments. The newspaper demanded that the "truly fallen girls" needed to be distinguished from those "who had merely slipped for the first time, be it because of stupidity, inexperience, or a faulty upbringing."[28]

Reining in Dr. Schnapp

Developments in Baumholder suggest that *Die Freiheit* and the *Pfälzische Volkszeitung* were merely giving voice to a much more widespread sentiment, namely that the national crackdown on immorality had gone too far. At a time when the initial shock over the American troop deployment was wearing off and a substantial number of local women were dating and marrying American GIs, attitudes had clearly shifted. In September 1953, the Birkenfeld Landrat called a meeting to reevaluate the manner in which the new prostitution guidelines were enforced in his county. At this meeting, the Landrat as well as the attending representatives of the local rural constabulary and the criminal investigation police all agreed that Dr. Schnapp was much too strict in his application of the prostitution laws. The Landrat reminded everyone present that many of the women who arrived with the American troops as girlfriends or fiancées were war widows from impeccable families.[29] Reflecting a new and much more relaxed attitude toward women who associated with GIs, one of the police officers agreed with the Landrat by complaining that Dr. Schnapp "considered every woman a whore (*Hure*)."[30] Dr. Schnapp was not only being accused of misogyny; he was also declared too authoritarian for local standards. The county's chief welfare worker asserted that the judge would like to consider all "police officers as well as the welfare workers his very own subjects."[31]

A police officer at the secret meeting argued that it was unacceptable that women who arrived in Baumholder in the evening had already been arrested by the next morning just because an American soldier had bought them a meal and paid for their room. The officer blamed this punitive attitude solely on Dr. Schnapp, who was so eager to control vice that he used binoculars from his office window to keep an eye on any female newcomer to the community. After sighting a newly arrived woman, Dr. Schnapp would then call the police chief and instruct him to have the woman arrested. The police officers clearly did not appreciate the judge's vigor. They agreed with the Landrat that the provision of the legal code that prohibited prostitution in communities under 20,000 inhabitants was much too strict, because the town needed the protection that "certain females" provided. The police reported that the new Protestant clergyman, who had replaced the Baumholder minister in 1953, had meanwhile also sided with the "smaller evil" of tolerating "Veronikas."[32]

For the local police, the criminal investigation police, and their state superiors, the challenge was not to rid the community of all traces of prostitution. Their primary goal was to ensure that the women acted in an "orderly manner" and that they were brought under the control of the local health office, so that the spread of venereal disease could be prevented. Keeping this mission in mind, the police representatives formally asked Landrat Heep at this meeting to have §361 No. 6c, which outlawed prostitution in rural communities, repealed.

The "conspirators" plotting behind the back of Dr. Schnapp, however, found themselves in a quandary. Because of their initial appeal to have the laws changed in the county of Birkenfeld, the county had attracted state as well as national attention. Dr. Schnapp and his ambitious plan to turn his tenure in Baumholder into a path-breaking model of how the Federal Republic could deal with the social cost associated with the continuing American "occupation" had made the "Veronika question" not just a local but a national concern. Schnapp's prominent role in the Verein also could not to be ignored. A clearly intimidated Landrat told his meeting partners that he feared that a repeal of §361 No. 6c would result in Dr. Schnapp reporting to "higher authorities." The Landrat also feared that such a request for repeal would result in "a quarrel with the governing president."[33]

With the state's as well as the nation's eye on the developments in Baumholder and Kaiserslautern and with a judge intent on jailing every new woman about town, the Landrat, the police, and the county welfare representative agreed to institute what they called "a golden mean."[34] The Landrat concluded, "We have to get away from our present system that every girl who is seen a number of times with an American can, without much ado, be indicted for prostitution." The participants of the meeting further agreed, "We have to consult with one another, so that our reports . . . corroborate."[35] Thus, the "plotters" agreed to falsify their regular reports on the "prostitution nuisance," which were called for by the regional government in Koblenz and forwarded to the state government in Mainz.

The Landrat and the police authorities of the county of Kaiserslautern apparently agreed on a similar arrangement. An internal memo from the Landstuhl police station to the Kaiserslautern Landrat reported that approximately forty to fifty prostitutes (*Dirnen*) lived in this small town and that the local police station had gathered information on these women, recorded on yellow cards kept at the local station. However the report that the Landrat passed on to the regional government of the Palatinate told a very different story: the Landrat assured the government that no prostitutes resided in Landstuhl, that no prostitutes came to Landstuhl, and that no records of prostitutes were kept at the Landstuhl police station.[36]

The note of discouragement that characterizes the accounts of the church-affiliated welfare agencies make all too clear that the Landräte of Birkenfeld and Kaiserslautern were not the only officials cautioning moderation. The moral rearmament campaign that the Verein tried to impose through the federal government encountered widespread resistance, even among members of the judiciary. The Innere Mission and the KFV complained repeatedly that in the overwhelming majority of locations with American troops "the judges were not applying the new interpretations that the Verein had suggested." The judge in Landstuhl, for example refused to indict a woman for prostitution just because she was living with a GI. The same held true for the judge in Bitburg.[37] Because "the judges pronounced punishments that were a joke," the police were relaxing their vigilance as well, complained another somber report. It was with great regret that the Christian welfare agencies concluded, "The freedom of a few dubious individuals was more important than the rightful interests of the citizen."[38]

While all garrison communities in Rhineland-Palatinate experienced similar increases in prostitution and "prostitute-like" behavior, Dr. Schnapp seems to have been the only judge who conscientiously and consistently applied the Verein's strict interpretation of prostitution. During his four-year tenure at the Baumholder Lower Court, he convicted 478 women as prostitutes. A superficial glance at the newspaper coverage in other garrison communities makes clear that nowhere else did the number of trials for prostitution come close to equaling the number held in Baumholder.[39] Even the exhortations of the Verein and the Ministries of the Interior and Justice to local officials that they emulate Dr. Schnapp did not change that fact.

The manner in which Dr. Schnapp enforced the law in Baumholder, then, is hardly representative of how most communities dealt with the social problems the American military posed. If anything, Schnapp's record was an aberration. His rigidity in matters of decency extended even to the social workers, who accompanied women charged for prostitution to their court appointments. Schnapp refused to admit the social workers into the courtroom if they wore makeup, nail polish, or high heels.[40] Nevertheless, Schnapp's record is interesting for our discussion because his rulings most closely resemble the attitudes about women's sexuality that the Verein was trying to enforce, if need be through the courts.

According to social workers, police officers, and former court officials, Schnapp treated the women brought before his bench as if they were lepers because he was driven by his mission to make Baumholder "*hurenfrei*" (free of whores).[41] Schnapp was not only arrogant and "tough as nails" (*knochenhart*), he also subjected the accused women to humiliating interrogation concerning their sex lives. Even the social workers were appalled by the way in which Schnapp conducted the proceedings. They noted his vicarious voyeurism (*aufgegeilt*) and often tried to protect "their girls" from the prying judge. More than half the convictions from those days, pondered one social worker, "would not stand today."[42]

Schnapp also set a standard for a new interpretation of prostitution. He ruled that the mere acceptance of gifts in kind or even a meal was enough to establish the guilt of a woman as a prostitute. As we have seen, this practice in particular had raised the ire of the Landrat as well as the police officers. Schnapp also expanded the definition of prostitution beyond the sexual act. In a 1952 ruling, he sentenced a woman for prostitution although no sexual act had taken place. The judge argued that her mere presence at a bar where "occupation soldiers" congregated was sufficient grounds for conviction. Schnapp ruled that "even the fact that she was unwilling to engage in sexual relations with the black soldier introduced to her by her girlfriend could not redeem her."[43] The punishment for such offenses was usually three months of jail and one year in the workhouse, so the women could, according to the judge's instruction, "learn to subordinate themselves" and "also learn to be hard on themselves."[44]

The women who transgressed racial boundaries may have been the worst offenders, but the women whom Schnapp considered *arbeitsscheu* (disaccustomed to work) received the same sort of scorn. His admonishments to the women reveal an obsession with decency, discipline, and order (*Sauberkeit, Zucht,* and *Ordnung*). Dr. Schnapp showed mercy only if the indicted woman was not a "hardened prostitute" and if he suspected that she could be redeemed to a life of propriety. If the "fallen" woman came from a solidly middle-class home, he was much more willing to concede that she might have slipped and might have the potential to save herself. Furthermore, if the woman came from a stable middle-class home, the "wayward daughter" could be released to the guardianship of a stern father.[45]

Under Schnapp's reign, the great majority of the women indicted for prostitution were refugees or expellees, and thus they were considered outsiders, or *Fremde,* to the community. Except for two cases, no local woman ever stood before the judge. Of the hundreds of women who appeared before Schnapp, less than a handful were indicted for having engaged in illicit sex with a German man. Although scores of German men, especially the workers during the boom years but respectable family men as well, ventured out to sample big-city life by visiting the tent or one of the local night clubs, the record of the courts would suggest that hardly any of them ever strayed. Even though, as some local people recalled with a chuckle, the "old [German] guys were worse than the soldiers," none of the women indicted before the court was there because of prostituting herself with a local German man.[46]

In 1955, the hard work of Dr. Schnapp received its due reward when he was appointed to the highest state court. Few in Baumholder were sad to see him go. That same year, the Landrat, who in 1953 had already expressed his displeasure that every woman seen with an American was considered a prostitute, declared that those women who remained inconspicuous and quiet were to be left alone.[47] The Landrat and the police came to that conviction because they considered the "soldiers' brides" who lived locally to be acting as a "filter" between the troops and the local women. Not surprisingly, the number of women punished for prostitution dropped significantly with Schnapp's departure. In 1955, a mere 69 women were sentenced for prostitution, and those numbers continued to decrease at the decade progressed.[48]

At a time when the Christian-dominated ministries of the Interior and Justice were still contemplating a complete redefinition of morality for *all* women, local efforts focused on observing all but punishing only a few. If one were to read only the pronouncements from the Verein concerning the overhaul of the sections of the German Criminal Code that dealt with prostitution, one could come to the conclusion that all of Germany had been caught up in a frenzy of self-righteousness. These voices of "moral rearmament" were raised foremost in the churches and their affiliated agencies gathered together in the Verein. Because of the influence that the conservative voices in the Verein continued to wield in matters of social policy at the national level, these moralizing voices also echoed loudly in the chambers of the CDU-dominated state and federal governments.

However, as we have seen, these voices are only one part of the story of the 1950s. Once daughters from respectable local families began to date and marry white GIs, much of the initial condemnation of all women who associated with American GIs as "Veronikas" ceased. Attitudes about prostitution shifted, then, because stigmatizing all sexual relationships between American soldiers and German women as acts of prostitution would have exposed local women to these charges as well.

Attitudes toward prostitution but also premarital sexuality shifted for another and perhaps more significant reason. Evidence from both counties suggests that after the initial shock, the local population had quickly made its peace with the women who arrived in the wake of the soldiers. The people in these communities may not have loved their "*Amimäd-chen,*" but these young women lived in their homes and communities, spent money on the local economy, and some even attended local church services. Most importantly, these young women assured that the GIs' dollars were spent in town. In light of all the money that could be made by renting to the young women and their American boyfriends, very few people were willing to return to the pre-Weimar social and moral values that the Verein and the churches were trying to enforce. Furthermore, many American consumer goods, including cigarettes, whiskey, coffee, and other "luxury goods," found their way into German homes by way of these young women and their beaus. Most people preferred not renting to women who had relations with black GIs, and many refused to do so. However, for many others the financial rewards were sufficient to overcome any feelings of racial unease or animosity.[49]

Many in the population probably judged the so-called "Veronikas" as audacious and lacking respectability even as whole villages prospered by renting to them. However, the local population did not share the convictions of the Verein or Dr. Schnapp that these women's lifestyle posed a threat to the survival of democracy. As long as the women respected community standards of proper behavior, officials left them alone. Women who lived with black GIs generally encountered more hostility, as the widespread and popular use of the pejorative name "*Negernutte*" (Negrowhore) makes all too clear. Yet, even these women were not prosecuted if they were in monogamous, serial relationships and behaved properly.[50]

The prostitutes who arrived on the soldiers' payday from Frankfurt, Munich, Cologne, or Mannheim were a whole other matter. In contradistinction to the concerns of the Verein, the population perceived the professional prostitutes as a significant problem. As far as the local populace was concerned, the professional prostitutes took the soldiers' dollars out of the local economy, leaving the town with nothing but hungover and broke GIs. Thus, by and large for the local residents and business community, the enemy was not the "Veronika" or "soldier's bride" but the professional prostitute.

The despondent tone that marks the reports from clergymen and Christian welfare institutions as the decade advanced reveals that the relaxed attitudes toward women's sexuality, which had provoked the containment measures in the first place, could not be overcome. No matter how vigorously conservatives tried to restore *Wohlanständigkeit,* attitudes toward women's sexuality outside marriage continued to relax. The local population no longer stigmatized premarital sexuality as prostitutelike behavior. Social welfare workers concluded that a dramatic shift in mores had taken place; the population no longer found the behavior of the soldiers' brides offensive. Even Germans who found the "Veronikas'" lifestyle morally offensive rejected the government's campaign to criminalize "marriage-like" arrangements.[51]

When trying to come to terms with their failure to rein in the relaxation of sexual norms during the 1950s, social workers and clergy foremost blamed the economic miracle and people's obsession with all things material. They charged that "the hunt for material goods as well as the apparent order of circumstances prevent any real serious concern over the moral disorder and endangerment."[52] Yet, the reaction of the population and local officials to the morality campaign suggests that West Germany's economic miracle was not the only cause of this greater tolerance. For the most part, Germans also no longer accepted the churches' and the state's prerogative to regulate private sexuality as appropriate for their new democracy.

Interaction of German and
American Assumptions about Race

While Germans in the garrison towns rejected the conservative effort to return to pre-Weimar sexual norms, they negotiated that rejection by redefining sexual norms around racial issues. The flip side of greater sexual tolerance, then, meant that the whole debate on prostitution was displaced almost solely onto women who frequented the black-only bars. Whereas about a third of the trials before 1955 involved women who associated with black GIs, after 1955 that percentage rose to between 70 and 80 percent of the cases prosecuted.[53] These numbers are even more astounding in light of the fact that at most 15 percent of the American troops were black. While the initial hysteria led to a conviction record that was almost "color blind," the greater "normality" of the second part of the decade brought a highly disproportionate ratio of indictments against interracial relationships.

The widespread stigmatization of interracial relationships was possible largely because of the intricate interplay of German and American racism. In Baumholder, as in all garrison communities, the clubs and bars that catered exclusively to American GIs were segregated along racial lines, with the soldiers and the military police enforcing those boundaries. While the German police and American military police regularly patrolled all bars where American GIs congregated, they paid special attention to black-only bars. Moreover, when granting licenses for such bars, authorities used a different, lower standard than that applied to "normal pubs." The objective of the more relaxed standards for these bars—in terms of building codes and public hygiene requirements—was to ensure that the "true prostitutes could meet there with their Negro friends." This strategy, it was hoped, would "make it easier for police officials to control these places, while at the same time it assured that the other pubs remained clean."[54]

The assumption behind this reasoning was that any German woman who frequented a black-only bar was by necessity a prostitute. The local newspaper expressed prevailing sentiments when it reported on a hangout for black GIs by suggesting that these sorts of places "were cesspools of humanity" and "whoever frequented them was by association a prostitute or a pimp."[55] The state's highest administrative court (*Oberverwaltungs-gericht*) came to a similar conclusion when it ruled in 1957 that "no further evidence was necessary to conclude, that an establishment that was frequented by Americans, but especially those bars with Negroes . . . attracted also prostitutes and other asocial elements."[56]

Many of the women who congregated in the black-only bars in Baumholder were in fact professional prostitutes from the city who showed up around payday and left when the soldiers' wallets were empty. Because Baumholder was a training camp, it had a constantly shifting troop population, with soldiers arriving for just a few weeks or months at a time. They worked and played hard and then left when their maneuvers ended. Thus, a disproportionate number of the soldiers in Baumholder were away from their regular military base and thus probably predisposed to explore the local nightlife. For these rotating troops, it was almost impossible to establish serious relationships with local women; consequently, they were much more likely to visit the prostitutes who arrived on the American payday. For black GIs on maneuver in Baumholder, establishing relationships with local women was an even more daunting challenge.

Throughout the decade, as I have shown, prostitutes from across Germany arrived on the American payday to seek out GIs, both white *and* black. However, by the mid-1950s, the prostitutes' solicitation of GIs at the white-only bars no longer seemed an issue that raised concerns. No such tolerance can be found when it came to the black-only bars, because both the German police and the American military police assumed that the black-only bars were the real trouble spots. They also assumed that any woman detected in a black-only bar could not be anything but a prostitute. It was the shared understanding of both American and German law-enforcement officers that interracial sexuality was unacceptable that defined much of the prostitution prosecution in all these communities. When German and American law enforcement officers decided "where to clean house," they were in general agreement over where the worst excesses occurred, namely in the black-only bars about town.[57]

Descriptions of the vice raids conducted in the bars frequented by black GIs show the high level of animosity evoked by the women who went to these places. Observers judged the women's actions not merely as sexual transgressions but as an assault on German national sovereignty. During a routine check conducted by German police in 1955, a slightly intoxicated woman resisted arrest by kicking and screaming at the officers. She also allegedly called for help from her black companions, who then allegedly assumed a threatening stance toward the German officers.

The only reason the officers were not attacked, according to the press coverage, was because their two German shepherds intimidated the soldiers. The prosecutor was appalled by the actions of the defendant and called her a "menace to the public." The judge considered the "massive resistance of the defendant especially incriminating because it was black Americans whom she had incited against German police officers."[58] The judge agreed that the defendant had undermined the authority of the German officers and that she had consciously exploited the tensions that the "latent [changed from "pronounced," the adjective that appears in the transcript] opposition between coloreds and whites entailed."[59] Just how "massive" the resistance of the defendant against the police officers was is revealed in records of the appeal trial. A higher court reduced the harsh sentence because the woman had not "incited Negroes against German police officers"; she had merely exclaimed, "So help me," when her arm was pinched in the door of the police car.[60]

Two years later, a Baumholder judge sentenced a woman to ten months in jail for "inciting colored soldiers" against German police. The police had noticed the woman at a favorite hangout for black soldiers and insisted on checking her papers. When she ignored the police officers and one of them grabbed her by the arm, she allegedly "incited black soldiers standing near by." Coverage of the trial in the press reveals the deep animosity expressed toward the women who associated with black GIs. It also shows that German law enforcement officers and the judge considered the presence of black GIs a serious threat. No such statements were ever made about white American soldiers. The paper reports that in light of the "dangerous situation, the police did not arrest the woman, especially since the soldiers had already taken a threatening stance." The court charged the woman with inciting "foreign colored troops against German police officers, whose duty in Baumholder because of the presence of such troops was already hard and life threatening." The prosecutor insisted, "It will not be tolerated that our police officers' lives are exposed to such mortal danger because of prostitutes."[61]

The fact that it was women who incited "occupation soldiers" against German policemen influenced the severity of the punishment. Because these soldiers were black, the punishment was even harsher, and the language during the trial reveals the outrage at the double offense. The combination of white female aggression and black male aggression was more than the guardians of the law could tolerate, and "justice" to address such behavior was swift. Although no violence had been perpetrated—the officers had merely *felt* threatened—the woman nonetheless received a long jail sentence.

Judges applied a very different standard of punishment when German men assaulted a police officer. While neither the prosecutors nor the judge were happy with such behavior, they were much more willing to write if off as rowdiness (*Halbstarke-Manier*) or to attribute it to an excess of alcohol. In one such case, a German man attacked a police officer and was sentenced to a choice of three weeks in jail or payment of a fine. In another incident, a young German man had kicked and punched a police officer who was checking whether the young woman accompanying him was old enough to be attending a village dance. The prosecutor called for three months' probation. The man was fined DM 350 instead.[62]

Not surprisingly, the prevailing association of black-only bars with prostitution had devastating consequences for all women who were in committed relationships with black soldiers. Interracial couples often chose to frequent a black-only bar because the male partner ran the risk of being insulted or even assaulted by white soldiers if the couple tried to go to a white-only bar. In "proper German pubs," the couple did not have to worry about physical safety, but they might have had to endure stares or sullen service. Young, interracial couples also frequented the black bars because they sought the company of like-minded couples and the entertainment the bars offered, such as jazz, blues, or rock and roll.

However, going to such places could be fraught with danger for the women. When a black soldier visited a black-only bar with his German girlfriend, fiancée, or even wife, the woman in his company ran as a matter of course the risk of being picked up as a prostitute during vice raids. While this was very unlikely to happen in small communities, where the women were well known to the local police, matters could be different in the anonymity of larger communities. One woman, for example was arrested during one such raid, indicted for prostitution, and sentenced to a jail sentence and the workhouse. Fortunately for her, a higher court overturned this harsh ruling, arguing that sexual relations with her fiancé did not constitute prostitution. Nonetheless, this woman endured two humiliating trials in which she was required to prove her innocence. The judge had established her guilt simply through her association with a black man.[63]

The indictment of this woman is also instructive in showing how German and American assumptions about race informed and reinforced each other during the 1950s. Increasingly, women arrested for conspicuous behavior or during a raid on a bar could prove to the judge that theirs was a serious relationship by producing wedding permits from the American military commander.[64] A woman living with a black soldier had more difficulty establishing the sincerity of her relationship because the American military continued to show reluctance in the granting of permits for interracial marriages. We have already seen in Chapter 3 how hard it was for interracial couples, even during the 1950s, to receive wedding permits. Without the commander's consent, young women were reduced to proving the sincerity of their relationship before the courts by producing letters from future mother-in-laws or other character witnesses.[65]

While the American military had officially committed itself to racial equality, granting of wedding permits continued to be the reserve of individual commanders. The woman cited in the above prostitution trial was indicted precisely because she could not produce the necessary papers that would establish the "respectability" of her relationship. When her fiancé appeared before his commanding officer to apply for a marriage permit, the white officer asked the young woman how she could possibly want to marry a black man. The woman's fiancé was so outraged at such questioning that he cursed the officer and as a consequence was demoted, further complicating his application for the much-desired marriage license.[66]

Conclusion

The local reaction to the national struggle for *Wohlanständigkeit*—most forcefully enunciated by the Verein and the conservative Christian Democratic state and federal governments—brings to light two important developments in German attitudes about premarital sexuality. The sexual relationships of German women with white American soldiers, even paid relationships, were no longer perceived as transgressions that placed the women outside the nation. Such unions were no longer judged as either a "sexual" or a "racial" transgression. Just as importantly, confronting the interracial sexuality of black GIs and white German women allowed Germans an easy shifting of their racial disparagement from Jews to blacks. The partnered perpetrators of *Rassenschande* were no longer Aryans and Jews but German women and blacks. Germans were able to make that shift with ease because both of their "occupiers," the French and the American military, were in general agreement that interracial sexuality was unacceptable. The French provided segregated brothels for their troops, and the American military was as vicious in its judgment of German women in the company of black GIs as were the Germans.

A 1956 overview of the "prostitution problem" by one of the state's top police officials (*Polizeipräsident*) reveals that the local shift in the assessment of what acts constituted prostitution expressed a broader national consensus. After giving the *Allgemeine Zeitung* a brief history of prostitution legislation going back to the 1927 reforms, the *Polizeipräsident* in Mainz reiterated that after 1933 prostitutes were dealt with without much ado. The police simply locked them into workhouses or the penitentiary (*Zuchthaus*). He then provided an interesting angle on the whole debate about what acts constituted prostitution. Completely ignoring any mention of sexual relationships between white GIs and German women, he conflated prostitution with racial transgression. Reminding the newspaper's readers that during the Nazi regime the "so-called *Rassenschande*" was punished by penitentiary or the death penalty, he distanced himself from that chapter of German history by stating that "such a solution obviously was no longer appropriate" for the "problem of 'white prostitutes and black soldiers.'"[67]

8

The Kaiserslautern
Steinstrasse Affair

In Kaiserslautern, just as in Baumholder, one of the biggest social problems incurred through the American presence was an explosion of the entertainment industry. However, reining in the side effects of having the American military in Kaiserslautern was a much more daunting task. Because the city's population was larger than 20,000, Kaiserslautern could not ask the state government to activate the provisions of §361 No. 6c of the Criminal Code, which criminalized prostitution. Efforts to rein in prostitution focused instead on curtailing the number of bars that catered to American soldiers and on limiting their business hours, requiring them to close by midnight. To the great dismay of many in Kaiserslautern, all these efforts had been for naught in getting a handle on the after-duty activities of the American GIs. Matters in Kaiserslautern came to a head in the fall of 1957, when the city appealed to the American military to make a whole street in the old part of town, the Steinstrasse, off-limits to American troops. The street that the city administration wanted closed to American GIs was also known as "Little Harlem" or "Bimbo-City" because the quarter was frequented predominantly by African American GIs and their German women friends.[1]

In many ways, the uproar that ensued over the black-only bars in the Steinstrasse mirrors developments in Baumholder. By 1957, the initial outrage over the moral threat that *all* American GIs posed to local life had been reduced to an exclusive concern over the so-called "Negro nuisance" (*Negerunwesen*).[2] However, the lessons that can be learned from a close exploration of the Steinstrasse affair are even more complex. Aside from providing an example of widespread, popular (*volkstümlicher*) racism, the Steinstrasse affair presents a disturbing instance of German politicians using race as a political tool during the 1957 Bundestag election. Anxious to garner voter support in this crucial election, the Christian Democrats (CDU) and the Social Democrats (SPD) indicted the allegedly scandalous conditions in the Steinstrasse to mobilize their electoral base. Both the left and the right, albeit for very different reasons, indicted as unacceptable the "immoral behavior" of black GIs and the German women who gathered in bars owned by Eastern European Jews.

The Steinstrasse affair reveals a complex layer of lingering German anti-Semitism and an ever more vocal racism, the focus of which was not Jews but blacks. The Steinstrasse incident is also instructive because the campaign against the black soldiers, the German women who associated with them, and the Jewish bar owners was not just an expression of local discontent. The nationwide coverage of the incident involved Germans across the country, at least vicariously, in the racialized morality debates surrounding the American military presence.

Kaiserslautern's Political Landscape

Kaiserslautern, just like Baumholder had prospered miraculously from the presence of the American military. Within just a few years Kaiserslautern had grown into the largest American military base outside the United States. By the mid-1950s, the Americans had become a substantial factor in the city's economy, employing more people than the city's largest factory, the Pfaff sewing machine plant. The approximately 40,000 American soldiers and their many family members and dependents who lived in and around Kaiserslautern assured the city an unprecedented prosperity. Despite this American-induced economic boom, relations between Germans and Americans were often strained. As in all other communities, land confiscations, maneuver damages, and the never-ending roar of the American military jets caused much grumbling. While the city had made its peace with the American families who lived in military base housing, the people of Kaiserslautern often experienced the thousands of single, young soldiers as a nuisance.

Politically, the city presented an interesting landscape. In a state dominated by the conservative Christian Democrats, 46 percent of the city's electorate supported the SPD. As the biggest party, the SPD provided the city's mayor throughout the 1950s. The Christian Democrats, who attracted only 20 percent of the vote, nonetheless, wielded much influence. Their alliance with the Free Democrats (FDP), who received another 20 percent of the vote, and with the Wählergruppe Geiger (an independent voting block of artisans and small businessmen), which received 7 percent, assured a powerful counterbalance to the SPD's electoral dominance in the city. Until the Communist Party (KPD) was banned in 1956, it managed to retain the allegiance of 5 percent of the voters, but the SPD refused any sort of cooperation with the KPD.

What distinguished German-American relations in Kaiserslautern was the relative weakness of the Christian Democrats in a state so powerfully dominated by that party. Kaiserslautern also had two city council members, the Christian Democratic Karl Lieberich and the Social Democratic Eugen Hertel, who gave voice to much of the existing discontent over the American presence. The conservative Lieberich fully supported Adenauer's West-integration, and thus the American military mission in Europe, but was appalled with the side effects of the American presence. The city's self-proclaimed fighter for decency, Lieberich relentlessly blamed the Americans for having brought the "material Zeitgeist" and immorality to his beautiful Kaiserslautern. Hertel, who was also a prominent member of the state parliament, was less troubled by matters of morality. Hertel appreciated the economic boom that came with the Americans, but he viewed the American military mission as undermining any chance for German unification. Because of the SPD's need to distance itself from the virulent anti-Americanism of the German Communists, much of the party's critique of the American military was muted before 1956. Discontent expressed itself largely by attacks on the CDU state government's alleged subservience to Adenauer and his strategy of West-integration. After the West German government banned the KPD in 1956, however, Hertel and the Rhineland-Palatinate SPD emerged as vocal critics of the American military mission in Europe when they opposed the American deployment of atomic weapons into Germany.[3] In 1957, when matters came to a head over the Steinstrasse in Kaiserslautern, Hertel and Lieberich found themselves in an unusual alliance.

Kaiserslautern's Steinstrasse

For the Germans living in and around the Steinstrasse, the presence of twenty-two bars that catered almost exclusively to young American soldiers must have been a nuisance, especially on the weekends and on the soldiers' payday. The city had granted concessions to most of these places in 1950–51 when the first American troops arrived and much of the Stein-strasse quarter was still a desolate landscape of bombed-out houses and storefronts. While some of the bars in Kaiserslautern were fancy estab-lishments, such as the Atlantik Club or the Rokkoko Bar, most were less elegant. They nonetheless promised the flair of America with names such as "Oasis, Night-Train-Club, New York City-Bar, Parisiana, Tabu-Club, Short-Timers-Club, New Orleans-Bar, Hollywood and Broadway." Still others were more down-to-earth, sporting such names as Fat Emil or Hole in the Wall, which was also referred to as "Hole in the Wole" by those whose English was not up to snuff.[4]

By the mid-1950s, much of the war destruction in the Steinstrasse had been overcome, largely due to the American-induced boom. With "nor-malcy" returning to their lives, the inhabitants of the Steinstrasse were much less willing to tolerate the American places of amusement in their neighborhood. In 1954, the inhabitants of the Steinstrasse found power-ful allies, when the Catholic and Protestant Churches in Kaiserslautern voiced a strongly worded condemnation of the bars, warning that the "*Ami-Bars*" might weaken German resolve against communism. The churches' affiliated youth organizations also called on the city to act, "so that we can preserve our inner strength against Bolshevist ideas."[5] Not surprisingly, the anxious outcry of the churches over the bars in the Stein-strasse and the German women who frequented them attracted the Ger-man gutter press. A particularly scandalous report in *Wochenend* called Kaiserslautern the whorehouse of the Federal Republic and accused the city of fostering immorality through its much too generous handling of licenses for the bar owners. The article concluded, "Any further toleration of this situation is sure to become a dangerous cancer for our young de-mocracy," and demanded that Joseph Wuermeling, the head of the new Ministry of the Family, take action.[6]

The 1954 outcry over the bars in Kaiserslautern shows a dramatic shift in the national morality debates surrounding the American military pres-ence. The American GIs' after-duty activities had become solely a "black problem." While the local newspaper *Rheinpfalz* merely asserted that "the *Heimat* was faced with a flood of immorality, the likes of which we have never experienced," the outside press was much more direct in identifying the culprits of the alleged immorality.[7] According to *Die Bunte* magazine, the "3,000 Negroes" stationed in Kaiserslautern, "who were generally harmless and fond of children when they were sober," were not alone to be blamed for the scandalous situation in the Steinstrasse. The black soldiers were merely a problem, reported *Die Bunte,* because of the "money-grubbing" bar owners who were "without any conscience" and the 3,000 "cunning prostitutes" who had made Kaiserslautern their new home.[8] Even the *Freisoziale Presse,* a publication associated with the Communist Party, drew on this racist discourse to describe the "ordeal" of West Germany's continuing occupation. The paper indicted as one of the main problems the bars, with their "howling and raging of jazz music." The reference to jazz assured that even the most uninformed reader understood that the newspaper was referring to the *"Neger-Bars."* Since approximately 3,000 black soldiers were among the military personnel in Kaiserslautern, the reference to the "3,000 *Amizonen*" who turned Kaiserslautern into a dung heap of immorality made even more explicit that the Steinstrasse was viewed foremost as a black problem.[9]

Prodded on by the churches' resolutions and by reports in the national tabloid press that thousands of prostitutes plied their trade in Kaiserslautern, the city had to act. Its first response was to raze some of the most decrepit buildings in one of the town's poorest neighborhoods, where some of the women who frequented the Steinstrasse allegedly lived.[10] The city also increased the number of police patrols, to keep the Steinstrasse safer for the German population. However, a four-week "special action" by the police to track down prostitutes revealed just how exaggerated many of the charges over matters of morality in the Steinstrasse were. The numerous vice raids (twenty-six were conducted during the week of 25–31 October alone) netted the police the arrest of a "mere 92 Veronikas," most of whom could only be charged for not carrying an identification card. The *Pfälzische Volkszeitung* suggested that because of these arrests "the citizens could again walk the streets at night without fear of harassment." However, the paper also concluded that the number of women arrested hardly warranted the wild speculations concerning the thousands of prostitutes in town.[11]

Alarmed by the scandalous reports in the national tabloid press, the regional government of the Palatinate in Neustadt exerted pressure on the city to control the situation in the Steinstrasse by limiting the number of bars that catered to the GIs. Although both white and black GIs frequented bars and clubs in Kaiserslautern, the regional as well as the state government associated the existence of these establishments foremost with the presence of black soldiers. The Ministry of the Interior in Mainz informed the city of Kaiserslautern, for example, that the "concentration of rather young and unrestrained colored soldiers and a great number of prostitutes . . . marked the situation in Kaiserslautern."[12]

To contain the situation in the Steinstrasse, the regional government in

January 1955 urged the city to be more discerning when granting licenses for bars that attracted "occupation soldiers." In its letter, the regional government suggested that Eastern European Jews owned all the "disreputable" bars that catered to American GIs. Repeating widely shared assumptions of the postwar years that Eastern European DPs had been active in the black market, the regional government cautioned the city that the bar owners' pasts "hardly recommended them" for running a business of that type.[13] Kaiserslautern's Social Democratic mayor did not appreciate this meddling from the regional government. He also was not happy with the explicit anti-Semitic allegations. He responded by informing the government that just because the bar owners were "stateless foreigners or belonged to another faith does not warrant the suspicion that these individuals have a disreputable past" and are therefore not reliable enough to run a bar or a nightclub.[14] He also lectured the regional government on the fact that Germany was a state of law and that existing laws did not allow for any such discrimination.[15]

After the 1954 *Wochenend* incident brought the city such unwanted publicity, an unusual alliance of Social Democrats, Christian Democrats, and Communists set out to curtail the bars with the only weapons available to city council. While city council could not stop the granting of licenses for such bars, that body had to be consulted when it came to granting these establishments extensions of their business hours past midnight. In October 1954, the city council voted that eight bars, which already had permission to be opened beyond midnight, were sufficient for Kaiserslautern. They also agreed to reject any further applications for extensions of business hours past midnight.[16]

The heated exchanges in the city council suggest a good deal of animosity toward the non-German bar owners, who were blamed for the drinking excesses of the GIs as well as the proliferation of prostitution. But these debates also reveal the multilayered attitudes that informed decision making on the bars. For the Kaiserslautern CDU, the whole affair of the bars was a deplorable one. While the CDU members were staunch defenders of the free market, they also wanted to use their judgment to control the social aspects of growth. For the CDU, any bar, even if it catered only to a German clientele, was a deplorable side effect of the new materialist age. CDU city councilman Lieberich, who was the most outspoken opponent of bars, gave voice to his party's conviction, declaring on a number of occasions that he did not care whether people thought the city backward; at least, he said, people will see that "in Kaiserslautern decency and order reign."[17] The CDU's coalition partners, the Free Democrats, disagreed with the CDU stance, insisting that the principle of freedom of trade was at stake; they were also appalled by the CDU's moral rigidity. FDP councilman Fritz Wilms implored his colleague from the CDU not to be "holier than the pope," by suggesting that not all the people of Kaiserslautern wanted to be in bed by midnight.[18] During another debate, Wilms was even more exasperated with Lieberich when he told his colleague that Germans should not be preachers of morality (*Moralprediger*). While not specifically mentioning Germany's appalling record during the Nazi past, Wilms asked his colleagues with a certain amount of sarcasm, "whether the German *Volk* is so noble that it never commits evil deeds."[19] The SPD, which had sympathy for neither the FDP's defense of free trade nor the CDU's morality campaign, nonetheless supported the ban on further bars.

The spirited debates on the bars reveal that limiting the business hours of these establishments was not a strategy aimed solely at bars that had DP proprietors. Even bars whose owners were German did not get extensions of their business hours if the city council suspected that American GIs, white or black, might frequent the establishment.[20] The council's voting patterns suggest that its underlying agenda on limiting the hours of these bars was to keep single American soldiers out of the city at night, especially after midnight. While the CDU was anxious to cleanse the city of all traces of vice and prostitution, the SPD's motivation for reining in the bars appears to have been more complex. Unable to oppose the American military mission politically, the ban on the bars seems to have provided the SPD with at least a minimal sense of self-determination. The SPD council members also may have speculated that their stance would assure them the sympathy of their local electorate, large sections of which still had not made their peace with the American military mission, West Germany's rearmament, and the looming introduction of nuclear missiles.

The SPD's stance on the bars was made explicit during an especially heated debate in late 1956, when Wilms again indicted his colleagues' hypocrisy. Wilms teased the city council for inviting the Americans to Christmas dinners but not wanting to grant them places of entertainment in the city. When Wilms asked his colleagues to make up their minds whether they wanted the Americans or not, the newly appointed Social Democratic mayor, Dr. Walter Sommer, gave voice to widespread SPD sentiments of the time when he answered, "We don't want them."[21]

While the city administration was under attack from a number of directions over the so-called *Ami-Bars,* the Jewish bar owners did not sit back quietly. In November 1954, they organized themselves as the Coalition of Jewish Bar Owners and took on the city administration. In an extensive letter, their lawyer reminded the city that his clients had survived the Nazi death camps by sheer coincidence. He appealed to common decency by demanding that these survivors now be given a chance to make a living. He accused the city of "anti-Semitic tendencies," because his clients were convinced that different standards were applied in granting licenses when Jews were the applicants. The Coalition of Jewish Bar Owners also claimed that their establishments were controlled more strictly and punished much more severely when they failed to close exactly at midnight.[22]

The Jewish bar owners also appealed to the state's Council of Jewish Communities, but they were rebuffed. The German-born Jews who dominated the council in Rhineland-Palatinate had little sympathy for the Eastern European Jews, who they feared were reinforcing traditional stereotypes through their business enterprises. Intent not to offer any ammunition to anti-Semites, the state's German Jewish community sided with the city of Kaiserslautern but demanded that the local press at least refrain from printing the names of the bar owners in their coverage of the topic. The state's Council of Jewish Communities also promised the Ministry of the Interior and the city that efforts to limit the bars would not be construed as anti-Semitism.[23] Even Heinrich Grüber, dean of the Protestant Church of Berlin, a formidable foe of Nazi policies during the Third Reich, had little sympathy for the controversy surrounding the bar owners. He commented that "the problem in Germany is that Jews have not learned anything from what happened to them" and suggested that the Jewish bar owners in localities with American military personnel were "putting hindrances in the way of our fight against anti-Semitism."[24] To the objection that the actions of a few bar owners were undermining the prestige of a whole people, a Jewish bar owner replied that he hoped that the "prestige of all Christians would not be undermined by the fact that almost all the prostitutes in town were Catholic."[25]

Kaiserslautern's "Little Harlem"

While the Steinstrasse clearly had its share of problems, much of the situation there was exaggerated in the public debate. The problems experienced in this quarter seem to have been consistent with those of any large garrison town, as the Social Democratic *Die Freiheit* had pointed out in the past.[26] The police reports for that section of town suggest a level of incidents that appear compatible with the existence of twenty-two pubs, of which fifteen were bars or bar-like establishments. During an eight-month period, the time that led up to the off-limits request in 1957, the whole Steinstrasse quarter reported "77 incidents, including fights, public drunkenness, crass mischief, disturbance of the peace, or public nuisance."[27] In 1960, when the mayor looked back on the previous decade, he also admitted that it had not been so much the big incidents that had caused the problems in the Steinstrasse. The residents of the city, according to the mayor, had been much more upset by little annoyances, such as noisy GIs, banging car doors, and squealing women. They also did not like that the GIs, especially the black GIs, assumed that they could approach any woman they encountered in the Steinstrasse with a friendly "Hello, Frollein."[28]

After the first uproar over the Steinstrasse in late 1954, Mayor Sommer took it upon himself to see just how bad matters were in the establishments of the Steinstrasse. His visit revealed that the so-called Negro bars (*Negerbars*) in the Steinstrasse were not cheap, run-down dives and places of "sexual excesses," as was often charged in the public debates. The first place the mayor visited was the Bimbo Bar, and while this "place was very loud," the mayor detected no "signs of indecency or offensiveness." In the Metro Bar, the mayor had to ask the owner to turn down the blaring jukebox, but he assured the city council that the "Negroes present did not seem to mind this." Nor did the city's first inspector find any evidence of offensive behavior in this establishment. At the Victoria, a live band had played that night, and while the mayor allowed that the dancing going on there hardly reminded him of his own dance lessons, no immorality or excesses were to be observed. The mayor concluded that "the fear that one dare not go into such places was absolutely unfounded." Despite the favorable impressions that the mayor had received on his tour of inspection, he insisted that none of these places should receive an extension of their business hours past midnight "because all of their customers are Negroes."[29]

While there probably were a number of bars that did not meet bourgeois standards or propriety, the mayor's visit to some of the most notorious bars in the Steinstrasse suggests that much of the public debate over these bars was exaggerated. Thus, when observers decried the sexual excesses going on in these bars, people were commenting on the fact that "the partners did not observe prevailing standards of distance and carriage of the body."[30] Many observers were also offended to see dancers whose whole body was in motion "from head to toe" or whose "arms jerked and legs stomped to the rhythm of the jitterbug, boogie-woogie, and bebop."[31]

"The Golden Plague," an essay in Benno Wundshammer's *Deutsche Chronik 1954,* is a stunning example of how deeply offensive these black-only bars and the people who frequented them were to many Germans.

Dancing couple in Kaiserslautern, 1954. The contrast between Wundshammer's obscene description of the dancers and the proper and composed appearance of this young couple could not be more incongruous. Photo from Wundshammer, *Deutsche Chronik 1954.*

The author reported with great consternation that in Kaiserslautern "Negro soldiers, whose clumsy hands reach for the white flesh, were lounging about in the bars" with young German women. According to the author, the women in these bars arrived in the luxurious street cruisers of their GI boyfriends and were wearing jewelry worth "thousands of dollars." All these accoutrements, however, cannot disguise the fact that when the women open their mouths, the "harsh language of the gutter" can be heard.[32]

The photo that accompanied the essay shows a black GI in dress uniform, who, with a serious and concentrated expression in his face, is leading a very properly dressed German woman in a traditional fox-trot. Completely ignoring the very respectable appearance and demeanor of this young couple, Wundshammer nonetheless calls the women in this Kaiserslautern *"Neger Bar"* "cheap barflies" (*lotterige Barschönheiten*) who are dressed in colorful and revealing clothing (*Flitterfähnchen*). Wundsham-mer considered the plain act of dancing with a black man so offensive that he completely effaced the young woman's respectability, evoking for the reader instead images of an "almost naked woman," who brushed her hair into her face through wild motions, gestured with her arms and finally collapsed on the floor like a contorting snake.[33]

Unlike the depictions of blacks during the French occupation of the Rhineland during the 1920s, the black soldiers in the 1950s generally were not portrayed as "beastly rapists." Although Wundshammer described how "excited Negroes" with "catlike movements" and faces like "shiny, contorted masks" conducted a "hunt for white women," he also con-cluded that the women offered themselves freely; they were an "all-too-easy prey."[34] Wundshammer acknowledged that the couples he observed were in consensual relationships, but the crossing of racial boundaries nonetheless placed both the woman and the man outside the realm of respectability. The woman is disgraced by identifying her dress and de-meanor with the lower class. In this manner her "racial transgression," "her dancing with a black man," is rendered a sexual transgression as well. In essence, Wundshammer depicts her racial transgression of dancing with a black man as an act of prostitution. Her partner, on the other hand, was removed from civilization and assigned to "*Unkultur*" (nonculture). The description of his appearance and behavior places him in the jungle, al-though the author assures the reader that the scene he has described is taking place not in "a capital of a Negro Republic" but in the middle of Germany.[35]

The 1957 Off-Limits Order

Negative depictions of the black-only bars, of the people who owned them, and of those who frequented them persisted, despite the mayor's assurances that all was well in the "Negro bars." In May of 1957, the in-habitants of the Steinstrasse were annoyed enough about the situation in their street to take political action. Their appeal to the city reveals just how deeply offended many Germans were by the fact that German women and African American soldiers could freely associate in their neighbor-hood. Although white GIs frequented the city and the Steinstrasse quar-ter as well, the bars they frequented and their behavior seem to have been acceptable to local standards. The Steinstrasse inhabitants asked that the city request the American military to make their neighborhood off-limits to *black soldiers only*. Mayor Sommer rejected that appeal, informing the Steinstrasse inhabitants that the Basic Law did not permit such an action.[36] Matters came to a head again in mid-August of 1957, just four weeks before the election for the German Bundestag. This timing made all the difference for the people in the Steinstrasse.

A German pub owner whose establishment was located on Steinstrasse initiated the whole affair. This man freely admitted that he had a "strong dislike of blacks." To keep them out of his establishment, he charged them 5 deutsche marks for using the restroom. He had also in the past pulled a gun on two black GIs who, when confronted with the five marks charge, had urinated outside his pub. Despite his vigorous efforts to keep black GIs out of his bar, the owner was not able to attract white customers, German or American. According to him, he had failed in his attempts because "blacks dominated the Steinstrasse." The pub owner saw no other way to reclaim his business except through drastic action. Together with about 100 inhabitants of the Steinstrasse, he founded the Emergency Council of Steinstrasse Inhabitants.[37] Many of the other members of the Emergency Council were also business owners who charged that they had lost their German customers, who, because of the presence of so many black soldiers, were afraid to frequent this part of town.

An emergency existed aside from these monetary concerns. The inhabitants of the street also objected to the fact that "black soldiers could be observed in the arms of white women not only in cars, but even in broad view in the middle of the street."[38] Something had to be done, the inhabitants insisted, charging: "By day and by night there is no rest. At night it is impossible to get any sleep before two in the morning. Noise, jazz music, the howls of the jungle, honking cars, yelling, bar stools and rocks fly through the air, knives flash, intoxicated soldiers and prostitutes stagger through the streets and wallow in the gutter."[39] In light of these alleged excesses, the Emergency Council drafted a resolution stating that "the inhabitants of the Steinstrasse have been living in a permanent state of emergency for the last three years" due to the "concentration and public demeanor of colored American troops and their female entourage." According to the Steinstrasse inhabitants, soldiers harassed the citizens at all times, but the biggest problem was the "shameless behavior of the prostitutes by day and by night."[40]

Although the Federal Republic had made racial tolerance a touchstone of its new democracy, neither the obvious racism of the Steinstrasse activists nor the disturbingly racist press coverage of the Steinstrasse evoked protests or an outcry from readers of these publications or from local officials.[41] The coverage of the 1957 affair also indicates that a much more assertive racism toward black GIs had emerged since the earlier complaints over the Steinstrasse in 1954. Germany's newly achieved sovereignty seems to have contributed to this shift; it had become much less controversial to assert national pride and to indict those who undermined that national pride. For example, a 1956 *Neue Blatt* essay entitled "Better Manners, Occupiers!" declared that sovereignty had changed the outlook of the Germans, who were again developing "national pride" (*Nationalbewusstsein*) in their hearts. Because Germans were again "masters in their house," it claimed, they were no longer willing to put up with the rowdy behavior of the GIs. The essay listed a recent spate of attacks by American soldiers on German civilians to indict the country's ally for behaving as if the Americans were still occupiers. Yet, the photograph accompanying the article illustrates what aspect of the American presence was most offensive to German pride: it shows a black soldier dancing with a German woman.[42]

While depictions of interracial couples during the early 1950s hardly minced words, this latest spate of reports revealed a new level of coarseness that was also expressed much more freely in a public forum. In 1957, the tabloid press described black soldiers and the German women who associated with them not merely as racial and sexual transgressors but as bestial creatures. One such report described the situation in the Steinstrasse as "worse than anything that could be found in a jungle village (*Urwaldkral*), because of the claustrophobic closeness, the noise, the jumble of voices—the unbearable perspiration of the masses that roll by."[43] The crowds in the Steinstrasse were also described as "the black wave . . . of frizzy head beside frizzy head that pushed through the half-dark alleys that all lead to the Steinstrasse."[44] Another report asserted that "more than 3,000 prostitutes were meeting there with more than 3,000 Negro soldiers . . . while turning the quarter into 'Little Harlem.'" The crowd that milled about in the streets was depicted as a "head-to-head screaming and howling gang that pushed through the streets." Evoking images of a stampede, the paper charged that it was so crowded in the street that "one black was almost stepping on the next."[45]

Because the majority of the local bar owners in the Steinstrasse were Eastern European and not German Jews, the Emergency Council also seemed little concerned with violating the Federal Republic's prescribed philosemitism. The Emergency Council identified as the "cause and origin for the illegal excesses a number of bars . . . that were frequented exclusively by coloreds."[46] The Coalition of Jewish Bar Owners quickly determined that its members were the targets of the Emergency Council's efforts, since its members owned fifteen of the twenty-two bars in the Steinstrasse.

While the citizens of the Steinstrasse defended themselves against charges of anti-Semitism by invoking their concern for morality, resentment toward the Jewish bar owners was widespread and vocal.[47] Although public opinion at the time and even today asserts that Jews owned all bars that catered to GIs, this was not the case. Municipal records show that although many of the bars and variétés were indeed run by Jews, non-Jews participated in the boom as well. Of the thirty bars and barlike establishments in Kaiserslautern, only six were owned by "stateless individuals" and nine by "foreigners," both terms used to indicate that the owners were Jews from Eastern Europe.[48] Furthermore, the process of stereotyping Jewish bar owners as having brought the vices of the city to the village clouded the reality that the overwhelming majority of the real estate was owned by *local* businessmen who themselves prospered handsomely through leasing of their establishments.

In this climate of finger pointing, traditional anti-Semitic stereotypes about Jews poisoning the morality of upright Germans quickly emerged. Because official German discourse self-consciously institutionalized philosemitism as the moral touchstone of the new democracy, it was no longer politically viable to publicly accuse Jews of corrupting morality.[49] Thus, official debates on the bar owners carefully avoided identifying the owners as Jews and talked instead of individuals "who could barely speak German and whose names are unpronounceable."[50] While the local press tended to tread carefully when talking about the bar owners, the national tabloid press showed little restraint. In their scandalous reportage, they suggested that moneymen (*Drahtzieher*) or "white slavery rings" from the big city imported German women for the "*Ami-Bars.*" While the tabloid press always used coded language when talking of the bar owners, such as "Sin Inc." or "Pleasure Mafia," everybody understood what those code words implied. The implication was that Jews corrupted German morality by running white slavery rings, a myth that had been a staple of European anti-Semitism since the nineteenth century.[51]

The level of animosity toward the Jewish bar owners is revealed in a letter that the president of the Munich police sent to the regional government of the Palatinate. He informed the Palatinate government with much consternation that some Jews allegedly used "the moneys they had received as restitution payment for concentration camp ordeals" to open these bars. He further suggested that the Jewish bar owners seemed to know ahead of time about planned American troop movements. According to his charges, the bar owners, who followed the American military to the Palatinate from the American zone, had scouted out real estate for potential bars in the French zone long before the Germans were informed about American plans.[52] These charges of Jews being informed by Washington about troop deployments in Germany even before the Germans knew about developments in their *Heimat* are reminiscent of traditional anti-Semitic charges of Jewish power. They also say much about the sense of helplessness that many Germans must have felt in this period over their own fate.

Even Germans who were generally sympathetic to the plight of the German Jews were not able to overcome deeply ingrained prejudices toward Eastern European Jews. The SPD's Eugen Hertel, himself a victim of Nazi persecution, described the Eastern European Jews as "victims who arrived here because of expulsion from Poland." While ignoring the German complicity in the fate of these individuals, as well as the unwillingness of German law to grant citizenship to these "stateless individuals," Hertel also expressed a new form of overt anti-Semitism. While "nobody wanted to rail" against these "victims of expulsion," Hertel noted, "the trend that half of the city's bar owners have unpronounceable names could not be ignored."[53]

The debates about the Jewish bar owners became particularly dirty in the neighboring city of Ramstein, where one city council member asserted publicly what many others expressed privately, namely, that nothing could be done about the Jewish bar owners because one was afraid "of being locked up."[54] That individual also made a laudatory reference to a recent incident in which a high school teacher in Offenburg had told a "half Jew" that "Hitler did not kill enough, otherwise they would not be acting so insolent again." The council member was admonished by a furious mayor never to repeat these sorts of statements again "or he would be dismissed." This individual made similar statements at a public meeting that a number of Jewish bar owners from Kaiserslautern also attended. In contradistinction to racist remarks made about black GIs, derogatory remarks about Jews in general elicited critical responses. A letter to the editor of the *Pfälzische Volkszeitung* denounced the fact that such things, which "so smacked of the recent past," could be said again in Germany.[55]

The theme of Jewish bar owners bringing vice and immorality to the *Heimat* was so widespread in the 1950s that Helmut Käutner's 1960 movie *Schwarzer Kies* commented critically but rather clumsily on the surge of anti-Semitism surrounding the bar owners. In one particularly jolting scene, the Jewish bar owner asks the old German farmer, from whom he has leased real estate, to stop playing a World War II soldier's song on the bar's shiny jukebox. He implores him to let the young GIs from the neighboring military base play some of their own music. The farmer replies in anger that he won't take orders from the bar owner, calling the man, a survivor of Auschwitz, a "dirty Jew" (*Sau-Jud*).[56]

Politics and Morality

Because matters over the Steinstrasse came to a head shortly before the federal elections, every political party jumped into the fray. The biggest coup for the Emergency Council was gaining the support of Eugen Hertel. Locally, Hertel was the most outspoken critic of Adenauer's West-integration and of the CDU state government's support of Adenauer's security policy. Hertel freely gave voice to his belief that "no Social Democrat could accept that the Federal Republic serve as an American military training ground until all hell freezes over."[57] Strongly opposed to the American military mission in Germany in general, and deeply opposed to the decision to station Nike missiles in Rhineland-Palatinate, Hertel seems to have used the Steinstrasse affair as a popular mobilizer to attract electoral support to the SPD and its antinuclear platform. On 22 August, Hertel wrote an open letter to the Ministry of the Interior in which he begged the government for help. Although Hertel indicted the shameless behavior of "prostitutes and allied soldiers" in general, he asked the state government's help only in alleviating matters in the Steinstrasse quarter.[58]

The Emergency Council was confident of victory, for now they had the support of the Kaiserslautern CDU, SPD, and the churches. Fortified in this manner, Lieberich, acting as a representative of the city, the Emergency Council, and the churches, organized a series of meetings with the Americans regarding the matter. During one such meeting between German and American representatives and individual citizens and soldiers in Kaiserslautern's "House of Encounter," all sides had a chance to air their grievances. An American soldier defended the bar owners against charges that they were the source of all the problems. He suggested that the bar owners had acted in good faith by wanting to offer the black soldiers, who had no other place to go, a place to gather. A black American woman forcefully rejected the soldiers' charges that black GIs had no places to frequent in the city, insisting that "Negroes have opportunities to go into any decent and respectable pub" in Kaiserslautern. She charged that the soldiers who frequented the bars in the Steinstrasse "were 'low-educated Negro soldiers,' who felt at home in these cheap dives." She also urged the city to solve the Steinstrasse problem by outlawing prostitution.[59]

The Americans agreed with the Germans that the bars were the source of many of the problems in the Steinstrasse, but they also made very clear that they were leery of local motivation. The military representatives suspected that the whole ruckus over the Steinstrasse was related to the ongoing Bundestag election. The military clergy, who were generally interested in the soldiers' off-duty activities, refused to attend the meeting because they too suspected that the whole affair was related to the election. However, a representative of the military rabbi was present, and he informed the Germans that he suspected that the Steinstrasse Emergency Council was acting out of a "certain prejudice" (*bestimmten Vorurteil*). The Germans forcefully rejected the charge that anti-Semitism or racism motivated the Steinstrasse inhabitants' actions. Because of the ongoing crisis over school integration in Little Rock, Arkansas, Councilman Lieberich was emboldened enough to suggest to the Americans that Germans were more tolerant than Americans toward blacks. "The situation [in Germany]," he told the Americans pointedly, "is very different from the one in the United States." The local paper reported with a certain amount of Schadenfreude that one of the black participants searched the faces of her white American colleagues during this exchange as they all sat in embarrassed silence.[60]

In a meeting between Mayor Sommer and Colonel Paul Breden, the commanding officer of the Western Area Command, matters became particularly tense. Colonel Breden demanded that the city stop the press campaign over the Steinstrasse; he also told the mayor that it was the city's responsibility to solve the Steinstrasse problem. As far as Breden was concerned, the mayor could easily resolve the issue by "locking up the prostitutes and closing down these joints." The exasperated mayor informed the colonel that he could do neither of these things according to German law. Breden, on the other hand, rejected the mayor's suggestion that he issue an off-limits order for the "worst offenders" only, that is, against the bars where most of the problems allegedly occurred. Although lower-level military commanders had at times invoked that prerogative, Colonel Breden was unwilling to do so. In light of the severe tensions among the troops caused by the ongoing crisis in Little Rock, Breden seemed unwilling to antagonize matters even more by making a number of black-only bars off-limits to his soldiers. He was also not willing to consider the mayor's suggestion that he issue an off-limits order for low-ranking personnel only.[61]

What was already a tense meeting turned icy when the city representatives suggested to Colonel Breden that they might have to alert the American women's organizations if the military could not solve the Steinstrasse problem. Breden was not averse to invoking the power of

America's women either. He warned the Germans that if the American women's organizations got wind of the affair, they would insist that all troops be withdrawn from the sinful climate. Such a development, the general believed, could "seriously affect the prosperity of the city." The mayor was clearly annoyed that Breden turned the tables on him and responded indignantly, "Kaiserslautern has done just fine for 800 years before the Americans came and will do so in the future."[62]

With the Emergency Council in permanent session and the national tabloid press besieging the city for yet another glance at depravity, the city had to act. While the Emergency Council denied having any racist agenda, it repeated its strategy of May 1957, calling for the Steinstrasse to be declared "off-limits" to black soldiers only.[63] This suggests that the thousands of single, white American soldiers and their female companions, who also frequented the town's numerous pubs, clubs, and bars, were, at least in the eyes of the local burghers, always on their best behavior. The mayor again refused this request as a violation of the German Basic Law, which specifically outlawed discrimination based on race. As a last desperate measure to quiet the most recent uproar, the clearly exasperated mayor asked Colonel Breden to make the Steinstrasse district off-limits to *all* American soldiers during evening hours.

Colonel Breden was not happy with the city's proposals because he was convinced that the request was politically motivated. However, it is also interesting to see how the Americans interpreted local actions. Nothing in the record suggests that the Americans suspected that the city's request was motivated by racist sentiments against the black soldiers. The Land Relations Officer (LRO), who reported weekly to Colonel Breden on developments in Kaiserslautern and other such communities, never made German racism an issue. Neither did the LRO, who prepared extensive overviews of the German press coverage of the brewing affair, ever condemn the outrageous coverage produced regarding black GIs. In general, the LRO suspected that German complaints about black soldiers were used in SPD strongholds as a "possible rabble rouser" against American military and political policies.[64]

Breden's decision, it appears, was informed by two considerations. First, he was convinced that the city's appeal, submitted by the Social Democratic mayor, was grounded solely in an anti-American political agenda. Breden believed that the whole affair was related to the SPD's opposition to the planned deployment of Nike missiles. The Americans quickly identified Eugen Hertel and Jockel Fuchs, a prominent SPD politician, as their most outspoken opponents in both Kaiserslautern and in the state legislature. American commentaries on the affair also suggest that, at least in public meetings with the Americans, the Germans never singled out black soldiers as a special problem. Consequently, the Americans were convinced that the Rhineland-Palatinate SPD had picked the "anti-American indecency theme" to push its "anti-Nike, anti-Atomic, [and] anti-NATO" agenda.[65]

Because the CDU was the Americans' most stalwart political ally, the LRO assumed that protests from the CDU over the Steinstrasse were not politically motivated but concerned only complaints over an "admittedly intolerable situation."[66] However, at this point so close to the election, Colonel Breden may have been suspicious of the CDU as well. While the CDU state government, under much pressure from the federal government, had secretly approved sixteen Nike missile launcher sites in April of 1957, negotiations between the American military and the state government over the locations of these sites had come to a virtual standstill. Because of the upcoming election and widespread opposition to nuclear weapons among the population, state president Altmeier was dragging his feet. As a matter of fact, Altmeier did not come around to giving his final go-ahead for the launcher sites until March of 1958, the same month that the SPD working group against nuclear weapons was founded.[67] The fact that the Protestant Church of the Palatinate sided with the SPD in opposing the deployment of Nike missiles only further convinced the Americans that the whole uproar over the Steinstrasse was a political maneuver.[68]

The second consideration that influenced Breden's decision making was the situation among his own troops. Breden had to proceed with caution because of a brewing crisis in the United States. While tempers flared in Kaiserslautern due to the upcoming Bundestag elections, the American military was experiencing tremendous tension between white and black soldiers because of events taking place in Little Rock, Arkansas.[69]

Wanting to punish the city for what he considered its opposition to the deployment of Nike missiles while also calming anger among his black troops over developments in the United States, Colonel Breden defined the borders of the off-limits area much more broadly than had been requested. When he issued the off-limits order on 9 September 1957, he declared the area off-limits around the clock. Breden also seems to have instructed his soldiers that the city ought to be taught a lesson in recompense for Sommer's comment that the city had done "just fine" for 800 years before the Americans arrived. In the next few days, there was hardly an American soldier or family dependent to be seen about town.[70]

Word of the off-limits order made headline news throughout the Federal Republic, with the tabloid press reporting with much satisfaction that the "3,000 coloreds . . . have through a military order suddenly lost the possibility to amuse themselves with 'white women' without being disturbed."[71] Another newspaper reported gleefully that the "excesses of the Negro soldiers and their white girlfriends had come to a sudden end." But the account of that observer also makes clear to what degree the black soldiers, the "sexually unrestrained women," and the bar owners from Eastern Europe had threatened what Germans considered a proper bourgeois identity. The author concluded, with a tone of irony, that without these outsiders, "Kaiserslautern had again become the respectable, bourgeois (*solide und bürgerlich*) city that it had been before the Americans came."[72]

Despite sensational reports in the press that "the Negroes and their lovers had threatened to take revenge by setting the whole of the city on fire," there were no signs of anger from the women or the black soldiers.[73] The much anticipated unrest over the Steinstrasse off-limits order came instead from a very different quarter. The first off-limits signs had hardly been set in place on 9 September 1957 when the city administration was besieged with calls from infuriated residents in and around the Steinstrasse who complained that their American friends could no longer visit them. Even angrier calls came from individuals whose stores and businesses were located in that part of town. The city of Kaiserslautern, with its 94,000 inhabitants, had lost the business of some 40,000 Americans.

The German tabloid press quickly found a villain to blame for the American boycott. They pointed their fingers at "the opaque syndicate of the mostly foreign bar owners . . . who were nothing less than front men for a powerful and secret organization." However, the indictment that the press hurled at the bar owners also reveals that Germans must have known on some level that their actions exposed them to charges of both racism and anti-Semitism. According to *Wochenend,* the bar owners had convinced the American soldiers that the city's action was an "anti-Semitic undertaking, a communist obstruction, political election maneuvers, and unleashed race hatred against the colored soldiers."[74]

As an immediate response to the off-limits order, a new emergency council was created: the Coalition of Those Injured by the Steinstrasse Off-Limits Order. This group sued the city for damages that the street's businesses had incurred because of the rash actions taken by the city council to appease the inhabitants of the Steinstrasse. Due to the off-limits order, other Steinstrasse businesses, such as car dealers, souvenir shops, restaurants, and laundromats, had lost their American customers and were going bankrupt. They pleaded with the city to ask the Americans to limit the off-limits order to the nighttime. The Coalition of Jewish Bar Owners joined these protests but called for a complete lifting of the order. By the end of the affair, six different coalitions had besieged the courthouse with their petitions.

The little morality play that ensued over the Steinstrasse generated both laughter and Schadenfreude across Germany. The national press, which earlier had delighted in the alleged excesses of the Steinstrasse, now reported with a measure of glee that little had the Emergency Council known that "the triumph of decency would empty their purses." One newspaper reported that instead of enjoying the fruits of their "struggle for decency and morality" the victorious fighters were "suffering a severe case of hangover."[75] Another observer commented that the "price of their morality was a steep one" because the money "of the Amis was missed everywhere."[76] According to another commentator, the people of Kaiserslautern had come to a crucial crossroads in their postwar transition into a consumer society, as they debated such dilemmas as "business *and* morality, business *or* morality, or business *without* morality?"[77]

In the end, business won out. The offensive bars had closed down or moved to other parts of town, taking the women and black soldiers with them. But more respectable businesses also had to close down because of the loss of American business. Consequently, the city pleaded with Colonel Breden to limit the off-limits order for the Steinstrasse to the nighttime. By 13 November, Colonel Breden repealed the daytime off-limits order, and Americans could again visit the businesses of the Steinstrasse quarter until 7 P.M.

"We Only Wanted to Keep the Black Soldiers Out"

Kaiserslautern's mayor Sommer missed most of the uproar over the Steinstrasse. While his city was debating the merits of morality versus business, he was traveling in the United States as a guest of the American government so he could convince himself of the safety of Nike missile sites. But the tremors accompanying the affair over the Steinstrasse reached as far as Washington, D.C. When Sommer met with officials from the Department of Defense, one African American official inquired with him whether the "Steinstrasse problem was a Negro problem." The mayor rejected any such speculation and responded with a resounding "No!" Indeed, the mayor was obviously anxious not to have his city appear intolerant and racist. He informed the official that the problem of the Steinstrasse was related to the fact that "young and lively soldiers, black and white, were seeking entertainment there."[78]

Despite the mayor's assurances, on a most basic level the Steinstrasse affair was an expression of widespread German racism. The Steinstrasse inhabitants freely admitted that while all the soldiers had caused them annoyance, they had "mostly been infuriated with the plentiful Negroes," whose presence had turned their Steinstrasse into a "Little Harlem."[79] They also insisted that although something had to be done about black Americans, "the white Americans were still much welcomed."[80] Another inhabitant announced, "The decline in business is painful. We should have just thrown out the Negroes, not all Americans."[81] In a tongue-in-cheek manner one newspaper pointed out the population's obvious racism by suggesting that white Americans, unlike black Americans, were "guests and customers who observed standards of morality."[82]

Even the much more subdued coverage of the local press revealed who had been targeted and who was the "problem." The paper demanded from its readers that they treat "all guests with the same courtesy—no matter what their skin color may be—as long as these guests behave according to standards of common decency (*gesittete Menschen*). The essay included two photographs to illuminate what was considered proper and improper behavior for American GIs. The first picture showed a black soldier in the embrace of a white woman. The other picture showed three black soldiers who were sitting by themselves drinking beer. The paper suggested that it was no wonder that the "local population was tired of seeing the shameless next steps of the embracing couple" but reported that nobody minded when "dark-skinned young men peacefully drink their beer."[83] The sole discussion of black GIs' behavior in the *Pfälzische Volkszeitung* implies that white American soldiers did not need admonishments on how to behave as "*gesittete Menschen.*"

The author also used his essay to take a stab at American racism, when he suggested that black GIs were more prone to frequent Kaiserslautern establishments because they had few suitable entertainment opportunities available to them on the American military base. Black soldiers came to town because their white colleagues made them feel uncomfortable in the existing clubs on the American base. The article insisted that it was "the responsibility of the American military who had sent these black soldiers over here to make sure that these soldiers have equal opportunities in their leisure time."[84] The writer of these lines was clearly sympathetic to the black GIs, reminding the reader that black soldiers had "proved their kindness" on many occasions in the past. However, as the accompanying photos and the text reveal, black GIs venturing downtown would be tolerated only if they stayed with "their own kind" and stayed away from German women.

The city council meeting on how to extricate the city from the quagmire into which it had gotten itself over the off-limits order reveals that the whole affair over the Steinstrasse was blown completely out of proportion. In an unusually frank manner, a CDU council member suggested, "In this case we have overshot our goal," conceding that "measures were taken whose extent went beyond the necessary." A spokesman for the Wählergruppe Geiger, a member of the CDU and FDP governing coalition, agreed, saying, "This house as well as large parts of the population have no doubt that the well-intended efforts of the city were absolutely misguided." Many "level-headed people," he said, as well as he himself "were convinced that with a couple of extra streetlights" and sufficient police patrols, matters in the Steinstrasse could have been improved to the point where everybody would have been happy. Phenomena like the Steinstrasse, he reiterated, "did not appear just because of the Americans; they also exist where German soldiers are stationed. . . . Wherever there are soldiers, there will be prostitutes, and it is good that way; . . . otherwise the situation could be even graver." He concluded with the judgment, "I do not think that the situation in the Steinstrasse was so outrageous that we needed to have created such a to-do."[85]

The spokesperson of the Wählergruppe Geiger aimed most of his criticism at the actions of the SPD mayor, who was now blamed for the whole debacle. However, his comments also suggest that expressing resentment against black soldiers in particular had become a way in which Germans voiced their opposition to the American military presence in general. He suggested, "We need not be thankful to the Americans, but we should also not offend them. We have to live with them, and we have benefited from many advantages because of them, and probably will call on them for favors in the future." In an obvious stab at the mayor, he also reminded his colleagues that the city was not strong enough to be so cocky as to declare that they have lived just fine for 800 years without the Americans.[86]

But the comments from the spokesperson of the Wählergruppe Geiger also suggest that the city council members worried foremost that their actions exposed them to charges of anti-Semitism. He asked them whether they really wanted the lawyer who represented the bar owners "to raise a stink so that by tomorrow we can read in the newspapers of New York: 'Kaiserslautern, the center of anti-Semitism, Kaiserslautern, city of Nazism.'" With what can only be described as a certain degree of regret, he added, "We are not big and strong enough to be able to afford that." In light of Germany's genocidal murder of Europe's Jews and the country's need to overcome that legacy, the city council's sole concern seems to have been not to appear as anti-Semites in this affair.[87] Nothing in the meeting's minutes suggests that the city's leaders were concerned that their actions appeared racist toward the black soldiers. The complete incomprehension on the part of the city council regarding racism toward the black GIs suggests that the American military command, whose sole anxiety was over the Nike missile sites, had never made the city's racism an issue either.

Conclusion

The Steinstrasse affair, even more poignantly than the prostitution enforcement in Baumholder, makes clear that the behavior of white GIs and their relationships with German women had ceased to be an issue for most Germans. The demeanor of black GIs and their relationships with white women, however, were a whole other matter. The fact that even the SPD in a roundabout way had indicted these relationships to mobilize its electorate suggests just how widespread opposition to these relationships was. Not only were these relationships perceived to be highly offensive, the attention dedicated to them suggests that many Germans did not judge these relationships as private matters that concerned only those involved. On the contrary, these interracial couples were perceived as a public concern. Their existence not only threatened bourgeois respectability but also undermined national integrity.

The Steinstrasse affair also reveals a complex interaction of German racism and anti-Semitism. While the rejection of racism and anti-Semitism in all official pronouncements of the Federal Republic became a touchstone of the new democratic Germany, a much less self-conscious public discourse, as reflected in the press and the correspondence of lower-level political institutions, reveals the limits of conviction in this national agenda. Popular anti-Semitism (*volkstümlicher Antisemitismus*) was widespread during the 1950s and receded only by the end of the decade. Because the great majority of the bar owners in these garrison communities were Jews from Eastern Europe, few Germans even experienced guilt or shame for violating the Federal Republic's prescribed philosemitism.[88] Thus, almost everybody in Kaiserslautern could agree that the "stateless foreigners" had brought immorality to the *Heimat*. However, derogatory public statements aimed at Jews in general, and thus German Jews, evoked strong-worded admonishments that such prejudices were unfitting for the new democracy.

Expressing racism toward black Americans, on the other hand, seems to have been much less controversial by the second part of the decade. The Steinstrasse affair, then, reveals a complex story of how German racial attitudes evolved in the postwar years. Twelve years after the end of the war German attitudes toward black GIs were far less uniformly friendly than they had been in 1945, when black soldiers had handed out Hershey bars and Lucky Strikes.[89] Germany's improving economic situation probably contributed to this shift. While most Germans did not yet live in a land of riches in the 1950s, they also no longer were dependent on black soldiers' rations. A 1957 *U.S. News and World Report* article commented on this shift, when it concluded that the economic situation in Germany had improved substantially and that this improvement had led to a lower level of tolerance toward black GIs.[90]

However, the improving economic situation was not the only or even the most important factor behind the increasingly hardening attitudes toward blacks. As relations in the postwar period normalized and Germans were again viewed as allies rather than a defeated, hostile people, Germans seemed no longer to identify their own fate of subjugation with that of blacks in America. Instead, the tendency to identify only *black* GIs with all the problems of the "continuing occupation" suggests that Germans envisioned their alliance with America foremost as an alliance between two white nations. For much of the 1950s, they were assured in that conviction by observing the deep gulf separating white and black American military personnel as well as the institutionalized aspects of American racism. The national press coverage of the Steinstrasse affair makes clear that wide segments of the German population shared the belief that black GIs somehow were not "true" Americans and thus could be attacked as the main source of immorality, which became synonymous with the "continuing American occupation."

Conclusion

In the garrison communities of Rhineland-Palatinate, the end of the Cold War did not bring about shouts of cheer but cries of despair. The Americans had been one of the biggest employers in the state and their absence, even ten years after the dramatic reduction of U.S. military strength in Europe is still felt in many communities. Those who in the past had occasionally complained about the hardships entailed in living with such a large and foreign military presence now insist nostalgically that the Americans really never were such a burden. In an ironic twist of fate, many of the vacated American military bases in Germany now house tens of thousands of *Aussiedler,* the ethnic Germans who began arriving from the Soviet Union after the collapse of communism. The presence of these "Russians," as the local Germans call them, evokes some of the same sort of anxieties and complaints that the American soldiers had brought about in the early 1950s. Germans grumble about the increase in crime and violence and the sexual threat the "Russians" pose to local women. They also bemoan the high cost of maintaining their new neighbors. However, the encounter with the *Aussiedler* in the 1990s differs in one important way from that with the Americans in the 1950s. The *Aussiedler* cannot balance any of the negative perceptions Germans have of them with the sense of wonder and fascination that the Americans evoked some fifty years ago. To most Germans, their ethnic brethren are more foreign than the Americans ever were, and plenty of locals wished they had their "Amis" back again. Baumholder and Kaiserslautern, at least for now, count themselves among the lucky communities. While experiencing extensive reductions in troop strength, they are still home to tens of thousands of American soldiers and their families.

For the historian studying the encounter of Germans with the American military in Rhineland-Palatinate, the 1950s are in many ways the most exciting decade. To Germans emerging from Nazism, the Americans and the American way of life that they brought to the provinces offered a tremendous sense of excitement. Because of the harshness of the French military occupation, a desperately poor population eagerly embraced the prosperity and opportunities that the American military deployment engendered. For most people in Baumholder and Kaiserslautern, the beginning of their recovery was not the 1948 currency reform but rather the "Korea Boom." Moreover, the 1950s are a unique decade because of the unprecedented degree of contact between Germans and Americans. The shortage of housing and leisure facilities on the American bases ensured that Americans eagerly turned to their German host communities. The strong dollar assured that Americans were well-liked customers in local stores and restaurants and much sought-after tenants for the new home-owners in town.

The Vietnam War disillusioned many in the younger generation who had formerly admired the Americans, but it did not lead to any sort of widespread anti-Americanism in the garrison communities. The more crucial caesura for German-American relations in these communities was the Nixon administration's decision during the early 1970s to uncouple the dollar from the gold standard. As a consequence of that policy, American GIs and their families could no longer afford Germany and started to rely almost exclusively on the goods and services that the American Post Exchange offered at subsidized prices. Local mayors implored the population to take account of the hardship faced by American military families and to lower rents for their apartments. Many took pity and complied, but the withdrawal of Americans behind the safe walls of their "Little Americas" could not be stopped. As the 1970s progressed, fewer and fewer Americans could be sighted in German communities, and Germans were stunned to learn that lower-rank soldiers and their families had to rely on food stamps when shopping for groceries. Most of the bars and clubs that had caused such outrage during the 1950s were forced to close their doors. In Baumholder, a good number of them have been converted into storefront churches for African American evangelical congregations.

The rash of terrorist attacks by the Baader-Meinhof group on American military installations during the late 1970s and the emergence of a reinvigorated German peace movement over the deployment of Pershing missiles during the early 1980s only increased the trend of the American military to withdraw from German host communities. Military communities that had been open and porous, allowing an easy flow between the American and German communities took on the appearance of heavily fortified fortresses. Beginning with the Gulf War in 1991, American fear over fundamentalist terrorism only increased that siege mentality.

Occasionally, the chasm that separates the German and American communities can still be overcome. During the Gulf War, for example, garrison towns throughout Germany stood by their American soldiers as the rest of Germany chanted, "No Blood for Oil." When American soldiers, both male and female, were sent to fight in Desert Storm, local communities offered their support. In Baumholder, the mayor sponsored a Christmas party for 120 family members, and the city sent Christmas greetings to 300 American soldiers serving in the Gulf. Individuals in Baumholder adopted American children while their fathers or mothers or sometimes both were sent off to serve in the war. Local taxi companies provided free rides to make sure that young mothers without cars could get to stores and doctor appointments. Restaurants offered free meals, florists sent bouquets to the military families left behind, and stores arranged for gift baskets to ease some of the pain. That same sort of outpouring transpired when American soldiers were deployed from German communities to serve as peacekeepers in Bosnia. Germans were finally able to return the generosity that so many had experienced during the 1950s.[1]

Still, the intimacy of the 1950s is long gone. While American GIs and their dependents continue to be seen about Baumholder and Kaiserslautern, they are no longer an economic force to be reckoned with. They are also no longer a source of wonderment. Germans now have access to the same sort of comfort and luxury that during the 1950s seemed like a distant utopia. If anything, the Americans now envy the Germans for their shiny and expensive Mercedes, Audis, and BMWs.

The ever-widening gulf between Germans and Americans, however, cannot be explained solely in economic terms. The composition of the American military also exacerbates that trend. During the 1950s and 1960s American soldiers were drawn from all classes of society, allowing different strata in German society to interact with their own social peers. These soldiers served their tour of duty because they were drafted, often against their will. Consequently, many of these soldiers took advantage of any opportunity to escape army life. Today's professional and all-volunteer army is diverse in different ways; it includes a much higher percentage of people of color but also a large number of women. However, their ethos as professional soldiers commits them in a very different way to the American military base. For these soldiers, their tour of duty in Germany is just another professional assignment during their long military career. Serving in Baumholder or Kaiserslautern is no different from being on a military base in America, Korea, or Japan. Since women and men serve side by side in the volunteer military, there is also no longer any need to venture outside the military compound for leisure activities and companionship. It is a combination of all these factors that has reduced the rich contacts during the 1950s to the formalized rituals between local dignitaries and base commanders of today.

Americanization, Westernization, or Modernization?

Trying to assess the impact of the close living together of these two cultures over the course of more than fifty years is not an easy undertaking. As Michael Ermarth reminds us in his study on the American impact on West German society, "the domain of 'culture,' for all its incontestable importance in bestowing a sense of collective identity and meaning, ultimately proves a rather nebulous area from which to draw firm conclusions about the lasting shape of historical influence."[2] However, if we keep the focus of this inquiry on the 1950s, the German-American encounter provides fascinating insights into how Germans experienced the transformation of their lives during this crucial decade.

For many young Germans in the garrison communities, just as the military had hoped, the American soldiers were not just members of the "occupation force"; they were ambassadors of a different world. Dancing to rock and roll, drinking Coca-Cola, and dressing the American way meant more to young people than merely rebelling against the cultural tastes of their parents. Much like teenagers all across Germany, the local young craved American styles as a way to distance themselves from the world of their parents and the Nazi past they associated with that world. Unlike most other Germans, who knew of the "American way of life" only through movies, popular music, or teen magazines like *Bravo,* teenagers in Rhineland-Palatinate observed the soldiers and their American ways in their own backyards. The American soldiers and their families literally carried the markers of that better and easier life on their bodies. This daily exposure to the consumer goods of the Americans and the much admired American casualness (*Lässigkeit*) allowed the young to imagine their own utopia of America, a dream of a better and easier life as well as a different experience of freedom.[3] One man expressed the sentiments of many of his generation when he reminisced, "One saw in the GIs a symbol of a country with a way of life one did not know of, but longed for so dearly."[4]

The infatuation of the younger generation with the American way of life holds a prominent place in Germans' recollections of the 1950s. This embrace of the American style is of course not simply a post–World War II phenomenon; it also defined much of the reaction of Germany's younger generation to American cultural imports during the years of the Weimar Republic. During that period the infatuation with American movies, jazz, and the cool and relaxed American style, however, was limited mostly to the cosmopolitan centers and middle-class youth, while rural society and the working class remained largely untouched by it. After World War II, America's political and economic dominance in Europe, as well as its extensive military presence, made American products and styles accessible to a much larger audience.[5]

It is probably safe to conclude that for the younger generation, accepting the Americans and their way of life was easier than for many older people. American soldiers who were stationed in these communities generally noted that older people were more reserved toward them than the young.[6] Germans who were teenagers during the 1950s are almost wholly convinced that their life is very different as a result of the American military presence. "One started dressing in the style that the Americans brought with them . . . that only started then with the jeans . . . all of the teenagers looked like Elvis or some other rock idol. . . . Of course, Americanization came with that."[7] One woman's observations on the American impact confirmed Kaspar Maase's findings of how the grassroots Americanization of German life was carried out by teenagers but nonetheless impacted the world of their elders: "The young adapted to the American style. Much was taken over from the Americans, the way we live, cook, always being on the run, . . . clothing styles as well, the young generation is more casual—that was then taken over [by us]."[8]

Members of the educated upper classes (*Kulturbürger*) who were interviewed for this project were most resistant to agreeing that the American military had had any sort of influence on their lives during the 1950s. Just as in the rest of Germany, upper-class Germans preferred French cinema to American movies, so the *Kulturbürger* in these communities tended to see in the former French occupation a much more desirable cultural model to emulate.[9] For the most part, the representatives of the educated élite in these communities attended the obligatory receptions with the American military and perhaps even served on the boards of the German-American friendship clubs. However, they did not embrace the Americans and their relaxed style as wholeheartedly as did the younger generation. The German *Kulturbürger* rejected much of the American way of life for its brashness and lack of "culture."

It is probably not that surprising a conclusion that the young embraced most things American and that Germany's *Kulturbürger* rejected it. But what about the rest of German society in these garrison communities? How did members of the German *Mittelstand* and people who were well beyond their teenage years respond to the Americans and their foreign ways? Any such inquiry must consider that German views on America are not as straightforward as my juxtaposition of teenagers versus *Kulturbürger* suggests. Within one person, great admiration of the American style could coexist with a rejection of America's social order or its foreign policy agenda. In just the same way, during the 1950s the most committed supporters of America's political agenda were usually also the most vocal critics of American social and cultural values. People interviewed for this project also acknowledged the problem of differentiating the impact of the U.S. military presence from the larger process of Americanization brought about by America's economic and cultural infiltration of West German society since 1945.

The German-American encounter, then, provides a forceful and much needed reminder that most people do not experience their lives according to the tidy but artificial categories historians like to impose. Nonetheless, by listening to the many different players in this extraordinary cultural encounter, one sees clear signs that Germans experienced the 1950s not merely as a process of modernization or Westernization but specifically as a process of Americanization.

The resistance that German conservatives activated to contain the social and cultural modernization that the Americans brought to the provinces makes it clear that Germany's transformation during the 1950s was hardly the inevitable consequence of a process of modernization that all Western industrial societies undergo. When the young and lower-class Germans in Rhineland-Palatinate embraced the "modernity" that the American-induced economic boom entailed, they did so against the resolute opposition of German conservatives. In light of their experience with Nazism, German conservatives had come around to supporting the reform of Germany's authoritarian political structures. However, as their response to the American presence reveals, for much of the decade they remained leery of the social and cultural implications of Germany's new consumer democracy.

Conservative attitudes toward consumer democracy changed only after 1957, when politicians who supported Ludwig Erhard's economic policies replaced the clerical conservatives in Adenauer's government. In light of West Germany's precarious position in the Cold War, those modern conservatives toned down their traditional resistance to consumer capitalism and American popular culture. Lest we forget, this modernization of German conservatism was possible largely because West Germany's cultural and political élites could hardly afford to malign American-style consumption and popular culture while at the same time calling for American political and military leadership in the Cold War struggle against communism. Just as importantly, conservatives revised their attitudes toward consumption because West German prosperity and consumption became the key weapons in exposing the deficiencies of the East German counter-model.

Since the French remained the official occupation power in the state even after the American forces returned in 1950, the garrison communities also have much to say about the limits of the Westernization school. Westernization scholars have focused their research on the important roles that Germany's political élites played in accomplishing the successful democratization of German society after 1945. After the horror of Nazism, conservative Germans like Konrad Adenauer and Peter Altmeier pushed for the postwar rapprochement of German political élites with the Western liberal tradition, but especially with France. By drawing on the language of the Christian *Abendland,* conservative "Westernizers" were able to pull reluctant democrats into a common struggle against communism. The Westernization scholars do not ignore America's pivotal role after 1945, since they consider America an integral part of the Western liberal tradition. Still, their narrative de-emphasizes the extent to which German élites drew on the American model when they debated democracy and liberalism. In their reading of the 1950s, the democratization of German society was not the result of any specific American policies but came about because West Germany's political and cultural élites embraced the liberal and democratic values of the West and passed this learning process down to society at large.[10]

Because of its focus on élites, the Westernization school precludes insights into how "common" Germans grew into their new democracy and the country's political and military alliance with the West. The Westernization model also ignores the fact that for much of the decade, as we have seen, German political and cultural élites were deeply suspicious of the freedom and social mobility that the Western liberal tradition entailed. I suggest that for most Germans in the garrison communities abstract references to the Western liberal tradition were not the determining factor in their gradual acceptance of the values inherent in their new democracy. Germans, just as the Americans had hoped, grew into the Western political and military alliance through their daily encounters and interactions with America in their own backyard. At a time when all Germans had to envision a new place for themselves in the community of nations, Germans in these garrison communities had a tremendous advantage. They saw the Western military and political alliance that the Christian Democratic Adenauer government endorsed as Germany's best hope for political rehabilitation enacted every day before their eyes.[11] By 1956, German, American, and French soldiers trained and worked together in all of these garrison communities, and the images of this cooperation were projected across the Federal Republic. Imagining themselves as part of the Western military and political alliance was not an abstract concept but a lived reality for the people in Rhineland-Palatinate.

However, and this point cannot be stressed strongly enough, because of the overwhelming predominance and preeminence of the American military forces, Germans experienced their alliance with the West foremost as an alliance with the United States. Furthermore, in the day-to-day encounter with the American way of life many Germans came to believe that this way of life was also within their reach. They came to that understanding because the newspapers at that time were full of awed descriptions of the luxurious interiors of American housing on the bases and of the easy life of the American hausfrau.[12] The American *Straßenkreuzer* that clogged the streets of every little town were the envy of all those still driving a Goggomobil or a moped. Germans were fully aware that the favorable exchange rate of the dollar was responsible for much of the American wealth, yet they also observed that this higher standard of living was accessible to the "common soldier" and not just to high-ranking officers or Hollywood movie stars. The relative ease with which even the lowliest corporal maneuvered his 1957 Chevy through the narrow streets of town convinced many Germans that owning such a car should not be the preserve of just the upper class.

For the people in Rhineland-Palatinate, especially during the crucial founding decade of the 1950s, the "West" that the Christian Democratic Adenauer government and the American military endorsed was not Europe but the United States. In 1954, when Germans were asked if they preferred a good cooperation with either France or the United States, 69 percent chose the Americans as their preferred partner. Only 17 percent chose France. In light of the deep-seated animosity toward the French in the border regions, those numbers were probably tilted even more favorably toward the United States in Rhineland-Palatinate. While West Germany's political and cultural élites may have looked to France for inspiration, most Germans in these communities kept their distance from the traditional "archenemy" until well into the 1960s. The overwhelming approval that the Germans accorded their American allies in the late 1950s, France could garner only a decade later.[13]

Although the French remained the official occupation power in Rhineland-Palatinate until the return of German sovereignty in 1955, the contemporary record makes clear that France was never truly a point of reference. None of the newspaper coverage of that time ever bothered to report on how the French lived or worked. When reference was made to the French during the 1950s, it was usually to point out how poor and wretched their lives were compared to those of the rich American GIs. The impact of the French was minimal, according to one observer, because they "were as poor as we."[14]

While the American military made a big effort to convince Germans of the American mission and of the superiority of the American way of life, I do not want to suggest that Germans unquestioningly accepted all things American. Germans in the garrison communities were not just acted upon; as we have seen in Chapter 2, they came to this encounter with their own cultural preferences and chose carefully from the offerings that the Americans made available to them. Thus, even as the German homes of the 1990s displayed all the American appliances that had evoked such wonder in the 1950s and the man of the house greeted the IANAS interviewers dressed in his comfortable blue jeans, his wife could still insist that her lace curtains and flower boxes were very German indeed.

Rather than investigating how top-down American military initiatives may have Americanized German society, my line of inquiry has focused instead on exploring what aspects of the American model Germans embraced and why they choose to do so. Most importantly, Germans in these communities admired the American model for holding much greater promise of prosperity and social mobility than the French model could offer. Motioning to his very comfortable living room, one man said: "This we owe to them [the Americans], this American way of life. . . . I never dreamed that I would someday own a car. . . . [Without the Americans,] things here would be like in the GDR."[15] Another observer made the connection between consumer goods and democracy even more strongly when he stated that trust in democracy grew "not through a desire for personal freedom" but through observing the high living standards of the Americans.[16] Germans were attracted to the American model, then, because they recognized in the American soldiers and their families the promise of an easier and better life, one that most Germans did not yet possess, but yearned for dearly.

Germans' reflections on the transformation of their lives in the 1950s also suggest that German admiration of things American went deeper than an infatuation with American products, such blue jeans, rock and roll, and hamburgers. The 1950s also gave many Germans a different experience of freedom and exposure to less rigid class and gender hierarchies. For much of the decade, German conservatives, as we have seen, had complained ad nauseum about these "unpleasant" side effects of the American troop presence. However, for many Germans looking back on the 1950s, it was precisely those aspects of Americanization that they found most enticing. The biggest distinctions Germans saw between the modernization boost of the Westwall and that of the Korea Boom was the simple fact that the 1950s were experienced not under a totalitarian dictatorship but in a democracy. Germans did not just modernize in the 1950s; through their daily encounters with the Americans, they were also exposed to different ways of comprehending the world and engaging with it. The Americans were attractive, then, because they introduced the population to greater ease in interpersonal relationships, a more relaxed way of being, and less authoritarian relationships. Because of the extensive American presence, Germans were able to not only observe but also experience this different civil habitus on a daily basis. It was these more ephemeral qualities, "not just the American consumer goods," that convinced many Germans that the Americans had brought the "flair of the big wide world" (*Duft der grossen weiten Welt*) to even the smallest village.[17]

The Adenauer Years, Sexuality, and German Debates on Difference

Studying the German-American encounter also makes it possible to assess the transformation of sexual mores during the 1950s and reveals how that transformation was negotiated around racial issues. As we have seen, German conservatives, but especially the clergy and workers in the church-affiliated welfare organizations struggled for much of the decade to protect the population from the American way of life, from the explosion of the entertainment industry, and from the German women who eagerly sought out the American GIs. Their anxious reports to state and federal governments confirm Dagmar Herzog's contention that the early 1950s was hardly a time of conservative consensus about sexual morality; indeed, they were a period of considerable flux and openness of sexual mores.[18] The conservative crackdown on society that produced the repressive sexual atmosphere we generally associate with the 1950s began in earnest only in 1952–53. Only then did conservatives fully realize that the defeat of Nazism and the end of the postwar years had not halted the greater sexual tolerance they had been hoping to rein in ever since the end of World War I. The encounter with National Socialism, however, had significantly changed the motivations behind conservatives' obsession with sexual sobriety. During the Weimar Republic, conservatives used the alleged increase in sexual immorality after World War I as a key argument to *challenge* the merits of democracy. After 1945, these same conservatives insisted on sexual sobriety with the aim of *protecting* their fragile new democracy in the Cold War struggle against the Soviet Union. Because clerical conservatives dominated the social and cultural agenda in the federal and state governments, their emphasis on sexual indecency as the country's most pressing moral crisis seemed to triumph until the later part of the decade.

The widespread opposition to conservative efforts to enforce sexual decency—if need be, through police action and judicial prosecution—reveals that the moral rearmament of German society was only one aspect of the 1950s. Although conservatives blamed the American-induced prosperity and the population's infatuation with the American way of life as the primary reasons behind the failure of their project, the records also indicate that most Germans—after the experience of National Socialism—rejected the role of the state in issuing directives regarding their private lives. Still others found the moral severity incompatible with their new democracy and also questioned the authority of the churches in sexual matters.

However, this greater tolerance in sexual matters was, again, only one aspect of a complex process of social and cultural transformation taking place during the 1950s. Despite the more relaxed attitude of citizens toward premarital sexuality, the municipal authorities in garrison communities relied extensively on the police and courts to enforce the rigid sexual norms being dictated to them by state and federal offices. Such efforts were especially pronounced during the most repressive phase of the 1950s, the years between 1953 and 1958. Significantly, the conservative agenda to enforce sexual sobriety did not affect all strata of society equally. For the most part, vice raids to uncover prostitution and procurement took place in the more marginal neighborhoods of town. Just as importantly, by the mid-1950s almost all police efforts focused on those bars and clubs where African American GIs and German women associated.

The garrison towns also offer a unique window on the transformation of German racism after 1945, because the American troop deployment in Rhineland-Palatinate confronted Germans with two "racial others"—

blacks and Jews. At the local level, the Federal Republic's official rejection of both racism and anti-Semitism coexisted with widespread and often public expressions of prejudice. The most startling examples of this racism and anti-Semitism can be found in the widely disseminated coverage in West Germany's tabloid press of the alleged sexual excesses that black GIs perpetrated in the "dens of vice" that Eastern European Jews made available to them. Still, the public debates surrounding the vice that Jewish bar owners and the black GIs had allegedly inflicted on the *Heimat* reveal an important shift in attitudes. As the decade progressed, it became ever less acceptable to publicly indict the Jewish owners of the amusement establishments that catered to the GIs. The Federal Republic's prescribed philosemitism prohibited such public condemnation. However, the black GIs and the German women who associated with them did not benefit from the Federal Republic's prescribed racial tolerance. On the contrary, the discourse on interracial sexuality in the publications of the national tabloid press became increasingly intolerant, especially after Germany achieved sovereignty in 1955.

By redirecting our exploration of the Adenauer years away from the realm of high politics and economics and toward the realities of gender history and the more mundane aspects of private life, we can discern serious flaws in the triumphant models of West Germany's so-called "Westernization" or "Americanization." Theorists in both these schools ignore the fact that the Western liberal tradition "as shared by both Europe and the United States" is "raced" and gendered, excluding women, nonwhites, and ethnic minorities from full participation.[19] In light of the long tradition of Western European racism, it should come as no surprise that Germans after 1945 continued to envision the West as being composed of white people. Just the same, the daily interaction with the widespread and institutionalized racism of their American mentors assured many a German that their alliance with America was indeed foremost an alliance between two white nations.

This book is a first effort to explore the complicated manner in which the German encounter with the American military might have Americanized traditional assumptions about race. Lest we forget, the German renegotiation of sexual mores around racial issues was possible largely because of a complex interaction between German and American attitudes toward interracial sexuality. After all, it was the combined efforts of German *and* American police personnel that defined the enforcement of the prostitution laws in these communities. A 1957 *U.S. News and World Report* article suggests that a reassessment of our understanding of Americanization might indeed be called for in light of the ubiquitous U.S. military presence in the Western world throughout the Cold War. The article commented on the declining number of applications for marriage between black GIs and German women and suggested that West Germany's economic improvement might have been contributing to this shift. However, the author speculated that more was at work, when, with a certain degree of satisfaction and without considering the implications of that comment, he concluded that "social customs have changed sufficiently to discourage German girls from marrying Negroes."[20]

Germany, which during the 1950s was the top choice for a tour of duty for African American GIs, became one of the least desired assignments by the late 1960s. To understand that dramatic shift, future research will need to explore the interaction of German and American racism beyond the 1950s. More research on how German notions of race shifted during this crucial period may also yield insights into a more comprehensive understanding of German xenophobia toward Turkish guest workers and other foreigners. In his thought-provoking introduction to *West Germany under Construction*, Robert Moeller suggests that future research on German racism might have to consider how the Cold War's prevalent anti-Soviet rhetoric easily merged with Germany's traditional anti-Slav sentiments, allowing pre-1945 racial hierarchies to survive in the Federal Republic.[21] Such an exploration is surely needed, but we must also acknowledge that German racism after 1945 was about more than engaging with a distant "other" Slav or an imaginary non-Christian East. Future work may have to consider how the debates around black GIs during the 1950s functioned as a sort of bridge to the racist discourse on the guest workers who came to the Federal Republic in the 1960s. Comments from the welfare workers presented in Chapter 6 suggest that their institutions, at least, had little problem shifting their emphasis from worrying about the presence of American GIs, especially black GIs, to worrying about the newly arrived guest workers (*Gastarbeiter*).

Notes

Introduction

1 BAK, Verhandlungen des Deutschen Bundestages, 232d Sitzung, 2 October 1952, 10663; and ibid., 259th Sitzung, 15 April 1953. See also *RZ*, 1 September 1953, "Sondermassnahmen für besatzungsgefährdete Jugendliche auf dem Kasernenhof der Bundesrepublik."

2 For assessments of the 1950s as a process of modernization, see the research of the Hamburg School, centered around Arnold Sywotteck and Axel Schildt, especially the essays in their edited collection, Schildt and Sywotteck, *Modernisierung im Wiederaufbau*. For a sophisticated analysis of the dark side of modernity during the Weimar Republic and Nazi Germany, see the works of Peukert: *Grenzen der Sozialdisziplinierung*, *Weimar Republic*, and *Inside Nazi Germany*.

3 For the Westernization school, see the writings of the Tübingen School, centered around Doering-Manteuffel, especially his own *Wie Westlich sind die Deutschen?*, "Deutsche Zeitgeschichte nach 1945," and "Dimensionen von Amerikanisierung." For scholars who stress Americanization, see Berghahn, *Americanization of West German Industry*, "Resisting the Pax Americana?," and "Philanthropy and Diplomacy"; and Rupieper, *Die Wurzeln* and *Der besetzte Verbündete*. Maase, *Bravo Amerika*, stresses the phenomenon of grassroots Americanization as young working-class males embraced American popular culture to set themselves apart from their parents' past. Poiger, *Jazz, Rock, and Rebels*, expands Maase's work by including a discussion of how female teenagers embraced American styles. Wagnleitner, *Coca-Colonization*, provides a fascinating example of the ambivalence of the European-American encounter. Fehrenbach and Poiger, *Transactions*, provides nuanced essays of the negotiation involved in the encounter of America with other indigenous traditions. On this process of negotiation or "creolization," see the important contributions by Kroes, especially his *If You've Seen One, You've Seen the Mall* and his edited collection, *Cultural Transmissions*.

4 IANAS, Letter from U.S. Embassy providing information for "Veranstaltungsreihe Die Pfälzer und Amerika—Ein Landkreis erinnert sich," which states that, according to the U.S. Information Service, approximately 15 million Americans have lived in Germany since 1945, the great majority of them military personnel.

5 For histories of the years of the U.S. military government, see, e.g., Zink, *United States in Germany*; Peterson, *American Occupation*; Davidson, *Death and Life of Germany*; Gimbel, *A German Community* and *American Occupation*; Woller, *Gesellschaft und Politik*, on the region of Fürth and Ansbach; Boehling, *A Question of Priorities*, for her depiction of policies in Munich, Stuttgart, and Frankfurt; Henke, *Die amerikanische Besetzung*; Pronay and Wilson, *Political Reeducation of Germany*; and Browder, "Impact of the American Presence" and *Americans in Post–World War II*. Becker and Burdack, *Amerikaner in Bamberg*, and D. Nelson, *Defenders or Intruders?* both ignore the social and cultural aspects of the American presence. Seiler, *Die*

GIs, provides a sociological study of how Americans GIs experienced their lives in Germany during the 1970s and 1980s.

6 See, e.g., Duignan and Gann, *Rebirth of the West;* Berghahn, *Americaniza- tion of West German Industry* and "Resisting the Pax Americana?"; Rupieper, *Die Wurzeln* and *Der besetzte Verbündete.*

7 For a discussion of the importance of these two military bases, see the tele- vision program "Vom Freund Umzingelt: Deutsch-Amerikanische Träume in der Pfalz," produced by ZDF (Zweites Deutsches Fernsehen), which aired on 8 August 1995.

8 The IANAS project Nachbar Amerika, which aims to explore all aspects of the five-decade-long American military presence in the state, was sponsored by the Staatskanzlei of Rhineland-Palatinate. Although the project explores the long-term implications of this presence, the focus so far has been on the 1950s, when the two cultures lived together most closely but were separated most dramatically by a wide gulf of differing values and ways of life. As part of the project, responses to and commentaries on the American GIs and their families were gathered from regional newspapers and national publica- tions and from television and radio. See the Bibliography for a more detailed description of individuals interviewed for this project.

9 For an overview of German anti-Americanism, see Hollander, *Anti-Ameri- canism,* 367–410; and Diner, *America in the Eyes.* For critical treatises on the American presence that came with the rise of the German peace movement during the 1980s, see Anhäuser, *Militär-Heimat Hunsrück;* Spoo, *Die Ame- rikaner in der Bundesrepublik;* and Stange, *Kriegsvorbereitung im Hunsrück.*

10 On the national level, German-American relations during the 1950s are also often referred to as the Golden Fifties. See Schwarz, *Die Ära Adenauer,* 427– 28; and D. Nelson, *Defenders or Intruders?* 51–61.

11 In 1933, the churches had celebrated the Nazis as overcoming the secular materialism of the "god-less" Weimar Republic. After 1945, the churches managed a complete turnaround when they interpreted the Nazis as the latest incarnation of secular materialism. See especially Vollnhals, "Die evan- gelische Kirche," 148–49. For a fascinating discussion of CDU debates on "*Materialismus*" and the *Abendland,* see Mitchell, "Materialism and Secu- larism" and "Christian Democracy"; see also Schildt, *Zwischen Abendland und Amerika.* For Christian Democratic apprehensions about the emerging consumer society during the first half of the 1950s, see Poiger, *Jazz, Rock, and Rebels;* and Fehrenbach, "Fight for the 'Christian West'" and *Cinema in Democratizing Germany.*

12 See Moeller, *Protecting Motherhood,* "Protecting Mothers' Work," and "Re- constructing the German Family"; Heineman, *What Difference* and "Hour of the Woman"; Fehrenbach, *Cinema* and "Fight for the 'Christian West'"; Höhn, "Frau im Haus."

13 Moeller, *Protecting Motherhood.* Moeller shows that the CDU was not alone in its insistence that the family was women's natural realm. The SPD and FDP (Free Democrats) equally shared that belief, however they also insisted on greater equality for women in the marriage and in the workplace.

14 For Weimar debates on America, see Kaes, Jay, and Dimendberg, *Weimar Republic Sourcebook,* 393–411; Willett, *New Sobriety;* Nolan, *Visions of Modernity;* Costigliola, *Awkward Dominion;* Lüdtke, Marßolek, and von Saldern, *Amerikanisierung.* For a good historical overview of German views on America, see Maase, *Bravo Amerika,* 41–62; Wagnleitner, *Coca-Colonization,* 9–36; Nolan, "America in the German Imagination"; Michael Ermarth, "Introduction," in Ermarth, *America and the Shaping of German Society,* 1–22.

15 For a wonderful discussion of the churches' role as arbiters of good and evil and how they reduced all moral questions to matters of sexuality, see D. Herzog, "'Pleasure, Sex, and Politics,'" 410–15.

16 See Poiger, *Jazz, Rock, and Rebels;* Fehrenbach, "Rehabilitating Fatherland" and "Of German Mothers and *'Negermischlinge.'*"

17 Fehrenbach, in "Rehabilitating Fatherland" and "Of German Mothers and *'Negermischlinge,'*" shows this shift by exploring the debates on the children born of German mothers and African American fathers

18 So far, very little is known of the experience of African American soldiers in Germany after World War II. For a contemporary novel written by an African American soldier, see Gardner Smith, *Last of the Conquerors.* For scholarship that treats some aspects of that experience during the years of occupation, see Kleinschmidt, *"Do not fraternize";* and Schmundt-Thomas, "America's Germany." In addition, Little, "Black Military Experience in Germany," has a very short discussion, and Posner, "Afro-America," has a chapter on German responses to African American GIs. Rainer-Maria Fassbinder's 1979 film *The Marriage of Maria Braun* is probably the best-known dramatization of the relationship between a white German woman and a black GI after World War II.

19 Powell, *My American Journey,* 53.

Chapter One

1 Historical Division, "American Military Occupation."

2 For an extensive discussion on the shift in American policy in light of the escalating Cold War, see T. A. Schwartz, *America's Germany;* Rupieper, *Die Wurzeln;* Historical Division, "Exchange of Troops," 1.

3 Küppers, "Rheinland-Pfalz," 164–87.

4 Herbert, "Good Times, Bad Times," argues that Germans viewed the economic miracle of the 1950s as a continuation of the economic improvements during the Nazi Regime in the late 1930s.

5 Heyen, *Geschichte des Landes Rheinland-Pfalz,* 155. See also Berichte, 1951–63, "Informationsbesuch Bundestagsabgeordnete Frau Seppi, Neuwied, 6 September 1963." There are three folders of reports and correspondence on the special problem that Baumholder posed for the county of Birkenfeld, each corresponding to one of three date ranges: 1951–63, 1951–73, or 1951–85. These reports, entitled as a whole "Berichte aus Baumholder" are a tremen-

dously rich source, and I have drawn on them extensively. They are not yet sorted and are kept at the youth agency of the Kreisverwaltung Birkenfeld. Thanks to the very helpful Karl Löffler, director of the youth agency, photocopies of all these reports are in my possession. Citations of sources from the Berichte include the date range of the folder in which it was found, the document title, and page number(s). See note 6 as an example.

6 Berichte, 1951–63, "Informationsbesuch Bundestagsabgeordnete Frau Seppi," 9.

7 See Barkin, "Modern Germany"; and the special issue of *New German Critique* (Vol. 36, Fall 1985) devoted to the TV series *Heimat,* which aired in the United States in 1985 on PBS.

8 Noß, "Parteien im Nachkriegsdeutschland," 3.

9 Heyen, *Nationalsozialismus im Alltag,* 76.

10 Brommer, *Dokumente der Geschichte,* 96. For voting patterns during the Weimar Republic, see Childers, *Nazi Voter.*

11 Herr Weber from the Stadtverwaltung Baumholder generously shared election lists from his own research, which show minuscule voting for the NSDAP in Catholic villages.

12 Nestler and Ziegler, *Die Pfalz unterm Hakenkreuz,* 123.

13 Noß, "Parteien," 3. Birkenfeld, though located in the Prussian Rhineland, was part of Oldenburg and had a National Socialist government by May of 1932.

14 Pyta, "Ländlich-evangelisches Milieu," 204.

15 Möhler, *Entnazifizierung in Rheinland-Pfalz,* 209.

16 Licht interview.

17 On the lack of industrialization in this region during the Third Reich, see Scharf and Schröder, *Die Deutschlandpolitik Frankreichs,* 125.

18 For a description of these projects, see Heyl, "Construction of the Westwall," 63–78.

19 Keddigkeit, "Bollwerk im Westen," 458.

20 Reitz's 1983 TV epic *Heimat* is a wonderful depiction of just how profoundly daily life in the village was affected by the rearmament projects of the regime.

21 Heyl, "Construction of the Westwall," 76 (Hitler quote), 69 (SD reports).

22 For a history of the Baumholder *Truppenübungsplatz,* see *Chronik des gemeindefreien Bezirks.*

23 Bürgermeisteramt Baumholder, *Chronik der Gemeinde Mambächel,* 2.

24 Karsch and Grimm, *Baumholder,* 89.

25 Schramm and Wisseroth, "Alltag im Nationalsozialismus." For a study of the Nazi impact on a village in neighboring Baden, see Rinderle and Norling, *Nazi Impact;* on the Palatinate, see Nestler and Ziegler, *Die Pfalz unterm Hakenkreuz.* For Northern Germany, see Allen, *Nazi Seizure of Power.*

26 Mais, *Die Verfolgung der Juden,* 292–95.

27 Erker, "Revolution des Dorfes?"

28 Winkler interview.

29 Erker, "Revolution des Dorfes?"

30 Mais, *Ende und Anfang,* 202. For the impact of the Third Reich on the Christian churches, see Blessing, "'Deutschland in Not'"; and Vollnhals, "Die evangelische Kirche." For complaints on the negative impact of the Nazi regime on religiosity, see KdP, Pfarrämter Jahresberichte, Kaiserslautern 1957–58.

31 For a discussion of how disruptive the Third Reich's policies were to social structures in the Palatinate, see Applegate, *Nation of Provincials,* 214–25. Beginning in 1936, constant troop movements and maneuvers took place in the region. With the beginning of the war in 1939, sections of the population were evacuated to regions east of the Rhine. When they returned in 1940, they often found rotting crops and dismantled industrial plants. Whole factories had been shipped east of the Rhine, away from the French border. Especially hard on the people in the Palatinate were the village renewal programs. Whole villages were relocated into the newly conquered Lorraine. But Applegate also points out how the Nazis' development of the region as a tourist attraction before 1939 had initiated a tremendous modernizing boost.

32 Blessing, "'Deutschland in Not,'" 56.

33 Erker, "Revolution des Dorfes?" 379; Stephenson, "Triangle." Stephenson argues that the treatment of slave labor in the countryside was less harsh than in the cities, and that sexual contacts were widespread. See also Heusler, "'Strafbestand' Liebe."

34 Mais, *Ende und Anfang,* 17.

35 Ibid., 84.

36 Henke, *Die amerikanische Besetzung,* 815–16.

37 Ibid., 823–29; Mais, *Anfang und Ende,* 114.

38 Henke, *Die amerikanische Besetzung,* 962.

39 Ibid., 961.

40 Ibid., 959.

41 Mais, *Anfang und Ende,* 238.

42 Henke, *Die amerikanische Besetzung,* 399 and 172.

43 IANAS video 57. It is important to keep in mind that most recollections of that first candy bar come from women or individuals who were children at the time, since most men were still at war, or in POW camps. A good source for these first positive recollections of American GIs in 1945 are the end-of-war anniversary specials (1985 and 1995) in local newspapers and *Heimatkalender.* See also IANAS videos 5, 8, 11, 14, 57, 63. The great majority of people interviewed for the IANAS project used the term "Ami," instead of "American." It also appeared in newspaper accounts and official records. I cite it as it appeared in the records. To many Americans, the word "Ami" has a negative connotation (as in "Ami go home"). However, for the people in Rhineland-Palatinate, it can also have a friendly meaning. The people interviewed for this project usually spoke of "our Amis" when referring to very positive memories.

44 For good depictions of first encounters with American troops in the county of Birkenfeld, see Mais, *Ende und Anfang,* 93–120.

45 Mais, *Ende und Anfang*, 186. For a discussion of the French military government, see Willis, *The French in Germany;* see also Scharf and Schröder, *Die Deutschlandpolitik Frankreichs*, especially the essay by Henke, "Politik der Widersprüche."

46 Mais, *Ende und Anfang*, 229 and 245 (quote).

47 Nieten and Heep, *Geheime Lageberichte*, 27.

48 Trees, *Stunde Null in Deutschland*, 62.

49 Henke, "Politik der Widersprüche," 82.

50 Nieten and Heep, *Geheime Lageberichte*, 22.

51 Ibid., 27. See also Erker, "Revolution des Dorfes," 392, for the increase in crime among farmers in Bavaria during the immediate postwar years.

52 In the 1947 state elections the CDU garnered 29.4 percent countywide, whereas its numbers statewide were 47.2 percent. With 44.7 percent in the county, the SPD had a 10 point higher turnout in the county than it did statewide. The KPD was able to hold on to 10.6 percent of the vote, while the LP (Liberal Party, later to merge with the FDP) received 15.3 percent. See Noß, "Parteien," Appendix 10.

53 Nieten and Heep, *Geheime Lageberichte*, 34.

54 Ibid., 22.

55 Mais, *Anfang und Ende*, 203–23; and Wünschel, *Quellen zum Neubeginn*, 237–54.

56 Denazification was guided by the principle of auto-epuration. The commissions were made up of German representatives from the civil service, churches, political parties, and the unions. Their recommendations were then evaluated by a committee made up of representatives of those groups that had experienced persecution under the Nazi regime.

57 Mais, *Ende und Anfang*, 206. See also Blessing, "'Deutschland in Not,'" 63–64.

58 Noß, "Parteien," 4. For denazification policies in the French zone, see Möhler, *Entnazifizierung;* and Henke, *Politische Säuberung unter französischer Besatzung*. See also Rauh-Kuhne and Ruck, *Regionale Eliten*, 303, on the continuities in high-level personnel. Of the 187,639 people investigated in Baden, 9,128 were deemed major offenders. Yet, of the 8,926 who appealed the rulings in their cases, a mere 178 had not been cleared by 1950.

59 W. Herzog, "Konkret vor Ort."

60 After the Americans arrived in March 1945, they separated the almost 175,000 DPs in the area according to nationality. The Baumholder Platz served as a collection point for about 18,000 Russian slave laborers. These men and women had been working in the coal mines and factories of the Saarland but also on local farms, and the American military government repatriated most of them by June 1945. When the French took over the area in July 1945, they continued repatriating the remaining DPs vigorously. Of the 175,000 DPs in the French zone, almost all were repatriated by the end of fall 1945. See Trees, *Stunde Null in Deutschland*, 160. For a discussion of the harsh attitudes of the French military government toward DPs, see Jacobmeyer, *Vom Zwangsarbeiter zum heimatlosen Ausländer*, 102. Harmsen, *Die Integra-*

tion heimatloser Ausländer, 24–25, states that by 1953 a mere 3.5 percent of all DPs in West Germany lived in Rhineland-Palatinate.

61 Palm, *Die Aufnahme von Vertriebenen,* 10–12.

62 Mais, *Ende und Anfang,* 246.

63 Verbandsgemeinde Baumholder, Vierteljahresberichte an den Landrat, "Report of 23 March 1950." See also *Bilanz der Aufbauarbeit,* 292.

64 *Geschichte der Polizei,* 373.

65 IANAS videos 14, 25, 30, 47, 60.

66 *RP,* 26 September 1951.

67 Verbandsgemeinde Baumholder, "Die Geschichte der Baumholderer U.S. Militärgemeinde," published by the Baumholder Military Community Public Relations Office. For the negotiations between the Americans and the French regarding the exchange of troops in their zones, see Historical Division, "Exchange of Troops," 1.

68 Karsch and Grimm, *Baumholder,* 23.

69 *RZ,* 28 July 1952, "Westwall Stimmung—Dichtung und Wahrheit/Die Kreisverwaltung steht Rede und Antwort/Tatsachen widerlegen den Irrglauben der Behörden und Oeffentlichkeit"; and *Wall Street Journal* 26 September 1952, "Huge U.S. Army Base Turns German Town into 'City of Miracles'—Natives Gape at $250 Million Building Projects and the Odd Ways of U.S. Women." See also IANAS videos 47 and 45.

70 *Der Stern,* 22 June 1952, "Wo gehobelt wird, da fallen Späne."

71 For complaints about this American tempo, see also BAK, B 153/1513, 208, "Tagung des Kuratoriums 28 Januar 1953." For a good overview of what the movement of troops into the Kaiserslautern region entailed, see LHA, 504/384, Anlage II of Deutscher Bundestag-Ausschuß für Besatzungsfolgen, "Bericht über die Besichtigungsfahrt des Ausschusses für Besatzungsfolgen in den Raum Idar-Oberstein/Baumholder und Bitburg am 21 Juni 1954." This report provides a detailed description of how much land was confiscated and what kinds of maneuver damages were suffered.

72 For a detailed account of the requisitioning, see *Bilanz der Aufbauarbeit.*

73 *RP,* 3 April 1952, "Im Pfälzerwald entsteht eine große Lazarettstadt."

74 This element of surprise was not unique to Birkenfeld. See Friedel, *Kaiserslautern im Wiederaufbau,* 111, for developments in the city and county of Kaiserslautern.

75 VGB, Stadtratsprotokolle, 4 April 1951.

76 KVB, Kreisausschußprotokolle, 6 June 1953, 6.

77 KVB, Kreistagsprotokolle, 5 December 1952.

78 *Heimatkalender des Landkreises Birkenfeld,* 1989, "50 Jahre Truppenübungsplatz Baumholder," 187–90. For a history of the Platz, see Karsch and Grimm, *Baumholder,* 12–25.

79 *RP,* 11 February 1952, "Probleme die der Übungsplatz Baumholder stellt."

80 Settlements were often held up because federal and state ministries were trying to pass the buck. The federal government was committed to a German integration into the West through participation in defense but was not that excited about the financial aspects of this policy. For a discussion of this

issue, see *RP*, 11 February 1952, "Probleme die der Übungsplatz Baumholder stellt."

81 KVB, Kreistagsprotokolle, 5 December 1952.

82 For an example of one such off-limits sign, see *RZ*, 30 May 1953.

83 See *RZ*, 4 August 1952, "Fadenscheinige Ostzonen-Propaganda im West-richgebiet"; and KVB, Kreistagsprotokolle, 16 April 1952. Fritz Licht, former spokesman for the Baumholder farmers still has some of these letters in his possession. For a report on Communist propaganda efforts in Kaiserslautern, see *Saarbrücker Zeitung*, 12 September 1952, "Dicke Luft in Kaiserslautern."

84 KVB, Kreistagsprotokolle, 19 February 1955.

85 Ibid. See also, *RZ*, 4 August 1952, "Kreistag fordert Rückkehr der Saargemeinden—Protest gegen Besatzungswillkür"; *RZ*, 16 October 1952, "Ist denn der Bauer heute vogelfrei?"; *RZ*, 18 October 1952, "Rechtlose Bevölkerung?—Das Janusgesicht hinter den allierten Baumassnahmen/Ein Kreis verändert sein Gesicht." See also LHA 504/479 for a letter from the city of Birkenfeld to the Landrat dated 7 January 1954. People were unsettled because they did not know how many more confiscations were imminent.

86 Herbert Sartorius, "Truppenübungsplatz Baumholder."

87 *RP*, 11 February 1952, "Probleme die der Übungsplatz Baumholder stellt"; and *Glaube und Heimat*, 6 September 1953, "Helft Baumholder." The author of this second essay clearly did not speak English, as he called Baumholder "Muttholder."

88 *RZ*, n.d., "Die Verteidigung hat das Wort." (clipping in Zeitungsausschnittsammlung, Verbandsgemeinde Baumholder).

89 *RP*, 26 September 1951, "Wenn es auf dem hohen Westrich Abend wird . . . Zwischen Kusel und Baumholder ist es sehr lebendig geworden—Starke Besorgnis bei der Bevölkerung"; H. Haag interview; IANAS video 48.

90 *RZ*, 22 March 1952, "Flur und Straßenschäden größten Ausmaßes—Die Orte um den Truppenübungsplatz Baumholder sind hart betroffen," provides a particularly graphic description of the damage that military vehicles inflicted on the county's roads. One photograph shows the pathetic attempts by two farm women trying to fix the damage to their fields with a hoe. See also KVB, Kreistagsprotokolle, 2 August 1952.

91 Karsch and Grimm, *Baumholder*, 22; see also *Heimatkalender des Landkreises Birkenfeld*, 1989, 188. The Kaiserslautern city archive also has a number of essays from National Socialist newspapers depicting the "columns of trucks" carrying materials to the construction sites of the Westwall.

92 *Der Weg: Evangelisches Sonntagsblatt für das Rheinland*, No. 20/21, 1959, "Die Stadt auf dem Berge."

93 *RZ*, 25 February 1956, "3000 US Privatwagen im Raum Baumholder." At the same time there were 2,800 German vehicles registered in the county; see *Bilanz der Aufbauarbeit*, 27.

94 *PV*, 24 October 1953, "Ein Dorf wandelt sein Gesicht / In zwei Jahren werdet Ihr Sembach nicht wiedererkennen."

95 A. Bartz interview.

96 Historical Division, "U.S. Army Construction," 168. See also LHA, 504/384, "Bericht des Besatzungsausschuss," 6.

97 Verbandsgemeinde Baumholder, Vierteljahresberichte an den Landrat, "Report of 23 March 1950"; IANAS video 45.

98 IANAS video 53.

99 *RZ,* 6 August 1953, "Ein kleines Dorf hat große Zukunft."

100 *RZ,* 23 July 1953, "Vorratskammer so groß wie ein Schwimmbad—Modernste Einrichtungen."

101 Sartorius, "Truppenübungsplatz Baumholder," 102. See also *RZ,* 10 July 1954, "Birkenfeld muß auf allerlei gefasst sein—Bürgermeister Morenz fordert Verständigungsbereitschaft gegenüber den Amerikanern"; and *RZ,* 10 December 1954, "Der Nikolaus kommt."

102 Karsch and Grimm, *Baumholder,* 23. Agricultural employment in Birkenfeld County decreased 36.6 percent between 1955 and 1961. See *Heimatkalender des Landkreises Birkenfeld,* 1964, 97.

103 *Bilanz der Aufbauarbeit,* 292.

104 KdP, Sittliche Notlage in der Pfalz, Jugendnot (hereafter 555.4), "Nöte der Bevölkerung und Arbeitskräfte in den westlichen Grenzzonen (Pfalz und Eifel)." See also Berichte 1951–73, letter from Landrat Birkenfeld to *Landkreistag,* 24 March 1952; and Berichte 1951–85, "Fürsorgetätigkeit als Ausstrahlung der Besatzung in Baumholder," n.d.

105 IANAS video 13.

106 IANAS video 54.

107 IANAS videos 8 and 16.

108 *Wall Street Journal,* 26 September 1952, "Huge US Army Base Turns German Town into 'City of Miracles'—Germans Gape at $250 Million Building Project and the Odd Ways of US Women."

109 IANAS video 20.

110 LHA, 504/384, "Bericht des Besatzungsausschuss."

111 *RZ,* 30 August 1955, "Besuch im amerikanischen Lager-Viel Jugend hat sich eingefunden-Interessante Filme über Atomenergie-Kaffee und Kuchen."

112 *Heimatkalender des Landkreises Birkenfeld,* 1961, 97. Employment for women nationwide increased from 26.4 percent to 36.5 percent between 1950 and 1961. See Frevert, "Frauen auf dem Weg zur Gleichberechtigung," 121. For social legislation and policies during the 1950s that aimed at returning women to the home, see Moeller, *Protecting Motherhood.*

113 See Chapter 6.

114 These numbers are from the town of Bitburg but are representative for all localities with American troops. See Heins, *Geschichte von Bitburg,* 78. A German engineer who worked for the American Corps of Engineers in Baumholder stated that between 1972 and 1978 his office alone spent DM 100 million in construction work. Ninety-five percent of those contracts went to the artisans and businesses of the surrounding communities. IANAS video 62.

115 *Bilanz der Aufbauarbeit,* 208.

116 *Die Pfalz klagt an,* 13.

117 *Der Sonntag,* 14 August 1960, "Revolution in der Eifel." See also *Der Stern,* 16 April 1959, "Die Bar auf der Tenne." Two good sources on how locals adapted to American tastes are the movies *Die Goldene Pest* (1954) and *Schwarzer Kies* (1959).

118 Karl Edinger photo archive, Baumholder.

119 *RZ,* 29 June 1957, "Rundgang durch Baumholder—Die große Wandlung auf dem Truppenübungsplatz."

120 *RZ,* 24 November 1954, "Kameraleute hatten in Baumholder nichts zu lachen—Der Film 'Die Goldene Pest' ist fertiggestellt."

121 The term "McDonald's" was used by Karl Edinger of Baumholder.

122 *Bilanz der Aufbauarbeit,* 208.

123 The best sense one gets of the scope of all this is to look at Kaiserslautern. In one night in May of 1952, contracts worth DM 250 million were granted to general construction contractors. That night was called "The night of the millions," "St. Bartholomew Night," and, eerily enough, "*Kristallnacht.*" Millions were lost because of improprieties, and for years the local courts were kept busy prosecuting individuals involved with fraud, corruption, and racketeering. See Frenzel, "Ein Standort im Goldenen Westen," 99.

124 See *Geschichte der Polizei,* 373–74, for a short overview of the increase in thefts on construction sites. See also LHA, 602.05, trial records from the Inferior Court Baumholder.

125 *RP,* 1 January 1955, "Vorhang auf vor 'Goldener Pest.'"

126 A favorite joke in the area explains why it was not considered a crime to "appropriate" goods from the Americans. All such goods were stamped with "U.S." to identify them as U.S. military property. The local dialect for "our" is "us"; thus locals jokingly asserted, "Die Sache sin [*sic*] all US" ("All these goods are ours").

127 *RP,* 26 September 1951, "Wenn es auf den Höhen des Westrich Abend wird. . . ." Black market activities of GIs and the local population have kept German and American customs official busy to this day, albeit to a lesser degree.

128 KVB, Kreistagsprotokolle, 11 February 1954; and Berichte, 1951–73, "Jugendamtsausschuß 12 March 1953."

129 *Heimatkalender des Landkreises Birkenfeld,* 1986, 46.

130 IANAS video 48.

131 Berichte, 1951–85, "Fürsorgetätigkeit als Ausstrahlung."

132 It was not unusual at that time to find ads by American officers offering to pay any price for a large apartment (see *RZ,* 13 April 1954, for example). Many of the people interviewed for the IANAS oral history project financed their homes in just this manner, and all the communities around military bases are marked by the unique architecture of single-family homes featuring an extra apartment. See also records of trials on "rent usury" in the Baumholder Inferior Court at the LHA, RG 602.05.

133 IANAS video 7. Matters were similar in the Kaiserslautern region. The *Wall*

Street Journal of 26 September 1952 reported that in Kaiserslautern rent of $100 was being paid for a two-room apartment that previously had brought the owner only $15.

134 IANAS video 25. The original quote is "Sollen wir uns eine Wutz oder einen Ami halten?"

135 IANAS video 9. See also *RZ,* 3 August 1955, "Wohnungsnot wäre bei weitem nicht so schlimm . . . wenn alle vermietbaren Wohnungen deutschen Familien vorbehalten blieben." In this letter to the editor, outrage is expressed that Germans have to live in the "most undignified circumstances" while wealthy Americans get all the good apartments.

136 *Geschichte der Polizei,* 373.

137 IANAS videos 60 and 47. See also NARA, RG 338, Weekly LRO Civil Affairs Report, 24 August 1957, which states, "Little Baumholder still possesses 70 taxis but the usual long-distance trips to Paris, Italy and the Netherlands were stopped a long time ago."

138 *Neue Revue,* 29 May 1954, "Das Volk muss es büssen."

139 Dreier interview.

140 IANAS video 14.

141 These numbers are from Stadt Baumholder/Steuerabteilung, cited in Becker, "Die Veränderung des Stadtbildes," 57. Unfortunately, tax figures for the 1940s were not available. I assume that revenues increased during the early 1940s, however city officials assured me that they never reached the level of the 1950s. The number of pubs in Baumholder increased from four in the early 1930s to eleven during the early 1940s.

142 *RZ,* 20 October 1956, "Die aktuelle Heimatreportage: Sag es mit Blumen, Schrott und Optimismus."

143 Historical Division, "U.S. Army Construction," 166.

144 Berichte, 1951–73, 14 May 1955 letter of Landrat Heep to the Ministry of Social Affairs of the state government. See also LHA, 504/384, "Bericht des Besatzungsausschuss," 3.

145 *RZ,* 7 February 1956, "Das Fazit unserer Leserumfage: Bevölkerung Baumholders zeigt sich der Situation gewachsen/Eine Stadt im Spiegel der Meinungen/Neuer Lebensrythmus wird gefunden."

146 *RZ,* 26 October 1957, "Tradition und Gegenwart: Baumholder—Stadt mit zwei Gesichtern feiert seine Kirmes."

147 See, for example, classified ads in *RZ,* 11 February 1957.

148 *Bilanz der Aufbauarbeit,* 27. See also Südbeck, "Motorisierung," which shows that car ownership increased eightfold between 1950 and 1960. Registrations of motorcycles doubled between 1950 and 1955.

149 IANAS video 5.

150 NARA, RG 338, Weekly LRO Civil Affairs Report, 22 July 1955.

151 Herbert, "Good Times, Bad Times."

152 *PV,* 26 August 1953, "Es ist nicht alles Gold was glänzt: Falsche Töne in der Harmonie unseres Alltages." The author also reminded the readers that not all yet profited equally from the American-induced wealth.

153 *PV,* 5 March 1953, "Kaiserslautern von den USA aus gesehen."

154 The archive of the Verbandsgemeinde Baumholder has a photo of a pub that catered to Wehrmacht soldiers. See also Licht interview.

155 The population in Baumholder doubled between 1952 and 1956. Ramstein had 3,700 inhabitants in 1950 and 7,800 in 1957. Kaiserslautern had a population of 65,000 people in 1951; by 1952, two years after the Americans arrived, it had increased to 80,000. W. Herzog, "Konkret vor Ort"; *PV*, 10 May 1957, "Ramstein—Eine Stadt von morgen?"

Chapter Two

1 Schwarz, *Die Ära Adenauer,* 375–428; and D. Nelson, *Defenders or Intruders?* 51–61. Nelson argues that the mid-1950s through 1967 were the "good old days" or the "golden period." Oral histories also refer to the 1950s as "the Golden Fifties" or the "Fantastic Fifties." See IANAS videos 47 and 37.

2 Schwartz, *America's Germany,* 248.

3 Knauer, *Lieben wir die USA?* 189–90.

4 Ibid., 80. Knauer suggests that the American soldiers were for many Germans a reminder of the lost war. He relates the increasing German acceptance of American troops to the heating up of the Cold War.

5 NARA, RG 338, Civil Affairs Division, Records of the LRO, box 19. For Altmeier and his views, see Hirschner, *Aus dem Chaos.* For Catholic views on remilitarization, see Doering-Manteuffel, *Katholizismus und Wiederbewaffnung;* Mitchell, "Materialism and Secularism."

6 Large, *Germans to the Front;* Von Schubert, *Wiederbewaffnung und Westintegration;* and Doering-Manteuffel, *Katholizismus und Wiederbewaffnung.*

7 Plassmann, "U.S. Air Base Sembach," 37–38.

8 The minutes of the Kaiserslautern city council are a wonderfully rich source of the early debates on the American presence because until the November 1952 election, the council contained six KPD members, who added a certain spice to many of the debates. Between 1952 and 1956 the council had two KPD members. It should be noted that these KPD members were able to raise a lot of ruckus, but with the exception of one resolution, an angrily worded condemnation of requisitions, none of their motions was ever adopted.

9 *Die Freiheit,* 18 October 1951, "Kaiserslautern ein Zentrum westlicher Verteidigung." For official SPD views on the United States, see Orlov, "Ambivalence and Attraction."

10 NARA, RG 338, Weekly LRO Civil Affairs Report, 22 June 1957.

11 NARA, RG 338, USAREUR Public Information Division, Classified Decimal File 1952, box 1, folder 014.13; and HICOG Report 152, 15 September 1952.

12 Rupieper, *Die Wurzeln.*

13 NARA, RG 338, USAREUR Public Information Division, Classified Decimal File 1952, box 1, folder 014.13.

14 *PV,* 22 March 1952, "Ein Jahr Rhine Military Post in Kaiserslautern." See

also *RZ,* 23 May 1955, "Ein Festtag für Amerikaner und Deutsche—Landräte von Birkenfeld und Kusel nahmen die Truppenparade ab."

15 NARA, RG 338, USAREUR Public Information Division, Classified Decimal File 1952, box 1, folder 014.13.

16 *RP,* 22 May 1956, "Amerikanische Streitkräfte stellen Stärke und Ausrüstung unter Beweis—Große Parade in der Barbarossa Stadt—Tausende auf den Flugplätzen Landstuhl, Ramstein und Sembach."

17 The Americans understood that just a few years after the end of the war, America's NATO alliance partners, especially the French, had to be convinced that Germany would no longer pose a threat and could become a reliable ally in a common defense strategy. To assure their allies, the Americans hoped "to weave Germany into a larger whole as to contain satisfactorily the energies, economy and political ambitions of the Germans." American policy makers judged West Germany's integration into the West, and thus control of West Germany, as the best guarantor to balance Soviet ambitions in Europe. See Rupieper, *Die Wurzeln,* 22; and Schwartz, *America's Germany.*

18 NARA, RG 338, USAREUR Public Information Division, Classified Decimal File 1952, box 1, folder 014.13, "A Note on Anti-Americanism in Germany," n.d. [probably 1952].

19 Ibid. This folder contains a number of documents dealing with the lack of confidence in American military readiness. See also NARA, RG 338, USAREUR Public Information Division, General Correspondence, box 1, 1952–53.

20 NARA, RG 338, USAREUR Public Information Division, Classified Decimal File 1952, box 1, folder 014.13 "Note on Anti-Americanism in Germany."

21 Eisenhower quoted in Schwartz, *America's Germany,* 220.

22 NARA, RG 338, Weekly LRO Civil Affairs Report, 16 July 1955.

23 NARA, RG 338, Weekly LRO Civil Affairs Report, 22 November 1958.

24 VGB, Deutsch-Amerikanisches Freundschaftskomitee, meeting minutes, 10 September 1957.

25 IANAS video 48.

26 NARA, RG 338, Weekly LRO Civil Affairs Report, 11 May 1957.

27 NARA, RG 338, Weekly LRO Civil Affairs Report, 18 May 1957.

28 NARA, RG 338, USAREUR Public Information Division, Classified Decimal File 1952, box 1, folder 014.13 "Note on Anti-Americanism in Germany."

29 A European Command board on German-American relations was established in 1950, and by August of that year a program aimed at improving the relationship between the troops and the German civilian population had been initiated. By 1952, military post commanders, instead of the Land Relations Officers (LROs) of the High Commissioner's Office, assumed responsibility for direct relations with German officials. See Historical Division, "American Military Occupation," 197.

30 VGB, Deutsch-Amerikanisches Freundschaftskomitee, Letter from Headquarters US Army Hospital, Neubrücke, 5 July 1955.

31 Amerika Häuser (America Houses) were established in the American zone during the period of the American military government. These institutions were to introduce the German population to American ideals of democracy. Visitors could choose among a wide variety of newspapers, journals, and books in the library.

32 *RP*, 18 October 1953, "Vor einem Jahr wurde das Amerika Haus Kaiserslautern eröffnet." The Amerika Haus activities were sponsored by the Department of State, while all other activities with local communities discussed below were sponsored by individual military commanders.

33 *Bilanz der Aufbauarbeit*, 192. See also Fehrenbach, *Cinema,* chap. 6, on the efforts of the German film industry to offer German *Kultur Film* as an antidote to the dominance of Hollywood.

34 VGB, Deutsch-Amerikanisches Freundschaftskomitee, meeting minutes, 27 April 1960.

35 *RZ*, 17 February 1955, "Die Autobücherei ist überall willkommen."

36 *RZ*, 29 October 1955, "Künstler Soldaten unter einem Taktstock."

37 *RZ*, 14 June 1956, "Ihre Leistung hielt höchsten Ansprüchen stand." However, the author of this article did attribute this achievement to the fact that America had benefited culturally from all the emigres who had left Europe during the Nazi Regime.

38 *RZ*, 31 December 1954, "Der Amerikaner: aktiv und menschlich."

39 *RZ*, 21 December 1955, "Soldatenchor ersang sich die Herzen des Publikums."

40 For a contemporary American account of this easy integration and the intensive contacts between Germans and Americans, see Historical Division, "American Military Occupation." For a depiction of this integration in Zweibrücken, see Browder, "Impact".

41 *PV*, 29 September 1952, "Amerikaner wünschen mehr Kontakte mit Deutschen."

42 *RZ*, 24 September 1951, "Deutsche bei Amerikanern zu Gast." See also *RZ*, 20 May 1955, "Amerikaner öffnen ihre Kasernen."

43 *PV*, 23 May 1955, "Wochenschau" photo essay. The Ramstein event was a highlight of the year until the terrible disaster at the Ramstein *Flugtag* in 1986, when 76 German spectators were killed and over 200 injured after military jets collided in midair, causing a devastating explosion.

44 *RZ*, 17 May 1955, "Das war eine Freude für die Buben! Die schweren Waffen waren der Tummelplatz Hunderter Jungen."

45 IANAS videos 12, 20, 27, 60.

46 IANAS video 56.

47 VGB, Deutsch-Amerikanisches Freundschaftskomitee, Letter of Headquarters Baumholder Post to German-American Friendship Committee, 31 March 1960.

48 *Der Weg: Evangelisches Sonntagsblatt für das Rheinland,* Nr. 20/21, 1959.

49 Verbandsgemeinde Birkenfeld photo archive. The military command of Mainz did not send troops to participate in the 1957 procession and was

admonished for having missed this important opportunity to reiterate the German-American friendship to the local population. See NARA, RG 338, Weekly LRO Civil Affairs Report, 22 June 1957.

50 Archiv des Kirchenkreis Birkenfeld, Verhandlungen der Kreissynode Birkenfeld, "Report for 1955," 24.

51 KdP, Beziehung zu Besatzungsmächten, "Aktennotiz über Vorsprache vom 26.7.1955."

52 Edinger interview. See also IANAS video 11.

53 VGB, Deutsch-Amerikanisches Freundschaftskomitee, meeting minutes, 9 May 1953.

54 VGB, Deutsch-Amerikanisches Freundschaftskomitee, "Stellungnahme der Gendarmerie Station Birkenfeld 28 July 1955."

55 See discussion in Chapter 6.

56 VGB, Deutsch-Amerikanisches Freundschaftskomitee, "Amerikanische Gäste von Burg Lichtenberg begeistert, 2. Tagung des Ausschusses für deutsch-amerikanische Verständigung," n.d.

57 LHA, 504/382, "Vermerk über die Besprechung mit General Berry, 24 August 1956."

58 RZ, 16 January 1956, "'Arrow'-Leute lösen 'Hölle auf Räder' ab." See also Browder, "Impact," 215–34.

59 VGB, Deutsch-Amerikanisches Freundschaftskomitee, "Stärkerer gesellschaftlicher Konnex angestrebt." See Browder, "Impact," for a depiction of these clubs in Zweibrücken.

60 IANAS videos 11, 17, 28, 48, 51.

61 IANAS video 24.

62 Ibid.

63 IANAS video 27.

64 Museum des Westrich, Ramstein, photo collection and interview with Michael Geib, director of the museum and curator of the collection. Geib bought the collection from the Kaiserslautern photographer Walter Matheis, who worked as a photographer on the Ramstein air base for thirty years.

65 VGB photo collection. See also IANAS videos 24, 28.

66 ASK, US Besatzung/Wohltätigkeit, "Translation of the minutes of the third meeting of the *Fasching* committee 14 November 1954." The German version of the motto was, "Von 'Lautern bis zum Mississippistrand schafft Karneval das Freundschaftsband."

67 LHA, 504/382, "Übereinkommen über gegenseitige Unterstützung 19 September 1955." Newspapers in those regions regularly reported on this mutual assistance. See, for example, *RZ*, 20 March 1954, "Wiesenbrände"; and *RZ*, 18 January 1951, "Nächtlicher Kasernenbrand in Algenrodt." Also IANAS videos 20, 40.

68 NARA, RG 338, Weekly LRO Civil Affairs Report, 25 January 1958.

69 IANAS video 17; Hermann Schüssler and Anneliese Kürsten interviews.

70 IANAS video 48; *Heimatkalender des Landkreises Birkenfeld*, 1975, "Zwei Jahrzente Pionierhilfe durch die 293. US-Einheit," 66–67. See also *RZ*, 11

June 1954, "Amerikanische Pioniere helfen mit"; *RZ,* 11 November 1955, "US Soldaten legen einen Sportplatz an—Grosszügiges Entgegenkommen amerikanischer Pioniere in Pfeffelbach."

71 *RZ,* 1 August 1954, "Amerikaner bauten Fußballplatz."

72 *RZ,* 22 November 1955, "Sportplatzbau in Hoppstädten—Freundliche Hilfe der Amerikaner"; *RZ,* 27 July 1955, "US-Truppen helfen beim Sportplatzbau—In Thallichtenberg wird ein jahrzehntelanger Plan verwirklicht."

73 *PV,* 11 February 1955, "Mehr Reserviertheit gegenüber den Besatzungsmächten?" This extensive construction of roads and bypasses was needed because of the great number of American vehicles. In 1955, 7,000 German automobiles and 18,000 allied automobiles were registered in the city of Kaiserslautern. See *PV,* 19 April 1955.

74 *Heimatkalender des Landkreises Birkenfeld,* 1975, "Zwei Jahrzente Pionierhilfe durch die 293. US-Einheit," 66–67.

75 *PV,* 29 September 1953, "Amerikaner helfen beim Schulneubau."

76 Photo archive of Dr. Gerhard Nagel, a former mayor of Baumholder.

77 Nagel photo collection and interview.

78 *RZ,* 10 December 1954, "Der Nikolaus kommt zu Tausenden."

79 Archiv der Evangelischen Kirche Baumholder, no folder information available. The photocopied materials from the foundation were given to me by Karl Edinger, the church archivist.

80 IANAS video 49; VGB, Deutsch-Amerikanisches Freundschaftskomitee memo, n.d.

81 KVB, Kreistagsprotokolle, 11 February 1954. See also KdP, Pfarrämter Jahresberichte, Landstuhl 1956.

82 IANAS video 32. See Alvah, "Unofficial Ambassadors," for the role American military wives played in these philanthropic efforts.

83 *RZ,* 30 July 1954, "Kontakt im heiteren Spiel—Amerikanische Pfadfinderinnen hatten Berliner Kinder eingeladen."

84 *RZ,* 20 October 1954, "Girl-Scouts besuchen den Kindergarten."

85 *RZ,* 22 December 1955, "Das Kinderparadies tat sich auf."

86 NARA, RG 338, Annual History Reports, US Army Europe, 1953–54.

87 KdP, Beziehung zu Besatzungsmächten, copy of the letter from General Reber in folder at KdP.

88 *RZ,* 20 December 1955, "Die gute Tat der Hunsrückflieger."

89 *RZ,* 22 December 1953, "Amerikanische 'Aktion Weihnachten' läuft." See also *RZ,* 2 September 1955, "Hilfsbereitschaft kennt keine Grenzen"; *RZ,* 24 December 1955, "Christliche Nächstenliebe kennt keine Grenzen—Amerikanische Soldaten, Frauen und Organisationen beschenken deutsche Familien."

90 *RZ,* 21 December 1954, "Zehntausende Sternlein leuchteten. . . ." See also IANAS videos 20, 40, 41, 48, 53, 56.

91 *RZ,* 7 December 1954, "St. Nikolaus kommt mit dem Hubschrauber." Santa Claus also descended in a helicopter at the General Hospital in Hoppstädten. *RZ,* 22 December 1953, "Kinderbescherung im General Hospital." See also *RZ,* 7 December 1953, "Der Nikolaus kam mit dem Hubschrauber."

92 ASK, Besatzung/Wohltätigkeit, Letter from Headquarters Western Area Command of 5 October 1954 to mayor of city.

93 IANAS video 24.

94 *RZ,* 17 December 1954, "Deutsche Weihnachtsbäume für Amerika." See also IANAS video 28.

95 Initially, American children attended the German kindergartens because of lacking American infrastructure. Once schools and nurseries existed on the military base, many Americans continued to send their children to German schools to learn the German language.

96 *RZ,* 22 December 1953, "Amerikanische 'Aktion Weihnachten' läuft." See also *RZ,* 2 September 1955, "Hilfsbereitschaft kennt keine Grenzen."

97 See, for example, KdP, Beziehung zu Besatzungsmächten, Letter of Landeskirchenrat to Dekanate, 8 December 1954. All people interviewed for the IANAS project who rented to Americans stated that they celebrated Christmas together with their tenants. See IANAS videos 22, 31, 33, 37, 41, 52, 63, 50, 57, 63 for descriptions of these celebrations.

98 NARA, RG 338, Annual History Reports, USAREUR, 1953–54, 148.

99 *RZ,* 12 December 1959, "Sollen wir nur Empfangende sein?" (The words in single quotes appeared in English in the original.)

100 Interview with James Larkins, former military commander of the Birkenfeld Air Force station. See IANAS videos 6, 20, 33, 62, 95 for comments on how many German women married GIs.

101 With only 6 million people living in the French zone, there were 800,000 more women than men at the end of the war. See Trees, *Stunde Null,* 60; and IANAS video 13. The individual in this video recalled that the young men of Bad Kreuznach had to travel far and wide to find communities without American GIs, saying that this was their only chance to get a German girlfriend, since the American GIs were favorites among local women. On opposition to these relationships in the immediate postwar years, see Biddiscombe, "Dangerous Liaisons."

102 Shukert and Scibetta, *War Brides of World War II,* 129. See also Domentat, *Hallo Fräulein,* 53–55, for observations by German women on why they preferred American men.

103 Decker, "Baumholder," 12. In Zweibrücken, during the 1950s, 20 percent of all marriages involved an American GI. Statistics at IANAS archive. Of the 1,002 marriages conducted in the Catholic parishes in Kaiserslautern in 1958, 188 were with American GIs. See BAS, Pfarrämter Jahresberichte, Kaiserslautern 1959.

104 By the mid-1950s, 40 percent of Germans remained opposed to marriages between German women and American GIs. D. Nelson, *Defenders or Intruders,* 59.

105 IANAS video 50. For marriages between GIs and German women before 1950, see Shukert and Scibetta, *War Brides of World War II;* and Heineman, "Standing Alone," 210–11.

106 IANAS video 63.

107 Ibid.

108 Interviews with former U.S. Air Force personnel Herb Stoudt, Greg Stagliano, and Jacki King. (Interview transcripts in author's possession).

109 One can of course question whether the military really represents the "American way of life." The people interviewed for the IANAS project all agreed that the 1950s was a time when U.S. soldiers and their families in Germany did indeed constitute a representative slice of America, since there was a military draft and people came from all sorts of backgrounds. German perceptions of the American military changed drastically in the 1970s with the introduction of a volunteer U.S. force.

110 E. Bartz interview; IANAS video 62.

111 One of the most common complaints leveled at the Americans during the occupation period was that they segregated themselves from the German population by recreating self-sufficient "Little Americas" in the middle of Germany. For research on the "Little Americas," see Alvah, "Unofficial Ambassadors"; and Leuerer, "Perspektive der Military Communities."

112 IANAS has extensive demographic statistics on communities surrounding American military bases. Such patterns of habitation were repeated wherever American troops were stationed. See Becker and Burdack, *Amerikaner in Bamberg*.

113 Plassmann, "U.S. Air Base Sembach," 78.

114 *RZ*, 9 May 1956, "Abschiedsfeier für amerikanischen Torwart." See IANAS videos 37, 42, and 63 for depictions of American GIs' participation in German clubs. See also Browder, "Impact," 215–34.

115 IANAS video 14; Browder, "Impact"; and IANAS, Mootz questionnaire for Zweibrücken. Even today, GIs participate in German music clubs but not on a large scale.

116 *RZ*, 16 January 1956, "'Arrow'-Leute lösen 'Hölle auf Räder' ab."

117 *RZ*, 20 November 1955, "US Komiker wirkte beim bunten Abend mit."

118 IANAS video 46.

119 Some of the people interviewed for the IANAS project had photo albums of every American family who ever lived with them. People shared with great pride how the children they helped to raise went to college and how they came to visit their "German *Oma* and *Opa*" on their trips to Europe.

120 Comment from Jürgen Henze during panel discussion at the "Nachbar Amerika" symposium at Ramstein Air Base, 17–19 March 1995, sponsored by the Johannes Gutenberg Universität Mainz and the Staatskanzlei Mainz.

121 IANAS video 33.

122 IANAS video 7.

123 IANAS video 22.

124 IANAS video 33.

125 IANAS video 30.

126 IANAS video 27.

127 IANAS video 10.

128 IANAS video 42.

129 All Germans who rented to Americans and who were interviewed for the IANAS project reported on the ease with which American children adopted

the local dialect, and that it was quite the norm that the young American children played with their own children and shared meals with them. Many German housewives also kept the American children during the day when American wives were busy with a job or because of their volunteer activities.

130 IANAS videos 7, 52.

131 IANAS videos 16, 52.

132 IANAS videos 27, 20.

133 IANAS video 10.

134 IANAS videos 7, 10, 33.

135 *RP*, 8 May 1951, "Amerikanische Kinder lernen spielend die deutsche Sprache—Ein Blick in die neue amerikanische Volksschule an der Vogelweh—Deutsch-Unterrricht ist Pflichtfach."

136 *RZ*, 27 March 1954, "Wie lerne ich amerikanisch?"

137 The Museum des Westrich, Ramstein, has a wonderful collection of photographs of these events in the American clubs. Michael Geib, the museum's curator, organized the exhibit, "Welcome to the Club." See also *RZ*, 15 December 1959, "Heute singen die 'Platters' im EM-Club"; *RZ*, 22 December 1956, "Auf vielseitigen Wunsch nochmal . . . deutsch-amerikanischer Abend im NCO Club"; and IANAS videos 52 and 47. The German customs agency and the *Gaststättenverband* (Organizations of Hotel and Restaurant Owners) used all their muscle to prohibit Germans from attending these clubs. The German restaurant owners viewed the American clubs as too much competition, and the custom officials feared loss of revenues if Germans consumed their alcohol in American clubs.

138 IANAS video 53.

139 IANAS video 58.

140 IANAS video 62; and Feis interview.

141 IANAS video 17.

142 Maase, *Bravo Amerika*, 83 and 119. See also Chapter 6.

143 IANAS video 22.

144 IANAS video 1.

145 IANAS videos 1, 28.

146 Feis interview. The headline "Drinking Rum and Coca-Cola" that appeared in English in a local newspaper conveyed this sense of sophistication, but the story also implied that these drinks were not without dangers. After too many of these American-style mixed drinks, some young men allegedly had gotten out of hand and broken a window at the Birkenfeld castle. See *RZ*, 10 May 1954.

147 Because of the American military presence, the American radio station AFN also offered many artists who were not yet played on German radio stations, thus exposing teenagers of that region to rock and roll very early on. See IANAS video 6 and interviews with Hechl, Feis, Müller, and Höhn. By 1960, AFN reported that 80 percent of all listener requests came from Germans. See Knauer, *Lieben wir die Amis?*, 158.

148 IANAS video 53.

149 "Welcome to the Club" photo exhibit, Museum des Westrich, Ramstein.

150 IANAS video 51.

151 IANAS video 6.

152 IANAS video 28.

153 Feis and Höhn interviews.

154 IANAS video 14.

155 IANAS video 13.

156 IANAS video 1; Arnold Sywotteck's comments at "Nachbar Amerika" conference in Ramstein, 17–19 March 1995. Sywotteck argued that the fact that Germans wore blue jeans had less to do with an Americanization of Germany than with the fact that jeans are a practical piece of clothing. See also his "Americanization of Everyday Life?"

157 IANAS video 6.

158 Schwerdtners interview. What makes this recollection even more fascinating is that the woman's husband was the spokesman of the dispossessed Baumholder farmers.

159 IANAS video 1.

160 IANAS video 28.

161 IANAS video 34.

162 Cited in Maase, *Bravo Amerika,* 189.

163 *PV,* 28 November 1951, "Zwischen Nacht und Morgengrauen."

164 IANAS video 1.

165 Fehrenbach, *Cinema in Democratizing Germany,* 165 ("American actors"); Feis and Mades interviews ("hands in pockets"). Fehrenbach suggests that "consumption, personal style, and leisure activity took on a symbolic significance as German youth employed American culture to mark their difference from received notions of German identity" (167–68). See also Poiger, *Jazz, Rock, and Rebels;* and Maase, *Bravo Amerika.*

166 IANAS video 39; Feis and Hechl interviews.

167 *RZ,* 19 November 1955, "Baumholder im Spiegel der deutschen Presse."

168 IANAS video 39.

169 Cited in Maase, *Bravo Amerika,* 215.

170 *PV,* 28 November 1951, "Zwischen Nacht und Morgengrauen." Text shown in single quotes appeared in English in the original.

171 According to Gabrielle Simon Edgcomb, author of *From Swastika to Jim Crow* and participant at a conference sponsored by the German Historical Institute in Washington, this was part of the Nazi propaganda taught to school children. See also Henke, *Die amerikanische Besetzung,* 167, which reports a German woman who referred to American soldiers as "tango dancers" or "jitterbugs" who lacked the soldierly discipline of the German Wehrmacht soldier.

172 IANAS video 47.

173 Cited in Maase, *Bravo Amerika,* 60.

174 *RP,* 14 March 1953, "Wie lebt der Amerikaner in der Pfalz."

175 NARA, RG 338, USAREUR Public Information Division, General Correspondence 1952–53, Box 1.
176 IANAS videos 60 and 63.

Chapter Three

1 *RZ,* 5 May 1953, "Noch immer nicht Herr im eigenen Haus—Landrat Heep sprach zum 1. Mai vor dem deutschen Batallion in Nahbollenbach."
2 Large, *Germans to the Front,* 223–33.
3 Weber, *Die Vollzugspolizei,* 36. LHA, 504/384, "Bericht des Besatzungsausschuss," 10, states that during the month of February 1952, American soldiers committed a total of 59 offenses against German nationals. According to crime statistics from the *Bundeskriminalamt,* U.S. soldiers committed 1,406 of the 79,653 crimes committed in all of Germany in 1957.
4 VGB, Deutsch-Amerikanisches Freundschaftskomittee, Letter from the police chief in Birkenfeld of 28 July 1955. According to a 1954 survey, 57 percent of Germans believed that the behavior of the troops was good, and 37 percent rated it as fair. Cited in Moskos, *American Enlisted Man,* 213.
5 *Die Pfalz klagt an,* 5.
6 Merritt and Merritt, *Public Opinion in Semi-Sovereign Germany,* 238. For complaints about the "American tempo," see *RP,* 19 July 1952, "Sondermaßnahmen für den Landkreis notwendig"; and *RP,* 15 January 1953, "Goldener Westen im Winterkleid."
7 *Die Pfalz klagt an,* 47.
8 *PV,* 3 December 1952, "Deutsche Ritter und amerikanische Herren" (*Amistädte*); *PV,* 9 April 1955, "Vor vier Jahren began in Sembach der 'Boon' [*sic*]" ("dull and monotone"); *PV,* 8 May 1953, "Akkord ist Trumpf in 'Coca-Cola Town'" ("hot and restless breath.").
9 *RP,* 5 February 1955, "Mal bei den Amis zu Besuch."
10 KdP, Pfarrämter Jahresberichte, Kaiserslautern 1953.
11 KdP, Pfarrämter Jahresberichte, Kaiserslautern 1955, 21.
12 ASK, US Besatzung Deutsch-Amerikanischer Ausschuß, 1954–1959 (emphasis in original). This appeal was published in the 14 September 1954 edition of the *Rheinpfalz,* thus reaching a very wide and varied audience.
13 Gräber, *Die Revolver Republik;* Lebzelter, "'Die Schwarze Schmach'"; K. Nelson, "Black Horror on the Rhine"; Campt, "'Afro-German.'"
14 Heyen, *Geschichte des Landes Rheinland-Pfalz,* 115.
15 Pommerin, "*Sterilisierung der Rheinlandbastarde*"; Campt, "'Afro-German.'" On German racism toward blacks during the Nazi regime, see also Massaquoi, *Destined to Witness.*
16 Henke, *Die amerikanische Besetzung,* 378; and Gassert, *Amerika im Dritten Reich,* 366.
17 Lester, *Trivialneger,* 38. For a discussion of rape by U.S. soldiers, see Reif, "Das Recht des Siegers," 360–71. In the whole territory conquered by the

U.S. Army approximately 1,000 rapes were reported in the spring of 1945. The military punished the offenders severely; some soldiers even received the death penalty. Military reports assumed that the white soldier was "teased [by German women] until his physical make-up has been over-tried." Black soldiers, on the other hand, were assumed to have committed the large majority of the rapes. See Report of XXIII Corps of 22 June 1945, reprinted in Wünschel, *Quellen zum Neubeginn,* 341.

18 Niethammer, "Privat-Wirtschaft: Erinnerungsfragmente einer anderen Umerziehung," in *"Hinterher merkt man",* 22–34. See also Kleinschmidt, *"Do not fraternize,"* esp. 175–77.

19 Lester, *Trivialneger,* esp. chap. 2, where she makes the point that in many of the serialized novels of the postwar years Germans compare their own suffering to that of blacks in the United States. See also Kleinschmidt, *"Do not fraternize,"* 184; and IANAS video 60.

20 *Ebony,* vol. 2, no. 10 (October 1946), "Germany Meets the Negro Soldier: GIs Find More Friendship and Equality in Berlin than in Birmingham or Broadway," 5–11. See also Schmundt-Thomas, "America's Germany," 73–74.

21 Gardner Smith, *Last of the Conquerors,* 67. See Schmundt-Thomas, "America's Germany," for a discussion of Gardner Smith's novel.

22 Motley, *Invisible Soldier,* 178.

23 *Stars and Stripes,* 12 August 1945, "The Negro GI in Germany."

24 *Newsweek,* 16 September 1946, "Racial: Mädchen and Negro," 29–30.

25 "Report of the Negro Publishers Association to the Honorable Secretary of War, Judge Robert Patterson, on Troops and Conditions in Europe, 18 July 1946," and "Memorandum, Sec. Of War Robert Patterson for deputy chief of staff," 7 January 1947; both reprinted in MacGregor and Nalty, *Blacks in the Military,* 211 and 217, respectively.

26 Gardner Smith, *Last of the Conquerors,* 67–68.

27 Interview with Lt. General Clarence Huebener, cited in MacGregor, *Integration of the Armed Forces,* 214.

28 Posner, "Afro-America," 35.

29 Moskos, *American Enlisted Man,* 126.

30 United States Department of Defense, *Integration,* 7. A *New York Times* essay of 31 October 1954 brought these findings to a larger audience.

31 Moskos, *American Enlisted Man,* 126. On the experience of black GIs in the United States, see David and Crane, *Black Soldier,* esp. 179–89; and President's Committee, *Equality of Treatment and Opportunity for Negro Personnel.*

32 Warren interview.

33 Schmitz interview.

34 Andrew Bowman, cited in Little, "Black Military Experience," 192.

35 Johnson, *Ebony Brass,* 99.

36 On black "occupation babies," see Fehrenbach, "Rehabilitating" and "Of German Mothers and 'Negermischlinge'"; Lemke Muniz de Faria, "Zwischen Fürsorge und Ausgrenzung"; Brauerhoch, "'Mohrenkopf.'" For contemporary studies, see Eyfurth, Brandt, and Hawel, *Farbige Kinder in Deutschland;*

and Frankenstein, *Soldatenkinder*. See also the 1958 German TV documentary *Wie Toxi wirklich lebt,* which depicts the life of Afro-German children and their mothers on the margins of West Germany's economic miracle. My thanks to Annette Brauerhoch for sharing this documentary with me.

37 *PV,* 3 January 1953, "Eine Stadt ändert ihr Gesicht—Landstuhler Strassenbild ist heute international."

38 IANAS videos 32, 22 and 29.

39 IANAS videos 22 and 39.

40 IANAS video 11.

41 IANAS video 41.

42 IANAS video 11.

43 IANAS video 46. Very few of the women interviewed for IANAS reported such fears. The women working on the military base never stated that the presence of blacks intimidated them.

44 *RZ,* 18 November 1954, "Baumholder"; and *RZ,* 9 March 1956.

45 On German racism, see Burleigh and Wippermann, *Racial State;* Gilman, *Difference and Pathology;* Mosse, *Toward the Final Solution;* Grimm and Hermand, *Blacks and German Culture;* Peukert, *Inside Nazi Germany.*

46 LHA, 930/8015, "Letter from mayor to the Social Ministry of Rhineland-Palatinate, 4 February 1952."

47 LHA, 930/8018, "Bericht über die Tagung des Landesjugendamtes Rheinland-Pfalz am 14.4.1959 zu Neustadt/a.d. Weinstraße." This report is an overview of the social work done in localities with American troops. See also BAK, B 153/327, 50 (back), "Niederschrift über die Arbeitstagung"; Berichte, 1951–1963, "Protokoll über die am 30. April 1953 stattgefundene Sitzung über die Zusammenarbeit der alliierten und deutschen Stellen zur Beseitigung der Jugendnot im Kreis Birkenfeld"; and *PV,* 19 January 1953, "Kaiserslauterner Polizei reicht nicht mehr aus," in which it was reported that "to a horrifying degree there has been sexual abuse of teenagers, especially by Negroes."

48 LHA, 930/8016, Letter of Staatliches Polizeiamt Bad Kreuznach, 23 September 1952 (emphasis in original). For similar allegations, see BAK, B 153/327, "Niederschrift über die Arbeitstagung," 46.

49 LHA, 930/8016, Letter of Staatliches Polizeiamt Bad Kreuznach, 23 September 1952.

50 *Allgemeine Zeitung, Mainz,* 21 February 1953, "Verstärkte Streifen rund um den Kirschgarten."

51 Historical Division, "Integration of Negro and White Troops," 5.

52 On Soviet propaganda, see Nichols, *Breakthrough,* 172–79. For a fascinating discussion of how the Cold War necessitated integration, see Dudziak, "Desegregation as a Cold War Imperative" and *Cold War Civil Rights.* See also "Symposium: African Americans and U.S. Foreign Relations."

53 *Saturday Evening Post,* 13 December 1952, "For Negroes, It's a New Army Now," 27.

54 Nichols, *Breakthrough,* 173. See also Dudziak, "Desegregation."

55 Nichols, *Breakthrough,* 179.

56 NARA, RG 338, Historical Division, folder 314.7, "Report from Professor Eli Ginzberg from Columbia University," 6.

57 MacGregor, *Integration of the Armed Forces,* 351. For a stunning reflection by a historian of American history on his military service in Mannheim, Germany, see Davis, "The Americanized Mannheim of 1945–46." His is a powerful comment on the violence he observed as a young soldier between white and black troops and how that aspect of the American occupation also was part of the Americanization of Germany.

58 Little, "Black Military Experience," 190.

59 Campbell interview.

60 MacGregor, *Integration of the Armed Forces,* 578. On race relations in Great Britain, see Gardiner, *"Overpaid, Oversexed and Over Here";* and Smith, *When Jim Crow Met John Bull.*

61 President's Committee, "Final Report" and "Investigation." See also MacGregor, *Integration,* 552 and 578; and H. Haag, Licht, and Gillespie interviews.

62 *Saturday Evening Post,* 13 December 1952, "For Negroes, It's a New Army Now," 26–27, 108–12. See also *U.S. News and World Report,* 11 October 1957, "When Negro Servicemen Bring Home White Brides." In Germany, the military was also integrating its social facilities on base. In the United States, clubs and dances on the military bases of the South were segregated throughout the 1950s. See MacGregor, *Integration,* 456; and Nichols, *Breakthrough,* 162.

63 Trefill interview.

64 IANAS video 60.

65 See NARA, RG 338, HQ USAREUR, Committee on Interracial Relations, memorandum of 22 September 1953, in which the military acknowledges that racial conflict was occurring almost exclusively off base. See also Moskos, *American Enlisted Man,* 122; Gropman, *Air Force Integrates,* 166–67; Mershon and Schlossman, *Foxholes and Color Lines,* 278.

66 Fasching, Schwerdtner, and Licht interviews.

67 *Nahezeitung,* 28 August 1995, "Bars schossen wie Pilze aus dem Boden"; Licht interview; and IANAS videos 37, 40, 47, 51.

68 NARA, RG 338, HQ USAREUR, Committee on Interracial Relations, memorandum of 22 September 1953. See Gardiner, *"Overpaid, Oversexed and Over Here,"* 155–56, for descriptions of this violence in Great Britain.

69 According to German police reports, during the 1950s all communities observed a noticeable increase in violence and destruction of property, "mostly caused by occupation soldiers (US Army)." The great majority of these incidents did not affect Germans, however, but "occurred between white and black soldiers because of the increased racial conflicts caused by the ongoing integration of the military as well as the emerging civil rights struggle in the United States." See *Geschichte der Polizei,* 374; and Weber, *Die Vollzugspolizei,* 36.

70 Andrew Bowman, cited in Little, "Black Military Experience," 191.

71 NARA, RG 338, Weekly LRO Civil Affairs Report, 2 November 1957; and President's Committee, "Final Report," 5–6.

72 According to the former police chief, Heinrich Haag, hundreds of soldiers were involved in that fight, and "blood was running in the gutter." Fritz Licht, who lived across the street from the bar where the fight occurred, also recalled the incredible violence and bloodshed. The community never found out how many people were killed or hurt. The military command and military police issued no statement and refused any information to the locals. See also IANAS videos 51, 60, 47, 40, 42, 37 and interviews with American veterans William Warren, Robert Gillespie, Dean Yearns, Manuel Trefill, and William Keen for descriptions of other incidents of violence.

73 *Geschichte der Polizei*, 374; and Weber, *Die Vollzugspolizei*, 36.

74 Trefill interview. The Saarland became a favorite hangout for the soldiers because the American military police had no jurisdiction there.

75 *RZ*, 9 March 1956, "Baumholder: Wer ist das nächste Opfer dieser Willkür?—Jeder farbige amerikanische Soldat trägt ein Messer mit sich. Wirken sich die Vorfälle an der Uni Alabama bis nach Baumholder aus?"

76 *PV*, 9 September 1957, "Steinstraßeabsperrung mit militärischer Pünktlichkeit" has some descriptions of racial violence during the Little Rock crisis. Fritz Licht, Gerd and Ingrid Schwerdtner, Georg Fasching, and former police chief Heinrich Haag also reported on this increase of violence following developments in the United States.

77 *PV*, 19 December 1958, "Rassenhass und Schlägermethoden bei der Militärpolizei?" The local authorities worked hard to convince Eastern European Jews not to put such signs in their establishments, because racial discrimination was illegal in West Germany. For critiques of Jewish bar owners who denied black GIs access to their bars, see *RZ*, 21 and 28 July 1959, "Wir wollen die Dinge beim Namen nennen"; *PV*, 14 May 1957, "Amerikanern den Begriff des Hausrechts klar machen"; and *RZ*, 13 October 1959, "Das sind keine Rassenstreitigkeiten."

78 Fasching, Hechl, and Feis interviews.

79 Mershon and Schlossman, *Foxholes and Color Lines*, 277–78; President's Committee, "Investigation," 12:331; President's Committee, "Final Report," 5–6.

80 Lohr interview. See also the 23 April 1964 letter of Benjamin Muse to Gerhard Gesell, reprinted in MacGregor, *Integration*, 13:122.

81 Mershon and Schlossman, *Foxholes and Color Lines*, 277–78; President's Committee, "Investigation," 12:331; President's Committee, "Final Report," 5–6. See also the 23 April 1964 letter of Benjamin Muse to Gerhard Gesell, reprinted in MacGregor, *Integration*, 13:122.

82 See also Mershon and Schlossman, *Foxholes and Color Lines*, 278, 283.

83 IANAS videos 37 and 60. See also cartoon in Pipifax, *Der fröhliche Westrich*, 70, for a depiction of that violence. Other accounts of such incidents include *RP*, 2 July 1952, "In Deutschlands Goldenem Westen"; and LHA, 602.6, Ordner 35, Strafsache Ds 21/56 28.5.56. The judge commented that

the "Negro soldiers have a fearsome (*heillosen*) respect for the American military police (*Polizeigewalt*)." See also Davis, "Americanized Mannheim," 89–91. For the violence of the U.S. military police in Great Britain, see Gardiner, "*Overpaid, Oversexed and Over Here*," 89.

84 *PV,* 19 December 1958, "Rassenhass und Schlägermethoden bei der Militärpolizei?"

85 See Rose, "Girls and GIs," 154, in which Rose describes the same phenomenon in Great Britain during World War II.

86 ASK, US Besatzung/Deutsch-Amerikanischer Ausschuss, "Es geht alle an"; BAS, Pfarrämter Jahresberichte, Kaiserslautern 1959.

87 During the Rhineland occupation, Germans mistook the French name *Maroc,* used for the soldiers from Morocco, as "*Mock.*" I am grateful to Ingrid Schwerdtner for this information. One of the women IANAS interviewed had a black doll while growing up during the Third Reich. Little girls called these black dolls "*Mockchen.*"

88 MacGregor, *Integration,* 215; Benjamin Muse's letter to Gesell Committee, 23 April 1964, reproduced in MacGregor and Nalty, *Blacks in the Armed Forces,* 13:121–23.

89 MacGregor, *Integration,* 578.

90 United States Department of Defense, *Integration,* 7. See also MacGregor, *Integration,* 479.

91 MacGregor, *Integration,* 479 and 552.

92 Gropman, *Air Force Integrates,* 167.

93 NARA, RG 338, Weekly LRO Civil Affairs Report, 4 October 1956. The military made three black-only bars in Mainz off-limits to its troops.

94 President's Committee, "Final Report"; Diggs Report, "Investigation."

95 In 1962, 24 percent of military bases in the United States still had segregated schools, 34 percent had segregated restaurants, and 31 percent had segregated theaters in their surrounding communities. See President's Committee, "Final Report" 45; and Stillman, *Integration,* 90.

96 IANAS videos 7, 10, and 58. See Colin Powell's comments on his very positive experience in Germany in 1958 in Powell, *My American Journey,* 53.

97 Cited in Posner, "Afro-America," 16. On interracial fraternization during the occupation years, see Kleinschmidt, "*Do not Fraternize,*" 179–85; and Rose, "Girls and GIs," 154, for Great Britain. Lester's *Trivialneger* explores serialized novels during the 1950s. In these narratives, black GIs are portrayed positively only if they accept that their relationship with a German woman can never be a sexual one.

98 NARA, RG 338, Civil Affairs, History Journals, Box 1.

99 IANAS video 48. The term "Nigger" was used in this manner during the interview. On racial attitudes in Germany, see Schütt, *Der Mohr;* Fremgen, . . . *und wenn du dazu noch schwarz bist,* especially the interview "Erika," 100–110; and Opitz, Oguntoye, and Schulz, *Showing our Colors.*

100 *PV,* 11 July 1952, "Wie ist heute die Ehe möglich?"

101 *PV,* 10 March 1953, letter to the editor.

102 *RP,* 3 April 1954, "Leserbrief: Rassentrennung."

103 Cited in Schmundt-Thomas, "America's Germany," 72. See also Historical Division, "Fraternization with the Germans," 153.

104 Alwin M. Owsley in a letter dated 16 September 1946, cited in Dalfiume, *Desegregation,* 133. See also Posner, "Afro-America," 22, for a 1947 U.S. military memo that admits that "some lower unit commander might disguise his . . . disapproval of an interracial marriage." Smith, *When Jim Crow Met John Bull,* 223–24, describes similar sentiments among soldiers stationed in Great Britain. One U.S. soldier had written home that he had seen "nice looking white girls going with a coon," and added, "They think they are hot stuff. The girls are so dumb it's pitiful. Wait till Georgia gets those *educated* negroes back there again." Another soldier commented that he did not mind that blacks were getting ahead, but that he did mind "negro men sexing with white women."

105 See KdP, 555.4, for a clipping from *Frankfurter Allgemeine Zeitung,* 23 May 1952, entitled "Immer wieder 'Veronikas.'"

106 Kelly, Bruner, Lohr, and Amicelli interviews. Lester, *Trivialneger,* 79–82, shows how that sort of language became popularized through the serialized novel *Die PX Story: Liebe hinterm Ladentisch* (*PX Story: Love behind the Store Counter*) in *Neue Illustrierte.*

107 Gardner Smith, *Last of the Conquerors,* 196. American officials generally charged that prostitution was a much bigger problem where black soldiers were stationed. Historical Division, "Fraternization with the Germans," 146–53.

108 *Westdeutsches Tagesblatt,* 21 September 1957, "Ganzes Stadtviertel in Kaiserslautern für US Truppen." In the early 1950s, only 44 percent of white soldiers outright opposed integration of the military, but 75 percent of white servicemen were not willing to tolerate black GIs and white women dancing together. See Moskos, *American Enlisted Man,* 122.

109 See LHA, 602.2, folder 40, DS 113/58 and 6NS 38/59, for an example of a woman and her landlord who were indicted for procurement. She had been living with an American for two years and could not produce a wedding permit because she had a spot on her lung. Because of her past ailment she could not live up to the health standard demanded by immigration laws. (To protect the privacy of the individuals in the court records, I include no names, instead citing the court cases according to the number assigned by the court.) For military attitudes toward women associating with American GIs in the immediate postwar years, see Willoughby, "Sexual Behavior of American GIs," 155.

110 Hough, "Socio-Cultural Integration," 144–45; Lester, *Trivialneger,* 38; Kelly interview. Military commanders at times gave lectures claiming that the women who sought out GIs were spies sent from East Germany.

111 Hough, "Socio-Cultural Integration," 144–45. The American military never kept records of how many of the marriages were interracial; however, according to American military chaplains' estimates, approximately 10–15 percent of all marriages between GIs and German women in the 1960s and 1970s involved a black partner.

112 Lester, *Trivialneger*, 38; IANAS video 56; interview with Christa Rühl [Schneider], a former social welfare worker in Birkenfeld County. According to Rühl, it was almost impossible for a young woman in Baumholder to get a permit to marry a black GI.

113 Frankenstein, *Soldatenkinder*, 26. On the postwar years, see Kleinschmidt, *"Do not fraternize,"* 185. In 1949, out of 280 black soldiers who had applied for wedding permits, only 22 (7.9 percent) had received permission. One hundred ten applications were still in process, 57 never received a response, and 91 were denied. By way of comparison, by 1948, 64.3 percent of white soldiers wanting to marry had been granted permission to do so. See Hough, "Socio-Cultural Integration," 92.

114 LHA, 602.06, folder 14, ES 56/57. In this case a black soldier was transferred to the United States for expressing outrage when his commanding officer rudely questioned his fiancée's decision to marry a black man.

115 Nichols, *Breakthrough*, 185.

116 *U.S. News and World Report*, 11 October 1957, "When Negro Servicemen Bring Home White Brides," 110–12; Warren interview.

117 See NARA, RG 338, USAREUR, Circular 3; *U.S. News and World Report*, 11 October 1957, "When Negro Servicemen Bring Home White Brides," 110–12.

118 Davies interview.

119 Email interview with Ronald Noble, 14 April 2001.

120 Rühl [Schneider], Lang, and Wolf interviews; IANAS video 53.

121 IANAS videos 37 and 38. One man recalled that Germans "adopted the official attitude [of race segregation] of the United States towards the blacks."

122 *RP*, 24 February 1953, "Der Mensch zwischen Freiheit und Verantwortung."

123 *PV*, 10 March 1953, "Hautfarbe, ein echtes Problem?"

124 Heide Fehrenbach shows this shift in her "Rehabilitating Fatherland" and "Of German Mothers and '*Negermischlinge*.'"

125 *RP*, 3 April 1954, "Leserbrief: Rassentrennung." See Fehrenbach, "Of German Mothers and '*Negermischlinge*,'" on this effacement in the national debates.

Chapter Four

1 KdP, 555.4, "Nöte der Bevölkerung"; KdP, 555.4, Letter of Arbeitsgemeinschaft Evangelischer Jugendaufbaudienst Pfalz to Ministry of the Interior, 1.

2 For a discussion of these racial outsiders in German debates on race, see Mosse, *Nationalism and Sexuality;* and Poiger, *Jazz, Rock, and Rebels*, 13–30.

3 NARA, RG 338, USAREUR, Annual History Report, US ARMY Europe 1953–54, 146. Of those questioned, 76 percent cited occupation costs as the biggest disadvantage of the U.S. presence; 16 percent claimed that U.S. troops presented no disadvantage; and 2 percent believed their presence provoked the Soviet Union. German assessment of the troops' behavior was much more favorable than those of the French or Japanese. In 1958, 57 per-

cent of Germans rated the GIs behavior as good, 37 percent rated it fair, and only 6 percent rated it poor. The numbers for France were 23 percent good, 49 percent fair, and 28 percent poor. In Japan, the numbers were 21 percent good, 60 percent fair, and 19 percent poor. See Moskos, *American Enlisted Man,* 213.

4 In *Jazz, Rock, and Rebels,* Uta Poiger presents a wonderful discussion of how German debates about American popular culture exposed the persistence of these racist attitudes. See also Heide Fehrenbach's work on the children born of German mothers and African American fathers, especially her "Rehabilitating Fatherland" and "Of German Mothers and '*Negermischlinge.*'"

5 BAK, Verhandlungen des Deutschen Bundestages, 2 October 1952 and 15 April 1953. See also BAK, B 153/1513, 207, "Tagung des Kuratoriums 28 January 1953."

6 Mönnich, *Das Land ohne Träume.*

7 *Glaube und Heimat,* "Helft Baumholder!", 285. I am grateful to Fritz Licht for making a copy of this essay available to me.

8 *RZ,* 14 March 1953, "Hessische Nachrichten berichten Moriaten aus Baumholder—Einseitig gefärbte 'Tatsachenberichte'—Eine einzige Verunglimpfung der heimischen Bevölkerung."

9 Mönnich, *Das Land ohne Träume,* 161. Interviewee Fritz Licht owns photos of the infamous tent as well as the bus bars.

10 For a wonderful and, according to Fritz Licht, a very realistic depiction of the tent, see *Die Goldene Pest.*

11 See, e.g., IANAS videos 37 and 53.

12 Stadtverwaltung Kaiserslautern, Vollzug des Gaststättengesetzes, Letter of Stadtverwaltung to Bezirksregierung, 19 November 1957. *Animierdamen* were, of course, not an American invention; they were already a feature of German nightclubs in the late nineteenth century.

13 In 1939, the town featured 11 pubs and inns. By 1955, this number had risen to 21 bars, and by 1959 the number had grown to 48. The heyday of the bars was the 1960s. Becker, "Die Veränderung des Stadtbildes von Baumholder," 34.

14 IANAS video 37; *Nahe Zeitung,* 28 August 1995, "Bars schossen wie Pilze aus dem Boden."

15 *RP,* 15 January 1953, "Goldener Westen im Winterkleid."

16 LHA, 930/8018, "Bericht über die Tagung des Landesjugendamtes Rheinland-Pfalz am 14.4.1959 zu Neustadt/a.d. Weinstraße."

17 Berichte, 1951–73, "Bericht über die Auswirkung der alliierten Baumassnahmen auf die fürsorgerische Arbeit."

18 German children had learned quickly how generous the American GI was, and whenever there was a maneuver, the children were not far off, as one German recalled, "because we were always hungry, and they always shared their food with us." The same man remembers that children asked for food, but that most of the time it was given without their having to ask. IANAS videos 51, 60, and 6.

19 *PV,* 6 August 1952, "'Mein Kind tut das nicht' sagt die Mutter"; *Allge-*

meine Zeitung, Mainz, 14 November 1951, "Diebstähle durch herumtrei-
bende Jugendliche"; *Allgemeine Zeitung, Mainz,* 2 October 1951, "Ami, e
Grosche" (quote).

20 Jacobmeyer, *Vom Zwangsarbeiter,* 102, describes how the harsh policies of
the French assured the highest repatriation rates, especially of Polish DPs. In
1950, when the American zone was still home to 93,909 DPs and the British
to 76,357, a mere 6,646 DPs lived in the French zone. Of all the DPs in the
Federal Republic in 1954, only 3.5 percent lived in Rhineland-Palatinate, according to Harmsen, *Die Integration,* 19 and 25.

21 On the fate of Jewish DPs in West Germany, see Jacobmeyer, *Vom Zwangs-
arbeiter;* Nachama, "Nach der Befreiung"; Brenner, "East European and
German Jews"; Harmsen, *Die Integration;* Wetzel, "'Mir szeinen doh'";
Grossmann, "Trauma, Memory, and Motherhood."

22 Mosse, *Nationalism and Sexuality.* See Bristow, *Prostitution and Prejudice,* for
a history of the role of Eastern European Jews in prostitution and traditional anti-Semitic charges related to that involvement.

23 BAK, B 153/327, Letter of Katholisches Pfarramt to Ministry of the Interior,
2 December 1954.

24 At the time, the term "professional prostitute" was applied to women who
acknowledged that this was their profession and registered with the health
office. "Amateur" prostitute was a label that was applied to a wide range of
sexual behavior that was deemed inappropriate. See Chapter 5 for a more
detailed discussion of how fluid the categories of sexual behavior were.

25 The prostitution trial records of the Amtsgericht Baumholder are at the
LHA, record group 602.06. They are a wonderfully rich source on the scope
of prostitution. Also see LHA, 504/384, "Bericht des Besatzungsausschuss,"
11; and the weekly coverage of the *Rheinzeitung* on the so-called "ladies' day"
(*Damensitzung*) in the courts. See, e.g., *RZ,* 21 June 1956, "Wieder Camping
im Dollarwäldchen."

26 LHA, 504/382, "Niederschrift über die amerikanische, französische und
deutsche Zusammenkunft 6 October 1955."

27 Berichte, 1951–1973, Letter Kreisjugendamt Birkenfeld an Landratsamt Esslingen 8 June 1955. According to Heinrich Haag, the former police chief, on
paydays and busy nights these checks were conducted every ten minutes.

28 See discussion in Chapter 5.

29 For a discussion of the churches' place in postwar society, see especially
Hollenstein, "Die Katholische Kirche"; Greschat, "Die evangelische
Kirche"; Kleßmann, "Kontinuitäten und Veränderungen im protestantischen Milieu"; Gabriel, "Die Katholiken in den fünfziger Jahren"; Hermand, *Kultur im Wiederaufbau;* and Mitchell, "Christian Democracy." On
the churches' role in cultural politics, see Fehrenbach, "Fight for the Christian West," and *Cinema in Democratizing Germany.*

30 D. Herzog, "'Pleasure, Sex, and Politics,'" 397, 415–19.

31 KdP, Pfarrämter Jahresberichte, Kaiserslautern 1958.

32 KdP, Pfarrämter Jahresberichte, Landstuhl 1953 and 1959. See also Evangelische Kirche im Rheinland, Zentralarchiv Düsseldorf, "Verhandlungen der

ordentlichen Kreissynode St. Wendel, 4–5 September 1951." For Catholic complaints, see BAS, Pfarrämter Jahresberichte, Landau, esp. 1958.

33 Debus, "Die Großen Kirchen unter dem Hakenkreuz." More than 40 percent of Catholic priests were persecuted in the Palatinate.

34 Dickinson, *Politics of German Child Welfare,* 214; Vollnhals, "Die evangelische Kirche."

35 For debates on *Amerikanismus* during the Weimar years, see Kaes, Jay, and Dimendberg, *Weimar Republic Sourcebook,* 393–411; Willett, *New Sobriety;* Nolan, *Visions of Modernity;* Costigliola, *Awkward Dominion;* and Lüdtke, Marßolek, and von Saldern, *Amerikanisierung.* For a thoughtful overview of German views on America, see Maase, *Bravo Amerika,* 41–62; Wagnleitner, *Coca-Colonization,* 9–36; Nolan, "America in the German Imagination."

36 KdP, Pfarrämter Jahresberichte, Sembach, 1952, 1953, 1954, 1955; ibid., Kusel and Landstuhl, esp. 1957; Evangelische Kirche im Rheinland, Zentralarchiv Düsseldorf, "Verhandlungen der ordentlichen Kreissynode St. Wendel, 13–14 Okt. 1957," 5. For Catholic complaints about *Amerikanismus* and people's striving for material goods and pleasure (*Genussucht* and *Geldsucht*), see BAS, Pfarrämter Jahresberichte, Landstuhl 1957 and 1961; Kaiserslautern 1958; and Landau 1958.

37 Evangelische Kirche im Rheinland, Zentralarchiv Düsseldorf, "Verhandlungen der ordentlichen Kreissynode St. Wendel, 4–5 September 1951," 3 ("political passions"); and "Verhandlungen der ordentlichen Kreissynode St. Wendel, 13–14 Okt. 1957," 7.

38 Evangelische Kirche im Rheinland, Zentralarchiv Düsseldorf, "Verhandlungen der ordentlichen Kreissynode St. Wendel, 13–14 Okt. 1957," 7.

39 KdP, Pfarrämter Jahresberichte, Kaiserslautern 1955, 21.

40 It is perhaps telling that the entry for the film in Jacobsen, *Geschichte des deutschen Films,* accidentally calls the little town "Gossenthal" (meaning Gutter Valley) instead of Dossenthal.

41 See Ritzenhofen, "*Goldene Pest* und *Schwarzer Kies.*" For a later East German version of the moral excesses in Baumholder, see Walter Heynowski's 1965 DEFA production *OK, OKAY.* I thank Annette Brauerhoch for this information.

42 Licht interview. The archives do not allow the names of clergy to be used.

43 *Glaube und Heimat,* "Helft Baumholder!" 283.

44 Ibid., 285.

45 Ibid., 283. According to Baumholder's former police chief Haag, the "dollar forest" was also known as "Black Forest."

46 Ibid., 284 and 285.

47 Ibid., 285.

48 For an example of East German commentary on the moral threat posed by the American military, see *Berliner Zeitung* (Berlin-Ost), 14 October 1956, "Ich war Taxifahrer in Kaiserslautern," (copy in ZSK). The essay describes in great detail the moral excesses of Kaiserslautern and shows photographs of the "so-called defenders of the 'occidental culture' . . . who think that they can do as they please in West Germany." Another photo showed a "GI

with his 'girl-friend'" with the caption saying that the other women in the bar were lucky since this GI already had found a willing "sacrificial lamb." At the same time, the paper pitied those poor women who were not thus protected by a "Veronika." A Leipzig SED publication described the sexual excesses by calling Baumholder an "Ami-Morass." Cited in *Glaube und Heimat,* 284. See also Merkel, "Eine andere Welt"; and the *Junge Welt* essay of 14 March 1950, cited in Fuchs, "Rock'n'Roll," 201.

49 *RZ,* 2 August 1954, "Baumholder im Spiegel der Presseerörterungen—Wochenblatt berichtet von einer 'Fremdenlegion der Sünderinnen' am Truppenübungsplatz."

50 *Die Pfalz klagt an,* 13.

51 Ibid., 12. The German historian Friedrich Meinecke coined the term "The German Catastrophe" when grappling with the rise of Nazism in his 1946 book of the same title. Heineman, "Hour of the Woman," shows how Germans considered the occupation years 1945–49 as the nadir of their history.

52 *Die Pfalz klagt an,* 12. For a similar attempt at erasure of the Nazi past, see KdP, Pfarrämter Jahresberichte, Pirmansens 1960, in which a Protestant clergyman asserts that the *Ami Bars* pointed to the "deterioration of our Western culture (*Abendland*), which used to be able to call itself proudly a Christian one."

53 *Die Bunte,* 14 September 1957, "Hilferuf aus Kaiserslautern."

54 *RZ,* 14 November 1954, "Baumholder ist hinreichend genug beschmutzt."

55 *Neue Revue,* 29 May 1954. Examples of this sort of coverage can be found in national publications such as *Die Bunte, Wochenend, Quick,* and *Das Grüne Blatt,* which showed almost exclusively pictures of black GIs with German women when reporting on the alleged excesses.

56 Mönnich, *Das Land ohne Träume,* 158.

57 *Tag der Arbeit,* 1 May 1959, "Das Dorf der 'Goldenen Pest' das stinkt zum Himmel, sagt der Staatsanwalt." For a communist commentary, see Freie Deutsche Jugend in Westdeutschland, *Denkschrift über das Ausmass,* 1–42. According to this essay, 280 girls in Baumholder had to leave school in 1953 because they were pregnant by American GIs, and 60 percent of "secret prostitutes" were less than fourteen years old.

58 *Allgemeine Zeitung, Mainz,* 15 September 1955, "Die Ursache allen Übels sind die Frolleins—Ein Rundgang mit dem Militärkommandeur durch Mainzer Negerbars." See Hitler, *Mein Kampf,* 448–49; and Nazi election poster in Moeller, *Protecting Motherhood,* fig. 3, which brought that message home by depicting a "savage black" attacking a white German woman while a stereotypical image of a Jew hovered in the background.

59 See my discussion in Chapter 8.

60 D. Herzog, "'Pleasure, Sex, and Politics.'" Heineman, "Hour of the Woman," makes that argument for the years of occupation.

61 On racial stereotypes, see Gilman, *Difference and Pathology;* Poiger, *Jazz, Rock, and Rebels;* Fehrenbach, "Rehabilitating Fatherland" and "Of German Mothers."

Chapter Five

1   BAK, B 153/327, 194. A common complaint by church-affiliated welfare organizations was that the strict marriage regulations of the American military needed to be changed. The provision that allowed soldiers to apply for a wedding permit only after having spent eighteen months in Germany was finally repealed on 15 November 1954, to appease the German welfare organizations and to improve troop morale. See Hough, "Socio-Cultural Integration," 91.

2   See Chapter 3.

3   *RZ,* 28 July 1952, "Westwall Stimmung—Dichtung und Wahrheit / Die Kreisverwaltung steht Rede und Antwort / Tatsachen widerlegen den Irrglauben der Behörden und Oeffentlichkeit"; and *Wall Street Journal,* 26 September 1952, "Huge U.S. Army Base." See also IANAS videos 47 and 45.

4   Other labels applied to women who were seen with Americans were *Amizonen, Amicen, Ami-Schickse, Amiliebchen, Amerikanerbräute, Marketenderinnen, Dirnen, Damen, leichte Mädchen, Frolleins,* and *Huren.* The fact that the term "Veronika" was used, at least during the first few years of the decade, is perhaps indicative of how the postwar period extended into the early 1950s. By the middle of the decade, the use of "Veronika" pretty much disappeared. I avoid the use of the term as much as possible, using "soldiers' brides" instead. See also Katz, "Die leichten Truppen."

5   Hillel, *Die Invasion,* 187; Heineman, "Standing Alone," esp. 209–28. See also Heineman, "Hour of the Woman" and *What Difference.*

6   For a wonderfully entertaining, if at times very critical and biased, depiction of the GIs' behavior and activities in Europe, see Hillel, *Die Invasion.* He argues that German women merely shifted from state-sponsored promiscuity to a free-for-all promiscuity in the chaos and suffering of the postwar years. Thus, whereas Hillel blames solely the American GIs for their behavior in other countries, in Germany he lays the blame for the GIs' sexual behavior largely on the shoulders of German parents who had welcomed the sexual liberation introduced by the Nazis.

7   *RZ,* 7 February 1952, "Man kann ruhig darüber sprechen: Zuviel oder zu wenig Dirnen im Kreis?—Ein offenes Wort zu einem heiklen Thema—Der goldene Mittelweg muss gefunden werden."

8   *RZ,* 1 April 1952, "Aus der Kreisstadt."

9   Berichte, 1951–63, Letter of Dr. Schnapp to Landrat Heep, 1 October 1951.

10 Berichte, 1951–73, "Niederschrift über eine Besprechung mit Gendamerie und Kriminalpolizei am 26 September 1953," 9.

11 Berichte, 1951–73 "Niederschrift über die Sitzung des Jugendausschusses, 12 March 1953."

12 BAK, B 106/17302, Letter of Verein to the Ministry of the Interior, 15 December 1953, in which they call the women "a grave threat to public order."

13 LHA, 930/4924 "Fürsorgearbeit in Gebieten mit ausländischen Truppen in Bad Godesberg 1–5 December 1957" (hereafter "Bad Godesberg Tagung"),

5. The minutes of the conference and the transcripts of the papers presented there were passed on to the Ministry of the Interior in Bonn.

14 See also Westphal, *Die Liebe auf dem Dorf*, 88, for examples of how women wearing makeup were scorned during the Nazi years.

15 *RZ,* 30 March 1955, "Schwere Haftstrafen."

16 See Rodnick, *Postwar Germans,* 107; Domentat, *"Hallo Fräulein,"* 53–55. For a novel written by a woman that depicts women's sexual attraction to black GIs, see Kellermann, *Die PX Story,* esp. 25.

17 BAK, B 153/327, 258, "Die Bekämpfung des Dirnenunwesens (3. Sitzung des Fachausschusses II des deutschen Verein für öffentliche und private Fürsorge)." AKK, Bekämpfung der Unzucht, "Niederschrift über die Abschlussbesprechung 5 September 1963," 6; *RP,* 26 April 1958, "Hatte angeblich keine Gewalt mehr über ihre Töchter."

18 Christa Rühl Schneider, who was a social worker in Baumholder during the 1950s, concluded in hindsight that much of the harsh and punitive measures dealt out to the women by her and her colleagues were sheer bourgeois envy at the freedom in sexual matters that these women seemed to enjoy.

19 Christa Rühl, "Soziale Auswirkungen eines Truppenübungsplatzes," 29. *RP,* 24 February 1953, "Der Mensch zwischen Freiheit und Verantwortung," indicts the women who seek out black GIs for their "addiction to pleasure" (*Vergnügungssucht*) and their "sexual drives" (*Triebhaftigkeit*).

20 On the "disciplining" of women into rational consumers, see Carter, *How German Is She?* and "Deviant Pleasures?" 368; Moeller, *Protecting Motherhood,* 139–40.

21 *RZ,* 26 September 1951, "Traurige Bilder Menschlichen Tiefstandes — Alle drei waren reif fürs Arbeitshaus."

22 Usborne, *Politics of the Body,* 84.

23 For a history of the link between consumption, sexuality, and feminity, see Huyssen, *After the Great Divide;* Poiger, *Jazz, Rock, and Rebels.*

24 *RZ,* 18 July 1959, "Wir wollen die Dinge beim Namen nennen: Das Leben hat sich nur scheinbar 'normalisiert.'"

25 Berichte, 1951–73, "Niederschrift," 3. See also LHA, 930/4924, "Bad Godesberg Tagung," 10–11.

26 KdP, 555.4, "Letter of Arbeitsgemeinschaft Evangelischer Jugendaufbaudienst Pfalz to Ministry of the Interior," 1.

27 *RZ,* 26 September 1951, "Traurige Bilder menschlichen Tiefstandes — Alle drei waren reif fürs Arbeitshaus."

28 LHA, 504/384, "Bericht über die Besichtigungsfahrt," 11.

29 BAK, B 153/327, Letter of Protestant minister from Miesau to Ministry of the Interior, 8 January 1954.

30 BAS, Pfarrämter Jahresberichte, Landstuhl 1959.

31 Ibid.; and KdP, Pfarrämter Jahresberichte, Kindsbach 1959.

32 KdP, 555.4, "Besuch bei Pfarrer K.-Miesau am 14 April 1950."

33 KdP, 555.4, "Verhältnisse in der Gemeinde Miesau," 9 February 1951.

34 KdP, Pfarrämter Jahresberichte, Landstuhl 1957.

35 Berichte, 1951–73, "Bericht, 8 August 1951."

36 See Heineman, "Standing Alone," for a discussion of how anxious young women were in the postwar years about transgressing boundaries of proper sexual behavior.

37 Berichte, 1951–73, "Niederschrift über die Sitzung des Jugendamtsausschusses am 12. März 1953."

38 Another bureaucratic category applied to these women was "girls without permanent domicile and disaccustomed to work *(nichtsesshafte und arbeitsentwöhnte)*. See Berichte, 1951–73, Letter of Landratsamt Birkenfeld to Landesjugendamt Koblenz, 13 August 1957; *RZ*, 26 October 1956, "Zwanzigjährige verscherzte sich Bewährungsfrist."

39 KdP, 555.4, Letter of the Protestant minister in Miesau to the Social Ministry, 4 March 1952.

40 KdP, Diakonisches Werk Pfalz, "Fürsorge für weibliche Gefährdete 31 Januar 1955," 14. See Reagin, *German Woman's Movement,* 155, for similar views in the nineteenth century.

41 LHA, 504/29, "Niederschrift uber die Amtsbürgermeisterkonferenz vom 110.1953."

42 KdP, 555.4, Letter of the Protestant minister in Miesau to the Social Ministry, 4 March 1952.

43 KdP, 555.4, "Nöte der Bevölkerung."

44 KdP, 555.4, Letter Protestantischer Landeskirchenrat to Social Ministry Rheinland-Pfalz, 1 April 1952.

45 KdP, 555.4, "Notizen für das Gespräch in Heidelberg, 18 February 1952."

46 Ibid.

47 KdP, 555.4, "Nöte der Bevölkerung," 4. Unfortunately, the records do not reveal which of the American women's groups the clergy approached.

48 For the churches' view on brothels, see KdP, 555.4, "Bericht über die sittliche Zustände in Miesau" (n.d.) and "Sittliche Zustände in Landstuhl und Umgebung, 2 Juli 1951." See also the request for brothels in the city of Kaiserslautern at ASK, Bekämpfung der Unzucht; and Stadtverwaltung Kaiserslautern, Stadtratsprotokolle, 22 October 1953.

49 NARA, RG 338, USAREUR Office of the Chaplain, General Correspondence, Box 1. A November 1954 memo reported: "East Coast women's group is digging in for battle with the U.S. Army. The organization has heard that our military authorities have 'approved' prostitution . . . in many areas of Europe."

50 The one exception to this policy was the establishment of segregated brothels in France after D-Day. See Cosamas and Cowdry, *Medical Services,* 540. The American military did not set up brothels for its soldiers in Hawaii, but it tolerated the existence of segregated institutions there. See Bailey, *First Strange Place.*

51 BAK, B 141/4724, 97. This document is a letter from the Office of the High Commissioner for Germany in reference to alleged moral endangerment of youth in Bavaria. The letter further stated that "relations between Germans and Americans were excellent."

52 KdP, 555.4, "Aktennotiz 19 February 1952." See also KdP, 555.4, memorandum of meeting with American chaplains, in which German clergymen
linked the existing prostitution situation to the dangers of Soviet espio-
nage. An essay in *PV*, 4 February 1955, cites Carl Yeager from the Protestant
Church commission for the U.S. military's speculations on this issue. What
is so fascinating about the American position is that in the immediate postwar period the Americans tended to describe "Veronikas" as Nazi seducers.
By the 1950s they were identifying these women as communist seducers.

53 *Die Freiheit*, 18 Dezember 1954, "Laufende Razzien beunruhigen Geschäftemacher." Another favorite in newspapers was to joke that even in this case
the Americans adhered to their "free market" principle. See *RZ*, 7 February
1952, "Man kann ruhig darüber sprechen."

54 During the period of the American military government, the Americans
were much more involved in trying to control prostitution. Under American leadership, vice raids were conducted regularly in order to control VD.
Beginning with the 1949 Occupation Statute, the Americans asserted that
prostitution was a German problem. However, they did still insist that vice
raids had to be conducted if they so desired in the former American zone.
See Kreuzer, "Die Entwicklung," 70 and 101. Beginning in 1951, the military
reintroduced its nightly bed checks to combat "problems involved in contacts between occupation troops and the civilian population." This meant
that lower rank military personnel had to be in by midnight and thus could
spend only weekend nights with their girlfriends away from their barracks.
See Historical Division, "American Military Occupation of Germany," 136.

55 For a reprint of §361 No. 6a–c of the German Criminal Code, see Kreuzer,
"Die Entwicklung," 102.

56 However, some sort of nonregimented prostitution was going on in Baumholder after the Nazis built the Platz in 1937. A prostitute who was known
by the less than glamorous name "Bunker-Lene" was arrested in 1957. In the
newspaper article covering the trial, it was reported that the name "Bunker-
Lene" had been given to the woman by soldiers of the "former grand German Wehrmacht." See *RZ*, 14 February 1957, "Hatte 'Bunkerlene' die Hand
in der Brieftasche?

57 Berichte, 1951–73, "Protokoll über die am 14 Nov. 1951 stattgefundene Sitzung des erweiterten Jugendamtsausschusses" provides details on a brothel
at Lager Aulenbach on the Platz during the Third Reich. See also BAK,
B 189/05838, "Sozialministerium Rheinland-Pfalz: Maßnahmen für die besonders gefährdete Jugend in Gebieten starker Truppenkonzentrationen," 9.
In Koblenz, for example, where a great number of French troops were stationed, two brothels were established to cater exclusively to the French African units. See LHA, 9330/8015, Letter of mayor of Koblenz to Social Ministry. According to Heinrich Haag, the former police chief of Baumholder,
the French had provided a separate brothel for African units in Baumholder
as well.

58 The law did not forbid the granting of shelter to prostitutes. However, to

avoid the exploitation of prostitutes, it forbid the establishment of organized brothels, as the organized brothel was believed to create a situation of dependency for the women.

59 AKK, Bekämpfung der Unzucht. For an overview of American policies in the immediate postwar period, see Kreuzer, "Die Entwicklung," 101.

60 This step was taken in all communities with American troops in order to control prostitution. The limit for the city of Kaiserslautern was set at seventy-two hours, thus anybody visiting the city longer than three days had to register with the police.

61 Berichte, 1951–73, "Niederschrift über die Sitzung des Arbeitskreises Baumholder am 1953."

62 Berichte, 1951–73, "Protokoll über die am 14 November stattgefundene Sitzung des erweiterten Kreisjugendamtsausschusses," 1.

63 Berichte, 1951–73, Letter of Landrat to Landkreistag Rheinland-Pfalz, 24 March 1952. This provision was widely used when the courts did not have enough evidence to convict the woman of prostitution. The woman would then be punished for failing to register with the police.

64 Berichte, 1951–63, "Arbeitsbericht des Katholischen Fürsorgevereins, 1 June 1960," 2.

65 See KdP, 555.4, "Bericht über die sittliche Zustände in Miesau" (n.d.) and "Sittliche Zustände in Landstuhl und Umgebung, 2 Juli 1951."

66 Lang and Werner interviews. Unfortunately, because of the German *Datenschutz* (privacy laws), I was not able to see the judge's file at the Landeshauptarchiv in Koblenz.

67 *RZ,* 16 March 1954, "Ein besseres gegenseitiges Verstehen / deutsch-amerikanische Pfarrer Konferenz in Baumholder."

68 *RZ,* 31 Dezember 1955, "Erschütternde Bilanz des Amtsgerichtes." On Schnapp's ambition, see especially Berichte, 1951–73. In a 20 December 1952 letter to the Landrat in Birkenfeld, Schnapp outlined his program for making Baumholder a "model and experimental case study" to examine how "disasters" such as the troop presence could be overcome. The judge hoped to get the Johannes Gutenberg University in Mainz interested in producing with him a *Denkschrift* (memorandum) titled "Modell Baumholder" that would attract national and state attention.

69 Berichte, 1951–63, "Auszüge des Berichtes des Landrat an den Herrn Regierungspräsidenten, Koblenz, 27 November 1951."

70 Ibid., 1–2. No more than perhaps four black soldiers were stationed at the Birkenfeld Air Force base during the early 1950s.

71 AKK, Bekämpfung der Unzucht, Letter of Polizeiverwaltung Landstuhl to Landrat Kaiserslautern. See also KdP, 555.4, "Nöte der Bevölkerung und der Arbeitskräfte in den westlichen Grenzzonen (Pfalz und Eifel)," 3.

72 *Glaube und Heimat,* "Helft Baumholder!", 285.

73 KdP, 555.4, "Nöte der Bevölkerung und der Arbeitskräfte in den westlichen Grenzzonen (Pfalz und Eifel)," 3.

74 Berichte, 1951–63, "Letter of Landrat to the Regierungspräsident Koblenz, 27 November 1951."

75 Berichte, 1951–73, Memo concerning *Dirnenunwesen* to Landrat Heep, 12 December 1951.

76 AKK, Bekämpfung der Unzucht, Letter of Regierungspräsident of the Palatinate to the Landräte Kaiserslautern und Kusel, 18 December 1951. Clearly, representatives of the KPD were not expected to participate in this meeting, even though they were the most articulate critics of the American presence and the danger it presented to local youth.

77 AKK, Bekämpfung der Unzucht, Letter Landratsamt Kaiserslautern to Regierungspräsident of the Palatinate, 9 January 1952.

78 AKK, Bekämpfung der Unzucht, contains a copy of that letter.

79 Ibid.

80 Archiv des Kirchenkreises Birkenfeld, Verhandlungen der Kreissynode, 10 Oktober 1955, 21.

81 Berichte, 1951–73, Letter of Regierungspräsident to Landrat Birkenfeld, 30 January 1952. The workhouse was outlawed in 1945 by Law No. 14 of the American military government; however, Section 3 of that law allowed state governments to make other provisions. LHA, 930/7180, contains a copy of the workhouse rules, which make very clear why the women despised the institution. The purpose of the workhouse was to educate the "inmates toward a lawful and ordered life . . . so that perhaps they can again become worthy of the *Volksgemeinschaft*." Among the long list of rules, the following one perhaps best reveals the spirit of the institution: "Singing, whistling and noisiness, the keeping of gold and writing utensils as well as lighters . . . is strictly forbidden." Herr Karl Werner from Birkenfeld, a former clerk for Dr. Schnapp, had visited the workhouse for women in Brauweiler on a number of occasions. The workhouse housed a laundry and a sewing shop, where the women worked long hours. At night they were locked up in regular cells similar to the ones in a jail. According to Werner, this place was not pleasant, and the women who were sentenced to the workhouse absolutely hated it.

82 BAK, Verhandlungen des Deutschen Bundestages, 232d Sitzung 2 October 1952, 10663. These asylums were envisioned as institutions were the women could stay for a few days before being sent to a reformatory institution.

83 Ibid. See also *Allgemeine Zeitung, Mainz,* 3 February 1952, "Ami-Ehe, ja oder nein?" which suggests that some girls "who came of age during the war" had "distorted the image of the German woman" through their trading love for Chesterfields. Similar sentiments were expressed in a 25 September 1951 issue of the same paper in "Vor der Kaserne . . . ." The author of that article pointed out that the German soldier's wartime ideal of the Lili Marlen had become a very different phenomenon and that it was necessary to ensure that these new soldiers' brides with their "sunglasses, cherry-red lips, [and] high-gloss fingernails. . . don't besmirch [Germany's] reputation and especially the reputation of the German woman." In neither of the other papers used for this study did I come across these sorts of arguments. I suspect that these sentiments were expressed in this newspaper because Mainz was the capital of the state and thus much more concerned

with the national perception of the "Veronika" phenomenon. See Heineman, "Standing Alone," 209–16, on the situation in the immediate postwar years.

84 BAK, Verhandlungen des Deutschen Bundestages, 232d Sitzung 2 October 1952, 10664.

85 Ibid.

86 Ibid., 10665.

87 On Zillken, see Wollasch, *Der Katholische Fürsorgeverein;* Hong, *Welfare, Modernity, and the Weimar State;* Dickinson, *Politics of German Child Welfare.* On the Verein, see Muthesius, *Beiträge zur Entwicklung.*

88 Quoted in Dickinson, *Politics of German Child Welfare,* 214.

89 Ibid., 237. See also Heusler, "'Strafbestand' Liebe"; and Bleuel, *Strength Through Joy,* 211–17, 238–45, on the rise in illegitimacy rates and "moral offenses."

90 BAK, B 153/327, "Die Bekämpfung des Dirnenunwesens," 258 (back).

91 The Verein had been involved in a redefinition of prostitution since the end of World War II. See Heineman, "Standing Alone," 209–28. In 1952, the Verein investigated the limits of the 1927 Venereal Disease Act, which forbade brothels in order to protect women from exploitation.

92 LHA, 930/8018, Dr. Wagner from Pirmasens: "Arzt und Gesundheitsamt gegen Verwahrlosung und Jugendgefährdung" presentation given at conference entitled "Notwendige Massnahmen zur Eindämmung der Jugendgefährdung in Gebieten mit Truppenkonzentrationen in der Pfalz," sponsored by the Landesjugendamt of Rheinland-Pfalz.

93 See Clement, *Sexualität im sozialen Wandel,* 1; Koch, *Sexualpolitik und politische Erziehung,* 164, on post–World War II ambitions to restore pre-Weimar sexual mores; and Heineman, "Standing Alone," 209–28.

94 Wollasch, *Der Katholische Fürsorgeverein,* 235. Even the arch-conservative DNVP feared that such a step would only encourage secret prostitution, which would lead to an increase in VD.

95 BAK, B 153/327, 387, "Aktennotiz Referat 4 of 28 July 1952."

96 BAK, B 153/327, 257, "Die Bekämpfung des Dirnenunwesens."

97 Ibid. Mannheim had become notorious because of the large number of black GIs stationed there. Any woman who arrived in Baumholder by way of Mannheim was immediately suspected of prostitution.

98 Ibid., (back). The Verein was instrumental in getting the VD Law of 1953 passed. The 1953 law omitted a key section of the 1927 Law, which prohibited the licensing of prostitutes.

99 Ibid., 259.

100 Ibid.

101 Ibid., 261.

102 Ibid., 258 (back).

103 Ibid., 261.

104 Ibid., 259.

105 BAK, B 153/327, 310, Memo from Dr. Hagen dated 8 December 1953. See

also Niehauss, "Kontinuität und Wandel," 331. Seventy percent was the figure for the rest of West Germany as well.

106 BAK, B 153/327, 264, "Meeting in the Ministry of the Interior, 10 February 1954."

107 BAK, B 153/327, 152, Letter of 12 January 1955 from the Ministry of Justice to the Ministry of Interior, replying to a request from that office in regard to the growth of prostitution in the locations of troop concentrations. Since they referred to the Verein's agitation in their response, the troop concentrations they were discussing must have been those of American troops.

108 BAK, B 153/327, 417, Letter of Ministry of the Interior to the Ministry of Justice, 5 April 1957.

109 Ibid.

110 Ibid.

111 AKK, Bekämpfung der Unzucht, Letter of Bezirksregierung der Pfalz 5 June 1954 instructing the police that the new standard of "continuing" rather than the old "habitual" was to be applied. See *Allgemeine Zeitung, Mainz,* 12 May 1954, "Haftstrafen und Arbeitshaus gegen das Dirnenunwesen," in which the new approach is described.

112 BAK, B 153/327, 412, Letter of Ministry of the Interior to the Ministry of Justice, 5 April 1957.

113 See especially the Bundesgerichtshof ruling BGH St. Bd. 6 S. 46ff of 1953. The state court referred to this ruling as late as 1960. See LHA, 602.6, 6 NS 6/60/13/60, Landesgericht Bad Kreuznach, 12 February 1960.

114 BAK, B 153/327, 418, Letter of Ministry of the Interior to the Ministry of Justice, 5 April 1957.

115 On the social policies that aimed at the "reconstruction of motherhood" by returning women to the home during the 1950s, see Moeller, *Protecting Motherhood;* see also his "Reconstructing the German Family." On the reconstruction of women's role in the immediate postwar years, see Höhn, "Frau im Haus."

116 The term "uncle marriages" (*Onkelehen*) emerged because children usually called their mother's new partner "uncle" (*Onkel*). See, e.g., Berichte, 1951–73, Letter from Landrat Birkenfeld to Pfarrer R. Farber, 1 September 1953. For a treatment of the war widows and the problem of *Onkelehen,* see Tumpek-Kjellmark, "From Hitler's Widows to Adenauer's Brides"; and Heineman, *What Difference.*

117 BAK, B 153/327, 417–18, Letter of Ministry of Justice to Ministry of the Interior, 5 April 1957 (emphasis in original).

118 BAK, B 141/90248, "Niederschrift über die Zwischentagung der II. Unter-Kommission vom 14. bis 16. März 1957 in Goslar zum Thema *Gemeinschäd-liches Verhalten.*"

119 See Chapters 6 and 7.

120 BAK, B 153/327, 149, "Deutscher Verein memo," n.d. [probably 1952 or 1953 since they are making recommendations for the creation of local committees to fight prostitution].

Chapter Six

1   On German anxieties over youth, see especially Baumgarten, "Jugendge-fährdung"; Chaussy, "Jugend"; Heinritz, "Bedrohte Jugend"; Nikles, *Jugendpolitik;* Schildt, "Von der Not der Jugend." On German anxieties over the impact of American popular culture on youth, see Poiger, *Jazz, Rock, and Rebels;* Maase, *Bravo Amerika.*

2   LHA, 930/4924, "Bad Godesberg Tagung," 12. See also LHA, 930/4921, "Besprechung zwischen Vertretern der Inneren Mission und des Katholischen Fürsorgeverein, 19 March 1953."

3   BAK, B 153/131, 120, "Vierte Tagung des Kuratoriums, 8 February 1952." On German welfare policies, see Hong, *Welfare, Modernity, and the Weimar State;* and Dickinson, *Politics of German Child Welfare.*

4   KdP, 555.4, "Aktennotiz 1 Februar 1952," 1.

5   BAK, B 153/327, "Niederschrift." In light of the housing shortage, it is very possible that many woods and meadows were used in such a manner; the question is, of course, whether the sex act was actually and deliberately conducted in front of children.

6   KdP, 555.4, Letter of the Miesau Protestant minister to Social Ministry of the Rhineland-Palatinate, 3 March 1952.

7   Bleuel, *Strength Through Joy,* 241, shows that during the Third Reich, Wehrmacht soldiers also sought out young teenage girls in garrison communities.

8   Ibid.

9   LHA, 930/816, Letter of Karl Kuhn, member of the state legislature to the Ministry of Interior in Mainz, 26 September 1952.

10 BAK, Verhandlungen des Deutschen Bundestages, 259th Sitzung, 15 April 1953, 12623–24.

11 Ibid.

12 According to that list, a mere 106 of those women were married, 206 were single, 21 were widowed, and 9 were divorced. See Berichte, 1951–73, Letter of Landratsamt to Social Ministry, Mainz, 6 January 1953.

13 BAK, Verhandlungen des Deutschen Bundestages, 259th Sitzung, 15 April 1953, 12624.

14 *RZ,* 13 August 1952, "Die Jugendnot in Rheinland-Pfalz/Landesregierung bittet den Bund in einer Denkschrift um finanzielle Hilfe."

15 BAK, Verhandlungen des Deutschen Bundestages, 259th Sitzung, 15 April 1953, 12624.

16 BAK, Verhandlungen des Deutschen Bundestages, 232d Sitzung, 2 October 1952, 10664.

17 *PV,* 17 November 1952, "Kampf gegen die sittliche Vergiftung der Jugend."

18 *RZ,* 13 August 1952, "Die Jugendnot in Rheinland-Pfalz/Landesregierung bittet den Bund in einer Denkschrift um finanzielle Hilfe."

19 BAK, B 153/129–2 and B 153/132, "Rede des Bundesminister des Innern 14 December 1954." See also B 153/1355, in which the Ministry of the Interior reported to the *Bundesrechnungshof* why it regarded the BJP as so important. The report states that in 1949 German youth were marked by "criminality,

spiritual and moral shallowness, mostly rejecting attitudes toward social and political community life." The author then compared the acute crisis with developments in 1930–33, when "parts of the youth streamed into extreme and democracy-rejecting camps." The BJP was initiated to ensure that there was no repetition of 1933. The BJP's annual budget of DM 20–30 million was intended to battle the persisting high unemployment rates among the youth and to insure that Germany's young would be raised as good democrats in the new Europe.

20 BAK, B 153/134, "Sitzung des Kuratoriums 20 Juli 1951"; and BAK, B 153/129–2, 563, "Lastenverteilung des Programmes zwischen Bund und Länder."

21 Comments by Elizabeth Zillken about the importance of Baumholder in BAK, B 153/1513, "Tagung des Kuratoriums, 28 Januar 1953."

22 Archiv des Kirchenkreis Birkenfeld, Letter of Innere Mission Cologne to pastor Bido in Idar-Oberstein, 31 Oktober 1953.

23 Once these federal funds were granted, these organizations received 85 percent of their operating costs. This allowed them to greatly expand their institutions while also expanding their job description and reach.

24 BAK, Verhandlungen des Deutschen Bundestages, 259th Sitzung, 15 April 1953, 12624.

25 For an overview of conservative fears, see LHA, 930/4924, "Bad Godesberg Tagung," 2–5.

26 BAK, B 153/1355, Letter Katholischer Fürsorgeverein, 15 March 1962.

27 Berichte, 1951–63, "Denkschrift über die Mißstände an den Großbaustellen der Besatzungsmacht in Rheinland-Pfalz und Vorschläge zu ihrer Behebung" (hereafter "Denkschrift über die Mißstände"), 2; BAK, B 153/327, "Bekämpfung des Dirnenunwesens," 294. For other comments on working mothers, see Stadtverwaltung Kaiserslautern, Dirnenunwesen, esp. "Niederschrift über eine Besprechung mit Herrn Innenminister Dr. Zimmer, 26 April 1955," 31. See also *Bilanz der Aufbauarbeit*, 196.

28 See DeLille, *Blick zurück aufs Glück,* 69, for the comments of Joseph Wuermeling, Minister of the Family, avowing that women who do not stay home with their children are selfish materialists.

29 BAK, B 153/327, Ministry of the Interior, "Vermerk," 13 September 1955.

30 BAK, B 153/327, 98, "Jugendgefährdung in Gegenden grosser Truppenansammlungen." Teachers were also instructed of their special duties in light of troop concentrations; see ibid., 98 (back).

31 BAK, B 153/1369, 246, "Bericht über die Arbeit der Gefährdetenfürsorge im Rechnungsjahr 1959." See also *Bilanz der Aufbauarbeit*, 194.

32 The model for this "travelling library" was, of course, the bookmobile of the Amerika Haus in Kaiserslautern.

33 Berichte, 1951–63, "Arbeitsbericht des Katholischen Fürsorgevereins, 1 June 1960," 3. In 1950 the whole county of Birkenfeld reported 39 acts of juvenile delinquency; in 1955 there were 125 such incidents, with only 11 of them involving "girls," the group that all the social workers fretted over. As in Kaiserslautern, the real increase in juvenile delinquency arose from traffic violations, which were closely related to the fact that more teenagers

had mopeds or motorcycles due to the new prosperity of their parents. Of the 125 indictments in Birkenfeld, 18 involved a prank committed during "witches night" (*Mainacht*), and 13 juveniles were sentenced for playing hooky from school. See *Bilanz der Aufbauarbeit*, 204. In Baumholder only 2 cases of juvenile delinquency were reported for 1956. See *RZ*, 17 January 1957, "682 Gesetzesbrecher 1956 vor dem Richter."

34 See also Berichte, 1951–63, "Denkschrift über die Mißstände."

35 Ibid., 2. For wonderful discussions of German perceptions of American culture in the 1950s, see Maase, *Bravo Amerika;* and Poiger, *Jazz, Rock, and Rebels.*

36 KVB, Protokolle des Jugendwohlfahrtsausschußes, meeting of 26 May 1956.

37 *Bilanz der Aufbauarbeit,* 200; Berichte, 1951–73, "Auswirkungen des Truppenübungsplatzes Baumholder auf die jugendfürsorgerische Arbeit," 1; and LHA, 930/9946, "Neuerkrankungen an Geschlechtskrankheiten." In the county of Birkenfeld, the illegitimacy rate was 8.3 percent in 1950, before the Americans arrived, and increased to 10.7 percent by 1955. After 1955, these numbers dropped significantly; the county's average was lower than the national average of 6.5 percent. Illegitimacy rates in Baumholder stood at 22.1 percent; however a good part of those numbers can be explained by the military's marriage restrictions, especially before 1954. During the Weimar period, illegitimacy rates averaged 11.4 percent. See Usborne, *Politics of the Body,* 82. For debates on "incomplete families," see Heineman, *What Difference.*

38 *PV,* 19 January 1953, "Kaiserlauterner Polizei reicht nicht mehr aus."

39 LHA, 930/8016, "Jugendnotstandsgebiet Bad Kreuznach."

40 *PV,* 30 September 1952, "Jugendnot-Alarmzeichen der Zeit/Eine große gemeinsame Aufgabe für Polizei, Elternhaus und Staat."

41 LHA, 930/4924, "Bad Godesberg Tagung," report entitled "Bericht über die Arbeit in der Truppenplatzfürsorge im Raum Trier," 3–4 and 9; LHA, 930/8015, Letter of Landrat Zell/Mosel to Social Ministry, 26 April 1954.

42 KdP, 555.4, Letter of Landesverband Innere Mission an Landeskirchenrat Speyer, 14 February 1952.

43 *PV,* 23 June 1954, "Jugendliche auf verbrecherischen Wegen."

44 KdP, 555.4, Letter of Landesverband Innere Mission an Landeskirchenrat Speyer, 14 February 1952; and *PV,* 23 June 1954, "Jugendliche auf verbrecherischen Wegen."

45 KdP, 555.4, "Aktennotiz 1 February 1952." See also LHA, 930/816, Letter of Karl Kuhn, member of the state legislature to the Ministry of Interior in Mainz, 26 September 1952.

46 Berichte, 1951–73, "Bericht" (n.d.), 3.

47 LHA, 930/8018, "Bericht über die Tagung des Landesjugendamtes Rheinland-Pfalz am 14.4.1959 zu Neustadt/a.d. Weinstraße," report entitled "Arzt und Gesundheitsamt gegen Verwahrlosung und Jugendgefährdung."

48 LHA, 930/8015, Letter from Ministry of the Interior to Social Ministry, 7 February 1956.

49 BAK, B 153/327, "Jugendgefährdung in Gegenden grosser Truppenansammlungen," 97 (back).

50 This last question also suggests that her mother was a single parent. Amtsgericht Birkenfeld DS 8/57. This case is one of the few for which the actual trial proceedings still exist.

51 BAK, B 141/82165, 81, "Niederschrift über die 9. Tagung der Länderkommission für die große Strafrechtsreform, 16.1–20.1.61." The former social welfare workers from Baumholder told me that most of these sorts of trials were conducted because of denunciations by neighbors. Interview with Christa Rühl Schneider and Annemarie Lang. For the crucial contribution of denunciation in assuring Nazi control of society, see Gellately, *The Gestapo and German Society.*

52 *RZ,* 3 July 1957, "Um des schnöden Mammons Willen . . . amerikanischer Freund der Tochter im Haus geduldet / Zeuge festgenommen."

53 *RP,* 26 April 1958, "Hatte angeblich keine Gewalt mehr über ihre Töchter."

54 *PV,* 5 April 1957, "Gefängnis für leidgeprüfte Kriegerwitwe / Wegen Kuppelei verurteilt verzeiht sie doch der widerspenstigen Tochter."

55 *Die Freiheit,* 17 January 1955, "Deutsch-Amerikanisches Sodom: Hinter dem Vorhang schlief das Kind."

56 *Freisoziale Presse,* 1 October 1954, "Eine Stadt unter Besatzungslaster"; and *PV,* 1 December 1954, "Kriminalpolizei macht dieses Geschäft zu."

57 *Die Freiheit,* 18 December 1954, "Laufende Razzien beunruhigen Geschäftemacher"; and *RP,* 25 May 1956, which lists the city boroughs where raids were conducted. The neighborhoods cited were always the same ones, some of them barrack housing for refugees and extremely poor.

58 *Die Freiheit,* 8 September 1954, "Die Moral des Stadtrats Lieberich."

59 KdP, Pfarrämter Jahresberichte, Kaiserslautern 1953, 2–3.

60 For conservative efforts to contain American popular culture, see Fehrenbach, *Cinema;* Poiger, *Jazz, Rock, and Rebels;* Maase, *Bravo Amerika.*

61 See, e.g., Schildt's argument that Germans did not view the American influence as a "foreign import" in his *Moderne Zeiten,* 422.

62 BAK, B 153/327, 82, Letter of Ministry of Labor to Ministry of the Interior of 18 January 1955. See also Evangelische Kirche Baumholder, Jugendarbeit, "Report of Innere Mission 16 January 1958." The social worker stated that she received monthly lists of the new female employees from the employment office.

63 Berichte, 1951–63, contains a list of all local women employed with the American military.

64 LHA, 930/4924, "Bad Godesberg Tagung," report entitled "Unsere Arbeit im Bereich der Truppenplätze im Raum Mainfranken." Dr. Schnapp expressed similar sentiments when he stated that Americans faultily assume that anybody willing to work is a "decent chap." See Berichte, 1951–73, "Niederschrift über die Sitzung 12 März 1953," 12.

65 Archiv der evangelischen Kirche Baumholder, Jugendarbeit, Letter of Innere Mission to Social Ministry, 11 April 1958.

66 LHA, 930/4924, "Bad Godesberg Tagung," report entitled "Unsere Arbeit im Bereich der Truppenplätze im Raum Mainfranken," 3. For similar complaints, see also Archiv des Kirchenkreises Birkenfeld, Verhandlungen der Kreissynode 1954.

67 Rühl, "Soziale Auswirkungen," 13. I am indebted to Rühl Schneider for graciously sharing her accreditation thesis with me, especially since she is horrified when she reflects back on social welfare work during those days.

68 *Die Pfalz klagt an,* 5.

69 Rühl, "Soziale Auswirkungen," 13–15.

70 BAK, B 153/327, 194, "Jugendgefährdung in Gegenden grosser Truppensammlungen."

71 Maase, *Bravo Amerika,* 14.

72 BAK, B 153/1355 "Bericht Katholischer Fürsorgeverein Wiesbaden 1957."

73 LHA, 930/4924, "Bad Godesberg Tagung," 5.

74 LHA, 930/4923, Letter of Katholischer Fürsorgeverein to Ministry of the Interior, 14 June 1954. See also Berichte, 1951–73, Letter of Landrat to Social Ministry in Mainz and "Niederschrift über die Sitzung des Jugendamtsausschusses, 12 March 1953," 9.

75 BAK, B 153/1355 "Sachlicher Bericht Katholischer Fürsorgeverein, 15 March 1962."

76 LHA, 930/4924, "Bad Godesberg Tagung," 4.

77 Berichte, 1951–73, Letter of Landrat, 9 February 1954; and Letter of Landrat to Social Ministry Mainz, 14 May 1955. See also BAK, B 141/4724, for an example of how other states (*Länder*) where Americans were stationed rejected the intrusive questions from the federal level about the status of morality in their communities.

78 Berichte, 1951–73, Letter of Landrat to Landratsamt Esslingen, 12 May 1955; and Letter of Landrat to Sozialministerium, 14 May 1954, 4.

79 VGB, Deutsch-Amerikanisches Freundschaftskomitee, "Deutsch-Amerikanische Konferenz," n.d. [probably either July or August 1956 since they refer to press reports of the month of July of that year]. See also a defense of the population by the local newspaper in *RZ,* 27 January 1956, "Man muss das Beste aus dieser Situation machen."

80 BAK, B 153/327, 156, Letter of Katholisches Pfarramt Baumholder, 2 Dezember 1954.

81 *Der Weg,* 20/21, 1959, "Die Stadt auf dem Berge"; and *RZ,* 1 June 1959, "'Baumholder ist gleich Unmoral'—Ist es das?"

82 BAK, B 153/327, 295, report of the Centralausschuss für die Innere Mission to the Ministry of the Interior, 18 January 1954.

83 BAK, B 189/05838 "Massnahmen für die besonders gefährdete Jugend in Gebieten starker Truppenkonzentrationen, 12 April 1957," 3.

84 BAK, B 153/1355, Letter Katholischer Fürsorgeverein, 17 März 1962.

85 LHA, 930/4924, "Bad Godesberg Tagung," 9.

86 Reports by local youth offices are full of complaints about parents who resisted attempts by police and youth welfare workers to prevent their teenage children from attending the movies or a village dance. LHA, 930/4920,

"Erfahrungsberichte der Jugendämter 1953"; and LHA, 930/4921 "Über Erfahrungen in der Durchführung des Gesetzes zum Schutz der Jugend 1951." See also LHA, 441/44532, Letter of Ministry of the Interior to regional governments, 19 July 1955; and Letter of regional government to Ministry of the Interior, 19 August 1955.

87 KdP, Pfarrämter Jahresberichte, Kaiserslautern 1953, 2–3. See also Erker, "Revolution des Dorfes?" 408, which describes the loss of authority suffered by the churches.

88 Stadtverwaltung Kaiserslautern, Jugendwohlfahrtsausschuß Protokolle, Sitzung des Jugendwohlfartsausschuß 1960, 2 and 9.

89 On the social and political transformation in the second part of the decade, see Erker, "Zeitgeschichte als Sozialgeschichte"; Sywotteck, "Wege in die fünziger Jahre"; Schildt, *Moderne Zeiten* and *Zwischen Abendland und Amerika*. On this shift in cultural attitudes and values, see Poiger, *Jazz, Rock, and Rebels*; and Maase, *Bravo Amerika*.

90 *RZ*, 27 July 1957, election advertisement for the economic policies of Erhard by "Die Waage, Gemeinschaft zur Förderung des sozialen Ausgleiches." For the nylon stocking metaphor as a tool in the Cold War rhetoric, see Carter, "Alice in the Consumer Wonderland."

91 For an insightful description of this shift, see Schildt, *Moderne Zeiten*, 320, 448. See Schwarz, *Die Ära Adenauer*, 439–46, for a depiction of this conflict between clerical conservatives and liberals within the CDU. See also Sywotteck, "Wege in die fünziger Jahre," 34–35; Maase, *Bravo Amerika*, 70.

92 Poiger, "Rock 'n' Roll," 409.

93 BAK, 153/1355, 402, 14 April 1962 letter of Katholischer Fürsorgeverein to Federal Youth Plan about their work in Mainz.

Chapter Seven

1 Berichte, 1951–63, "Protokoll über die am 30.4.1953 stattgefundene Sitzung über die Zusammenarbeit der allierten und deutschen Stellen zur Beseitigung der Jugendnot im Kreis Birkenfeld," 7.

2 According to German law, everyone must carry a personal identification card at all times. In the 1950s, failure to do so was punishable by a short jail sentence.

3 For a more detailed description of the many ways in which these agencies helped young women, see Chapter 4 in Höhn, "GIs, Veronikas and Lucky Strikes."

4 I have talked to two social welfare workers who worked in Baumholder during the 1950s: Christa Rühl of Birkenfeld (a county social worker), and Annemarie Lang of Idar-Oberstein (a county social worker until 1955, after that employed with the *Innere Mission*). Looking back on their work in those years, they were horrified at the manner in which they intruded on the lives of these women. In hindsight, both suggested that they at all times overstepped the boundaries of propriety and that in their unquestioning accep-

tance of authority they never second-guessed policies handed down from the state and federal youth agencies. As Lang put it, all too often "*Fürsorge* became *Befürsorgung*."

5 Berichte, 1951–73, "Bericht an das Sozialministerium über Jugendgefährdung im Raume Baumholder, 14 May 1955."

6 Berichte, 1951–73, "Besprechung am 2 November 1952 mit dem aufsichtsführenden Richter von Baumholder, dem 2. Vorsitzenden des Stadtjugendringes, den Kreisfürsorgerinnen, der Wohlfahrtsfürsorgerin des Caritasverbandes, und Oberinspektor Koob," 1.

7 Berichte, 1951–73, "Anmerkungen," n.d. The document seems to have been drawn up in October of 1951 since they refer to events taking place in that month.

8 KdP, 555.4, "Soldatenliebchen in der französischen Zone." This document of the Landesverband Pfalz der Inneren Mission listed the information gathered from the various offices of the agency.

9 BAK, B 153/327, 152 (back), Letter of Ministry of Justice to Ministry of Interior, 12 January 1955.

10 *RZ*, 4 August 1951, "'Frolleins' verursachen 'Sturm im Wasserglas'—Wer rettet die Moral Birkenfelds?" The former commanding officer of Birkenfeld Air Station, James Larkin, told me that "all his men" arrived in Birkenfeld with their German girlfriends and that the women stayed in private homes or local inns and hotels.

11 *Die Freiheit*, 5 November 1954, "Polizei Etat soll vergrößert werden."

12 Stadtverwaltung Kaiserslautern, Stadtratsprotokolle, "Sitzung des Haupt- und Finanzausschusses der Stadt Kaiserslautern, 7 October 1954," 3.

13 Stadtverwaltung Kaiserslautern, Stadtratsprotokolle, closed meeting of 31 January 1955. Jewish hotel owners in Kaiserslautern suggested that anti-Semitism informed these police actions; however, I found that non-Jewish hotel owners were punished just as severely. The main police effort appears to have been to close down places that tolerated liaisons between German women and black GIs.

14 See Eyferth, Brandt, and Hawel, *Farbige Kinder in Deutschland*, 93. The authors conclude that in exclusively working-class residential areas, the children of German women and black GIs were accepted much more freely than in middle-class neighborhoods. For examples of raids in marginal neighborhoods, see *PV*, 3 November 1959, "Kinder und Jugendliche sittlich gefährdet"; and *PV*, 23 September 1958, "Empörend und grotesk: schwarz-weiß im Schrank."

15 BAK, B 153/1355 Letter of Katholischer Fürsorgeverein, 17 March 1962. See also Chapter 5 for more examples of this shift. Since many of the young women dating American GIs merely sublet rooms in the landlord's home, the vice raids also exposed the landlord to the prying eyes of the police, who were generally accompanied by customs officials. Often enough, the police discovered American cigarettes, whiskey, and coffee not just in the young women's quarters but also in the landlord's kitchen. H. Haag interview.

16 Berichte, 1951–63, "Arbeitsbericht des Katholischen Fürsorgevereins, 1 June

1960." BAK, B 153/327, 390, Letter of Ministry of Justice to Ministry of Justice in Rhineland-Palatinate, 17 July 1952.

17 The story was different in Kaiserslautern, where prostitution was legal. The American military police and the German police continued to conduct vice raids in hotels and private homes throughout the decade.

18 Berichte, 1951–63, "Protokoll über die am 30.4.1953 stattgefundene Sitzung über die Zusammenarbeit der alliierten und deutschen Stellen zur Beseitigung der Jugendnot im Kreis Birkenfeld," 2. In 1953, the Ministry of the Interior implored the Social Security Committee of HICOG to agree that German police officers could at least check on girls under the age of eighteen if military police were present. HICOG agreed to inform the military police accordingly. See BAK, B 153/327, 309, "Besprechung über das Gesetz zum Schutz der Jugend."

19 *RP,* 2 November 1954, "Polizei über das Ergebnis der Großrazzien." See also Posner, "Afro-America," 7, which describes an incident during the occupation in Bavaria in which black GIs had allegedly beaten up the German police units who tried to arrest the GIs' girlfriends. An angry police chief feared that this sort of behavior would undermine respect for lawful authority of the local population.

20 *RP,* 18 October 1954, "Die bisherigen Ergebnisse der Polizeiaktion."

21 H. Haag and Rühl [Schneider] interviews.

22 BAK, B 153/327, Letter of Katholischer Fürsorgeverein Bamberg to their central office in Dortmund, 19 January 1954; Licht interview. According to Herr Licht, the 1950s knew three cries of terror: for the Germans, it was "the tanks are coming"; for the GIs, it was the warning that the MP was on its way; and for the young women in town, it was the name of Frau Wefelscheid.

23 Many of the young women who arrived in these localities had their first contact with the local social workers during social workers' visits to the jails. See KdP, 555.4, "Aktennotiz 1 Februar 1952," 1. In order to meet the women before they were sent to jail (usually for not carrying an identification card or having failed to report at the health office for a gynecological examination), the social workers accompanied the police on these raids. See BAK, 153/327, Letter of Katholischer Fürsorgeverein Bamberg to their central office in Dortmund, 19 January 1954.

24 See *PV,* 26 July 1957, "Großrazzia in und um Kaiserslautern."

25 Rühl [Schneider] interview.

26 Stadtverwaltung Kaiserslautern, Stadtratsprotokolle, 9 May 1955 (closed meeting).

27 *Die Freiheit,* 5 January 1954, "Staatlich konzessierte Mädchenjagd—Die Freiheit der Person ist unantastbar." See also Heineman, "Standing Alone," 219–22, on similar vice raids during the immediate postwar years. In the American zone German and American authorities participated in raids that were conducted mostly in dance halls and pubs. It was also a common phenomenon then that "good girls" were arrested.

28 *PV,* 17 September 1952, "Warum eigentlich nur die Mädchen?"

29 Berichte, 1951–73, "Niederschrift über eine Besprechung mit Gendamerie und Kriminalpolizei am 26 September 1953," 9.

30 Ibid., 8. A journalist who wrote for the *Rheinzeitung* in the 1950s also attested to the overzealousness of the judge. A newspaper story on the Baumholder judge entitled "Dr. Schnapp schnappt sie alle" ("Dr. Schnapp catches them all") was produced during the judge's tenure. See IANAS video 29.

31 Berichte, 1951–73, "Niederschrift über eine Besprechung mit Gendamerie und Kriminalpolizei am 26 September 1953," 4.

32 The prostitution trial records show that a number of women in fact had been punished for merely accepting drinks or meals from soldiers.

33 Berichte, 1951–73, "Niederschrift über eine Besprechung, 26 September 1953," 8. Unfortunately, it is not clear from this statement whether the Landrat feared trouble from the Christian Democratic president of the regional or the state government.

34 See the suggestion of the Ministry of the Interior, Mainz: "Life has to be made as hard as possible for the prostitutes. Constant raids and control checks have to be conducted." In addition, the women were also to be constantly called before the health office for gynecological exams. In *RZ*, 19 January 1952, "Rheinland-Pfalz bekämpft Dirnenunwesen / Division lockerer Mädchen in Baumholder / Anordnung für Landkreise."

35 Berichte, 1951–73, "Niederschrift über eine Besprechung," 12.

36 AKK, Bekämpfung der Unzucht, 22 January 1958 report to regional government. Unfortunately, the records in the Kreisverwaltung Kaiserslautern are much thinner than those for Birkenfeld, because most of them were burned sometime during the 1970s.

37 LHA, 930/4924, "Bad Godesberg Tagung," 4.

38 BAK, B 153/327, "Tagung Innere Mission und Katholischer Fürsorgeverein" (n.d.). See also BAK, B 153/327, for a 30-page document without title or date that seems to be a report from the church-affiliated welfare organizations to the Ministry of the Interior on their work in all the locations with troops. See also LHA, 930/4924, "Bad Godesberg Tagung," 4.

39 See, e.g., *Allgemeine Zeitung, Bad Kreuznach; Pfälzische Volkszeitung;* and *Rheinpfalz.*

40 Rühl [Schneider] and Lang interviews.

41 Ibid. The judge's voyeurism was also described by Karl Werner, a former clerk at the Inferior Court in Birkenfeld who worked under Dr. Schnapp's tenure in Baumholder, and by Heinrich Haag, the former police chief of Baumholder.

42 Rühl [Schneider] and Lang interviews. For a discussion of such voyeurism during the Nazi years, see Heusler, "'Strafbestand' Liebe."

43 LHA, 602.06, folder 9, ES/23/52. Schnapp was very careful with his language. I found only one other incident in which he specifically mentioned black GIs as a special problem: Berichte, 1951–73, "Protokoll über die am 14 November 1951 stattgefundene Sitzung," in which he reported on the special dangers that "sexually incited Negroes" posed to local women and men.

44 *RZ,* 11 December 1954, "Haftstrafen und Einweisung ins Arbeitshaus." See also *RZ,* 26 November 1955, "Margarete lebte unter falschen Namen / Auf Umwegen kehrte sie immer wieder nach Baumholder zurück."

45 See also Amtsgericht Birkenfeld, ES 2/52. Young women under the age of twenty-one were escorted by the county and Christian welfare workers back to their families if the judge deemed the family stable enough to control the daughter. Rühl [Schneider] and Lang interviews.

46 IANAS videos 60 and 42. See also *Neue Revue,* 2 May 1959, "Die doppelte Moral von Baumholder," for a depiction of a scandal involving members of city council being caught with their hands in the cookie jar. For one of the few cases I came across, see LHA, 602.06, folder 9, ES 22/52.

47 Berichte, 1951–73, Letter of Kreisjugendamt Birkenfeld to Landratsamt Esslingen, 8 June 1955.

48 Rühl, "Soziale Auswirkungen," 25.

49 Fasching, Licht, and Rühl [Schneider] interviews.

50 Larkin, Bruner, and Campbell interviews. Interracial couples, both married and unmarried, resided in all communities around American military bases. Licht, Löffler, Lang, and Rühl [Schneider] interviews.

51 Rühl, "Soziale Auswirkungen," 25. See also BAK, B 106/17302 for a 9 July 1956 letter of the Ministry of the Interior to the Foreign Office, in which they comment on the fact that the population tolerated the "new face of prostitution." For the population's rejection of criminalizing "marriage-like" arrangements, see BAK, B 141/82165, 81, "Niederschrift über die 9. Tagung der Länderkommission für die große Strafrechtsreform, 16.1–20.1.61."

52 LHA, 930/4924, "Bad Godesberg Tagung," 10–11. See also BAK, B 153/1369, "Bericht Katholischer Fürsorgeverein Landstuhl 5 December 1959"; and BAK, B 153/327, 194, "Jugendgefährdung in Gegenden grosser Truppensammlungen."

53 I checked LHA RG 602.06 to establish the ratio: folder 9 (1952)—33 cases, of which 10 involved a black GI; folder 10 (1953)—28 cases, 10 involving a black GI; folder 14 (1956)—36 cases, 20 involving a black GI; folder 16 (1957/58)—47 cases, 35 involving a black GI; folder 19 (1959)—18 cases, 14 involving a black GI. Because the judge did not always identify the race of the woman's sex partner or potential sex partner, the number of black GIs in folders 9 and 10 may actually be higher. Before integration was accomplished in 1954, the percentage of black soldiers may also have been higher at times. If, for example, all-black units arrived to train in Baumholder, the ratio of black soldiers to white soldiers would have been higher.

54 Berichte, 1951–73, Letter of Birkenfeld Landrat to Landratsamt Esslingen, 8 June 1955, 4.

55 *RZ,* 19 April 1952, "Die leichten Mädchen haben es nicht mehr leicht."

56 Stadtverwaltung Kaiserslautern, Vollzug des Gaststättengesetzes, Letter of Ministry of the Interior in Mainz to regional government of the Palatinate, 13 March 1958.

57 The best sources for this conclusion are the Baumholder prostitution rec-

ords at the Landeshauptarchiv in Koblenz. The great majority of women were arrested in establishments that were described as places "where colored occupation soldiers" congregated. The former social worker from Birkenfeld also told me that the majority of vice raids were conducted in bars frequented by African American soldiers. The patterns of vice raids were similar in Kaiserslautern. During one such raid in 1957, 350 women and their male companions were checked, and 24 women were arrested by the German police and the MP. Almost all the soldiers involved were black. NARA, RG 338, Weekly LRO Civil Affairs Report, 7 December 1957. See Sonya Rose, "Girls and GIs," 159, which shows that in Great Britain during the war the British police likewise maintained a much larger presence at black-only clubs.

58 *RZ*, 27 October 1955, "Farbige Soldaten auf deutsche Polizei gehetzt."

59 LHA, 602.06, folder 34, DS 76/55.

60 LHA, 602.06, folder 34, NS 289/55–497/55. For similar cases, see *RZ*, 21 December 1955, "Farbige Soldaten gegen Taxifahrer aufgewiegelt — Ein Jahr Gefängnis für die 'größte Gewissenslosigkeit einer Frau Deutschen gegenüber'"; and *RZ*, 12 Oktober 1957, "Farbige Soldaten auf Polizisten gehetzt."

61 *RZ*, 24 July 1957, "Zehn Monate zur Abschreckung / Dirne wiegelte farbige amerikanische Soldaten gegen Baumholderer Kriminalbeamte auf."

62 *RZ*, 20 November 1951, "Am Ende des Weges steht das Arbeitshaus"; and *RZ*, 23 October 1957, "Schöffengericht Idar-Oberstein: Es war gewissermaßen Halbstarken-Manier."

63 LHA, 602.06, folder 14, Landgericht Kreuznach NS 229/57 and DS 394/57, 28 December 1957.

64 A woman who had been living with a particular GI for the preceding five years avoided a jail term when she convinced the courts that her boyfriend was legally separated and merely waiting for his divorce decree. Another woman did not yet have the wedding papers, but the many letters she had received from her fiancé convinced the court that he was serious about marrying her. Although this woman had already been in the workhouse, the court felt confident that a marriage would rehabilitate her. Another woman was granted a two-month grace period so she could produce the necessary papers that were still missing to "convince the judge of her 'real intentions.'" See *RZ*, 23 May 1957, "Da hilft kein anderes Mittel: Wer nicht hören will muß fühlen!" See also *RZ*, 22 June 1955, "Hat sich das Sittenleben wieder normalisiert?"; *RZ*, 24 November 1955, "Pussta Mädchen will zurück ins Pusstastädtchen"; *RZ*, 27 November 1957, "Katharine flüchtete aus dem Arbeitshaus und lernte den Mann 'ihres Lebens' kennen"; and *RZ*, 30 March 1955, "Idar-Oberstein: Schwere Haft und Gefängnisstrafen ausgesprochen."

65 *RZ*, 11 November 1956, "Nur die Heirat kann Elfriede noch retten"; *RZ*, 17 May 1956, "Dagmar führte die Starparade an." This latter one is a fascinating case. The young woman indicted was an Afro-German born in 1934. The judge argued that she should not be punished as a prostitute because only a black man would be appropriate for her. Since Dagmar was able to produce a letter from her future mother-in-law, the judge showed mercy.

66 LHA, 602.06, folder 14, NS 229/57 and DS 394/57.

67 *Allgemeine Zeitung, Mainz,* 11 September 1956, "Polizei befürwortet Dirnen-Sperrbezirke."

Chapter Eight

1 See, e.g., *Hamburger Abendblatt,* 10 December 1955, "Ein Zahltag in der Westpfalz"; and *PV,* 3 December 1959, "Bimbo City trockengelegt." The *Hamburger Abendblatt* explained that that part of town was called Bimbo-City "because only Bimbos, black soldiers, frequent it." (Copies available in ZSK.)

2 The term *"Negerunwesen"* was used during the 18 May 1956 meeting of the Stadtrat Kaiserslautern by FDP delegate Fritz Wilms. See Stadtverwaltung Kaiserslautern, Stadtratsprotokolle, 31.

3 Schraut, "U.S. Forces in Germany." The stationing of Nike missiles in Germany beginning in 1954 and NATO's military maneuver "Carte Blanche" in June 1955 led to an outcry over Adenauer's security policy. Germans were appalled to read in the newspapers that American military exercises were conducted under the premises that 400 nuclear warheads had exploded over Germany, killing 1.7 million and wounding 3.5 million German civilians.

4 Stadtverwaltung Kaiserslautern, Vollzug des Gaststättengesetzes, Letter of Stadtverwaltung to Bezirksregierung, 19 November 1957; and *Wochenend,* 28 August 1954, "Das Laster regiert in Kaiserslautern" (copy in ZSK).

5 *RP,* 11 November 1954, ". . . bis das Menschenmöglichste für diese Not getan worden ist!" See the appeal, "Es geht alle an" of the Protestant and Catholic clergy in Kaiserslautern in ASK, US Besatzung/Deutsch-Amerikanischer Ausschuß.

6 *Wochenend,* 11 September 1954, "Jagd auf wilde Mädchen"; and *Wochenend,* 28 August 1954, "Das Laster regiert in Kaiserslautern: 72 Millionen DM im Jahr allein für schnelle Küsse-'Königin der Negerliebchen' fährt im eigenen Mercedes." See also *Die Bunte,* 19 September 1954, "SOS in Kaiserslautern."

7 *RP,* 14 March 1953, "Die Invasion der Unmoral."

8 *Die Bunte,* 19 September 1954, "SOS aus Kaiserslautern."

9 *Freisoziale Presse,* 1 October 1954, "Eine Stadt unter Besatzungslaster / Misthaufen der Unmoral durch den Besatzungsdollar / Polizeiknüppel gegen 3000 'Amizonen' und ihre Zuhälter."

10 *Die Bunte,* 19 September 1954, "SOS aus Kaiserslautern."

11 *PV,* 2 November 1954, "Leichte Mädchen wandern weiter." The city is responsible for these exaggerated numbers. Since members of the American military were not included in the census, police department personnel remained at the same level as if no troops were stationed in their communities. To expand their police force, the city had to convince the state government of the severity of the situation in Kaiserslautern. Consequently, they presented highly inflated numbers of prostitutes.

12 Stadtverwaltung Kaiserslautern, Vollzug des Gaststättengesetzes, Letter of

Ministry of the Interior in Mainz to regional government of the Palatinate, 13 March 1958, which was passed on to the city. The ministry is citing an October 1957 ruling of the state's supreme administrative court (*Oberverwaltungsgericht*).

13 *PV,* 13 January 1955, "Stadtverwaltung Kaiserslautern gesetzestreuer als Regierung." Stern, *Whitewashing,* and Goschler, "Attitude toward Jews," discuss how prevalent such charges were in the postwar years.

14 *Die Freiheit,* 7 January 1955, "'Notenaustausch' Kaiserslautern-Neustadt."

15 *PV,* 13 January 1955, "Stadtverwaltung Kaiserslautern gesetzestreuer als Regierung." For a good explanation of the legalities involved in all of this, see Stadtverwaltung Kaiserslautern, Vollzug des Gaststättengesetzes.

16 Stadtverwaltung Kaiserslautern, Stadtratsprotokolle, 29 October 1954.

17 For especially lively exchanges on the bar question, see ibid., 6 March 1953 and 9 May 1955.

18 Ibid., 13 May 1955.

19 Ibid., 18 May 1956.

20 Ibid.

21 Ibid., 3 December 1956.

22 Stadtverwaltung Kaiserslautern, Vollzug des Gaststättengesetzes, Letter of Dr. Wemmer, legal council of the Coalition of Jewish Bar Owners to the city of Kaiserslautern, 22 November 1954.

23 Stadtverwaltung Kaiserslautern, Vollzug des Gaststättengesetzes, Letter of regional government of the Palatinate to the city of Kaiserslautern, 28 February 1955. For an overview of how the traditional antagonism between German and Eastern European Jews continued after World War II, see Nachama, "Nach der Befreiung"; Brenner, "East European and German Jews"; Harmsen, *Die Integration;* Wetzel, "'Mir szeinen doh'"; and Grossmann, "Trauma, Memory, and Motherhood." *Der Spiegel,* No. 31, 1963, "Heimstätte auf verfluchter Erde?" has an extensive report on Jews in Germany that also discusses this split between German Jews and Eastern European Jews over the Jewish-owned bars.

24 Rubenstein, "The Dean and the Chosen People," 281. Quotes are from an interview that Rubenstein conducted with Dean Grüber in the 1960s.

25 *Der Spiegel,* No. 31, 1963, "Heimstätte auf verfluchter Erde?"

26 *Die Freiheit,* 5 November 1954, "Polizei Etat soll vergrößert werden."

27 *PV,* 30 August, 1957, "'Oberst Bredens plumpe Drohung.'"

28 *Die Welt,* December 1960, "Im Wilden Westen der Bundesrepublik" (copy in ZSK); and *PV,* 7 September 1957, "Steinstrasse für US Militär gesperrt."

29 Stadtverwaltung Kaiserslautern, Stadtratsprotokolle, 28 December 1955, 259–60.

30 Ibid., 260.

31 *PV,* 28 November 1951, "Zwischen Nacht und Morgengrauen." For a fascinating glimpse at the music and dancing at one such bar frequented by black GIs, see the 1958 German TV documentary *Wie Toxi wirklich lebt.*

32 Wundshammer, *Deutsche Chronik,* 115–16.

33 Ibid.

34   Ibid. See also *RP*, 2 July 1952, "In Deutschlands Goldenem Westen," which draws parallels between the French colonial troops after World War I and black American GIs.

35   Wundshammer, *Deutsche Chronik*, 115–16.

36   *PV*, 14 May 1957, "Amerikanern den Begriff des Hausrechts klar machen."

37   *Der Spiegel*, 9 October 1957, "Die Schatten der NATO."

38   Ibid.

39   *Deutsche Tagespost*, 10 September 1957, "Es ist höchste Zeit" (copy in ZSK).

40   *RP*, 30 August 1957, "Nicht mit den übelsten Erscheinungen eines Garnison-betriebes zu vergleichen."

41   In 1957–58, *Neue Illustrierte* published a serial novel about a black GI and his white German girlfriend. The novel, *Die PX Story: Liebe hinterm Ladentisch* (*The PX Story: Love behind the Store Counter*) ends in bloodshed when the jealous soldier kills his German girlfriend. Twenty-three saleswomen from the Kaiserslautern Post Exchange wrote a letter of protest to the *Neue Illustrierte*. The women defended their black customers as polite and decent human beings and accused the magazine of inciting racial animosity with its story. See Lester, *Trivialneger*, 82.

42   *Das Neue Blatt*, 2 August 1956, "Mehr Anstand, Besatzer!" For similar ex-pressions of national pride expressed in relation to the "reining in" of black GIs, see *RZ*, 27 May 1955, "Souveränität anstatt Souvenir? Wenn der Joshua sein blitzendes Messer zieht."

43   *Westdeutsches Tagesblatt*, 21 September 1957, "Ganzes Stadtviertel in Kaisers-lautern für US-Truppen" (copy in ZSK).

44   *Abendzeitung München*, 10 September 1957, "Kaiserslautern besiegt das Laster" (copy in ZSK).

45   *Welt am Sonnabend*, 28 September 1957, "Schluß mit der Unmoral" (copy in ZSK).

46   *RP*, 30 August 1957, "Nicht mit den übelsten Erscheinungen eines Garnison-betriebes zu vergleichen."

47   *Deutsche Tagespost*, 10 September 1957, "Es ist höchste Zeit" (copy in ZSK).

48   Both Kaiserslautern and Birkenfeld counties kept lists of the pub and bar owners and identified them according to their nationality. See Stadtverwal-tung Kaiserslautern, Vollzug des Gaststättengesetzes, "Report of Rechts-rat Mangold during 7 October 1954 Sitzung des Haupt- und Finanzaus-schusses," 2. See also *RZ*, 28 July 1959, "Wir wollen die Dinge beim Namen nennen," in which the author argues that identifying "foreigners" and DPs as bar owners should not expose Germans to charges of anti-Semitism. See Stern, *Whitewashing*, 108. Beginning in 1948, the word "Jew" was no longer used in official documents but was replaced with such categories as "group of foreigners" or "shiftless elements."

49   Stern, *Whitewashing*, 299.

50   Stadtverwaltung Kaiserslautern, Vollzug des Gaststättengesetzes, "15. Sit-zung des Haupt- und Finanzausschusses 7 October 1954."

51   The most outrageous speculation informed German readers that "10,000 such women and their bosses were organized in corporations of vice" in

Kaiserslautern. See *Das Grüne Blatt*, 18 January 1956, "Alarm in deutschen Großstädten: Sünden GMBH schlägt los!" See also *Das Neue Blatt*, 16 May 1958, "Skrupellose Agenten 'kaufen' deutsche Mädchen für amerikanische Soldaten in der Pfalz"; *Wochenend*, 4 September 1954, "Alarm in der 'Nahkampf-Diele.'" See also the allegations of the Katholisches Männerwerk in *RP*, 14 September 1954, "Gegen Dirnenunwesen und verantwortungslose Barbesitzer."

52 Stadtverwaltung Kaiserslautern, Vollzug des Gaststättengesetzes, Letter of Polizeipräsidium München to Bezirksregierung der Pfalz, 10 March 1958.

53 Stadtverwaltung Kaiserslautern, Vollzug des Gaststättengesetzes, "15. Sitzung des Haupt- und Finanzausschusses 7 October 1954."

54 A letter to the editor of the *Allgemeine Wochenzeitung der Juden* suggests that this sort of vicious anti-Semitism was not the exception but a widespread phenomenon. The letter informed readers that "one can hardly imagine how often people talked about the Jews in an ugly and slanderous manner." See *Der Spiegel*, No. 31, 1963, "Heimstätte auf verfluchter Erde?" This letter appears to have been written by a non-Jew who wanted to alert the German Jewish community to the anti-Semitism expressed over the so-called Jewish bar owners. The letter writer was from Birkenfeld County.

55 Verbandsgemeinde Ramstein, Stadtratsprotokolle, 7 February 1958; and *PV*, 5 October 1957, "Der Leser hat das Wort."

56 Käutner dramatized the scene by showing the bar owner's tattooed camp number reflected in the glass of the jukebox. The exchange caused an outrage in the Jewish community in Germany, forcing Käutner to cut the scene from the film. When the film airs today on German television, the controversial scene is again included. For coverage of the incident, see *Frankfurter Allgemeine Zeitung*, 18 April 1961, "Strafantrag gegen den Käutnerfilm 'Schwarzer Kies,'" and 22 April 1961, "Einigung im Fall 'Schwarzer Kies.'" See also *Die Zeit*, 21 April 1961, "Schwarzer Kies uraugfeführt—Dr. van Dam stellt Strafantrag." The newspaper editions of that week also carried prominent coverage of the Eichmann trial in Jerusalem.

57 *PV*, 28 August 1957, "Wohnungen, Schulen wichtiger als Kasernen."

58 *Die Freiheit*, 26 August 1957, "Notgemeinschaft will Weißbuch zusammenstellen"; and *PV*, 22 August 1957, "Neue Möglichkeiten gegen skandalöse Zustände." For a good overview of the developments, see the report of legal council Dr. Mangold, which is included in the city council meeting of 27 September 1957.

59 *PV*, 7 September 1957, "Steinstrasse-Viertel 'off-limits'—Ab heute für Amerikaner gesperrt."

60 Ibid.

61 Stadtverwaltung Kaiserslautern, Stadtratsprotokolle, 31 October 1957, has a lengthy report by Mayor Sommer on his negotiations with Colonel Breden. In 1955, the commander at Mainz had made three black-only bars off-limits to his troops. See NARA, RG 338, Weekly LRO Civil Affairs Report, 10 September 1955. In 1957 in Kaiserslautern, the commanding officer of the Twelfth U.S. AAA Group, Colonel Arthur Sanford, did not have the au-

thority to issue a general off-limits, but he issued a daily order in which he recommended that the men in his command stay away from the Steinstrasse. See NARA, RG 338, Weekly LRO Civil Affairs Report, 31 August 1957.

62 *RP*, 27 August 1957, "Sperr Verfügung für Kaiserslautern? Wer gefährdet den Ruf der Stadt?"; and *Der Spiegel*, 9 October 1957, "Die Schatten der NATO." According to *Wochenend*, 3 October 1957, "Verdammt sei diese Seligkeit," the "American women's organizations had a power that was unfathomable to Europeans," and thus a "reaction from the White House was expected." The story about the threat to inform the women's organizations and descriptions of what sort of power they had in America were repeated incessantly. See, e.g., *Welt am Sonnabend*, 28 September 1957, "Schluß mit der Unmoral." The theme of emasculating American women has been part of German stereotypes since the nineteenth century. See Maase, *Bravo Amerika*, 249; and Nolan, *Visions of Modernity*, 108–30.

63 *PV*, 14 May 1957, "Amerikanern den Begriff des Hausrechts klar machen." Posner, "Afro-America," cites complaints about black-only bars from Frankfurt and Munich.

64 NARA, RG 338, Weekly LRO Civil Affairs Report, 10 September 1955.

65 NARA, RG 338, Weekly LRO Civil Affairs Reports, 17, 24 August 1957. Unfortunately, the crucial folder that contains the weekly LRO reports for September is missing from the National Archives.

66 NARA, RG 338, Weekly LRO Civil Affairs Report, 31 August 1957.

67 NARA, RG 338, Weekly LRO Civil Affairs Report, 29 March 1958.

68 *RP*, 6 September 1957, "Sperrung des Steinstrassegebietes steht unmittelbar bevor." See also NARA, Weekly LRO Civil Affairs Reports, 20 April, 24, 31 August 1957.

69 See *PV*, 9 September 1957, "Steinstrasseabsperrung mit militärischer Pünktlichkeit," for some descriptions of racial violence at the time.

70 *Wiesbadener Kurier*, 28 September 1957, "Wenn die Soldaten . . ." (copy in ZSK); *RP*, 9 September 1957, "Telefone läuten am Samstag Sturm."

71 *Abendzeitung München*, 9 September 1957, "Kaiserslautern hat das Laster besiegt" (copy in ZSK).

72 *Wetzlarer Neue Zeitung*, 21 September 1957, "Kaiserslautern wurde solide" (copy in ZSK).

73 *Welt am Sonnabend*, 28 September 1957, "Schluß mit der Unmoral." See also *PV*, 14 November 1957, "Steinstrasse 'off-limits' tagsüber wieder aufgehoben," where this fear of revenge is also expressed.

74 *Wochenend*, 3 October 1957, "In Kaiserslautern kommt jetzt die Moral vor dem Fressen, aber man weiß nicht wie lange."

75 *Anzeiger und Kurier*, 20 September 1957, "Dem Sieg der Moral folgt der Katzenjammer" (copy in ZSK).

76 *8 Uhr Blatt*, 15 October 1957, "Der Kampf gegen die Unmoral kostete einen Haufen Geld" (copy in ZSK).

77 *Oberbergische Volkszeitung*, 21 September 1957, "Moral und Geschäft" (copy in ZSK).

78 Stadtverwaltung Kaiserslautern, Stadtratsprotokolle, 31 October 1957, 81.

The mayor left for his visit to the United States the day before matters in the Steinstrasse came to a head.

79 *Heidenheimer Zeitung,* 9 September 1957, "Ein Stadtviertel wehrt sich der Verwahrlosung" (copy in ZSK).

80 *Weser Kurier,* Bremen 26 September 1957, "Moral ist teuer" (copy in ZSK).

81 *Kassler Zeitung,* 26 September 1957, "Kaiserslautern löscht rote Laternen aus" (copy in ZSK).

82 *Weser Kurier,* Bremen 26 September 1957, "Moral ist teuer" (copy in ZSK).

83 *PV,* 7 September 1957, "Steinstrasse-Viertel 'off-limits' / Ab heute für Amerikaner gesperrt" and "Jetzt müssen die Behörden zupacken."

84 Ibid.

85 Stadtverwaltung Kaiserslautern, Stadtratsprotokolle, 27 September 1957.

86 Ibid.

87 Ibid.

88 Stern, *Whitewashing,* argues that at a time of apparent German philosemitism toward German Jews, Jewish DPs were assigned all the traditional anti-Semitic stereotypes. According to opinion surveys, anti-Semitism was in decline by the late 1950s in West Germany. See Bergmann and Erb, *Antisemitismus,* 281.

89 Lester, *Trivialneger,* 38, also comments on this shift in attitude.

90 *U.S. News and World Report,* 11 October 1957, "When Negro Servicemen Bring Home White Brides," 11.

Conclusion

1 Document from Ramstein Air Base at IANAS, "Desert Storm Host Nation Support / Project Friendship Activities, May 1991." This is a 10-page document listing the activities of German communities in support of American families during the Persian Gulf War. During the Bosnian deployment, an American soldier from Baumholder kept the community updated by contributing reports and artistic sketches to the local newspaper, *Nahezeitung.* After his return, the local bank sponsored an exhibit of his artwork.

2 Ermarth, *America and the Shaping of German Society,* 15–16.

3 See Maase, *Bravo Amerika,* for his suggestion that consumer goods of Americans were experienced as the realization of this utopia for a better and easier life.

4 IANAS, Mootz Questionnaire File, Section 2c. See also Maase, *Bravo Amerika.* Wagnleitner's introduction in his *Coca-Colonization* is a wonderful personal reflection on how enticing the Americans seemed to young teenagers.

5 For a good historical overview of German views on America, see Maase, *Bravo Amerika,* 41–62; Wagnleitner, *Coca-Colonization,* 9–36; and Poiger, *Jazz, Rock, and Rebels,* 1–70.

6 Rogers, McDonald, Rauman, and Shelbourne interviews. See also Plassmann, "U.S. Air Base Sembach," 49.

7 IANAS video 51. With few exceptions, almost all people interviewed for the

IANAS project concluded that they were Americanized, especially those of the younger generation. For some examples, see IANAS videos 53, 58, 60, 62. See also Maase, *Bravo Amerika,* 177–99.

8   IANAS video 9.

9   Maase, *Bravo Amerika,* 18.

10 On the Westernization school, see the work of scholars in the Tübingen school, esp. Doering-Manteuffel, *Wie Westlich sind die Deutschen?*; and "Deutsche Zeitgeschichte nach 1945"; and "Dimensionen von Amerikanisierung."

11 IANAS, Mootz Questionnaire File, Section 2c.

12 See, e.g., *PV,* 1 April 1952, "Meine Tochter schafft beim Ami"; *RZ,* 4 December 1954, "Millionen Bauprogram geht dem Ende entgegen." These sorts of images were reconfirmed by Peter von Zahn's TV series *New York, New York,* which brought the marvels of American consumer capitalism into the German home during the 1950s and 1960s.

13 D. Nelson, *Defenders or Intruders,* 61. The press coverage is an important indicator here. After 1965, coverage of the U.S. presence declined substantially, while more attention was paid to German-French encounters and exchanges. See Eva Dannenberg's overview of press coverage on the United States and France. IANAS, unpublished manuscript.

14 For similar comments, see IANAS videos 14, 25, 30, 47, 60.

15 IANAS video 9. Schildt, *Moderne Zeiten,* 315, also argues that Germans grew into democracy through increasing prosperity.

16 IANAS, Mootz questionnaire.

17 IANAS videos 28, 47, 48 and 50. Comments from Jürgen Hentze, former mayor of Baumholder, at the "Nachbar Amerika" symposium in Ramstein.

18 D. Herzog, "'Pleasure, Sex, and Politics,'" 411.

19 See, e.g., Stoler, *Race and the Education of Desire;* Cooper and Stoler, *Tensions of Empire.*

20 *U.S. News and World Report,* 11 October 1957, "When Negro Servicemen Bring Home White Brides," 11.

21 Moeller, *West Germany under Construction,* 29.

Bibliography

Primary Sources

Document Archives

Amtsgericht Birkenfeld
  Prostitution trial records
Archiv der Evangelischen Kirche Baumholder
  Allgemeine Gemeindearbeit
  Jugendarbeit
Archiv der Kreisverwaltung Kaiserslautern (AKK)
  Bekämpfung der Unzucht
  Kreistagsprotokolle 1950–60
Archiv der Stadt Kaiserslautern (ASK)
  Bekämpfung der Unzucht
  Besatzung/Wohltätigkeit
  US Besatzung/Deutsch-Amerikanischer Ausschuß
  Zeitungsausschnittsammlung (ZSK)
Archiv des Kirchenkreises Birkenfeld
  Jahresberichte
  Kirchenvisitation
  Konferenzen
  Mädchenwohnheim Idar-Oberstein
  Pfarrkonvente
  Verhandlungen der Kreissynode
Bistumsarchiv Speyer (BAS)
  Pfarrämter Jahresberichte

Bundesarchiv Koblenz (BAK)
   B 106: Bundesministerium des Innern
   B 141: Bundesministerium der Justiz
   B 153: Bundesministerium für Familie und Jugend
   B 189: Bundesministerium für Jugend, Familie, Frauen und Gesundheit
   Verhandlungen des Deutschen Bundestages
Evangelische Kirche der Pfalz, Zentralarchiv Speyer (KdP)
   Abteilung 1/Altregistratur Landeskirchenrat
      555.4: Sittliche Notlage in der Pfalz, Jugendnot
   Beziehung zu Besatzungsmächten
   Diakonisches Werk Pfalz
   Pfarrämter Jahresberichte
Evangelische Kirche im Rheinland, Archivstelle Koblenz
   Berschweiler No. 28
Evangelische Kirche im Rheinland, Zentralarchiv Düsseldorf
   Kreissynode St. Wendel
Interdisziplinärer Arbeitskreis für Nordamerikastudien (IANAS), Johannes
      Gutenberg Universität, Mainz
   Oral History Project
   Mootz Questionnaire File
   Zeitschriftensammlung
Kreisverwaltung Birkenfeld (KVB)
   Hauptabteilung
      Kreistagsprotokolle 1950–60
      Kreisausschußprotokolle 1950–60
   Jugendamt
      Berichte aus Baumholder 1951–63
      Berichte aus Baumholder 1951–73
      Berichte aus Baumholder 1951–85
      Jugendamt Idar-Oberstein
      Protokolle des Jugendwohlfahrtsausschußes 1955–60
Landeshauptarchiv Koblenz (LHA)
   Amtsgericht Baumholder, RGs 602.02, 602.05, 602.06
   441: Bezirksregierung
   504: Landesamt Birkenfeld
   932: Ministerium für Jugend und Soziales
   930: Ministerium für Soziales, Gesundheit und Umwelt
   860: Staatkanzlei
National Archives and Record Administration (NARA), College Park, Md.
   RG 338: Records of the United States Army, Europe
      Annual History Reports
      Civil Affairs Division
      Historical Division
      Public Information Division
      Office of the Chaplain
      Records of the Land Relations Officer of the Rhineland-Palatinate

Stadtverwaltung Kaiserslautern
  Hauptabteilung
    Stadtratsprotokolle 1950–60
  Rechtsamt
    Bars und Bar-ähnliche Betriebe
    Dirnenunwesen
    Polizeistundenverlängerung
    Vollzug des Gaststättengesetzes
  Jugendamt
    Jugendwohlfahrtausschuß Protokolle 1955–60
    Statistik der öffentlichen Jugendhilfe
Verbandsgemeinde Baumholder
  Deutsch-Amerikanisches Freundschaftskomitee
  Jugendschutz
  Polizeistundenverlängerung
  Stadtratsprotokolle 1950–60
  Vierteljahreberichte an den Landrat
  Zeitungsausschnittsammlung
Verbandsgemeinde Birkenfeld (VGB)
  Stadtratsprotokolle 1950–60
  Deutsch-Amerikanisches Komitee
Verbandsgemeinde Ramstein
  Stadtratsprotokolle 1950–60

Periodicals

Allgemeine Zeitung, Bad Kreuznach, 1950–55
Allgemeine Zeitung, Mainz, 1951–55
Die Bunte, 1950–60
Die Freiheit, 1950–60
Heimatkalender des Landkreises Birkenfeld, 1955–94
Der Spiegel, 1949–70
Der Stern, 1952–70
Die Rheinpfalz, 1950–59
Eifeler Zeitung, 1950–55
Pfälzische Volkszeitung, 1951–61
Pirmasenser Zeitung, 1960–70
Neue Revue, 1950–60
Rheinzeitung, 1950–60
Wochenend, 1950–60

Films

Die Goldene Pest (1954), directed by John Brahm
The Marriage of Maria Braun (1979), directed by Rainer-Maria Fassbinder
Schwarzer Kies (1960), directed by Helmut Käutner

Photo Archives

Interdisziplinärer Arbeitskreis für Nordamerikastudien (IANAS), Johannes
     Gutenberg Universität, Mainz
     Photo Collection
Museum des Westrich, Ramstein
     "Welcome to the Club," photo exhibit of American NCO (Non-
     Commissioned Officer) and Officers Clubs during the 1950s;
     Michael Geib, curator
     Photo collection Matheis; Michael Geib, curator
Private Photo Archives
     Karl Edinger, Baumholder
     Dr. Gerhard Nagel, Baumholder
Verbandsgemeinde Birkenfeld
     Photo archive; Heinrich Brucker, curator

Video Archive

IANAS Oral Histories Video Archive, Interdisziplinärer Arbeitskreis für Nord-
     amerikastudien (IANAS), Johannes Gutenberg Universität, Mainz

This oral history collection contains more than seventy videos of interviews conducted during 1993–94, most of them around Kaiserslautern and Baumholder and
a smaller number in the neighborhood of Hahn Air Base in the Hunsrück. I have
transcribed portions of sixty-three of these interviews and have the transcripts in
my possession. Transcribing only statements that pertained to the topic of Americans during the 1950s, I sorted the statements according to the categories listed
below, creating a database that gave me a good overview, both qualitatively and
quantitatively, of people's recollections of German-American interaction in the
1950s.

A   Anxiety due to Americans
C   Changes due to Americans
D   America as the "Other"
E   Economic impact due to Americans
H   Harmonious relations with the U.S. military and individual GIs
J   Persisting anti-Semitism
K   Contacts with Americans in clubs and other social settings
O   Observations on America and Americans
P   Comments relating to prostitution
Q   Critical comments about Americans
R   Comments on race relations
Y   Comments on youth

According to the wishes of the individuals interviewed, IANAS identified the
videos by number, not name, but it did keep a listing that provides personal information on all individuals interviewed, including in what capacity they interacted

with Americans during the 1950s. Listed below are the numbers of the videos I have transcribed and a description of the interviewee(s) in each.

Video	Interviewee
1	Civil servant who conducted German-American wedding ceremonies (male)
2	Liaison officer in the 1950s (female)
3 & 4	Mayor and former Landrat (state-appointed head of county government, male) and his secretary (female)
5	Former president of the state legislature (male)
6	Civil servant (male) who had American friends
8	Worked as a maid for Americans (female)
9	Couple who rented to Americans
10	Couple who rented to Americans
12	Former archivist of city archive in Kaiserslautern (male)
13	Worked for Americans as dentist (male)
14	High-ranking civil servant (male)
16	Worked for Americans as logger (male)
17	Neighbor of Americans
18	Rented to Americans for decades
19	Forester (male)
20	Worked as translator (female)
21	Mayor (male)
22	Rented to Americans (couple)
23	Worked as bus driver (male)
24	City council member (male)
25	Three women from a German-American Women's Club
27	Civil servant and his wife, who had long-term contact with Americans
28	President of German-American Women's Club
29	Former editor of the *Rheinzeitung* (male)
30	Former police chief (male)
31	Couple that had American neighbors and friends
32	Women involved with German-American friendship club
33	Rented to Americans (male)
34	Worked in the Post Exchange (female)
35	Worked for Americans (male)
37	Founder of the German-American Committee in Baumholder (male)
38	Director of a high school, worked on base as a teenager (male)
39	Firefighter with American military (male)
40	Worked for Americans (male)
41	Worked for Americans (couple)
42	Rented to Americans (couple)
44	Worked for Americans (male)
45	Former chief of the water works in Baumholder (male)
46	Rented to Americans (female)
47	Rented to Americans, former city council member (male)

48	Former mayor (male)
49	Worked as translator (male)
50	Rented to Americans, had three daughters who married GIs (male)
51	Knew Americans as a teenager (male)
52	Rented to Americans
53	Knew Americans as teenagers in 1950s (couple)
54	Worked in an American snack bar (female)
56	Secretary for local commander 1953–94 (female)
57	Worked for Americans (female)
58	Ran a dry cleaning store on an American military base (couple)
60	Worked for Americans (male)
61	Worked for Americans (male)
62	Worked for Americans (couple)
63	Rented to Americans, had two daughters who married GIs

Interviews with Germans

All interviews were conducted by the author during the summers of 1993 and 1994 in the communities where the individuals live. Notes from these interviews are in the author's possession.

Bartz, Alfred. Hoppstädten (worked for American military for thirty years)

Bartz, Erika. Hoppstädten (worked for American military water treatment plant for forty years)

Britzius, Hans. Baumholder (police officer in Baumholder)

Divivier, Erich. Ramstein (mayor of Ramstein)

Dreier, Manfred. Birkenfeld (mayor of Verbandsgemeinde Birkenfeld)

Edinger, Karl. Baumholder (former city council member and businessman)

Fasching, Georg. Ellweiler (former head of the Baumholder Housing Office; part-time taxi driver in Baumholder during the 1950s)

Feis, Hans. Weiersbach (teenager in 1950s)

Geib, Michael. Ramstein (archivist and curator at the Museum des Westrich, Ramstein)

Grimm, Herbert. Baumholder (former Baumholder city council member)

Haag, Gerhard. Landstuhl (mayor of Landstuhl and former police chief in Landstuhl)

Haag, Heinrich. Baumholder (former police chief in Baumholder)

Hechl, Karl. Eckelhausen (teenager in 1950s)

Höhn, Winfried. Hoppstädten (child during 1950s; had American friends)

Kölling, Werner. Saarbrücken (former chief of the German customs station in Baumholder)

Kürsten, Anneliese (worked as a nurse in the Neubrücke General Hospital)

Lang, Annemarie. Idar-Oberstein (former social welfare worker in Baumholder)

Licht, Fritz. Baumholder (county council member and farmers' advocate during the 1950s)

Mades, Heinz. Gimbweiler (teenager in the 1950s)

Müller, Hans. Hoppstädten (teenager in the 1950s)
Nagel, Dr. Gerhard. Baumholder (former mayor of Baumholder)
Schneider, Christa Rühl. Birkenfeld (former social welfare worker in Baum-
    holder)
Schüssler, Hermann and Anna. Hoppstädten (businessman and wife, who
    rented to Americans, had two daughters who married American GIs)
Schwerdtner, Gerd and Ingrid. Baumholder (children during the 1950s, they
    lived in the center of town and knew Americans at that time)
Werner, Karl. Birkenfeld (former clerk at the Inferior Court in Baumholder)
Winkler, Anna. Hoppstädten. (leader of the Bund deutscher Mädchen in Hopp-
    städten during the Nazi regime)
Zimmermann, Josef. Birkenfeld (employee of Birkenfeld Police Department)

Interviews with American Veterans

In 1998, I advertised in the *VFW (Veterans of Foreign Wars) Magazine* and received
written responses and telephone calls from approximately 100 veterans who were
stationed in Rhineland-Palatinate during the 1950s. Listed below are those who
contributed valuable information for this manuscript. The great majority of them
were not career soldiers. Their letters and transcripts of our telephone conversations are in my possession.

Abbett, James	Martin, Harold
Amicelli, Anthony	McDonald, James
Bishop, John	Moskos, Charles
Bruner, Homer	Parsons, Russell
Campbell, Charles	Price, Oscar
Davies, Gerald	Rauman, Eino
German, Tom	Rogers, Theodore
Gillespie, Robert	Schmitz, Leland
Gillie, Robert	Shelbourne, Bradley
Glisson, Charles	Stagliano, Greg
Holmes, Carl	Stoudt, Herb
Keen, William	Trefill, Manuel
Kelly, John	Warren, William
King, Jacki Greg	Wolf, Fred
Larkin, James	Years, Dean
Lohr, Raymond	

Secondary Sources

Abelshauser, Werner. *Die langen 50er Jahre: Wirtschaft und Gesellschaft der Bundes-
    republik 1949–60.* Düsseldorf: Cornelsen, 1987.
Adams, Willi Paul. *Deutschland und Amerika: Perzeption und historische Realität.*
    Berlin: Colloquium Verlag, 1985.

Allen, William S. *The Nazi Seizure of Power: The Experience of a Single German Town, 1922–1945*. Chicago: University of Chicago Press, 1984.

Alvah, Donna. "Unofficial Ambassadors: American Military Families Overseas and Cold War International Relations, 1945–65." Ph.D. diss., University of California, Davis, 2000.

Anhäuser, Uwe. *Militär-Heimat Hunsrück: Fichten, Fachwerk, Flugzeugträger— Beiträge zu einer regionalen Militäranalyse*. Neckarsulm: Jungjohann, 1986.

Antonio, Peter, and Werner Wold, eds. *Arbeit, Amis, Aufbau: Alltag in Hessen 1949–1955*. Wiesbaden: Hessische Landeszentrale für politische Bildung, 1990.

Applegate, Celia. *A Nation of Provincials: The German Idea of Heimat*. Berkeley: University of California Press, 1990.

Bailey, Beth. *The First Strange Place: The Alchemy of Race and Sex in Hawaii*. New York: Free Press, 1993.

Bänsch, Dieter, ed. *Die fünfziger Jahre: Beiträge zu Politik und Kultur*. Tübingen: Narr, 1985.

Barden, Judy. "Candy-Bar Romance—Women of West Germany." In *This Is Germany*, edited by Arthur Settel, 161–76. New York: Sloane, 1950.

Barkin, Kenneth. "Modern Germany: A Twisted Vision," *Dissent* (Spring 1987): 252–55.

Bauer, Ingrid. *Welcome Ami Go Home: Die amerikanische Besatzung in Salzburg. Erinnerungslandschaften aus einem Oral History Projekt*. Salzburg: Verlag Anton Pustet, 1998.

Bauer, Willi. *Geschichte und Wesen der Prostitution*. Stuttgart: Weltspiegel Verlag, 1956.

Bauerkämper, Arnd. "Landwirtschaft und ländliche Gesellschaft in der Bundesrepublik in den fünfziger Jahren." In *Modernisierung im Wiederaufbau: Die westdeutsche Gesellschaft der 50er Jahre*, edited by Axel Schildt and Arnold Sywotteck, 188–202. Bonn: J. H. W. Dietz Nachf., 1993.

Baumgarten, Achim. "Jugendgefährdung und Jugendschutz im Raum Baumholder in den 50er Jahren." Birkenfeld: Mitteilungen des Vereins für Heimatkunde im Landkreis Birkenfeld und der Heimatfreunde Oberstein, 1995.

Becker, Hans Jürgen. "Die Veränderung des Stadtbildes von Baumholder seit 1945." Diplomarbeit, Erziehungswissenschaftliche Hochschule Rheinland-Pfalz Abteilung Koblenz, 1975.

Becker, Hans, and Joachim Burdack. *Amerikaner in Bamberg: Eine ethnische Minorität zwischen Segregation und Integration*. Bamberg: Fach Geographie an der Universität Bamberg, 1987.

Becker, Josef, Theo Stammen, and Peter Waldemann. *Vorgeschichte der Bundesrepublik Deutschland: Zwischen Kapitulation und Grundgesetz*. Munich: Fink, 1979.

Benz, Wolfgang. *Die Geschichte der Bundesrepublik Deutschland*. Vols. 1–4. Frankfurt/Main: Fischer Taschenbuch Verlag, 1993.

———. *Von der Besatzungsherrschaft zur Bundesrepublik*. Frankfurt/Main: Fischer Taschenbuch Verlag, 1984.

———. *Zwischen Hitler und Adenauer*. Frankfurt/Main: Fischer Taschenbuch Verlag, 1991.

Berghahn, Volker. *The Americanization of West German Industry, 1945–1973.* New York: Cambridge University Press, 1986.

———. "Philanthropy and Diplomacy in the 'American Century.'" *Diplomatic History* 23, no. 3 (Summer 1999): 393–420.

Bergmann, Werner, and Rainer Erb, eds. *Antisemitismus in der politischen Kultur nach 1945.* Opladen: Westdeutscher Verlag GmbH, 1990.

Bergstrasser, Arnold. "Zum Problem der sogenannten Amerikanisierung Deutschlands." *Vierteljahreshefte für Zeitgeschichte* 1 (1953): 222–43.

Biddiscombe, Perry. "Dangerous Liaisons: The Anti-Fraternization Movement in the U.S. Occupation Zones of Germany and Austria, 1945–48." *Journal of Social History* 34 no. 3 (Spring 2001): 611–48.

Bigsby, C. W. E. *Cultural Change and the U.S. Since World War II.* Amsterdam: Free University Press, 1986.

Bilanz der Aufbauarbeit eines Grenzkreises, 1950–1955. Birkenfeld: Kreisverwaltung Birkenfeld, 1956.

Blessing, Werner. "'Deutschland in Not, wir im Glauben . . .': Kirche und Kirchenvolk in einer katholischen Region, 1933–49." In *Von Stalingrad zur Währungsreform: Zur Sozialgeschichte des Umbruchs in Deutschland,* edited by Martin Broszat, Klaus-Dietmar Henke, and Hans Woller, 3–112. Munich: R. Oldenbourg, 1988.

Bleuel, Hans-Peter. *Strength Through Joy: Sex and Society in Nazi Germany.* Translated by J. Maxwell Brownjohn. London: Secker & Warburg, 1973.

Bodemann, Y. Michael, ed. *Jews, Germans, Memory: Reconstruction of Jewish Life in Germany.* Ann Arbor: University of Michigan Press, 1996.

Boehling, Rebecca. *A Question of Priorities: Democratic Reforms and Economic Recovery in Early Postwar Germany.* Providence, R.I.: Berghahn, 1996.

Brauerhoch, Annette. "'Mohrenkopf': Schwarzes Kind und weisse Nachkriegsgesellschaft in TOXI." *Frauen und Film* 60 (October 1997): 106–30.

Braun, Hans. "Das Streben nach 'Sicherheit in' den 50er Jahren: Soziale und politische Ursachen und Erscheinungsweisen." *Archiv für Sozialgeschichte* 18 (1978): 279–306.

Brenner, Michael. "East European and German Jews in Postwar Germany, 1945–50." In *Jews, Germans, Memory: Reconstruction of Jewish Life in Germany,* edited by Michael Y. Bodemann, 49–64. Ann Arbor: University of Michigan Press, 1996.

———. *Nach dem Holocaust: Juden in Deutschland 1945–50.* Munich: Beck, 1995.

Bristow, Edward. *Prostitution and Prejudice: The Jewish Fight against White Slavery, 1870–1939.* New York: Schocken, 1982.

Brommer, Peter. *Dokumente der Geschichte: 50 Jahre Kreis Birkenfeld, 1937–87.* Koblenz: Landeshauptarchiv, 1987.

———, ed. *Quellen zur Geschichte von Rheinland-Pfalz während der französischen Besatzung, März 1945–August 1949.* Mainz: Veröffentlichungen der Kommission des Landtages für die Geschichte des Landes Rheinland-Pfalz, 1985.

Broszat, Martin. *Zäsuren nach 1945: Essays zur Periodisierung der deutschen Nachkriegsgeschichte.* Munich: R. Oldenbourg, 1990.

Broszat, Martin, Klaus-Dietmar Henke, and Hans Woller, eds. *Von Stalingrad zur Währungsreform: Zur Sozialgeschichte des Umbruchs in Deutschland.* Munich: R. Oldenbourg, 1988.

Browder, Dewey A. *Americans in Post–World War II Germany: Teachers, Tinkers, Neighbors, and Nuisances.* Lewiston, N.Y.: E. Mellen Press, 1998.

———. "The Impact of the American Presence on Germans and German-American Grass-Roots Relations in Germany, 1950–1960." Ph.D. diss., Louisiana State University, 1987.

Bürgermeisteramt Baumholder. *Chronik der Gemeinde Mambächel.* Baumholder, 1937.

Burleigh, Michael, and Wolfgang Wippermann. *The Racial State: Germany 1933–1945.* Cambridge: Cambridge University Press, 1991.

Campt, Tina. "'Afro-German': The Convergence of Race, Sexuality and Gender in the Formation of a German Ethnic Identity, 1919–1960." Ph.D. diss., Cornell University, 1996.

Carter, Erica. "Alice in the Consumer Wonderland: West German Case Studies in Gender and Consumer Culture." In *Gender and Generation,* edited by Angela McRobbie and Mica Nava, 185–214. London: Humanities Press, 1984.

———. "Deviant Pleasures? Women, Melodrama, and Consumer Nationalism in West Germany." In *The Sex of Things: Gender and Consumption in Historical Perspective,* edited by Victoria de Grazia, 359–80. Berkeley: University of California Press, 1996.

———. *How German Is She? Postwar West German Reconstruction and the Consuming Woman.* Ann Arbor: University of Michigan Press, 1997.

Chaussy, Ulrich. "Jugend." In *Die Geschichte der Bundesrepublik,* edited by Wolfgang Benz, 3:207–44. Frankfurt/Main: Fischer Taschenbuchverlag, 1989.

Childers, Thomas. *The Nazi Voter: The Social Foundations of Fascism in Germany, 1919–1933.* Chapel Hill: University of North Carolina Press, 1983.

Chronik des gemeindefreien Bezirks Gutsbezirk Baumholder. Landkreis Birkenfeld, 1976.

Clement, Ulrich. *Sexualität im sozialen Wandel: Eine empirische Vergleichsstudie an Studenten 1966–1981.* Stuttgart: Enke, 1986.

Confino, Alon. "The Nation as Local Metaphor: Heimat, National Memory, and the German Empire, 1871–1918." *History and Memory* 5, no. 1 (1993): 42–86.

———. *The Nation as Local Metaphor: Württemberg, Imperial Germany, and National Memory, 1871–1918.* Chapel Hill, University of North Carolina Press, 1997.

Conze, Werner. *Sozialgeschichte der Bundesrepublik: Beiträge zum Kontinuitätsproblem.* Stuttgart: Klett-Cotta, 1983.

Cooney, James A., ed. *The Federal Republic of Germany and the United States: Changing Political, Economic, and Social Relations.* Boulder, Colo.: Westview, 1984.

Cooper, Frederick, and Ann Laura Stoler, eds. *Tensions of Empire: Colonial Cultures in a Bourgeois World.* Berkeley: University of California Press, 1997.

Cosamas, Graham, and Albert Cowdry. *Medical Services in the European The-*

ater of Operations: The Medical Department. Washington, D.C.: Center for Military History, 1992.

Costello, John. *Virtue under Fire. How World War II Changed Our Social and Sexual Attitudes.* Boston: Little, Brown, 1985.

Costigliola, Frank. *Awkward Dominion: American Political, Economic, and Cultural Relations with Europe, 1919-33.* Ithaca: Cornell University Press, 1984.

Crespi, Leo. "Germans View the U.S. Reorientation Program: Extent of Receptivity to American Ideas." *International Journal of Opinion and Attitude Research* 5 (1951): 181-90.

Dalfiume, Richard. *Desegregation of the U.S. Armed Forces: Fighting on Two Fronts, 1939-1953.* Columbia: University of Missouri Press, 1975.

David, Jay, and Elaine Crane. *The Black Soldier: From the American Revolution to Vietnam.* New York: William Morrow, 1971.

Davidson, Eugene. *The Death and Life of Germany: An Account of the American Occupation.* New York: Knopf, 1959.

Davis, David Brion. "The Americanized Mannheim of 1945-46." In *American Places: Encounters with History—A Celebration of Sheldon Meyer,* edited by William E. Leuchtenburg, 79-91. New York: Oxford University Press, 2000.

Debus, Karl-Heinz. "Die großen Kirchen unter dem Hakenkreuz." In *Die Pfalz unterm Hakenkreuz: Eine deutsche Provinz während der nationalsozialistischen Terrorherrschaft,* edited by Gerhard Nester and Hannes Ziegler, 227-72. Landau: Pfälzische Verlagsanstalt, 1993.

Decker, Ursula. "Baumholder—Ein Ort zwischen Deutsch und Amerikanisch." M.A. thesis, Universität Trier, 1977.

De Grazia, Victoria. *The Sex of Things: Gender and Consumption in Historical Perspective.* Berkeley: University of California Press, 1996.

Deiseroth, Dieter. *Fremde Truppen im eigenen Land.* Starnberg: Forschungsinstitut für Friedenspolitik, 1984.

DeLille, Angela. *Blick zurück aufs Glück: Frauenleben und Familienpolitik in den 50er Jahren.* Berlin: Elefanten Presse, 1985.

———, ed. *Perlon Zeit: Wie deutsche Frauen ihr Wirtschaftswunder erlebten.* Berlin: Elefanten Presse, 1985.

Dickinson, Edward Ross. *The Politics of German Child Welfare from the Empire to the Federal Republic.* Cambridge: Harvard University Press, 1996.

Die Pfalz klagt an: Tatsachenbericht eines deutschen Pfarrer. Frankfurt, 1954.

Dillmann, Edwin, and Richard van Dülmen. *Lebenserfahrungen an der Saar: Studien zur Alltagskultur 1945-1995.* St. Ingbert: Röhrig Universitätsverlag, 1996.

Diner, Dan. *America in the Eyes of the Germans: An Essay on Anti-Americanism.* Princeton: Princeton University Press, 1996.

Dischner, Gisela, ed. *Eine stumme Generation berichtet.* Frankfurt/Main: Fischer Taschenbuchverlag, 1982.

Doering-Manteuffel, Anselm. *Die Bundesrepublik Deutschland in der Ära Adenauer.* Darmstadt: Wissenschaftliche Buchgesellschaft, 1983.

———. "Deutsche Zeitgeschichte nach 1945: Entwicklung und Problemlagen der historischen Forschung zur Nachkriegszeit." *Vierteljahreshefte für Zeit-geschichte* 41 (January 1993): 1–29.

———. "Dimensionen von Amerikanisierung in der deutschen Gesellschaft." *Archiv für Sozialgeschichte* 35 (1995): 1–34.

———. *Katholizismus und Wiederbewaffnung: Die Haltung der deutschen Katho-liken gegenüber der Wehrfrage 1948–1955.* Mainz: Mathias Grünewald Verlag, 1981.

———. *Wie Westlich sind die Deutschen? Amerikanisierung und Westernisierung im 20th Jahrhundert.* Göttingen: Vandenhoeck & Ruprecht, 1999.

Dombrowski, Erich. *Wie es war: Mainzer Schicksalsjahre 1945–1948.* Mainz: Main-zer Verlagsgesellschaft, 1965.

Domentat, Tamara. *"Hallo Fräulein": Deutsche Frauen und amerikanische Sol-daten.* Berlin: Aufbau Verlag, 1998.

Dudziak, Mary. *Cold War Civil Rights. Race and the Image of American Democ-racy.* Princeton: Princeton University Press 2000.

———. "Desegregation as a Cold War Imperative." *Stanford Law Review* (November 1988): 61–120.

Duignan, Peter, and L. H. Gann. *The Rebirth of the West: The Americanization of the Democratic World, 1945–1958.* Cambridge: Blackwell, 1992.

Duke, Simon. *United States Military Forces and Installations in Europe.* New York: Oxford University Press, 1989.

Duke, Simon, and Wolfgang Krieger. *United States Military Forces in Europe: The Early Years, 1945–70.* Boulder, Colo.: Westview, 1993.

Edgcomb, Gabrielle Simon. *From Swastika to Jim Crow: Refugee Scholars at Black Colleges.* Malabar, Fla.: Krieger,1993.

Erker, Paul. "Revolution des Dorfes? Ländliche Bevölkerung zwischen Flücht-lingsstrom und landwirtschaftlichem Strukturwandel." In *Von Stalingrad zur Währungsreform: Zur Sozialgeschichte des Umbruchs in Deutschland,* edited by Martin Broszat, Klaus-Dietmar Henke, and Hans Woller, 367–426. Munich: R. Oldenbourg, 1988.

———. "Zeitgeschichte als Sozialgeschichte." *Geschichte und Gesellschaft* 19 (1993): 202–38.

Ermarth, Michael, ed. *America and the Shaping of German Society, 1945–1955.* Providence, R.I.: Berg, 1993.

Evans, Jennifer V. "Protection from the Protectors: U.S. Court-Martial Cases and the Lawlessness of Occupation in Postwar Berlin, 1945–48." In *GIs and Germans: The American Military Presence, 1945–90,* edited by Detlev Junker. Cambridge, Mass.: Cambridge University Press, forthcoming.

———. "Reconstruction Sites: Sexuality, Citizenship, and the Limits of Na-tional Belonging in Divided Berlin, 1944–58." Ph.D. diss. State University of New York, Binghamton, 2001.

Eyferth, Klaus, Ursula Brandt, and Wolfgang Hawel. *Farbige Kinder in Deutsch-land: Die Situation der Mischlingkinder und die Aufgaben ihrer Eingliederung.* Munich: Juventa Verlag, 1960.

Fehrenbach, Heide. *Cinema in Democratizing Germany: The Reconstruction of*

National Identity in the West, 1945–62. Chapel Hill: University of North Carolina Press, 1995.

———. "The Fight for the 'Christian West': German Film Control, the Churches, and the Reconstruction of Civil Society in the Early Bonn Republic." *German Studies Review* 14 (1991): 39–63.

———. "Of German Mothers and '*Negermischlinge*': Race, Sex, and the Postwar Nation." In *The Miracle Years: A Cultural History of West Germany, 1949–1968,* edited by Hanna Schissler, 164–86. Princeton: Princeton University Press, 2000.

———. "Rehabilitating Fatherland: Race and German Remasculinization." *Signs* 24 (Fall 1998): 107–28.

Fehrenbach, Heide, and Uta Poiger. *Transactions, Transgressions, Transformations: American Culture in Western Europe and Japan.* Providence, R.I.: Berghahn, 2000.

Flamm, Franz. *Social Welfare Services and Social Work in the Federal Republic.* Frankfurt: Deutscher Verein für öffentliche und private Fürsorge, 1974.

Foitzik, Doris. "'Sittlich verwahrlost': Disziplinierung und Diskriminierung geschlechtskranker Mädchen in der Nachkriegszeit am Beispiel Hamburg." *Hamburger Stiftung für Sozialgeschichte des 20. Jahrhunderts* 12, no. 1 (1997): 68–82.

Foner, Jack. *Blacks and the Military in American History: A New Perspective.* New York: Praeger, 1974.

Först, Walter, ed. *Die Länder und der Bund: Beiträge zur Entstehung der Bundesrepublik Deutschland.* Essen: Reiner Hobing, 1989.

Frankenstein, Luise. *Soldatenkinder: Die unehelichen Kinder ausländischer Soldaten mit besonderer Berücksichtigung der Mischlinge.* Munich: Internationale Vereinigung für Jugendhilfe, 1954.

Fraser, Nancy. *Unruly Practices: Power, Discourse, and Gender.* Minneapolis: University of Minnesota Press, 1989.

Freie Deutsche Jugend in Westdeutschland. *Denkschrift über das Ausmass der Landbeschlagnahmungen und über die Auswirkungen der Anwesenheit der Besatzer auf die Jugend.* Mainz: Körner, 1955.

Freier, Anna Elisabeth, and Anette Kuhn. *"Das Schicksal Deutschlands liegt in der Hand seiner Frauen": Frauen in der deutschen Nachkriegsgeschichte.* Düsseldorf: Schwann, 1984.

Fremgen, Gisela. . . . *und wenn du dazu noch schwarz bist: Berichte schwarzer Frauen in der Bundesrepublik.* Bremen: Edition Con, 1984.

Frenzel, Manfred. "Ein Standort im Goldenen Westen? Kaiserslautern als Garnisonsstadt." In *Aspekte und Perspektiven einer Stadt—Kaiserslautern,* edited by Dietrich Mack, 93–102. Kaiserslautern: Stadtverwaltung Kaiserslautern, 1976.

Frevert, Ute. "Frauen auf dem Weg zur Gleichberechtigung—Hindernisse, Umleitungen, Einbahnstraßen." In *Zäsuren nach 1945: Essays zur Periodisierung der deutschen Nachkriegsgeschichte,* edited by Martin Broszat, 113–31. Munich: R. Oldenbourg, 1990.

————. *Women in German History: From Bourgeois Emancipation to Sexual Liberation.* Oxford: Berg, 1989.

Friedel, Franz. *Kaiserslautern im Wiederaufbau, 1946–1966.* Kaiserslautern: F. Arbogast, 1981.

Fuchs, Thomas. "Rock'n'Roll in the German Democratic Republic, 1949–1961." In *"Here, There and Everywhere": The Foreign Politics of American Popular Culture,* edited by Reinhold Wagnleitner and Elaine Tyler May, 192–206. Hanover, N.H.: University Press of New England, 2000.

Gabriel, Karl. "Die Katholiken in den fünfziger Jahren: Restauration, Modernisierung, und beginnende Auflösung eines konfessionellen Milieus." In *Modernisierung im Wiederaufbau: Die westdeutsche Gesellschaft der 50er Jahre,* edited by Axel Schildt and Arnold Sywotteck, 418–33. Bonn: J. H. W. Dietz Nachf., 1993.

Gardiner, Juliet. *"Overpaid, Oversexed and Over Here": The American GI in World War II Britain.* New York: Canopy, 1992.

Gardner Smith, William. *The Last of the Conquerors.* Chatham, N.J.: Chatham Booksellers, 1948.

Gassert, Philipp. *Amerika im Dritten Reich: Ideologie, Propaganda, und Volksmeinung, 1933–45.* Stuttgart: Franz Steiner Verlag, 1997.

Gellately, Robert. *The Gestapo and German Society: Enforcing Racial Policy, 1933–45.* New York: Oxford University Press, 1991.

Geschichte der Polizei des Birkenfelder Landes. Birkenfeld, 1987.

Gilman, Sander. *Difference and Pathology: Stereotypes of Sexuality, Race, and Madness.* Ithaca: Cornell University Press, 1985.

Gimbel, John. *The American Occupation of Germany: Politics and the Military, 1945–49.* Stanford: Stanford University Press, 1968.

————. *A German Community under American Occupation.* Stanford: Stanford University Press, 1961.

Glaser, Hermann. *Kulturgeschichte der Bundesrepublik Deutschland.* Vol. 2. Munich: C. Hanser, 1986.

Goedde, Petra. "From Villains to Victims: Fraternization and the Feminization of Germany, 1945–47." *Diplomatic History* 23 (Winter 1999): 1–20.

Goschler, Constantin. "The Attitude toward Jews in Bavaria after the Second World War." *Leo Baeck Institute Yearbook* 36 (1991): 443–58.

————. *Wiedergutmachung: Westdeutschland und die Verfolgten des Nationalsozialismus (1945–1954).* Munich: R. Oldenbourg Verlag, 1992.

Gräber, Gerhard. *Die Revolver Republik am Rhein—Die Pfalz und ihre Separatisten.* Vol. 1. Landau: Pfälzische Verlagsanstalt, 1992.

Grimm, Reinhold, and Jost Hermand, eds. *Blacks and German Culture.* Madison: University of Wisconsin Press, 1986.

Greschat, Martin. "Die evangelische Kirche." In *Die Geschichte der Bundesrepublik,* edited by Wolfgang Benz, 3:87–123. Frankfurt/Main: Fischer Taschenbuchverlag, 1989.

Gropman, Alan. *The Air Force Integrates, 1945–1964.* Washington, D.C.: Office of Air Force History, 1978.

Grossmann, Atina. *"Girlkultur* or Thoroughly Rationalized Female: A New

Woman in Weimar Germany." *In Women in Culture and Politics: A Century of Change,* edited by Judith Friedlander et al., 62–80. Bloomington: Indiana University Press, 1986.

———. *Reforming Sex. The German Movement for Birth Control and Abortion Reform, 1920–50.* New York: Oxford University Press, 1995.

———. "Trauma, Memory, and Motherhood: Germans and Jewish Displaced Persons in Post-Nazi Germany, 1945–1949." *Archiv für Sozialgeschichte* 38 (1998): 215–39.

Habe, Hans. *Off Limits: Roman der Besatzung Deutschlands.* Munich: K. Desch, 1955.

Hansen, Eckhard. *Wohlfahrtspolitik im NS Staat.* Augsburg: Maro Verlag, 1991.

Harmsen, Hans. *Die Integration heimatloser Ausländer und nichtdeutscher Flüchtlinge in Westdeutschland.* Augsburg: Hofmann Druck, 1958.

Haungs, Peter, ed. *40 Jahre Rheinland-Pfalz.* Mainz: H. Schmidt, 1986.

Heineman, Elisabeth. "The Hour of the Woman: Memories of Germany's 'Crisis Years' and West German National Identity." *American Historical Review* 101, no. 2 (April 1996): 354–95.

———. "Standing Alone: Single Women from Nazi Germany to the Federal Republic." Ph.D. diss., University of North Carolina, 1993.

———. *What Difference Does a Husband Make? Women and Marital Status in Nazi and Postwar Germany.* Berkeley: University of California Press, 1999.

Heinritz, Charlotte. "'Bedrohte Jugend—drohende Jugend'? Jugend der fünfziger Jahre im Blick des Jugendschutzes." In *Jugendliche und Erwachsene '85: Generation im Vergleich: Band 3 Jugend der fünfziger Jahre—Heute,* edited by Arthur Fischer, Werner Fuchs, and Jürgen Zinnecker, 293–319. Opladen: Leske und Budrich, 1985.

Heins, Dr. Josef. *Geschichte von Bitburg.* Trier: WTV, 1965.

Hellwig, Gisela. *Zwischen Familie und Beruf: Die Stellung der Frau in beiden deutschen Staaten.* Cologne: Verlag Wissenschaft und Politik, 1974.

Henke, Klaus-Dietmar. *Die amerikanische Besetzung Deutschlands.* Munich: R. Oldenbourg Verlag, 1995.

———. "Politik der Widersprüche: Zur Charakteristik der französischen Militärregierung in Deutschland nach dem Zweiten Weltkrieg." In *Die Deutschlandpolitik Frankreichs und die französische Zone 1945–49,* edited by Claus Scharf and Hans Jürgen Schröder, 49–89. Wiesbaden: F. Steiner, 1983.

———. *Politische Säuberung unter französischer Besatzung: Die Entnazifizierung in Württemberg-Hohenzollern.* Stuttgart: Deutsche Verlagsanstalt, 1981.

Herbert, Ulrich. "Good Times. Bad Times: Memories of the Third Reich." In *Life in the Third Reich,* edited by Richard Bessel, 97–110. New York: Oxford University Press, 1987.

Herget, Winfried, ed. *Amerikaner in Rheinland-Pfalz: Beiträge zu einem halben Jahrhundert deutsch-amerikanischer Nachbarschaft.* Trier: Wissenschaftlicher Verlag, 1996.

Herget, Winfried, Werner Kremp, and Walter Rödel, eds. *Nachbar Amerika: 50 Jahre Amerikaner in Rheinland-Pfalz.* Trier: Wissenschaftlicher Verlag, 1995.

Hermand, Jost. *Kultur im Wiederaufbau. Die Bundesrepublik Deutschland 1945–1965.* Munich: Nymphenburger, 1986.

Herzog, Dagmar. "'Pleasure, Sex, and Politics Belong Together': Post-Holocaust Memory and the Sexual Revolution in West Germany." *Critical Inquiry* 24 (Winter 1998): 393–444.

Herzog, Werner. "Konkret vor Ort: Die Rolle des Militärs." Unpublished manuscript. Kreisverwaltung Birkenfeld, 1988.

Heupel, Carl. *Die Pfalz auf der Suche nach sich selbst.* Landau: Pfälzische Verlagsanstalt, 1983.

Heusler, Andreas. "'Strafbestand' Liebe: Verbotene Kontakte zwischen Münchnerinnen und ausländischen Kriegsgefangenen." In *Zwischen den Fronten: Münchner Frauen in Krieg und Frieden, 1900–50,* edited by Sybille Kraft, 324–42. Munich: Buchendorf Verlag, 1995.

Heyen, Franz-Josef. *Nationalsozialismus im Alltag: Quellen zur Geschichte des Nationalsozialismus vornehmlich im Raum Mainz-Koblenz-Trier.* Boppard: Harold Boldt Verlag, 1967.

———. *Rheinland-Pfalz entsteht: Beiträge zu den Anfängen des Landes Rheinland-Pfalz in Koblenz 1945–51.* Boppard: Harold Boldt Verlag, 1984.

———, ed. *Geschichte des Landes Rheinland-Pfalz.* Freiburg: Ploetz, 1981.

Heyl, John. "The Construction of the Westwall, 1938: An Exemplar of National Socialist Policymaking." *Central European History* 14 (March 1981): 63–78.

Hillel, Marc. *Die Invasion der Be-Freier: Die GIs in Europa, 1942–1947.* Hamburg: E. Kabel, 1983.

Hirschner, Fritz. *Aus dem Chaos zum Land mit Zukunft.* Neuwied: Strieder, 1975.

———. *Dr. hc. Peter Altmeier und das Werden von Rheinland-Pfalz.* Neuwied: Strieder, 1975.

Historical Division, Headquarters, United States Army Europe (HQ USAREUR). "The American Military Occupation of Germany, 1945–1953." Karlsruhe: HQ USAREUR, 1953.

———. "The Employment of Local Nationals by the U.S. Army Europe (1945–1966)." Heidelberg: HQ USAREUR, 1953.

———. "Exchange of Troops and Facilities, United States and French Zones 1950–51." Karlsruhe: HQ USAREUR, 1952.

———. "Fraternization with the Germans in World War II." Occupation Forces in Europe Series, 1945–46, No, 67. Frankfurt/Main: Office of the Chief Historian, European Command, 1947.

———. "Integration of Negro and White Troops in the U.S. Army, Europe, 1952–54 (U)." Karlsruhe: Historical Division, HQ USAREUR, 1956.

———. "Negro Personnel in the European Command, 1 January 1946–30 June 1950." Occupation Forces in Europe Series, No. 105. Karlsruhe: European Command, 1952.

———. "Short History of EUCOM, 1947–1974." Washington, D.C.: Office of the Chief of Military History, Department of Army, 1974.

———. "The U.S. Army Construction in Germany, 1950–53." Heidelberg: HQ USAREUR, 1954.

Historisches Museum, Frankfurt am Main. *Frauenalltag und Frauenbewegung 1890–1980.* Frankfurt am Main: Stadt Frankfurt/Main, Dezernat für Kultur und Freizeit, 1981.

Hitler, Adolf. *Mein Kampf.* New York: Houghton Mifflin, 1939.

Höhn, Maria. "Frau im Haus und Girl im Spiegel: Discourse on Women in the Interegnum Period of 1945–49 and the Question of German Identity." *Central European History* 26 (1993): 57–90.

———. "GIs, Veronikas, and Lucky Strikes: German Reaction to the American Military Presence in Rhineland-Palatinate during the 1950s." Ph.D. diss., University of Pennsylvania, 1995.

———. "Heimat in Turmoil: African-American GIs in 1950s West-Germany." In *The Miracle Years: A Cultural History of West Germany, 1949–1968,* edited by Hanna Schissler, 145–63. Princeton: Princeton University Press, 2001.

———. "'Rheinland-Pfalz ist ein sittliches Notstandsgebiet': Die Reaktion der Kirchen auf die amerikanische Militärpräsenz." In *Nachbar Amerika: 50 Jahre Amerikaner in Rheinland-Pfalz,* edited by Winfried Herget, Werner Kremp, and Walter Rödel, 57–75. Trier: Wissenschaftlicher Verlag, 1995.

Hollander, Paul. *Anti-Americanism: Critiques at Home and Abroad, 1965–1990.* New York: Oxford University Press, 1992.

Hollenstein, Günter. "Die Katholische Kirche." In *Die Geschichte der Bundesrepublik,* edited by Wolfgang Benz, 3:124–61. Frankfurt/Main: Fischer Taschenbuchverlag, 1989.

Hong, Young-Sun. *Welfare, Modernity, and the Weimar State, 1919–1933.* Princeton: Princeton University Press, 1998.

Hough, Patricia. "The Socio-Cultural Integration of German Women Married to American Military Personnel." Ph.D. diss., Free University, Berlin, 1979.

Hudemann, Rainer. "Sozialstruktur und Sozialpolitik in der französischen Besatzungszone 1945–1949." *Jahrbuch der westdeutschen Landesgeschichte* (1979): 373–408.

Huyssen, Andreas. *After the Great Divide: Modernism, Mass Culture, Postmodernism.* Bloomington: Indiana University Press, 1986.

Jacobmeyer, Wolfgang. *Vom Zwangsarbeiter zum heimatlosen Ausländer: Die Displaced Persons in Westdeutschland, 1945–1951.* Göttingen: Vandenhoeck und Ruprecht, 1985.

Jacobsen, Wolfgang. *Geschichte des deutschen Films.* Stuttgart: Metzler, 1993.

Johnson, Jesse. *Ebony Brass: An Autobiography of Negro Frustration amidst Aspiration.* New York: William-Frederick, 1967.

Kaelble, Hartmut, ed. *Der Boom 1948–73: Gesellschaftliche und wirtschaftliche Folgen in der Bundesrepublik Deutschland und in Europa.* Opladen: Westdeutscher Verlag, 1992.

Kaes, Anton. *From Hitler to Heimat: The Return of Film as History.* Cambridge: Harvard University, 1989.

Kaes, Anton, Martin Jay, and Edward Dimendberg. *The Weimar Republic Sourcebook.* Berkeley: University of California Press, 1994.

Karsch, Otto, and Herbert Grimm. *Baumholder: Die Geschichte der Stadt und des*

Truppenübungsplatzes. Baumholder: Kuratorium zur Förderung von Sport und Kultur, 1972.

Katz, Ottmar. "Die leichten Truppen von Grafenwöhr oder 'Fräuleins' im Gelände." In *In Deutschland unterwegs: Reportagen, Skizzen, Berichte, 1945–48*, edited by Klaus Scherpe, 58–74. Stuttgart: Reclam, 1982.

Keddigkeit, Jürgen. "Bollwerk im Westen: Krieg und Kriegsende im Pfälzischen Raum, 1939–1945." In *Die Pfalz unterm Hakenkreuz: Eine deutsche Provinz während der nationalsozialistischen Terrorherrschaft*, edited by Gerhard Nester and Hannes Ziegler, 446–62. Landau: Pfälzische Verlagsanstalt, 1993.

Kellermann, Marion. *Die PX Story: Liebe Hinterm Ladentisch*. Wien: n.p., 1959.

Kleinschmidt, Johannes. *"Do not fraternize": Die schwierigen Anfänge deutsch-amerikanischer Freundschaft, 1944–1949*. Trier: WTV, 1997.

Kleßmann, Christoph. *Die doppelte Staatsgründung: deutsche Geschichte 1945–1955*. 5th ed. Bonn: Bundeszentrale für politische Bildung, 1991.

———. "Kontinuitäten und Veränderungen im protestantischen Milieu." In *Modernisierung im Wiederaufbau: Die westdeutsche Gesellschaft der 50er Jahre*, edited by Axel Schildt and Arnold Sywotteck, 403–17. Bonn: J. H. W. Dietz Nachf., 1993.

———. *Nicht nur Hitlers Krieg: Der zweite Weltkrieg und die Deutschen*, Düsseldorf: Droste, 1989.

———. *Zwei Staaten, eine Nation: deutsche Geschichte 1955–1970*. Göttingen: Vandenhoeck und Ruprecht, 1988.

Knapp, Manfred. *Die deutsch-amerikanischen Beziehungen nach 1945*. New York: Campus Verlag, 1975.

Knauer, Sebastian. *Lieben wir die USA?: Was die Deutschen über die Amerikaner denken*. Hamburg: Gruner und Jahr, 1987.

Koch, Friedrich. *Sexualpolitik und politische Erziehung*. Munich: List, 1975.

Kolinsky, Eva. *Women in Contemporary Germany: Life, Work, and Politics*. Oxford: Berg, 1989.

Kraft, Sybille, ed. *Zwischen den Fronten: Münchner Frauen in Krieg und Frieden, 1900–1950*. Munich: Buchendorf Verlag, 1995.

Kreisverwaltung Birkenfeld (KVB). *Bilanz der Aufbauarbeit eines Grenzkreises 1950–1955*. Birkenfeld: Kreisverwaltung, 1955.

Kreuzer, Margot Dominika. "Die Entwicklung der heterosexuellen Prostitution in Frankfurt am Main von 1945 bis zur Gegenwart unter besonderer Beachtung des Einflusses von Syphilis und AIDS." Ph.D. diss., Johann Wolfgang Goethe Universität, Frankfurt/Main, 1987.

Kroes, Rob. *If You've Seen One, You've Seen the Mall: European and American Mass Culture*. Urbana: University of Illinois Press, 1996.

———, ed. *Cultural Transmissions and Receptions: American Mass Culture in Europe*. Amsterdam: Free University Press, 1993.

Kuhn, Annette. *Frauen in der deutschen Nachkriegszeit: Frauenpolitik 1945–1949*. Düsseldorf: Schwann, 1986.

Kuisel, Richard. *Seducing the French: The Dilemma of Americanization*. Berkeley: University of California Press, 1993.

Küppers, Heinrich. "Rheinland-Pfalz." In *Die Länder und der Bund: Beiträge zur*

Entstehung der Bundesrepublik Deutschland, edited by Walter Först, 164–87. Essen: Reimar Hobbing, 1989.

Lake, Marilyn. "The Desire for a Yank: Sexual Relations between Australian Women and American Servicemen during World War II." *Journal of the History of Sexuality* 2 (April 1994): 621–32.

Large, David Clay. *Germans to the Front: West German Rearmament in the Adenauer Era.* Chapel Hill: University of North Carolina Press, 1996.

Laurien, Ingrid. "'Wie kriege ich einen Mann?': Zum weiblichen Leitbild und zur Rolle der Frau in den fünfziger Jahren." *Sozialwissenschaftliche Informationen* 15 (1986): 32–44.

Lebzelter, Gisela. "'Die Schwarze Schmach': Vorurteile—Propaganda—Mythos." *Geschichte und Gesellschaft* 11 (1985): 37–58.

Lemke Muniz de Faria, Yara Colette. "Zwischen Fürsorge und Ausgrenzung: Zur Situation und Darstellung afrodeutscher Kinder 1945–60 in Deutschland und den USA." M.A. thesis, Free University, Berlin, 1995.

Lester, Rosemarie. *Trivialneger: Das Bild des Schwarzen im westdeutschen Illustriertenroman.* Stuttgart: Akademischer Verlag H.-D. Heinz, 1982.

Leuerer, Thomas. "Die Perspektive der Military Communities: *Little America* in Rheinland Pfalz bestimmt die amerikanische Politik mit." In *Nachbar Amerika: 50 Jahre Amerikaner in Rheinland-Pfalz,* edited by Winfried Herget, Werner Kremp, and Walter Rödel, 75–98. Trier: Wissenschaftlicher Verlag, 1995.

———. "Die Stationierung amerikanischer Streitkräfte in Deutschland: Militärgemeinden der U.S. Army in Deutschland seit 1945 als ziviles Element der Stationierungspolitik der Vereinigten Staaten." Ph.D. diss., Würzburg University, 1996.

Lindemann, Beate. *Amerika in uns: Deutsch-amerikanische Erfahrungen und Visionen.* Mainz: v. Hase & Koehler Verlag, 1995.

Little, Monroe, Jr. "The Black Military Experience in Germany: From the First World War to the Present." In *Crosscurrents: African-Americans, Africa, and Germany in the Modern World,* edited by David McBride, 177–96. Columbia, S.C.: Camden House, 1998.

Löwenthal, Richard, and Hans-Peter Schwarz, eds. *Die zweite Republik: 25 Jahre Bundesrepublik Deutschland—Eine Bilanz.* Stuttgart: Seewald Verlag, 1974.

Lüdtke, Alf, Inge Marßolek, and Adelheid von Saldern, eds. *Amerikanisierung: Traum und Alptraum im Deutschland des 20. Jahrhunderts.* Stuttgart: Franz Steiner Verlag, 1996.

Maase, Kaspar. *Bravo Amerika: Erkundigungen zur Jugendkultur der Bundesrepublik in den fünfziger Jahren.* Hamburg: Junius Verlag, 1992.

MacGregor, Morris. *Integration of the Armed Forces, 1940–1965.* Washington, D.C.: Center for Military History, 1981.

MacGregor, Morris, and Bernhard Nalty, eds. *Blacks in the United States Armed Forces: Basic Documents.* Vols. 12 and 13. Wilmington, Del.: Scholarly Resources, 1977.

Mack, Dietrich. *Kaiserslautern: Aspekte und Perspektiven einer Stadt.* Kaiserslautern: Stadtverwaltung Kaiserslautern, 1976.

Mahncke, Dieter, ed. *Amerikaner in Deutschland: Grundlagen und Bedingungen der transatlantischen Sicherheit.* Bonn: Bouvier, 1991.

Mais, Edgar. *Ende und Anfang 1945: Die Kriegs- und Nachkriegszeit des Jahres 1945 im Kreis Birkenfeld.* Birkenfeld: Stadt Birkenfeld, 1985.

———. *Die Verfolgung der Juden in den Landkreisen Bad Kreuznach und Birkenfeld, 1933–1945.* Bad Kreuznach: Kreisverwaltung Bad Kreuznach, 1988.

Manz, Mathias. "Stagnation und Aufschwung in der französischen Besatzungszone 1945–48." Ph.D. diss., Universität Mannheim, 1968.

Markovits, Andrei. "Anti-Americanism and the Struggle for a West German Identity." In *The Federal Republic of Germany at Forty,* edited by Peter Merkl, 35–54. New York: New York University Press, 1989.

Massaquoi, Hans. *Destined to Witness: Growing Up Black in Nazi Germany.* New York: William Morrow, 1999.

May, Elaine. *Homeward Bound: American Families in the Cold War.* New York: Basic, 1988.

McBride, David, ed. *Crosscurrents: African-Americans, Africa, and Germany in the Modern World.* Columbia, S.C.: Camden House, 1998.

Merkel, Ina. "Eine andere Welt: Vorstellungen von Nordamerika in der DDR der fünfziger Jahre." In *Amerikanisierung: Traum und Alptraum im Deutschland des 20. Jahrhunderts,* edited by Alf Lüdtke, Inge Marßolek, and Adelheid von Saldern, 245–56. Stuttgart: Franz Steiner Verlag, 1996.

Merkl, Peter, ed. *The Federal Republic of Germany at Forty.* New York: New York University Press, 1989.

Merritt, Anna, and Richard Merritt. *Public Opinion in Semi-Sovereign Germany: The HICOG Surveys, 1949–55.* Urbana: University of Illinois Press, 1980.

Mershon, Sherie, and Steven Schlossman. *Foxholes and Color Lines: Desegregating the U.S. Armed Forces.* Baltimore: Johns Hopkins University Press, 1998.

Meyer, Sybille, and Eva Schulze. *Von Liebe sprach damals keiner: Familienalltag in der Nachkriegszeit.* Munich: C. H. Beck, 1985.

———. *Wie wir das alles geschafft haben. Alleinstehende Frauen berichten über das Leben nach 1945.* Munich: C. H. Beck, 1988.

Meyerowitz, Joanne. *Not June Cleaver: Women and Gender in Postwar America.* Philadelphia: Temple University Press, 1994.

Mitchell, Maria. "Christian Democracy and the Transformation of German Politics, 1945–1949." Ph.D. diss., Boston University, 1995.

———. "Materialism and Secularism: CDU Politicians and National Socialism, 1945–1949." *Journal of Modern History* 67 (June 1995): 278–308.

Moeller, Robert. "Introduction: Writing the History of West Germany." In *West Germany under Construction: Politics, Society, and Culture in the Adenauer Era,* edited by Robert Moeller, 251–86. Ann Arbor, University of Michigan Press, 1997.

———. "The Homosexual Man Is a 'Man,' the Homosexual Woman Is a 'Woman': Sex, Society, and the Law in Postwar West Germany." In *West Germany under Construction: Politics, Society, and Culture in the Adenauer Era,* edited by Robert Moeller, 1–30. Ann Arbor, University of Michigan Press, 1997.

————. "'The Last Soldiers of the Great War' and Tales of Family Reunions in the Federal Republic of Germany." *Signs* 24 (Fall 1998): 129–45.

————. *Protecting Motherhood: Women and the Family in Reconstruction Germany.* Berkeley: University of California Press, 1993.

————. "Protecting Mothers' Work: From Production to Reproduction in Postwar West-Germany." *Journal of Social History* 22 (1989): 413–37.

————. "Reconstructing the German Family in Reconstruction Germany." *Feminist Studies* 15 (1989): 137–69.

————. "War Stories: The Search for a Usable Past in the Federal Republic of Germany." *American Historical Review* 101 (October 1996): 1008–48.

————, ed. *West Germany under Construction: Politics, Society and Culture in the Adenauer Era.* Ann Arbor: University of Michigan Press, 1997.

Moersch, Karl. *Sind Wir denn eine Nation? Die Deutschen und ihr Vaterland.* Stuttgart: Bonn Aktuell, 1982.

Möhler, Rainer. *Entnazifizierung in Rheinland-Pfalz und im Saarland unter französischer Besatzung.* Mainz: v. Hase und Koehler, 1992.

Mommsen, Hans. "Von Weimar nach Bonn: Zum Demokratieverständnis der Deutschen." In *Modernisierung im Wiederaufbau: Die westdeutsche Gesellschaft der 50er Jahre,* edited by Axel Schildt and Arnold Sywotteck, 745–58. Bonn: J. H. W. Dietz Nachf., 1993.

Mönnich, Horst. *Das Land ohne Träume: Reise durch die deutsche Wirklichkeit.* Munich: P. List, 1957.

Mooser, Josef. "Arbeiter, Angestellte und Frauen in der 'nivellierten Mittestandsgesellschaft': Thesen." In *Modernisierung im Wiederaufbau: Die westdeutsche Gesellschaft der 50er Jahre,* edited by Axel Schildt and Arnold Sywotteck, 362–76. Bonn: J. H. W. Nachf., 1993.

Moseler, Claudius. "Die Auswirkungen der Präsenz des amerikanischen Militärs im Bereich des Ober-Olmer Waldes und in Mainz-Finthen." Arbeitspapiere zur Nordamerikaforschung No. 1. Johannes-Gutenberg Universität, Mainz, 1995.

Moskos, Charles. *The American Enlisted Man: The Rank and File in Today's Military.* New York: Russell Sage Foundation, 1970.

Mosse, George L. *Nationalism and Sexuality: Respectability and Abnormality in Modern Europe.* New York: H. Fertig, 1985.

————. *Toward the Final Solution: A History of European Racism.* New York: N. Fertig, 1978.

Motley, Mary, ed. *The Invisible Soldier: The Experience of the Black Soldier, World War II.* Detroit: Wayne State University Press, 1975.

Müller, Emil-Peter. *Anti-Amerikanismus in Deutschland.* Cologne: Deutscher Institutsverlag, 1986.

Müller, Horst, Andreas Wirsching, and Walter Ziegler, eds. *Nationalsozialismus in der Region: Beiträge zur regionalen und lokalen Forschung und zum internationalen Vergleich.* Munich: R. Oldenbourg, 1996.

Muthesius, Hans, ed. *Beiträge zur Entwicklung der Deutschen Fürsorge: 75 Jahre Deutscher Verein.* Cologne: Carl Heymann Verlag, 1955.

Nachama, Andreas. "Nach der Befreiung: Jüdisches Leben in Berlin 1945–1953."

In *Jüdische Geschichte in Berlin: Essays und Studien,* edited by Rainhard Rürup, 254–72. Berlin: Ed. Hentrich, 1995.

Nalty, Bernard C. *Strength for the Fight: History of Black Americans in the Military.* New York: Free Press, 1986.

Nalty, Bernard C., and Morris J. MacGregor. *Blacks in the Military: Essential Documents.* Wilmington, Del.: Scholarly Resources, 1981.

Nelson, Daniel. *Defenders or Intruders? The Dilemma of U.S. Forces in Germany.* Boulder, Colo.: Westview, 1987.

———. *A History of U.S. Military Forces in Germany.* Boulder, Colo.: Westview, 1989.

Nelson, Keith. "The Black Horror on the Rhine." *Journal of Modern History* 42 (1970): 606–27.

Nestler, Gerhard, and Hannes Ziegler, eds. *Die Pfalz unterm Hakenkreuz: Eine deutsche Provinz während der nationalsozialistischen Terrorherrschaft.* Landau: Pfälzische Verlagsanstalt, 1993.

Nichols, Lee. *Breakthrough on the Color Front.* New York: Random House, 1954.

Niehauss, Merith. "Kontinuität und Wandel der Familie in den 50er Jahren." In *Modernisierung im Wiederaufbau: Die westdeutsche Gesellschaft der 50er Jahre,* edited by Axel Schildt, Arnold Sywotteck, 316–34. Bonn: Verlag J. H. W. Dietz Nachf., 1993.

Nieten, Karl, and Jakob Heep. *Geheime Lageberichte aus dem Kreis Birkenfeld 1945–47.* Birkenfeld: Verbandsgemeinde, 1995.

Niethammer, Lutz. *"Die Jahre weiß man nicht wo man die heute hinsetzen soll." Faschismuserfahrungen im Ruhrgebiet: Lebensgeschichte und Sozialkultur im Ruhrgebiet 1930–1960.* Berlin: Verlag J. H. W. Dietz Nachf., 1985.

———, ed. *"Hinterher merkt man, daß es richtig war, daß es schief gegangen ist": Nachkriegserfahrungen im Ruhrgebiet.* Bonn: Verlag J. H. W. Dietz Nachf., 1983.

Niethammer, Lutz, and Alexander von Plato, eds. *"Wir kriegen jetzt andere Zeiten": Auf der Suche nach der Erfahrung des Volkes in nachfaschistischen Ländern.* Berlin: Verlag J. H. W. Dietz Nachf., 1985.

Nikles, Bruno. *Jugendpolitik in der Bundesrepublik Deutschland.* Opladen: Leske und Budrich, 1978.

Noelle, Elisabeth, and Erich Peter Neumann. *The Germans—Public Opinion Polls, 1947–1966.* Allensbach: Verlag für Demoskopie, 1967.

———. *Jahrbuch der öffentlichen Meinung, 1947–1955.* Allensbach: Verlag für Demoskopie, 1956.

Nolan, Mary. "America in the German Imagination." In *Transactions, Transgressions, Transformations: American Culture in Western Europe and Japan,* edited by Heide Fehrenbach and Uta Poiger, 3–25. Providence, R.I.: Berghahn, 2000.

———. *Visions of Modernity: American Business and the Modernization of Germany.* New York: Oxford University Press, 1994.

Noß, Holger. "Parteien im Nachkriegsdeutschland am Beispiel des Landkreises Birkenfeld." Facharbeit in Sozialkunde, Gymnasium Birkenfeld, 1995.

Oppens, Edith, ed. *Die Frau in unserer Zeit.* Oldenburg: G. Stalling, 1954.

Opitz, May, Katharina Oguntoye, and Dagmar Schulz. *Showing Our Colors: Afro-German Women Speak Out.* Amherst: University of Massachusetts Press, 1992.

Orlov, Dietrich. "Ambivalence and Attraction: The German Social Democrats and the United States, 1945–1974." In *The American Impact on Postwar Germany,* edited by Rainer Pommerin, 35–54. Providence, R.I.: Berghahn, 1995.

Palm, Dirk. *Die Aufnahme von Vertriebenen und Flüchtlingen im Landkreis Birkenfeld nach dem Zweiten Weltkrieg.* Birkenfeld: Verbandsgemeinde, 1990.

Pence, Katherine. "The 'Fräuleins' meet the 'Amis': Americanization of German Women in the Reconstruction of the West German State." *Michigan Feminist Studies* 7 (1992–93): 83–108.

Peterson, Edward. *The American Occupation of Germany: Retreat to Victory.* Detroit: Wayne State University Press, 1977.

Peukert, Detlev. *Grenzen der Sozialdisziplinierung: Aufstieg und Krise der deutschen Jugendfürsorge, 1878–1929.* Cologne: Bund Verlag, 1986.

———. *Inside Nazi Germany: Conformity, Opposition and Racism in Everyday Life.* New Haven: Yale University Press, 1987.

———. *The Weimar Republic: Crisis of Classical Modernity.* Translated by Richard Deveson. New York: Hill and Wang, 1992.

Pfaff, Martina, and Martin Haag. "Kaiserslautern nach den Amerikanern." Diplomarbeit, Universität Kaiserslautern, 1992.

Pilgert, Henry. *Women in West Germany.* Bad Godesberg: Office of the United States High Commissioner for Germany, 1952.

Pipifax [pseudonym]. *Der fröhliche Westrich: Eine heitere Chronik von Baumholder und anderes.* Baumholder, 1959.

Plassmann, Max. "U.S. Air Base Sembach: Von der ersten Landbeschlagnahme zu Abzug und Konversion." Arbeitspapiere zur Nordamerikaforschung No. 3. Mainz: Johannes Gutenberg Universität, 1995.

Poiger, Uta. *Jazz, Rock, and Rebels: Cold War Politics and American Culture in a Divided Germany.* Berkeley: University of California Press, 2000.

———. "Rebels with a Cause? American Popular Culture, the 1956 Youth Riots, and the New Conception of Masculinity in East and West Germany." In *The American Impact on Postwar Germany,* edited by Reiner Pommerin, 93–124. Providence, R.I.: Berghahn, 1995.

———. "Rock 'n' Roll, Female Sexuality, and the Cold War Battle over German Identities." *Journal of Modern History* 68 (September 1996): 577–616.

Poiger, Uta, and Heide Fehrenbach, eds. *Transactions, Transgressions, Transformations: American Culture in Western Europe and Japan.* Providence, R.I.: Berghahn, 2000.

Polm, Rita. *". . . neben dem Mann die andere Hälfte eines Ganzen zu sein?!"* Münster: Unrast, 1990.

Pommerin, Reiner, ed. *The American Impact on Postwar Germany.* Providence, R.I.: Berghahn, 1995.

———. "The Fate of the Mixed-Blood Children in Germany." *German Studies Review* 5 (1982): 315–23.

———. *"Sterilisierung der Rheinlandbastarde": Das Schicksal einer farbigen deutschen Minderheit 1918–1937.* Düsseldorf: Droste, 1979.

Posner, David Braden. "Afro-America in West German Perspective, 1945–1966." Ph.D. diss., Yale University, 1997.

Poste, L. J., and R. Spahn. "The Germans Hail America: Some Aspects of Communications Media in Occupied Germany." *Modern Language Journal* 33 (1949): 423–24.

Powell, Colin. *My American Journey.* New York, Random House, 1995.

President's Committee on Equal Opportunity in the Armed Forces. *Equality of Treatment and Opportunity for Negro Personnel Stationed within the United States.* Washington, D.C.: U.S. Government Printing Office, 1963.

———. "Final Report: Military Personnel Stationed Overseas, 1964." In *Blacks in the United States Armed Forces: Basic Documents,* edited by Morris MacGregor and Bernard Nalty, 13:125–52. Wilmington, Del.: Scholarly Resources, 1997.

———. "Investigation of Alleged Discriminatory Practices in the Armed Forces." In *Blacks in the United States Armed Forces: Basic Documents,* edited by Morris MacGregor and Bernard Nalty, 12:316–46. Wilmington, Del.: Scholarly Resources, 1997.

Preuss-Lausitz, Ulf, ed. *Kriegskinder, Konsumkinder, Krisenkinder: Zur Sozialisationsgeschichte seit dem zweiten Weltkrieg.* Weinheim: Beltz, 1983.

Prinz, Michael, and Rainer Zitelmann. *Nationalsozialismus und Modernisierung.* Darmstadt: Buchgesellschaft, 1991.

Pronay, Nicholas, and K. Wilson. *The Political Reeducation of Germany and Her Allies.* London: Croom Helm, 1985.

Pyta, Wolfram. "Ländlich-evangelisches Milieu und Nationalsozialismus bis 1933." In *Nationalsozialismus in der Region: Beiträge zur regionalen und lokalen Forschung und zum internationalen Vergleich,* edited by Horst Müller, Andreas Wirsching, and Walter Ziegler, 198–222. Munich: R. Oldenbourg, 1996.

Rauh-Kuhne, Cornelia, and Michael Ruck. *Regionale Eliten zwischen Diktatur und Demokratie.* Munich: R. Oldenbourg, 1993.

Reagin, Nancy. *A German Women's Movement: Class and Gender in Hanover, 1880–1933.* Chapel Hill: University of North Carolina Press, 1995.

Reich-Hilweg, Ines. *Männer und Frauen sind gleichberechtigt.* Frankfurt/Main: Europäische Verlagsgesellschaft, 1979.

Reif, Sieglinde. "'Das Recht des Siegers': Vergewaltigungen in München 1945." In *Zwischen den Fronten: Münchner Frauen in Krieg und Frieden, 1900–1950,* edited by Sybille Kraft, 360–71. Munich: Buchendorf Verlag, 1995.

Reinders, Robert. "Racialism on the Left: E. D. Morel and the 'Black Horror on the Rhine.'" *International Review of Social History* 13 (1968): 1–28.

Rheinland-Pfalz: Amt für Verteidigungslasten. Birkenfeld, 1982.

Rinderle, Walter, and Bernhard Norling. *The Nazi Impact on a German Village.* Lexington: University of Kentucky Press, 1993.

Ritzenhofen, Ute. "*Goldene Pest* und *Schwarzer Kies:* Amerikaner in Rheinland im deutschen Spielfilm." In *Nachbar Amerika: 50 Jahre Amerikaner in*

Rheinland-Pfalz, edited by Winfried Herget, Werner Kremp, and Walter Rödel, 37–56. Trier: Wissenschaftlicher Verlag, 1995.

Rödel, Walter. "Die Amerikaner kehren zurück: Aus Besatzern werden Nachbarn." In *Nachbar Amerika: 50 Jahre Amerikaner in Rheinland-Pfalz,* edited by Herget Winfried, Werner Kremp, and Walter Rödel, 45–70. Trier: Wissenschaftlicher Verlag, 1995.

Rodnick, David. *Postwar Germans: An Anthropologist's Account.* New Haven: Yale University Press, 1948.

Rollin, Roger. *The Americanization of the Global Village.* Bowling Green, Ohio: Bowling Green State University Press, 1989.

Rose, Sonya. "Girls and GIs: Race, Sex, and Diplomacy in Second World War Britain." *International History Review* 19 (February 1997): 146–60.

Rosenhaft, Eve. "Lesewut, Kinosucht, Radiotismus: Zur (geschlechter-) politischen Relevanz neuer Massenmedien in den 1920er Jahren." In *Amerikanisierung: Traum und Alptraum im Deutschland des 20. Jahrhunderts,* edited by Alf Lüdtke, Inge Marßolek, and Adelheid von Saldern, 119–43. Stuttgart: Franz Steiner Verlag, 1996.

Roth, John, ed. *Holocaust: Religious and Philosophical Implications.* New York: Paragon, 1989.

Rubenstein, Richard. "The Dean and the Chosen People." In *Holocaust: Religious and Philosophical Implications,* edited by John Roth, 277–90. New York: Paragon, 1989.

Ruge-Schatz, Angelika. *Umerziehung und Schulpolitik in der französischen Besatzungszone, 1945–49.* Frankfurt/Main: Lang, 1977.

Rühl, Christa. "Soziale Auswirkungen eines Truppenübungsplatzes: Erfahrungsbericht einer Fürsorgerin." Diplomarbeit Nürnberg, 1960.

Ruhl, Klaus-Jörg. *Die Besatzer und die Deutschen: Amerikanische Zone 1945–48.* Düsseldorf: Schwann, 1980.

———. *Frauen in der Nachkriegszeit.* Munich: Deutscher Taschenbuchverlag, 1983.

———. *Unsere verlorenen Jahre: Frauenalltag in Kriegs- und Nachkriegszeit 1939–49 in Berichten, Bildern und Dokumenten.* Darmstadt: Luchterhand, 1985.

Rupieper, Hermann-Josef. *Der besetzte Verbündete: Die amerikanische Deutschlandpolitik 1949–1955.* Opladen: Westdeutscher Verlag, 1991.

———. *Die Wurzeln der westdeutschen Nachkriegsdemokratie: Der amerikanische Beitrag, 1945–1952.* Opladen: Westdeutscher Verlag, 1993.

Rupp, Elfriede. "Der Grenzkreis Birkenfeld." Hausarbeit Jugendamt Idar-Oberstein, 1948.

Sartorius, Herbert. "Truppenübungsplatz Baumholder." In *Militär-Heimat Hunsrück: Fichten, Fachwerk, Flugzeugträger—Beiträge zu einer regionalen Militäranalyse,* edited by Uwe Anhäuser, 100–110. Neckarsulm: Jungjohann, 1986.

Schäfer, Hans-Dieter. "Amerikanismus im Dritten Reich." In *Nationalsozialismus und Modernisierung,* edited by Michael Prinz and Rainer Zitelmann, 199–215. Darmstadt: Wissenschaftliche Buchgesellschaft, 1991.

———. *Das gespaltene Bewußtsein: Über deutsche Kultur und Lebenswirklichkeit, 1933–1945.* Frankfurt: Ullstein, 1984.

Schäfers, Bernhard, "Die westdeutsche Gesellschaft: Strukturen und Formen." In *Modernisierung im Wiederaufbau: Die westdeutsche Gesellschaft der 50er Jahre,* edited by Axel Schildt and Arnold Sywotteck, 307–15. Bonn: J. H. W. Dietz Nachf., 1993.

Scharf, Claus, and Hans Jürgen Schröder, eds. *Die Deutschlandpolitik Frankreichs und die französische Zone, 1945–49.* Wiesbaden: F. Steiner, 1983.

Schildt, Axel. *Moderne Zeiten: Freizeit, Massenmedien und 'Zeitgeist' in der Bundesrepublik der 50er Jahre.* Hamburg: Christians, 1996.

———. "Die USA als 'Kulturnation': Zur Bedeutung der Amerikahäuser in den 50er Jahren." In *Amerikanisierung: Traum und Alptraum im Deutschland des 20. Jahrhunderts,* edited by Alf Lüdtke, Inge Marßolek, and Adelheid von Saldern, 257–69. Stuttgart: Franz Steiner Verlag, 1996.

———. "Von der Not der Jugend zur Teenager Kultur: Aufwachsen in den 50er Jahren." In *Modernisierung im Wiederaufbau: Die westdeutsche Gesellschaft der 50er Jahre,* edited by Axel Schildt and Arnold Sywotteck, 335–48. Bonn: J. H. W. Dietz Nachf., 1993.

———. *Zwischen Abendland und Amerika: Studien zur westdeutschen Ideenlandschaft der 50er Jahre.* Munich: R. Oldenbourg, 1999.

Schildt, Axel, and Arnold Sywotteck, eds. *Modernisierung im Wiederaufbau: Die westdeutsche Gesellschaft der 50er Jahre.* Bonn: J. H. W. Dietz Nachf., 1993.

Schmid-Harzbach, Ingrid. "Serie Nackkrieg II: Nun geht mal beiseite, Ihr Frauen." *Courage* Sonderheft [special issue] 6 (1982): 32–40; and Sonderheft 7 (1982): 47–54.

Schmundt-Thomas, Georg. "America's Germany: National Self and Cultural Other after World War II." Ph.D. diss., Northwestern University, 1992.

Schramm, Steffen, and Michael Wisseroth. "Alltag im Nationalsozialismus." *Westricher Heimatblätter* (1982): 3–30.

Schraut, Hans Jürgen. "U.S. Forces in Germany, 1945–55." In *U.S. Military Forces in Europe: The Early Years 1945–70,* edited by Simon Duke and Wolfgang Krieger, 153–80. Boulder, Colo.: Westview, 1993.

Schubert, Doris. *Frauen in der deutschen Nachkriegszeit: Frauenarbeit 1945–1949.* Düsseldorf: Schwann, 1986.

Schuster, Verena. "Serie Nachkrieg IV: Freiheit, Gleichheit und unsere verfluchte Last glücklich zu sein." *Courage* Sonderheft 9 (1982): 39–44.

Schütt, Peter. *Der Mohr hat seine Schuldigkeit getan . . . Gibt es Rassismus in der BRD? Eine Streitschrift.* Dortmund: Weltkreis Verlag, 1981.

Schwartz, Thomas Alan. *America's Germany: John McCloy and the Federal Republic of Germany.* Cambridge: Harvard University Press, 1991.

Schwarz, Hans-Peter. *Die Ära Adenauer: Gründerjahre der Republik.* Stuttgart: Deutsche Verlagsanstalt, 1981.

Seiler, Signe. *Die GIs: Amerikanische Soldaten in Deutschland.* Hamburg: Rowohlt, 1985.

Shukert, Elfrieda Berthiaume, and Barbara Smith Scibetta. *War Brides of World War II.* Novato, Calif.: Presidio, 1980.

Siegrist, Hannes. "Ende der Bürgerlichkeit? Die Kategorien 'Bürgertum' und 'Bürgerlichkeit' in der westdeutschen Gesellschaft und Geschichtswissen-schaft der Nachkriegsperiode." *Geschichte und Gesellschaft* 20 (1994): 549–83.

Smith, Graham. *When Jim Crow Met John Bull: Black American Soldiers in World War II in Britain.* New York: St. Martin's, 1987.

Spoo, Eckhart, ed. *Die Amerikaner in der Bundesrepublik.* Cologne: Kiepen-heuert Witsch, 1989.

Stange, Sabine. *Kriegsvorbereitung im Hunsrück: Der Einfluß der Raketen-stationierung auf den Alltag der Menschen.* Essen: Klartext, 1985.

Stephenson, Jill. "Triangle — Foreign Workers, German Civilians, and the Nazi Regime: War and Society in Württemberg, 1939–1945." *German Studies Review* 15 (May 1992): 339–59.

Stern, Frank. *The Whitewashing of the Yellow Badge: Antisemitism and Philo-semitism in Postwar Germany.* New York: Pergamon, 1992.

Stillman, Richard. *Integration of the Negro in the U.S. Armed Forces.* New York: Praeger, 1968.

Stoler, Ann Laura. *Race and the Education of Desire: Foucault's History of Sexuality and the Colonial Order of Things.* Durham, N.C.: Duke University Press, 1995.

Stolten, Inge. *Das alltägliche Exil: Leben zwischen Hakenkreuz und Währungs-reform.* Berlin: J. H. W. Dietz Nachf., 1982.

Südbeck, Thomas, "Motorisierung, Verkehrsentwicklung, und Verkehrspolitik in Westdeutschland in den fünfziger Jahren." In *Modernisierung im Wieder-aufbau: Die westdeutsche Gesellschaft der 50er Jahre,* edited by Axel Schildt and Arnold Sywotteck, 170–87. Bonn: J. H. W. Dietz Nachf., 1993.

"Symposium: African Americans and U.S. Foreign Relations." *Diplomatic History* 20, no. 4 (Fall 1996): 531–650.

Sywotteck, Arnold. "The Americanization of Everyday Life? Early Trends in Consumer and Leisure Time Behavior." In *America and the Shaping of Ger-man Society, 1945–55,* edited by Michael Ermarth, 132–54. Oxford: Berg, 1993.

———. "Wege in die fünfziger Jahre." In *Modernisierung im Wiederaufbau: Die westdeutsche Gesellschaft der 50er Jahre,* edited by Axel Schildt and Arnold Sywotteck, 13–42. Bonn: J. H. W. Dietz Nachf., 1993.

———. "Zwei Wege in die 'Konsumgesellschaft'." In *Modernisierung im Wieder-aufbau: Die westdeutsche Gesellschaft der 50er Jahre,* edited by Axel Schildt and Arnold Sywotteck, 269–74. Bonn: J. H. W. Dietz Nachf., 1993.

Tent, James. *Mission on the Rhine: Reeducation and Denazification in American-Occupied Germany.* Chicago: University of Chicago Press, 1982.

Thies, Jochen. *Südwestdeutschland Stunde Null: Die Geschichte der französischen Besatzungszone 1945–48.* Düsseldorf: Droste, 1979.

Trees, Wolfgang. *Stunde Null in Deutschland: Die Westlichen Besatzungszonen.* Düsseldorf: Droste, 1980.

Tröger, Annemarie. "Between Rape and Prostitution: Survival Strategies and Chances of Emancipation for Berlin Women after World War II." In *Women in Culture and Politics: A Century of Change,* edited by Judith Friedlander et al., 97–120. Bloomington: Indiana University Press, 1986.

Tumpek-Kjellmark, Katharina. "From Hitler's Widows: Towards a Construction of Gender and Memory in Postwar Germany, 1938–1963." Ph.D. diss., Cornell University, 1994.

United States Department of Defense. *Integration in the Armed Services: A Progress Report.* Washington, D.C.: Department of Defense, 1955.

Usborne, Cornelie. *The Politics of the Body in Weimar Germany: Women's Reproductive Rights and Duties.* Ann Arbor: University of Michigan Press, 1992.

Vogel, Angela. "Familie." In *Die Geschichte der Bundesrepublik,* edited by Wolfgang Benz, 3:35–86. Frankfurt/Main: Fischer Taschenbuchverlag, 1989.

Vollnhals, Clemens. "Die evangelische Kirche zwischen Traditionswahrung und Neuorientierung," In *Von Stalingrad zur Währungsreform: Zur Sozialgeschichte des Umbruchs in Deutschland,* edited by Martin Broszat, Klaus-Dietmar Henke, and Hans Woller, 113–68. Munich: R. Oldenbourg, 1988.

Von Saldern, Adelheid. "Überfremdungsängste: Gegen die Amerikanisierung der deutschen Kultur in den zwanziger Jahren." In *Amerikanisierung: Traum und Alptraum im Deutschland des 20. Jahrhunderts,* edited by Alf Lüdtke, Inge Marßolek, and Adelheid von Saldern, 256–69. Stuttgart: Franz Steiner Verlag, 1996.

Von Schubert, Klaus. *Wiederbewaffnung und Westintegration: Die innere Auseinandersetzung um die militärische und außenpolitische Orientierung der Bundesrepublik, 1950–1952.* Stuttgart, Franz Steiner Verlag, 1970.

Wagnleitner, Reinhold. *Coca-Colonization und Kalter Krieg: Die Kulturmission der USA in Österreich nach dem zweiten Weltkrieg.* Wien: Verlag für Gesellschaftskritik, 1991.

Ware, Vron. *Beyond the Pale: White Women, Racism, and History.* New York: Verso, 1992.

Weber, Heinrich. *Die Vollzugspolizei im Landkreis Birkenfeld/Nahe.* Birkenfeld: Kreisverwaltung, 1986.

Westphal, Hannelore. *Die Liebe auf dem Dorf: Vom Wandel der Sexualmoral und der Prostitution auf dem Lande.* Braunschweig: G. J. Holtzmeyer, 1988.

Wetzel, Juliane. "'Mir szeinen doh': München und Umgebung als Zuflucht von Überlebenden des Holocausts 1945–48." In *Von Stalingrad zur Währungsreform: Zur Sozialgeschichte des Umbruchs in Deutschland,* edited by Martin Broszat, Klaus-Dietmar Henke, and Hans Woller, 327–64. Munich: R. Oldenbourg, 1988.

———. "Trauma und Tabu: Jüdisches Leben in Deutschland nach dem Holocaust." In *Ende des Dritten Reiches: Ende des Zweiten Weltkriegs,* edited by Hans-Erich Volkmann, 128–46. Munich: Piper, 1995.

Wiehn, Erhard. *Kaiserslautern: Leben in einer Pfälzischen Stadt.* Landau: Meininger, 1982.

Wildt, Michael. *Am Beginn der Konsumgesellschaft: Konsum in Westdeutschland in den fünfziger Jahren.* Hamburg: Ergebnisse Verlag, 1994.

Willett, John. *The New Sobriety: Art and Politics in the Weimar Period.* New York: Pantheon, 1978.

Willis, Roy. *The French in Germany, 1945–49.* Stanford: Stanford University Press, 1962.

Willoughby, John. "The Sexual Behavior of American GIs during the Early

Years of the Occupation of Germany." *Journal of Military History* 62 (January 1998): 155–74.

Wolf, Charles. *Garrison Community. A Study of an Overseas American Military Colony.* Westport, Conn.: Greenwood, 1969.

Wolf, Robert, ed. *Americans as Proconsuls: U.S. Military Government in Germany and Japan.* Carbondale: Southern Illinois University Press, 1984.

Wollasch, Andreas. *Der Katholische Fürsorgeverein für Frauen, Mädchen, und Kinder (1899–1945).* Breisgau: Lambertus, 1991.

Woller, Hans. "Germany in Transition from Stalingrad (1943) to Currency Reform (1948)." In *America and the Shaping of German Society, 1945–55,* edited by Michael Ermarth, 23–34. Oxford: Berg, 1993.

———. *Gesellschaft und Politik in der amerikanischen Besatzungszone.* Munich: R. Oldenbourg, 1986.

Wünschel, Hans-Jürgen, ed. *Quellen zum Neubeginn der Verwaltung im rheinisch-pfälzischen Raum unter der Kontrolle der amerikanischen Militärregierung April bis Juli 1945.* Mainz: v. Hase & Koehler Verlag, 1985.

———. *Schicksalsjahre der Pfalz.* Neustadt/Weinstraße: Meininger, 1979.

Wundshammer, Benno. *Deutsche Chronik 1954.* Stuttgart: Europäischer Buchklub, 1954.

Zauner, Stefan. *Erziehung und Kulturmission: Frankreichs Bildungspolitik in Deutschland 1945–49.* Munich: R. Oldenbourg, 1994.

Zink, Harold. *The United States in Germany, 1944–1955.* Princeton, N.J.: Van Nostrand, 1957.

Index

Abendland (Christian Occident), 9, 127, 161, 175–76, 229, 269 (n. 52)

Acheson, Dean, 52

Adenauer, Konrad, 8, 18, 53, 175, 228, 229

Adolescents. *See* Youth, German

AFN (American Forces Network), 79, 256 (n. 147)

African American GIs: serving in Germany, 7, 8, 13, 240 (n. 18); German children fathered by, 12, 93, 101, 147, 260 (n. 36), 290 (n. 31); relationships with German women, 14, 86, 103, 182, 207; and their families, 86, 93, 103; and Nazi racial propaganda, 90, 103; generosity toward Germans, 90–91; German identification with, 91; encountering American racism, 91, 93, 97–100, 102, 104–7, 192–93, 195–96; positive experience in Germany, 91–93, 103, 107–8, 235; comparing Germany to the United States, 93, 107; blamed for increase in crime, 94; as alleged sexual threat, 94, 140, 157–58, 206–7; conflicts with white GIs, 97–99, 216, 261 (nn. 57, 69), 262 (n. 72); and American military police, 98–100, 192, 193, 262–63 (n. 83); discrimination against, in German communities, 99, 101, 102; and marriage to German women, 104–7, 195, 235, 264 (n. 111); blamed for cultural decline, 110, 121, 201–2, 208; blamed for increase in prostitution, 120–23, 141, 201–2, 207–8; special danger posed by, 183, 194–95; portrayed as sexual predators, 207–8, 210; defense of, 291 (n. 41)

African American press, 91

Altmeier, Peter, 18, 53–54, 216, 229

America Houses. See *Amerika Häuser*

American GIs. *See* African American GIs; GIs

American popular culture, 80–82, 155, 163, 206, 226–27

American tempo, 8, 32, 36, 87

American way of life: as advertised by the military, 4, 62–63, 71–73, 255

(n. 109); as a threat, 8, 156, 161–62, 164, 168–73, 256 (n. 146); German infatuation with, 79–81, 156, 168, 170–73, 226–27, 230–32; as different experience of freedom, 81–83, 156, 168–73, 226, 232; as means to distance oneself from Nazism, 226; as way to expose deficiencies of communism, 228–29, 231; and democracy, 231

American-German relations. *See* German-American relations

Americanization: as an explanatory model, 4, 226, 231, 234, 238 (n. 3); churches' views of, 5, 88–89, 110, 168–69; and failure of conservative project, 117–18, 168–69, 172–73, 233; containment of, 161–63; 168–73; German society and, 169, 172, 227, 231–32

Amerika Häuser, 61–62, 251 (nn. 31–32)

Amerikanismus, 116, 156, 169, 173, 268 (n. 36)

Amizonen. *See* "Veronikas"

Anti-Americanism: political, 55, 57, 61, 86–87, 120, 124, 215–16, 228, 239 (n. 9); cultural, 63, 73, 79, 86, 89, 118, 120, 124, 228; and effacing of Nazi past, 125

Anti-Communism, 9, 13, 116, 136–37, 175–76, 201, 229

Anti-Semitism: toward DPs, 109, 113–14, 119, 199, 212, 234, 292 (n. 54); regional government of the Palatinate and, 203; fight against, 205, 234; Eastern European Jews' charges of, 205, 284 (n. 13); European tradition of, 211; rejecting charges of, 211, 291 (n. 48); resurgence of, 211–12, 220, 292 (n. 54); condemnation of, 212, 292 (n. 56); depicted in *Schwarzer Kies,* 212–13; U.S. military rabbi's charges of, 214; alleged power of American Jews, 220; weakening of, 221, 234

Armed Forces Day, 56–57, 60, 64

Aussiedler (ethnic Germans returning to Germany after collapse of Soviet Union), 223

Baader-Meinhof, 224

Bars: explosion of entertainment industry, 10, 111, 158, 200–201; clergy's attitude toward, 115, 120, 122, 201–2, 269 (n. 52); municipalities' attitude toward, 115, 192, 203–4; and Jewish owners, 119, 123–25, 183–85, 204–5, 211–13; vice raids in, 183. *See also* Steinstrasse

Bars, black-only: segregated bars, 97–98, 124, 192, 195, 290 (n. 31); military police and, 99–100, 192; associated with prostitution, 122–25, 192–96, 201–2, 206–7, 209–10, 216–18, 233; vice raids in, 192, 193–195, 287–88 (n. 57); municipalities' attitudes toward, 192–93, 208; in Kaiserslautern, 198, 208; defense of, 206; Off-Limits Order, 208–9, 213–18

Basic Law. See *Grundgesetz*

Baumholder: as moral disaster area, 3, 118–19, 143; during Weimar Republic, 19–21; under Nazism, 21–26; *Truppenübungsplatz,* 22–24, 32, 36, 38–42; and U.S. occupation, 28–29, 35–37; and denazification, 29–30; and expellees/refugees, 30; economic impact of U.S. troop deployment, 32, 36, 38–42, 48–50, 118–19; 109, 113; anger over U.S. troop deployment, 36–37; and increase in German crime rate, 44–45, 118–19; and Jewish DPs, 99, 109, 113–14; *Denkschrift,* 119–21; and prostitution, 130, 136, 140–42, 173, 185–86, 189–90; vice raids in, 180–81, 184. *See also* Model Baumholder

Besatzungsamt (Occupation Office), 36

Bierhallen Putsch (1923), 21

Bimbo City, 198, 289 (n. 1)
Birkenfeld County. *See* Baumholder
"Black Horror on the Rhine," 27,
  89–90
Black Market, 44, 114, 203
Bolshevism, 201
Boogie-woogie, 206
Breden, Colonel Paul, 214–16
Bundesjugendplan, 157, 160, 278
  (n. 19), 279 (n. 23)
Bundestag, 3, 142–44, 158–162, 199,
  209, 214
Bundeswehr. *See* Military, German

Catholic Center Party, 21
CDU (Christian Democrats): and
  conservative restoration, 11, 149–54,
  158–59, 160, 163, 167–68, 181–82,
  190, 191; and West-integration, 18,
  54, 229–30; Rhineland-Palatinate
  CDU, 18, 199, 200; and rearmament, 54, 181; on dangers posed by
  U.S. troops, 158–161; modernization of, 175–76, 228–29
Christian churches: role in conservative restoration, 9, 11–12, 116, 232;
  impact of Nazism on, 116–17, 120,
  stance toward Weimar Republic,
  117; on *Amerikanismus,* 117–18;
  on consumer society, 120, 228–29;
  on materialism, 120, 239 (n. 11);
  reining in sexual immorality, 136,
  201, 232; waning influence of, 175–
  76, 192, 233; Protestant opposition
  to atomic weapons, 216. *See also*
  Christian welfare agencies; Clergy,
  Catholic; Clergy, Protestant
Christian Democrats. *See* CDU
Christian Occident. See *Abendland*
Christian welfare agencies: containing
  women, 9–10, 11, 160–66, 169–73,
  179–80; on dangers of American
  way of life, 10, 130–35, 162–65, 168–
  74, 232; on prostitution, 10–11,
  141, 144–49, 178–80, 184; failure to
  contain Americanization, 12, 174–

76, 232; effacing Nazi past, 127;
  on premarital sexuality as a political threat, 130–31, 191; impact of
  Nazism, 145–46, 148–49, 233; protecting the family, 161–63; failure of
  struggle for decency, 177, 187, 191,
  233, 287 (n. 51). *See also* Deutscher
  Verein für öffentliche und private
  Fürsorge
Civil habitus, 172, 226, 232, 257
  (n. 165)
Civil rights, 86, 96, 97–98, 101–2, 260
  (n. 52)
Class: weakening of, 130, 134–35,
  169, 172, 175–76; U.S. presence
  and, 132–33, 156, 169–73, 175–76,
  227–28, 230; control of lower, 156,
  161–63, 165–67, 181–82, 233
Clergy, Catholic, 10, 88–89, 110, 114,
  139, 141, 268 (n. 36)
Clergy, Protestant: criticism of
  Americanization, 10, 88–89, 168–
  69; condemning interracial relationships, 104, 110, 121, 135; on
  entertainment industry, 114, 269
  (n. 52); on American militarism,
  121–22; on Nazi past, 122; reining
  in sexual immorality, 136, 141; on
  brothels, 139
Coalition of Jewish Bar Owners, 204,
  210, 217, 284 (n. 13)
Coalition of Those Injured by the
  Steinstrasse Off-Limits Order, 217
Coca-Cola, 79, 226
Cold War: and troop deployment, 9,
  18, 235; and German conservatism,
  9, 175–76, 228–29; Colin Powell on,
  13; and anti-Slav sentiment, 13, 235;
  and civil rights, 96, 260 (n. 52); and
  sexual containment, 136–37, 201,
  233; exploiting U.S. anxiety over,
  136–37, 273 (n. 52); end of, 224
Colonial troops (French), 7, 20, 89–
  90
Consumer capitalism: 118, 120, 156,
  165, 175, 295 (n. 12)

Consumer democracy, 4, 47–50, 175, 181, 191, 228–29

Consumer goods: and sexual disorder, 120, 134, 164–66, 169–71; and sexual tolerance, 190, 191; desire for, 226, 231. *See also* Class

Council of Jewish Communities, Rhineland-Palatinate, 205

Criminal Code, German, 138, 142, 151–53, 182, 186, 190, 198

Currency reform (1948), 30–31, 224

Das Land Ohne Träume (Mönnich), 123

Decadence. *See* Degeneration

Decency, sexual. *See* Sexual decency

Degeneration: American culture as, 79, 122, 134; clergy on, 87, 110; Jews as source of, 90, 120–21, 123–124, 202, 210–13; black GIs as source of, 120–21, 122, 124, 201–2, 206–8, 210, 217; "Veronikas" as source of, 122–124, 131–32, 134–35, 140

Denazification, 29–30, 243 (nn. 56, 58)

Denunciation, 166, 281 (n. 51)

Department of Defense, 5, 17, 92, 96, 102, 218

Deutscher Verein für öffentliche und private Fürsorge: and sexual norms, 11, 12, 127, 145–48, 178; and postwar social conservatism, 127, 148–53, 157–60, 190; Schnapp's role in, 140, 147, 150; and Nazi regime, 144–45, 148–49, 233; on Weimar democracy, 145, 147–48; role in redefining prostitution, 146–49, 150–51; on brothels, 147; on HWG individuals, 147–150; rejection of its initiatives, 167–68, 175, 177, 180, 182, 185, 187, 189, 233, 287 (n. 51). *See also* Christian welfare agencies

Die Freiheit. See SPD

Die Pfalz klagt an, 121–122

Dietz, Maria (CDU), 142–43

Displaced Persons (DPs): and enter-

tainment industry, 10, 109, 113–15, 123, 203, 210–11, 234; after World War II, 13, 109, 243 (n. 60), 267 (n. 20); and German women, 180. *See also* Bars; Bars, black-only

DNVP (German Nationalist People's Party), 20, 146

DPs. *See* Displaced Persons

East Germany: 10, 95, 128, 268–69 (nn. 41, 48)

Economic miracle, 7, 19, 47–50, 118, 134, 161, 175–76, 191

Eisenhower, Dwight, 58, 104

Emergency Council of Steinstrasse Inhabitants, 208–10, 213, 214, 215

Erhard, Ludwig (CDU), 176, 228

Ermarth, Michael, 226

EUCOM (European Command), 32

Expellees, 30, 105, 189

Family: role of traditional family in overcoming Nazism, 9; special dangers faced by, 116–17, 147, 158, 160–63; protection of, 160–63; incomplete families, 163–64, 166–67; and sexual containment, 287 (n. 45)

"Fantastic Fifties." *See* "Golden Fifties"

FDP (Free Democrats), 158

Federal Ministry of Culture, 166

Federal Ministry of Justice, 150–53, 180, 188, 190

Federal Ministry of Labor, 169–70

Federal Ministry of the Interior, 150–53, 166, 182, 188, 190

Fehrenbach, Heide, 13, 93, 238 (n. 3), 240 (n. 17), 257 (n. 165), 266 (n. 4)

France: military government of Germany by, 5, 6, 18, 27–31, 35, 224; use of colonial troops by, 20, 27, 89–90; post–World War I occupation of Rhineland by, 20, 208; attitudes of Germans toward, 28, 229–31; and French attitude toward expellees and refugees, 30; and policies toward DPs, 30, 267 (n. 20); and military policies on brothels, 114–15, 138, 273 (n. 57); and policies on interracial sexuality, 138, 196, 273 (n. 57); French soldiers and German women, 180

Fraternization, 9, 103

Fräuleins. *See* "Veronikas"

Freeman, General Paul, 102

Fuchs, Jockel (SPD), 215

Gardner Smith, William, 91, 105

Gastarbeiter (guest workers), 176, 235

GDR (German Democratic Republic). *See* East Germany

Gender conservatism: and postwar social order, 9–11, 41–42, 130, 146–51, 161, 166–67, 188; weakening of, 169, 173–74, 191, 232–34

Genocide, 11, 107, 220

German catastrophe, 9, 122, 269 (n. 51)

German-American relations: in wake of World War II, 27, 52; fostered by U.S. military, 61, 63–68, 71–74; and friendship committees, 66–67, 173, 227; in German communities, 76–80, 174, 199, 220, 225–26; in American clubs, 79–80; celebration of, 83; in wake of Gulf War, 225; strength of, 230–31

German-French relations, 27–31, 230–31

GIs, American: positive views of, 26–27, 57, 119, 265–66 (n. 3); as neighbors, 43–46, 67, 76–77, 199; marriages with German women, 74–75, 104–7, 127, 185, 190; as ambassadors of the American way of life, 79–82, 226–27, 230; as male role models, 81–82, 226–227; negative views of, 87, 111, 199, 205–6; increase in crime due to, 87, 205, 258 (n. 3); resisting integration

of the military, 96–97, 192, 264 (n. 108); conflict between white and black GIs, 97–99, 216, 261 (nn. 57, 69), 262 (n. 72); rejection of interracial relationships by, 104–5, 264 (nn. 104, 108). *See also* African American GIs; USAREUR

"Golden Fifties," 8, 46, 76

Goldene Pest, Die (film), 111, 118–119, 206

Grüber, Heinrich, 205

Grundgesetz, 53, 96, 101, 108, 215

Gulf War, 225

Hagen, W., 249–50

Halbstarke. See Youth, German

Handy, General John W., 93

Heep, Jakob (SPD): on Nazism, 28–29; on U.S. occupation, 28–29, 35–37; on control of prostitution, 130, 136, 140–42, 173, 185–86, 189–90

Heimat, 7, 21, 86–89, 114, 118, 212, 221, 234

"Hell on Wheels" (U.S. Army tank division), 31, 38

Hertel, Eugen (SPD), 200, 212, 213, 215

Herzog, Dagmar, 232, 240 (n. 15)

HICOG (Office of the High Commissioner for Germany), 55, 285 (n. 18)

Himmler, Heinrich, 139

Hitler, Adolf, 21, 23, 28, 124

Holocaust, 10, 107

House of Encounter, 213

Hübner, Karl (FDP), 158

Hunsrückhöhenstraße, 22

HWG individuals (*häufig wechselnder Geschlechtsverkehr*), 130, 147–48, 151, 166, 180

IANAS (Interdisziplinärer Arbeitskreis für Nordamerikastudien), 7, 300

Idar-Oberstein, 20, 32

Ilk, Herta (FDP), 143
Illegitimacy, 145, 164, 280 (n. 37)
Immorality. *See* Sexual immorality
Innere Mission. *See* Christian welfare agencies; Deutscher Verein für öffentliche und private Fürsorge

Jazz, 8, 10, 13, 80, 83, 111–12, 202, 209
Jews, Eastern European: in Germany after World War II, 10, 13, 109, 113–15; blamed for explosion of entertainment industry, 10, 119, 123–25, 203, 210–11, 234; blamed for Rhineland occupation, 90; discriminating against African Americans, 99, 262 (n. 77); Coalition of Jewish Bar Owners, 204, 210; and tensions with German Jews, 205, 290 (n. 23)
Jews, German, 13, 24, 205, 210, 290 (n. 23)
Jim Crow, 5, 86, 95–97, 99, 101–3

Kaiserslautern (city): as moral disaster area, 3, 201–2, 210; as garrison town, 5, 6, 199, 200–202, 205; political landscape of, 199, 243 (n. 52), 249 (n. 8); Korea Boom in, 199, 247 (n. 123), 249 (n. 155); CDU on U.S. military in, 200, 203; SPD on U.S. military in, 200, 204; Wählergruppe Geiger on U.S. military in, 200, 220–21; FDP on U.S. military in, 203–4; curtailing the GI bars in, 203–4, 208. *See also* Steinstrasse
Kaiserslautern (county), 3, 134, 141–42, 144, 146, 154, 187
Katholischer Fürsorgeverein für Frauen, Mädchen und Kinder (KFV). *See* Christian welfare agencies; Deutscher Verein für öffentliche und private Fürsorge
Käutner, Helmut, 212–13
Koblenz, 18
Korea Boom: in Rhineland-Palatinate, 7, 12, 18, 109, 224; in Baumholder,

32, 36, 38–42, 46–50, 118–19; compared to Westwall boom, 50, 232; in Kaiserslautern, 199
Korean War, 5, 17, 18, 58, 96, 98
KPD (Communist Party): during Weimar Republic, 21, 90; during the Nazi regime, 24; and anti-Americanism, 29, 37, 54, 200; reaction to U.S. troop deployment, 29, 37, 143, 269 (n. 57); on rearmament, 54–55; denouncing American racism, 95–96; banning of, 100, 200; and racism, 202
Kulturbürger (educated upper classes), 227–28, 230. *See also* Class
Kuppelei (procurement), 151, 166–68, 180, 182, 233, 264 (n. 109)

Land Relations Officer (LRO), 54, 215–16
Lieberich, Karl (CDU), 200, 203–4, 214
Little Americas, 84, 224, 255 (n. 111)
Little Harlem, 198, 205, 219
Little Rock, Ark., 99, 214, 216
Lucy, Autherine, 99

Maase, Kaspar, 75, 168, 172, 227, 238 (n. 3)
Mainz, 18, 124, 187, 196–97
Mambächel, 21
Mannheim, 147, 276 (n. 97)
Marriage: with GIs, 74–76, 104–7, 127, 185, 190, 254 (n. 103), 270 (n. 51), 287–88 (n. 57); interracial, 104–8, 195, 235, 264 (n. 111); common law, 126, 152–53, 191, 277 (n. 116), 287 (n. 51)
Materialism: as part of American-style capitalism, 9, 120, 132, 148, 156, 170–73; conservative views of, 9, 120–21, 124, 161, 168–73, 175, 191; inherent in Soviet system, 120; shift in conservative view, 175, 228–29
Military, German: Wehrmacht, 10, 20, 26–27, 58–60, 82–83, 138–39; Bundeswehr, 18, 58–60, 230

Military, U.S. *See* USAREUR

Military government (American), 5, 26–27, 258 (n. 17), 273 (n. 54)

Military Police (MP), American: in German communities, 66, 105; brutality toward black GIs, 98–100, 192, 193, 262–63 (n. 83); enforcing racial boundaries, 99, 192, 234; and treatment of black-only bars, 100, 192, 287–88 (n. 57); cooperating with German police, 183–84, 192–93, 234, 285 (n. 18), 287–88 (n. 57)

Mockchen, 101, 263 (n. 87)

Model Baumholder, 160, 274 (n. 68)

Modernization, 4, 19, 49–51, 228, 232, 238 (n. 2)

Moeller, Robert, 235, 239 (n. 13), 277 (n. 115)

Moral rearmament: effort to impose, 11, 154, 167–68, 190; failure of, 175–76, 177, 180, 187, 189, 287 (n. 51)

Nadig, Friederike (SPD), 143

National Socialism. *See* Nazi regime

NATO (North Atlantic Treaty Organization), 18, 35, 60, 216

Nazi regime: and rearmament, 7, 22–24; impact on German social life, 9, 24–25, 117, 130, 242 (n. 31); racism of, 12, 14, 24–25, 90, 103, 124, 269 (n. 58); and secularization, 22, 24–25, 116–17, 120; economic/social changes due to rearmament, 22, 39, 49–50; opposition to interracial marriage/sexuality, 25, 107, 131, 197; youth organizations, 28, 156; on jazz, 80, 83, 257 (n. 171); views on women, 131; on prostitution, 138–39, 273 (n. 57); modernizing aspects of, 148–49, 233

Negerunwesen ("Negro nuisance"), 199, 289 (n. 2)

Nightclubs. *See* Bars

Nike missiles, 55, 121, 200, 213, 215–16, 218

NSDAP (National Socialist German Workers Party), 21–22, 90, 140

Nuremberg Laws, 107

Occupation Statute, 18, 183, 273 (n. 54)

Off-Limits Order. *See* Steinstrasse

Onkelehen ("uncle marriages"). *See* Marriage: common law

Ortsgruppenleiter (local Nazi leader), 22

Palatinate, 18, 242 (n. 31)

Paris Treaty (1955), 18

Peace movement, 224

Pershing missiles, 8, 224–25

Philosemitism, 210, 221, 234, 294 (n. 88)

Poiger, Uta, 238 (n. 3), 266 (n. 4)

Police, German: and GIs, 87, 95, 98–99; cooperation with American military police, 183–84, 192, 193, 285 (n. 18), 287–88 (n. 57); enforcement of prostitution laws, 183–84, 196, 233; rejection of new definition of prostitution, 186; hostility toward African-American GIs, 194–95, 285 (n. 19); on Jewish DPs, 211

Potsdam Treaty, 30

Powell, Colin, 13

Presley, Elvis, 59, 64, 80, 81, 227

Prosperity for All (Erhard), 176

Prostitution: professional, 109, 115, 127, 130, 137, 147, 178, 191, 193, 267 (n. 24); municipalities' response to, 135, 137, 139, 233; clergy's view of, 135–37, 139; USAREUR's attitude toward, 137–39, 214, 264 (n. 107), 272 (n. 50); legal status of, 138–39, 273 (n. 58); racial transgression depicted as, 140–41, 178, 182, 189, 192–93, 195–96, 207–8, 232, 287–88 (n. 57); criminalization of, 141–42; redefining parameters of, 146–49, 150–51, 153, 188–89, 277 (nn. 111, 113), 286 (n. 32); enforcement of laws against, 166–68, 184, 193–96, 233, 286 (n. 34); rejection of new definition of, 177–78, 185–88, 196, 287 (n. 51). *See also* HWG individuals; *Kuppelei;* "Veronikas"; Vice raids

Public Information Office (U.S.). *See* USAREUR

Rabbi, U.S. military, 214

Racial decline, 10, 109–10, 114, 120–22, 124, 206–8, 210

Racial hierarchies, 12–13, 93, 101, 104, 110, 125, 235, 266 (n. 4)

Racial segregation: imported by U.S. military, 14, 86, 95–96, 99; in the United States, 92–93, 95–96, 98–99, 102, 263 (n. 95); and white GIs, 96–97; supported by Germans, 103, 104, 108

Racial tolerance, 13, 91–93, 107–8, 135, 209, 219

Racism, American: within the military command, 95–96, 99, 105–7, 114–15, 196, 258–59 (n. 17), 261 (n. 62); German comments on, 95–96, 100–101, 214, 219; by individual GIs, 96–98, 192, 261 (nn. 57, 69), 264 (nn. 81, 104)

Racism, German: transformation of, 12–13, 108, 196–97, 199, 209–10, 221–22, 233–35; pre-Nazi racism, 101, 104; toward interracial sexuality, 103–4, 107, 140–41, 178, 189, 194–95, 209, 213–19, 234; efface-ment of, 108; critique of, 108, 219, 291 (n. 41); expressed over racial transgressions, 183, 189, 192–93, 195–96, 207–8, 287–88 (n. 57). *See also* African American GIs; Anti-Semitism; Nazi regime; *Rassenschande; Rassenstolz; Schwarze Schmach;* Sexuality, interracial; Steinstrasse

Racism, interaction of German and

American: and interracial sexuality, 13, 192, 193, 195–96, 234, 287–88 (n. 57); looking to American model of segregation, 101–2, 107–8; and transformation of German racism, 196–97, 221–22, 234–35

Rassenschande (miscegenation), 131, 196–97

Rassenstolz (racial pride), 107

Rearmament (of West Germany), 3, 18, 58, 83, 110, 121, 124, 204

Rhineland-Palatinate, 3, 142–44, 202–3, 205, 213, 286 (n. 34)

Rock and roll, 8, 13, 80, 124, 226

Russia. *See* Soviet Union

SA (Nazi stormtroopers), 22

Saarland, 20–21, 22, 24, 25, 30, 76, 98, 262 (n. 74)

Schelsky, Helmut, 176

Schnapp, Dr. Detmar: role in Deutscher Verein für öffentliche und private Fürsorge, 140, 147, 150, 188; efforts to battle prostitution, 140–42, 186, 188–89, 274 (n. 68), 286 (n. 32); rejection of views of, 149–50, 153, 186, 188; on interracial sexuality, 188–89, 286 (n. 43)

Schumacher, Kurt (SPD), 54

Schwarze Schmach ("Black Horror on the Rhine"), 27, 89–90

Schwarzer Kies (film), 212–13, 292 (n. 56)

Secularization: during Nazi regime, 9, 23, 24–25; in post–World War II West Germany, 11–12, 117–18, 120, 134–35, 153, 175, 191–92, 233, 287 (n. 51)

Sexual decency: lack of, 11, 107, 145, 166, 134; legal enforcement of, 166–68, 182, 232–33; rejection of rigid standard, 167–68, 175, 177, 180, 182, 185, 187, 189, 233, 287 (n. 51)

Sexual immorality, 112, 115, 118, 120–21, 130–35, 163–66, 175. *See*

alien presence, 87, 89; and increase in crime, 87, 205, 258 (n. 3); on the experience of African American GIs, 92–93; implementing integration, 96–97; tolerating social segregation, 99, 102–3, 261 (n. 65); enforcing integration in German communities, 102–3; and interracial relationships, 107, 114–15, 195–96, 265 (nn. 112, 113, 114); attitude toward prostitution, 137–38, 264 (n. 107), 272 (n. 50), 273 (n. 54); and transformation of German racism, 196–97, 221–22, 234–35; on GI bars, 213–14; military rabbi, 214; ignoring German racism, 215, 221; and troop reductions, 223; and professional military, 225–26

Venereal disease, 127, 129, 139, 145–46, 151, 164, 186, 197
Verein. *See* Deutscher Verein für öffentliche und private Fürsorge
Veronika Dankeschön (song), 128–29
"Veronikas": clergy's view of, 21, 120, 135; U.S. military on, 105, 137, 273 (n. 52); as source of racial disorder, 120–21, 122–24, 131–32, 134–35, 140, 202; municipalities' view of, 127, 137–42; viewed as disgracing German honor, 127, 154, 275 (n. 83); as derogatory name, 128–29, 270 (n. 4), 275 (n. 83); popular perception of, 128–35; Bundestag debate on, 143; and Deutscher Verein für öffentliche und private Fürsorge, 144, 145–49; federal government on, 149–53; defense of, 186–87, 190
Versailles Treaty, 20
Vice raids: and racism, 167, 181–82, 192, 193, 195, 281 (n. 57), 284 (n. 14); and class bias, 167, 181–82, 281 (n. 57), 284 (n. 14); to contain prostitution, 180–81, 184–85,

193, 233, 285 (n. 17); opposition to, 180–81, 184–85, 284 (n. 15); in black-only bars, 192, 193, 195, 233, 287–88 (n. 57); in the immediate post–World War II period, 285 (n. 27)
Vietnam War, 224
Volksgemeinschaft (People's Community), 23, 25
Volkssturm (Home Defense), 26
Volkstrauertag (West Germany's national day of mourning), 59
Voyeurism, 188

Wefelscheid, Johanna, 184, 285 (n. 22)
Weimar Republic, 10, 20, 89–90, 118, 145–46, 227
Western alliance, 53, 55–60, 230, 234, 250 (n. 17)
Western Area Command, 58, 214
Western liberal tradition, 14, 104, 107–8, 229, 234
Westernization, 4, 229, 234, 238 (n. 3)
Westwall, 5, 22, 23, 49–50, 232
White slavery, 211
Wie Toxi wirklich lebt (TV documentary), 260 (n. 36), 290 (n. 31)
Wild, Herbert, 23
Wilms, Fritz (FDP), 199, 204, 289 (n. 2)
Wirtschaftswunder (economic miracle), 7, 19, 47–50, 118, 134, 161, 175–76, 191
Wohlanständigkeit (decency), 11, 107, 116, 134, 191, 196. *See also* Sexual decency; Sexual immorality
Women, American: German views of, 41, 78, 230, 253 (82); alleged power of, 137–38, 213, 214–15, 272 (n. 49), 293 (n. 62)
Women, German: employment of, 3, 41, 128, 158, 160–61, 169–73; sexuality of, 5, 9, 131, 164–67; social legislation regarding, 9; sexual liberation of, 9, 131, 146; "sexually